© 橘右之吉 2017

春(shun) = spring; 夏(ka) = summer; 秋(shu) = autumn; 冬(to) = winter
These characters symbolise the beauty of Japan's four distinct seasons.

FOREWORD

This book - which provides insights into the beauty of Japan's lesser-populated areas from the perspective *of* foreigners *for* foreigners - is the first collaboration of its kind in the publishing world of Japan. All the content was created by a team of foreign researchers, and then appraised by a mostly Japanese selection committee. This finished product, *Japan - 100 Hidden Towns*, is the fruit of a rigorous selection process.

Firstly, candidate towns recommended by each of Japan's 47 local governments were adopted. Then, after adding other nominations from the selection committee, over 150 towns were visited and researched. Tense and lengthy committee meetings were held on 20 occasions, and eventually the final selection of 100 towns was agreed.

Though many of these destinations are familiar to Japanese, most are less well-known among foreigners, and still invoke a sense of 'hidden'.

Japan has proudly developed a modern state while still maintaining its traditions and beautiful countryside. With this book as your companion, please enjoy the variety of these locations throughout Japan.

- **Atsushi Takahashi**
  The Sumitomo Trust & Banking Co., Ltd. former President
  Sumitomo Mitsui Trust Bank, Limited. Senior Corporate Advisor

For many foreign tourists, the so-called 'Golden Route' that combines visits to Tokyo, Mt. Fuji, Kyoto, and Osaka, is the definitive Japan experience. However, the variation of climate, countryside, history, culture, food, festivals and local industries throughout the archipelago ensures that Japan offers a wealth of other fascinating destinations.

Our team of foreign-resident researchers has travelled the length and breadth of the country and collected together the reviews and travel advice contained within this book, *Japan - 100 Hidden Towns*, where we aim to introduce the charms of some of the lesser-known towns of Japan.

The Japanese authorities are continually striving to provide a welcoming and illuminating experience for travellers from overseas. Through this book, we hope you can enjoy encounters only found far from Japan's busy areas.

- **Shigeto Kubo**
  Japan Tourism Agency (JTA) former Commissioner
  Japan Travel and Tourism Association President and COO

introduction

JAPAN 100 HIDDEN TOWNS

CONTENTS

INTRODUCTION

Special Interests
- 6 History
- 8 Performance / Arts
- 8 Traditional Crafts
- 9 Local Delicacies
- 9 Hot Springs
- 10 Seaside
- 11 Museums / Galleries
- 12 Wildlife / Nature
- 13 Festivals

14 HOKKAIDO

Hokkaido
- 20 Nakafurano
- 22 Bibai
- 24 Kamoenai
- 26 Mikasa
- 28 Numata
- 30 Kamishihoro
- 32 Esashi
- 34 **Other Towns**

36 TOHOKU

Akita
- 42 Kosaka
- 46 Oga
- 50 Semboku

Aomori
- 54 Hachinohe
- 58 Mutsu

Fukushima
- 62 Iwaki
- 66 Nihonmatsu

Iwate
- 68 Rikuzentakata
- 70 Tono

Miyagi
- 74 Matsushima
- 78 Shiroishi

Yamagata
- 82 Sagae
- 84 Sakata
- 88 **Other Towns**

90 KANTO-KOSHINETSU

Chiba
- 98 Kamogawa
- 102 Tateyama

Gunma
- 106 Kusatsu
- 110 Shibukawa

Ibaraki
- 114 Itako
- 118 Kasama

Kanagawa
- 122 Miura

Nagano
- 124 Hakuba
- 128 Komoro
- 132 Nozawaonsen
- 136 Ogawa
- 138 Shimosuwa

Niigata
- 142 Sado
- 146 Tokamachi

Saitama
- 150 Kawagoe
- 154 Nagatoro

Tochigi
- 156 Ashikaga
- 160 Tochigi

Tokyo
- 162 Katsushika
- 164 Ogasawara
- 168 Oshima

Yamanashi
- 172 Hokuto
- 176 Koshu
- 178 **Other Towns**

180 CHUBU-HOKURIKU

Aichi
- 188 Inuyama
- 192 Tokoname

Fukui
- 196 Awara
- 198 Katsuyama
- 202 Ono
- 204 Wakasa

Gifu
- 208 Gero

Ishikawa
- 210 Hakusan
- 212 Wajima

Mie
- 214 Ise
- 218 Kumano

Shizuoka
- 222 Atami
- 224 Shimoda

Toyama
- 226 Himi
- 228 Kamiichi
- 232 **Other Towns**

234 KANSAI

Hyogo
- 240 Akashi

Kyoto
- 244 Miyazu

Nara
- 246 Asuka
- 250 Ikoma
- 252 Soni

Osaka
- 254 Chihayaakasaka
- 258 Izumisano
- 262 Suita

Shiga
- 264 Hikone

Wakayama
- 266 Minabe
- 270 **Other Towns**

272 CHUGOKU

Hiroshima
- 278 Hatsukaichi
- 282 Sera

Okayama
- 284 Kurashiki
- 288 Mimasaka

Shimane
- 292 Izumo
- 296 Masuda
- 300 Nishinoshima

Tottori
- 304 Misasa
- 306 Sakaiminato

Yamaguchi
- 308 Hagi
- 312 **Other Towns**

314 SHIKOKU

Ehime
- 320 Imabari

Kagawa
- 324 Naoshima
- 326 Shodoshima

Kochi
- 330 Konan
- 332 Shimanto

Tokushima
- 334 Miyoshi
- 338 **Other Towns**

340 KYUSHU AND OKINAWA

Fukuoka
- 350 Ukiha
- 354 Yanagawa

Kagoshima
- 358 Amami
- 362 Tatsugo
- 364 Yakushima

Kumamoto
- 368 Aso
- 370 Hitoyoshi

Miyazaki
- 372 Aya
- 376 Shiiba

Nagasaki
- 378 Iki
- 382 Shimabara

Oita
- 384 Kitsuki
- 388 Usuki

Saga
- 392 Arita
- 396 Ureshino
- 400 **Other Towns**

Okinawa
- 402 Miyakojima

OTHER INFORMATION
- 406 Travel Advice
- 409 General Advice
- 412 Useful Phrases
- 414 Index

introduction

SPECIAL INTERESTS

🏯 HISTORY

Japan is wonderful for history buffs, whether focusing on ancient Jomon artefacts, the Kofun tombs that gave name to that period, the culture and lifestyle of the Edo period, or the dramatic changes of westernisation during the Meiji era. There are plenty of ruins and reconstructions of castles dotted around Japan, and many towns have local museums where they proudly expound on their own historical luminaries. Use this book to find the unique historical claims of the featured towns and how the past shapes the present throughout Japan.

JAPANESE HISTORY TIMELINE

This simplified timeline of Japanese history is for quick reference when reading about the historical attractions listed in this book.

14,000 BC-300 BC Jomon Era
The earliest Japanese era of fishing, hunting and gathering.

300 BC-250 Yayoi Era
Rice farming begins.

250-538 Kofun Era
Japan begins to unify under leaders, who were buried in large keyhole-shaped tombs (*kofun*).

710-784 Nara Era
Nara becomes Japan's first permanent capital.

794-1185 Heian Era
The capital moves to Heian (modern day Kyoto). This is an era of peace and artistic pursuits among the aristocracy.

1180-85 The Gempei War
Lengthy war between the Minamoto clan and the Taira, eventually resulting in Minamoto supremacy.

1192-1333 Kamakura Era
Kamakura becomes the Japanese capital, with Yoritomo Minamoto as its first shogun.

1338-1600
Febrile times as the Muromachi and then the Azuchi take over. The 16th century is referred to as the Sengoku (Warring States) era and is a period characterised by violence, political intrigue and, later, the rise of the three great unifiers of Japan - Nobunaga Oda, Hideyoshi Toyotomi and Ieyasu Tokugawa.

1600 The Battle of Sekigahara
Ieyasu's victory ensures the Tokugawa begin to dominate Japan.

1603-1867 Edo Era
Ieyasu becomes shogun and establishes the Tokugawa government in Edo (Tokyo). The shogunate persecutes Christianity, closes the country to foreigners except at small trading posts in Nagasaki, and sets up the *sankin kotai* system whereby local lords have to spend part of the year in Edo.

1854
US Commodore Matthew Perry and his black ships force the Japanese government to open for trade.

1868-1912 Meiji Era
The Meiji Restoration and the Boshin War bring an end to the Tokugawa shogunate and Japan moves ahead with foreign trade and industrialisation.

1912-1926 Taisho Era
Japan embraces the fashion and culture of the roaring twenties.

1926-1989 Showa Era
Period beginning with militarism and increased imperialism leading to war. Japan's defeat is followed by the US occupation, and rapid post-war growth.

1989-2019 Heisei Era

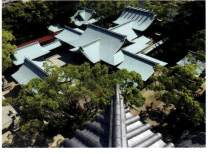

Key Towns

Hokkaido
Esashi (p32)

Tohoku
Hachinohe (p54), Iwaki (p62), Nihonmatsu (p66), Shiroishi (p78), Sagae (p82)

Kanto-Koshinetsu
Kamogawa (p98), Tateyama (p102), Itako (p114), Kasama (p118) Komoro (p128), Shimosuwa (p138), Kawagoe (p150), Nagatoro (p154), Ashikaga (p156), Katsushika (p162), Hokuto (p172)

Chubu-Hokuriku
Inuyama (p188), Tokoname (p192), Katsuyama (p198), Ono (p202), Hakusan (p210), Ise (p214), Kumano (p218), Kamiichi (p228)

Kansai
Akashi (p240), Asuka (p246), Ikoma (p250), Chihayaakasaka (p254), Izumisano (p258), Hikone (p264)

Chugoku
Hatsukaichi (p278), Kurashiki (p284), Izumo (p292), Masuda (p296), Misasa (p304), Hagi (p308)

Shikoku
Imabari (p320), Konan (p330), Shimanto (p332)

Kyushu and Okinawa
Ukiha (p350), Hitoyoshi (p370), Shimabara (p382), Kitsuki (p384), Usuki (p388), Arita (p392), Miyakojima (p402)

introduction

SPECIAL INTERESTS

PERFORMANCE / ARTS

Japan has cultivated its own unique performances and arts over centuries of human history and culture. The closed country *sakoku* policy during the Edo era cloistered Japan even further and, in many ways, incubated and enabled the arts to flourish further. This book spotlights some of the colourful arts and performances maintained in the remoter parts of the country. Aside from the major arts such as *kabuki* theatre and *noh* performance that many people with an interest in Japan will be aware of, there are also many other unique art forms exclusive to Japan's secluded areas showcased in this book.

Key Towns

Hokkaido
Numata (p28)

Tohoku
Sakata (p84)

Kanto-Koshinetsu
Tokamachi (p146)

Chubu-Hokuriku
Gero (p208)

Kansai
Asuka (p246)

Chugoku
Masuda (p296)

Shikoku
Imabari (p320)

Kyushu and Okinawa
Shiiba (p376)

# TRADITIONAL CRAFTS

Ceramics, woodblock art prints (*ukiyo-e*), flower arranging, the tea ceremony… the list goes on. Japan's lengthy history and proud cultural heritage mean there is a huge variety of traditional crafts to choose from - for purchasing or having a go at making. Whether it's pottery, kimono-wearing, traditional Japanese paper, sword-making or any number of other artisanal activities, the hidden towns of Japan often have their own unique slant on the traditional crafts of the country. Many offer workshops where visitors can try their hand at crafting something, with veteran teachers eager to impart their knowledge and skills.

Key Towns

Hokkaido
Bibai (p22)

Tohoku
Shiroishi (p78)

Kanto-Koshinetsu
Kasama (p118), Tochigi (p160), Ogasawara (p164)

Chubu-Hokuriku
Tokoname (p192), Wajima (p212)

Kansai
Akashi (p240), Minabe (p266)

Chugoku
Mimasaka (p288)

Shikoku
Naoshima (p324)

Kyushu and Okinawa
Tatsugo (p362), Aya (p372), Arita (p392), Ureshino (p396)

8

LOCAL DELICACIES

A huge plus for any visit to Japan is its wonderful, diverse cuisine - you could spend a month eating different dishes every day. Japan has a massive souvenir-giving industry which ensures local producers can keep in the black. Most towns have a station souvenir shop, tourist office, or a *michi-no-eki* (roadside service station) that provides an outlet for local produce. Indulge yourself in the wide range of exquisite delicacies mentioned in this book.

Key Towns

Hokkaido
Nakafurano (p20), Kamishihoro (p30), Esashi (p32)

Tohoku
Kosaka (p42), Oga (p46), Semboku (p50), Hachinohe (p54), Matsushima (p74), Shiroishi (p78), Sagae (p82), Sakata (p84)

Kanto-Koshinetsu
Kusatsu (p106), Itako (p114), Miura (p122), Komoro (p128), Ogawa (p136), Nagatoro (p154), Ashikaga (p156), Tochigi (p160), Katsushika (p162), Hokuto (p172), Koshu (p176)

Chubu-Hokuriku
Awara (p196), Ono (p202), Gero (p208), Hakusan (p210), Shimoda (p224), Himi (p226)

Kansai
Akashi (p240), Miyazu (p244), Soni (p252), Chihayaakasaka (p254), Izumisano (p258), Minabe (p266)

Chugoku
Hatsukaichi (p278), Sera (p282)

Shikoku
Naoshima (p324), Shodoshima (p326)

Kyushu and Okinawa
Ukiha (p350), Yanagawa (p354), Yakushima (p364), Shiiba (p376), Shimabara (p382), Arita (p392), Ureshino (p396), Miyakojima (p402)

HOT SPRINGS

On the downside - earthquakes, on the plus side - hot springs. Japan's location on the Pacific Ring of Fire means that its mountainous landscape is the home to active volcanoes and spurting geysers. Being blessed with therapeutic waters has meant that the Japanese have long been regular bathers, so much so that early European visitors were seen as literally unclean. Many of the towns offer hot spring facilities and indeed some of the towns in this book have hot spring spas as their main draw. Follow our icon and enjoy a long soak.

Key Towns

Hokkaido
Bibai (p22)

Tohoku
Oga (p46), Iwaki (p62)

Kanto-Koshinetsu
Kusatsu (p106), Shibukawa (p110), Hakuba (p124), Nozawaonsen (p132), Oshima (p168)

Chubu-Hokuriku
Awara (p196), Gero (p208), Atami (p222)

Kansai
Soni (p252)

Chugoku
Mimasaka (p288), Misasa (p304)

Shikoku
Miyoshi (p334)

Kyushu and Okinawa
Amami (p358), Aso (p368), Hitoyoshi (p370), Ureshino (p396)

9

introduction

SPECIAL INTERESTS

🌊 SEASIDE

Predictably for an island nation, many of the towns in this book face the sea. The geological traits of the country ensure that there are many breathtaking seaside vistas to enjoy. Beach vacations, coastal walks, spectacular cliffs and bizarre rock formations are often key attractions of such destinations.
As well as the views, Japan provides many opportunities for water sports enthusiasts - its marine wonderlands are a Mecca for divers, while snorkelling, surfing, all manner of boating activities, and summer beach fun can be experienced throughout the archipelago.

Key Towns

Hokkaido
Kamoenai (p24)

Tohoku
Rikuzentakata (p68), Matsushima (p74)

Kanto-Koshinetsu
Kamogawa (p98), Tateyama (p102), Miura (p122), Sado (p142), Ogasawara (p164), Oshima (p168)

Chubu-Hokuriku
Tokoname (p192), Wakasa (p204), Hakusan (p210), Wajima (p212), Ise (p214), Kumano (p218), Atami (p222), Shimoda (p224), Himi (p226)

Kansai
Miyazu (p244)

Chugoku
Nishinoshima (p300), Sakaiminato (p306), Hagi (p308)

Shikoku
Imabari (p320), Naoshima (p324), Shodoshima (p326), Shimanto (p332)

Kyushu and Okinawa
Amami (p358), Tatsugo (p362), Yakushima (p364), Iki (p378), Kitsuki (p384), Miyakojima (p402)

10

MUSEUMS / GALLERIES

As a nation that lays claim to such a unique history, wide biodiversity, super-modern technology and an abundance of traditional and modern arts, it is hardly surprising that there are so many museums and galleries in Japan - even in the most hard-to-reach spots.
Many of these establishments were hastily created during the Japanese economy's bubble years, and these can vary greatly in quality. However we have attempted to spotlight the museums and galleries, often tucked away in the most unexpected places, that most impressed our researchers during their travels.

Key Towns

Hokkaido
Bibai (p22), Kamoenai (p24), Mikasa (p26), Numata (p28), Kamishihoro (p30), Esashi (p32)

Tohoku
Kosaka (p42), Semboku (p50), Mutsu (p58), Iwaki (p62), Nihonmatsu (p66), Rikuzentakata (p68), Tono (p70), Sakata (p84)

Kanto-Koshinetsu
Kamogawa (p98), Shibukawa (p110), Kasama (p118), Hakuba (p124), Shimosuwa (p138), Sado (p142), Tokamachi (p146), Kawagoe (p150), Ashikaga (p156), Tochigi (p160), Katsushika (p162), Koshu (p176)

Chubu-Hokuriku
Inuyama (p188), Awara (p196), Katsuyama (p198), Ono (p202), Wakasa (p204), Ise (p214), Atami (p222), Shimoda (p224), Kamiichi (p228)

Kansai
Akashi (p240), Asuka (p246), Suita (p262), Hikone (p264)

Chugoku
Kurashiki (p284), Mimasaka (p288), Izumo (p292), Nishinoshima (p300), Sakaiminato (p306), Hagi (p308)

Shikoku
Konan (p330), Miyoshi (p334)

Kyushu and Okinawa
Yanagawa (p354), Aya (p372), Iki (p378), Kitsuki (p384), Usuki (p388)

introduction

SPECIAL INTERESTS

WILDLIFE / NATURE

The rural location of many of the hidden towns recommended within these pages ensures that there are plenty of natural delights for visitors to enjoy. Each season lends Japan its own unique colour scheme and conditions - the snowscapes and the frosting of woodlands in winter, the nationwide sweep of plum and cherry blossoms in spring, summer's hot days and nights serenaded by the relentless chatter of insects, and autumn's cool, temperate months of gold, russet and vermilion foliage falling from the trees - the mountains, forests and rice terraces of Japan are a fabulous stage for them all.
Make use of our climate information to help plan your trip.

Key Towns

Hokkaido
Nakafurano (p20), Bibai (p22), Kamoenai (p24), Mikasa (p26), Numata (p28), Kamishihoro (p30)

Tohoku
Kosaka (p42), Semboku (p50), Mutsu (p58), Nihonmatsu (p66), Rikuzentakata (p68), Tono (p70), Matsushima (p74), Sagae (p82)

Kanto-Koshinetsu
Tateyama (p102), Kusatsu (p106), Shibukawa (p110), Itako (p114), Kasama (p118), Miura (p122), Hakuba (p124), Komoro (p128), Nozawaonsen (p132), Ogawa (p136),
Sado (p142), Tokamachi (p146), Nagatoro (p154), Ogasawara (p164), Oshima (p168), Hokuto (p172), Koshu (p176)

Chubu-Hokuriku
Katsuyama (p198), Wakasa (p204), Gero (p208), Wajima (p212), Kumano (p218), Kamiichi (p228)

Kansai
Miyazu (p244), Asuka (p246), Ikoma (p250), Soni (p252), Chihayaakasaka (p254), Izumisano (p258), Suita (p262), Hikone (p264), Minabe (p266)

Chugoku
Hatsukaichi (p278), Sera (p282), Mimasaka (p288), Izumo (p292), Masuda (p296), Nishinoshima (p300), Misasa (p304)

Shikoku
Imabari (p320), Shodoshima (p326), Shimanto (p332), Miyoshi (p334)

Kyushu and Okinawa
Ukiha (p350), Amami (p358), Tatsugo (p362), Yakushima (p364), Aso (p368), Hitoyoshi (p370), Aya (p372), Shiiba (p376), Iki (p378), Usuki (p388)

OTHER FEATURES OF THIS BOOK

Climate - a guide of each area's average monthly temperatures is provided, as well as information on extreme seasonal conditions such as typhoons and heavy snow.

Travel times - visitors to Japan will often be dependent on public transport or rental cars during their stay. We have listed approximate travel times between all of the prefectural capitals in each region.

FESTIVALS

A proud sense of heritage is clearly in evidence in the huge number and variety of ancient festivals that are still celebrated in modern-day Japan.
These can range from the bizarre and gaudy to the downright raucous and dangerous. Health and safety often takes a back seat at the many festivals involving fire, icy waters, and precarious physical challenges. The famed Japanese modesty also seems to evaporate when dancing and performing are the order of the day. Each town in this book has its own specific festivals which are listed with dates and a brief outline. The more eye-catching festivals may well be the major annual draw for the towns, so make sure to plan your visit accordingly and join in the fun.

Key Towns

Hokkaido
Numata (p28), Esashi (p32)

Tohoku
Oga (p46), Hachinohe (p54), Tono (p70)

Kanto-Koshinetsu
Kamogawa (p98), Tateyama (p102), Nozawaonsen (p132), Ogawa (p136), Shimosuwa (p138), Kawagoe (p150)

Chubu-Hokuriku
Himi (p226)

Kansai
Ikoma (p250)

Chugoku
Izumo (p292)

Shikoku
Miyoshi (p334)

Kyushu and Okinawa
Yanagawa (p354), Aso (p368)

Maps - we have included rudimentary maps to indicate the relative positions and distances between local attractions. Please refer to the more detailed maps on our website when navigating an area.

Key Dates - while some of Japan's local events occur on the same date every year, many shift slightly depending on which day of the week they fall. Please check with local authorities in order to avoid disappointment.

HOKKAIDO

北海道

Hokkaido is the second-largest island of Japan, and also its largest and northernmost prefecture. The island was formerly known as Ezo, and is famous for its unique Ainu culture that its descendants have meticulously maintained, through celebrating their history with museums and cultural events dotted across the area.

Climate-wise, Japan's four distinct seasons are no more clearly exemplified than in Hokkaido. The dry, warm summer is more pleasant than the uncomfortable humidity of further south. Winter, on the other hand, transforms the island into a snow-shrouded wonderland, drawing in winter sports enthusiasts.

Quite different from other islands and prefectures of Japan, Hokkaido is a sparsely populated rural mix of farms, forests, volcanoes, hot springs and ski resorts, combining to create dazzling natural vistas that stay with any tourist lucky enough to have the opportunity to visit.

The island is divided into several sub-prefectures, but for the purposes of this book we have split Hokkaido into four geographical sections - north, central, east and south.

Transport
Car rental is strongly advised as the best way to experience the stunning nature and wide expanses of the island.

✈ Airports
New Chitose Airport is the main hub for getting to Hokkaido. From there, as you move further away from Sapporo, the train and bus services are limited compared to the rest of Japan.

🚅 Main Train Stations
In 2016, the bullet train service was finally connected to Hokkaido with the establishment of a line to Shin-Hakodate-Hokuto Station.

Seasonal Information
Winter is long, snowy and extremely cold in Hokkaido, though the heavy snows bring with it wonderful skiing opportunities. In contrast, the summer is warm and pleasant and a great escape from the uncomfortable humidity of the rest of Japan. If your purpose is to see the island outside of its winter sports season, a leisurely drive around any of the areas of Hokkaido will reveal the natural delights of this rustic land.

Mikasa

NORTH HOKKAIDO

Here at the northernmost point of Japan, on a clear day you can catch a view of Russia's Sakhalin Island from the lighthouse at Cape Soya. The Soya Misaki Wind Farm attracts a number of visitors, while the Rumoi area boasts a thriving fishing industry. The fireflies, fossils and festivals of Numata, and the rolling lavender fields of Nakafurano are deservedly popular draws to the area.

✈ Airports
Wakkanai Airport

🚆 Main Train Stations
Yuchi Station, Wakkanai Station

Other Tourist Attractions
Kamikawa
Known for its Ice Waterfall Festival during the months of heavy snow.
Wakkanai
The coastal viewing spots and hot springs of Wakkanai are worth a visit.

Extreme Seasonal Conditions Heavy snow in winter. Cool even in summer.

Kamikawa

CENTRAL HOKKAIDO

Daisetsu Mountains

Central Hokkaido is home to several of the prefecture's most popular attractions. The prefectural capital of Sapporo is a vibrant city close to many popular ski resorts and possessing a range of appealing architecture, both modern and Meiji-era. Its famous snow festival displays outstanding sculptures and draws a huge number of visitors every year. Nearby Otaru has a beautifully preserved canal area with historical storehouses. For hidden towns, take the time to travel and learn about the coal-mining legacy of Bibai, the herring industry of Kamoenai, and the remarkable fossils of Mikasa.

✈ Airports
New Chitose Airport, Asahikawa Airport

🚆 Main Train Stations
Sapporo Station

Other Tourist Attractions
Sorachi
Outside the capital, central Hokkaido is also home to the vineyards of Sorachi.
Daisetsu Mountains
Get up close to the volcanic power of the Daisetsu mountain range.

Extreme Seasonal Conditions Heavy snow in winter (less heavy on Pacific side).

HOKKAIDO

北海道

EAST HOKKAIDO

The vast region of East Hokkaido is where Japan gets really isolated. The Sea of Okhotsk laps at the area's northern shore and the coast here offers spectacular views. The gorgeous mountains and lakes of the area (including the bubbling mud pools of Lake Akan) and the region's migrating swans are another draw. The farms and redundant railway bridges of Kamishihoro are a testament to the industry and historical changes this area of Hokkaido has undergone. The awesome beauty of Kushiroshitsugen National Park and the mountaineering Mecca of the Hidaka mountain range also attract visitors.

✈ Airports
Kushiro Airport
Nakashibetsu Airport
🚆 Main Train Stations
Kushiro Station
Other Tourist Attractions
Abashiri
For those interested in the more morbid points of history, the notorious Abashiri Prison, built in the Meiji era and now converted to a museum, was once the residence of political prisoners seen as troublesome to the authorities and thus sent to this isolated area.
Extreme Seasonal Conditions Cold in winter, but less snow than other Hokkaido regions.

Sea of Okhotsk

SOUTH HOKKAIDO

The southern tip of Hokkaido is dominated by the city of Hakodate, which finally became connected by bullet train to the rest of Japan in 2016. Mount Hakodate looms over the town and affords iconic nighttime views of the area from the top of its ropeway. The city also houses plenty of early 20th-century European-style architecture to enjoy. Use Hakodate as a base for venturing to the inland lakes and mountains of the area, or head along the coast to catch the Meiji-era architecture and odd rock formations of Esashi.

✈ Airports
Hakodate Airport
🚆 Main Train Stations
Shin-Hakodate-Hokuto Station
Other Tourist Attractions
Matsumae
Enjoy the rare sight of an Edo-era Hokkaidan castle at Matsumae.
Extreme Seasonal Conditions Heavy snow in winter.

Matsumae Castle

NATIONAL PARKS

Akan National Park

Akan National Park
Area: 90,481 ha
Features: caldera lakes, gorgeous mountain backdrops
Did you know? Lake Akan is the location of one of the largest Ainu settlements in Hokkaido, Ainu Kotan, and the village hosts craft shops, festivals and a theatre for traditional performances.

Daisetsuzan National Park
Area: 226,764 ha
Features: Mount Asahidake, rare animals and plants
Did you know? The park is known by two different nicknames - 'the roof of Hokkaido' is derived from Mount Asahidake, the prefecture's highest peak, while the Ainu describe it as 'the playground of the Gods'. Both give an indication of the scale and beauty of this vast park.

Kushiroshitsugen National Park
Area: 28,788 ha
Features: rivers, marshes, mountain views, red-crowned cranes
Did you know? The red-crowned crane was thought extinct due to over-hunting, but conservation efforts have aided its recovery.

Rishiri-Rebun-Sarobetsu National Park
Area: 24,166 ha
Features: flower gardens, dunes, cliffs, ocean views
Did you know? Japan's northernmost national park, Rishiri-Rebun-Sarobetsu is home to Hokkaido's answer to Mount Fuji - the beautiful, cone-shaped Mount Rishiri.

Shikotsu-Toya National Park
Area: 99,473 ha
Features: caldera lakes, volcanoes and a variety of hot springs
Did you know? The park's location, close to central Sapporo City and New Chitose Airport, makes it convenient to visit.

Shiretoko National Park
Area: 38,636 ha
Features: rare wildlife, including brown bears and birds of prey
Did you know? The name of this northeastern point of Japan derives from an Ainu phrase meaning 'the end of the Earth' - a testament to its isolated location.

Shiretoko National Park

HOKKAIDO

北海道

HIDDEN TOWNS
HOKKAIDO

- 20 **Nakafurano**
- 22 **Bibai**
- 24 **Kamoenai**
- 26 **Mikasa**
- 28 **Numata**
- 30 **Kamishihoro**
- 32 **Esashi**

CLIMATE (monthly average temperatures)

SAPPORO (central Hokkaido)

SHARI (east Hokkaido)

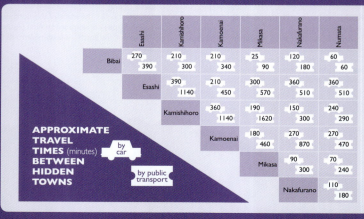

APPROXIMATE TRAVEL TIMES (minutes) **BETWEEN HIDDEN TOWNS**

by car / by public transport

	Esashi	Kamishihoro	Kamoenai	Mikasa	Nakafurano	Numata
Bibai	270 / 390	210 / 300	210 / 340	25 / 90	120 / 180	60 / 60
Esashi		390 / 1140	210 / 450	300 / 570	360 / 510	360 / 510
Kamishihoro			360 / 1140	190 / 1620	150 / 300	240 / 290
Kamoenai				180 / 460	270 / 870	270 / 470
Mikasa					90 / 300	70 / 240
Nakafurano						110 / 180

18

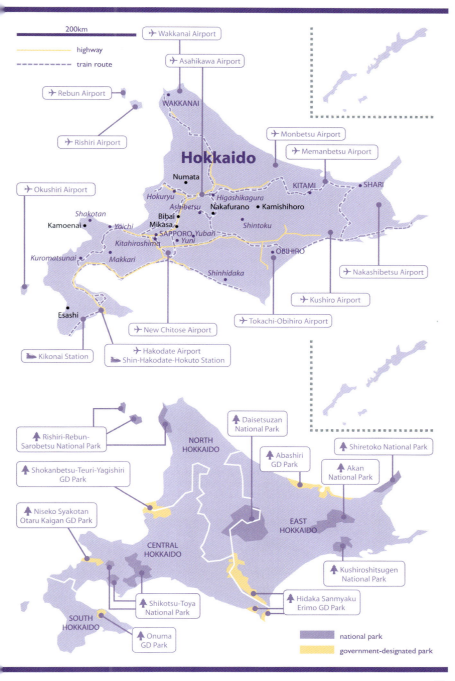

Hokkaido

中富良野町

North Hokkaido
NAKAFURANO

With rolling fields of lavender and flowers set against a mountainous backdrop, summer in Nakafurano feels more like a European break than a holiday in Asia. A flower lover's paradise, Nakafurano is a wonderful experience of nature.

👍 Must see! Farm Tomita [1]

Farm Tomita is the most iconic of the farms in the area and has garnered attention both at home and abroad. It feels like what you would experience if Disney opened a flower-based wonderland. Set out over a large site, there are numerous gardens bursting with seasonal flowers, while round the edge, picturesque wooden buildings sell an eclectic mix of Farm Tomita products. Whilst the lavender perfume factory, and house of dry flowers are interesting, it is the flower gardens that really are the main draw here.

🍶 Food and Drink - Dococa Farm [2]

Dococa Farm is a working farm, cafe and hotel all rolled into one. Tamago Café attached to it, is worth the visit alone. Stroll past the goats and chickens housed inside a converted, pleasingly cluttered farmhouse. Using its own produce for much of the cuisine, it's a great opportunity to try authentic farm dishes.

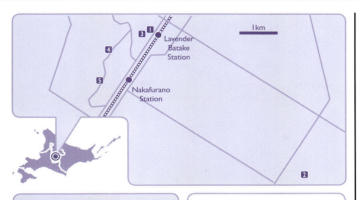

🌷 Nature Spot
Tomita Melon House 3

Just across from the lavender farm is the Melon House, a melon-themed outlet providing an enjoyable spot to relax in. Jam, cakes, ice creams and of course the fruit itself, are all on offer. Either relax in the cafe or take a short stroll round the garden on the premises.

🌷 Nature Spot
Saika-no-Sato Lavender Farm 5

This farm is a large site that covers the hills just west of the main town. Contrasting with the more managed fields and hedgerows of Farm Tomita, the flowers roll like a carpet over the gentle hills of this site. There are large lavender fields, but also those of other flowers, including a poppy field, that help form a colourful landscape. A short stroll to the top of the hill is rewarded with views across the Furano basin and as far as the Tokachi mountains beyond.

🌷 Nature Spot
Nakafurano Lavender Garden 4

A rival lavender field and flower garden built on the hillside close to Nakafurano Station. There is a summer sightseeing lift to take the effort out of going to the top of the hill. In winter, it doubles as a ski lift for the short snow course that attracts winter sports enthusiasts.

🚆 Getting there and around

✈ Asahikawa Airport.

🚄 Asahikawa Station. Travel to Nakafurano Station on the Furano Line.

🚶 Most of the farms and fields are in the central area of Nakafurano and are no more than half an hour apart on foot, making this town one of the few in Hokkaido that is easily visited using just public transport.

❓ Did you know?

Terrain for trains

The flower fields are so popular in summer that an extra train station is opened in the fields at this time. The name of the station? Lavender Field (*Batake*) Station.

There is also a special *Norokko* train that runs between Furano and Biei in high season. This train has seats facing the window for you to enjoy the scenery as you trundle by.

Key dates

mid-July - Nakafurano Lavender Festival (fireworks displays and various stalls)

We say

"To experience an explosion of flowers in the heart of Hokkaido, Nakafurano is certainly worth visiting. The flowers clothe the fields in colour, and are beautifully framed by the Tokachi mountains."

Recommended for

Nature lovers

Gardeners

Further information
www.100hiddentowns.jp/hokkaido/nakafurano.html

Hokkaido

美唄市
Central Hokkaido — BIBAI

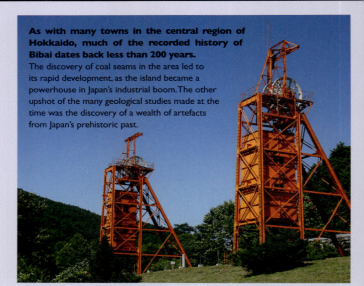

As with many towns in the central region of Hokkaido, much of the recorded history of Bibai dates back less than 200 years.
The discovery of coal seams in the area led to its rapid development, as the island became a powerhouse in Japan's industrial boom. The other upshot of the many geological studies made at the time was the discovery of a wealth of artefacts from Japan's prehistoric past.

Culture Spot - Coal Mine Memorial Forest Park [1]

This photogenic spot in the hills outside the town marks the location of the coal mine that brought prosperity to the area in the last century. Its twin red shaft head winches are a silent memorial to an era now passed.

Old Tomei Station/Train [2]

This preserved old station and train are pretty mementoes of the rail service that used to run here. The station marks the starting point of a popular cycling route.

Culture Spot — Bibai City Folk Museum [3]

This is a beautifully curated museum where a clearly marked path transports visitors through the history of the area, back from its prehistoric geological and botanical origins, through to the modern agricultural and industrial lifestyle of the town today. Exhibits include tools of the area's earliest human inhabitants, lifestyles of the indigenous Ainu, farming equipment, geological surveys for coal mining, train tracks and full-size reconstructions of the dwellings of early settlers, and a Taisho-era general store.

Nature Spot - Miyajima-Numa [4]

A short drive out of town takes you to this serene marsh area, which is furnished with hides from where visitors can observe birds and other wildlife in their wetland habitat. Sunset is particularly lovely here.

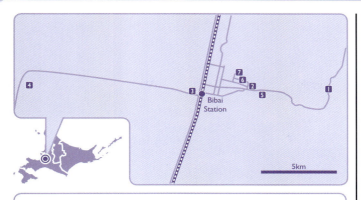

👁 Did you know?

Marble-ous
Sculptor Kan Yasuda is Bibai's most celebrated son. Born in 1945, he is one of the pre-eminent contemporary Japanese sculptors. His minimalist, smoothly undulating works in marble and bronze are critically acclaimed throughout Japan and Europe. Many such works are placed throughout the school building and the surrounding grounds of Arte Piazza Bibai.

Key dates

early February - Snow Festival

early May - Sakura Festival

early August - Song Festival

We say

" Bibai is a quiet town where the attractions can all be visited within a day. While in the region, it is an ideal place to combine with a trip to neighbouring Mikasa. "

Recommended for

Art lovers

Industrial history buffs

Geology and palaeontology enthusiasts

👍 Must see! Kan Yasuda Sculpture Museum Arte Piazza Bibai

This expansive, grassy space is home to a large number of child-friendly, outdoor exhibits, with paddling areas and a charming, old converted schoolhouse which serves as a gallery for smaller pieces of art. Elsewhere in the grounds there is a quiet cafe, which backs onto a workshop where local artists can congregate and create. The aura is a relaxing mix of art, design, and family day out.

👨‍👩‍👧 Kids - Tomei Park

Tomei is a wide, open park with a beautiful lily pond, a playground for kids, tennis courts and, as its centrepiece, an observation tower that offers views over the whole area.

🛏 Accommodation
Pipa-no-Yu Yurinkan

A spacious, modern hotel, located adjacent to Tomei Park, with a park-golf course and a restaurant which serves exquisite set meals.

The hot spring water in the hotel *onsen* is famed amongst locals as being the silkiest to gurgle through the pores of the volcanic strata in the whole region.

⇌ Getting there and around

Bibai is an 80-kilometre drive from New Chitose Airport.

Further information
www.100hiddentowns.jp/hokkaido/bibai.html

Hokkaido

Central Hokkaido
KAMOENAI
神恵内村

Though not a hot spot for thrills and spills – some of the brightest lights on display in Kamoenai are the lanterns strung out for attracting *ika* (squid) on the little, bobbing boats in the sea – this small fishing village, set in a wooded valley with a river running through it, does not lack charm. Kamoenai makes a pleasant base from which to explore the whole Shakotan Peninsula.

👍 Must see!
Doushinkan Folk Toy Museum [1]

One of the town's elders took a disused school and filled it to the rafters with traditional toys to populate this museum.

The second floor has a collection of kites from all over the world and there's also a room where kids can play with the toys and have their picture taken with their favourites.

🏠 Culture Spot
Fukuroma (Herring Pens) [2]

For visitors interested in Japanese fishing techniques, it's worth exploring the seashore on the coastal road leading into Kamoenai from Osukoi roadside station. A pattern of low, rock walls built into the sea are the remnants of the herring pens that fishermen built to hold their live catch before processing them.

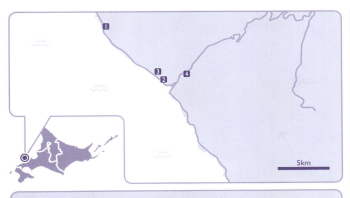

Culture Spot - Kamoenai Folk Museum 3

This folk museum is located in a park that also contains the town's campsite. About 400 local artefacts, dating from the prehistoric era through to the present day, are displayed inside the facility, including exhibits that help to explain the area's herring fishing industry. Note that the museum is closed during the winter.

Nature Spot - Refresh Plaza 998 4

This establishment claims to have the saltiest hot spring water in Japan (1.3 times saltier than the sea). Located on route 998 (hence the name), it is a popular place for locals to stop by on their way home from work. The water is a thick, muddy green - so much so that it leaves stains on bathers' washcloths.

Getting there and around

Kamoenai is a 150-kilometre drive from New Chitose Airport.

Further information
www.100hiddentowns.jp/hokkaido/kamoenai.html

Did you know?

There be dragons
Many of the lampposts in Kamoenai are decorated with dragons. This relates to the story of a woodsman who was woken one night by the vision of a beautiful lady. She claimed to be trapped under a tree in a forest marsh. Persuaded to go and free her, he found the tree and cut through it, releasing an enormous snake. This creature swam out to sea, and villagers built a shrine to it. As a result, prosperity came to the town in the form of (you guessed it...) plentiful herring.

Key dates

first Sunday in July - Okiage Festival (selling of local food such as sea urchin on a bed of rice)

July 14-16 - Kamoenai Itsukushima Shrine Festival (including a fire festival on the final day)

We say

" Kamoenai is a pleasant spot in Hokkaido. Characteristic of the island's tranquility and natural attractions, the town is a good place to stop off and enjoy a hot spring bath and its quiet museums. "

Recommended for

Nature lovers

Those looking for a quiet break

25

Hokkaido

MIKASA 三笠
Central Hokkaido

All of the main attractions for visitors to Mikasa are dotted along the meandering valley of this lush, green-steeped region of Hokkaido. Its mountainous forests are the natural habitat of foxes, deer and bears.

The area commemorates its industrial past with museums and exhibits devoted to coal mining, logging, and vintage trains. Many local attractions serve to focus visitors' interest on the geological heritage of the town - with the Mikasa City Museum being home to Japan's largest collection of ammonite fossils.

The tough winter climate consigns most holidaymakers to visiting in the summer months when, around a tower in the town square, revellers enjoy the fireworks and traditional songs and dances of the Hokkai-bon-odori Festival.

👍 Must see! Mikasa Railway Village and Memorial Museum

This refurbished railway yard is a train enthusiast's heaven. Upon the closure of the local Horonai Railway line in 1987, the buildings here were converted into a museum which now houses a fabulous collection of rail paraphernalia and engines collected from the days of the steam and electric freight trains that served the whole island of Hokkaido.

Objects on display include a large collection of train nameplates, station signs and meticulously recreated miniature replicas of the engines that served back in the day. Operational vintage rail signals and a huge diorama with moving model trains

are just a taster of the many charming exhibits here. There is also a kids' area upstairs with train sets to play with.

Outside, visitors can enjoy the hands-on experience of walking around and sitting inside some of the vintage engines, and can even take a short ride on an original steam train.

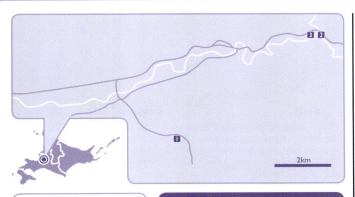

 Did you know?

Mighty ammonite
Ammonites are the prehistoric relatives of such creatures as cuttlefish, squid and octopus. Many ammonites are thought to have been good swimmers, with flattened, discus-shaped, streamlined shells.

Key dates

August 13-15 - Hokkai-bon-odori Festival (Mikasa-chuo park)

We say

"A lovely location for visitors to spend a full and rewarding day. The harsh weather conditions of the area mean that many attractions are only open from April to October. In winter, the ski resorts are popular."

Recommended for

Train fans

Geology lovers

Nature Spot
Geopark Open-Air Museum 2

From directly outside the Mikasa City Museum, visitors can embark upon a pleasant walking trail via a wealth of interesting sights that relate to the geology of Mikasa. The 2.4-kilometre round trip includes tunnels (where the strata of the ancient rock are exposed), the mine pithead and winch, and a mineshaft entrance colourised by the flow of a sulphurous stream. The route follows the contours of what was formerly a logging railway, and runs beside a pretty river which is now occasionally used for canoe racing.

Culture Spot
Mikasa City Museum 3

This museum, located adjacent to the Mikasa Geopark Open-Air Museum, contains five exhibition areas, with ammonite fossils as the stars of the show. Jaw-dropping for their size, number and extraordinary appearance, these remnants of the sea creatures that lived here in the Cretaceous period (about 100 million years ago) are a fascinating attraction. One of the ammonite fossils on display measures 1.3 metres in diameter!

The museum has animated holograms that bring some of the dinosaurs and fossils back to life. The interactive viewfinders are a hair-raising way to visualise how these creatures moved around before they became extinct.

In the museum's other exhibitions there are displays on the local coal mining industry, rural village life, the prison that provided labourers to the mines, and the native flora and fauna.

Getting there and around

Mikasa is a 70-kilometre drive from New Chitose Airport.

  Further information
www.100hiddentowns.jp/hokkaido/mikasa.html

Hokkaido

Central Hokkaido — NUMATA / 沼田町

In this part of Hokkaido, you can travel for miles on the roads, taking in the wide-open mountain terrain without encountering any other vehicles.

Like several of its neighbouring towns, Numata has a notable industrial past, and it is also the site of a wealth of prehistoric discoveries. During the winter, most visitors come for the skiing, but in the wonderfully humidity-free summer months, tourists come to enjoy the lush green farmland and highland scenery.

Culture Spot - Numata Yohtaka Andon Festival

Taking place in late August, this spectacular festival features a procession of huge floats carrying giant, colourful lanterns. Accompanied by the sounds of singing and *taiko* drumming, the brilliantly painted, smoke-spewing constructions are rocked, rotated and rammed into each other during the evening revelry. The lanterns, which are used for that year's festival only, sit atop a five-ton timber mobile shrine.

If your trip does not coincide with the night of the festival, the lanterns' creators may be happy to show you the work in progress during the preceding months. The lanterns are crafted and painted in various workshops and local schools throughout the town, before being assembled in a huge, permanent warehouse devoted to storage for the festival.

Accommodation - Horoshin Hotarukan Hotel

This out-of-town *onsen* hotel is a perfect base from which to explore most of the local attractions - many of which are practically on its doorstep.

The rooms are spacious, the restaurant serves excellent course meals, and the hot spring has both indoor and outdoor baths to unwind in.

Just across the road there are park golf facilities, and a walking path to the scenic head of the Numata Dam. A similarly dramatic view of another dam can be found a few minutes drive uphill from here at Horopiri Lake viewpoint.

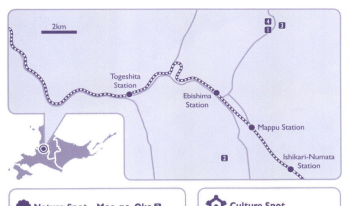

Nature Spot - Moe-no-Oka

The hilltop of Moe-no-Oka provides visitors with a truly spectacular panorama of the mountains to the east of Numata, from a spot remote enough to have no electric cables and scarce air traffic to blemish the view (see main photo).

Must see! Fireflies Walk

Guests and visitors to the Horoshin Hotarukan Hotel can enjoy the enchanting sight of tiny, flickering fireflies flying over and around the sparingly lit walkway that loops around its grounds. The remoteness of the location, with almost no ambient light coming from the surrounding area, also serves to make the stars of the night sky an incredible sight. Note that the firefly season is just a few weeks long, from July until early August.

Getting there and around

Numata is a 160-kilometre drive from New Chitose Airport. Visitors can use local buses for transit from Ishikari-Numata Station to Horoshin Hotarukan Hotel. From here, many of Numata's attractions are a short walk away. To really enjoy all of the area's charms, a car is necessary.

Culture Spot
Numata Fossil Museum

Hokkaido has provided rich pickings for palaeontologists, due to the submersion of parts of the island over its history. Numata was the location of many key finds, and this friendly museum provides visitors with an informal opportunity to get up close to the fossils and the recreated skeletons of various whales and other prehistoric marine creatures. A spacious side room allows youngsters to practise their excavation skills by using tools to erode pre-prepared chunks of soil, which each contain a genuine prehistoric artefact, such as a shark tooth or an ammonite. Located in the adjacent building, there is a small local history museum containing exhibits of the area's wildlife and coal mining past, as well as a vintage steam train engine directly outside.

Did you know?

Park Golf

Park golf, one of the diversions available to visitors to Numata, is a sport that was invented in Hokkaido in 1983. Although the rules are basically the same as for golf, it looks like a hybrid of golf and croquet. The founders wanted to keep the rules simple so that people of all ages could enjoy the game. However, the vast majority of today's participants ('parkers') seem to be of retirement age.

Key dates

the fourth Friday and Saturday of August - Numata Yohtaka Andon Festival (parades, floats and music)

We say

" The climate and lack of any crowds in Numata make this a refreshing and serene getaway in the summer months. The massive view of the wide-open surrounding expanse is breathtaking. "

Recommended for

Nature lovers

Fossil fans

Festival aficionados

 Further information
www.100hiddentowns.jp/hokkaido/numata.html

Hokkaido

KAMISHIHORO 上士幌町
East Hokkaido

Kamishihoro is a small village situated in the eastern area of Hokkaido island. Its quiet, natural surroundings and ancient history make it a welcoming spot, with various attractions and activities spread out across the area.

The diversity of the seasons gives rise to dramatic changes in scenery, providing special experiences throughout the year. The area is covered in rolling hills and lush green grass, bringing a sense of nostalgia for those who hanker for the North European countryside. The autumn leaves at the end of September and the beginning of October add splashes of orange, yellow and red to the beautiful views of the valleys, while the winter has a snowy wonderland feel.

Culture Spot - Vintage Railway Bridges [1] [2] [3]

Kamishihoro was actually named 'Nukabira' during the industrial era, when there were more train lines running across Hokkaido. One such line that used to carry the steam trains through Kamishihoro left a number of railway bridges behind - 34 of which have been preserved. The surrounding countryside and the effects of ageing on the stone make them an attractive feature of the area.

30

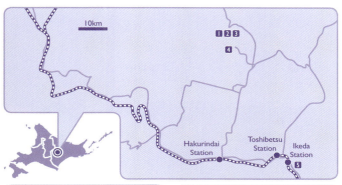

👍 Must see!
Naitai Highland Farm 4

In order to get the best out of the countryside in Kamishihoro, be sure to visit this local ranch. It is renowned for having the widest area of public farm fields in the whole of Japan. The fresh meat and dairy products produced here are of excellent quality due to the special care and attention that is given to their livestock, and can be enjoyed at the rest house at the top of the hill. Climb the high slopes surrounding the valleys to enjoy the astounding scenery from above.

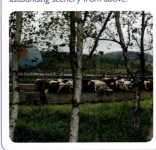

⇌ Getting there and around

Kamishihoro is a 75-kilometre drive from Tokachi-Obihiro Airport.

🍶 Food and Drink

Kamishihoro is located in the Tokachi district which, if renting a car, is very easy to get around. Tokachi is famous for its wine. Near to Kamishihoro is Ikeda Wine Castle 5, which is open every day for public viewing. There you will find vast vineyards, a walkway into their cellar, an exhibition room to see how the wine is made, free wine tasting, and a souvenir shop where the wine is sold at great prices.

The famed farming of the area produces high-quality dairy products, especially the meat. *Wagyu* beef, renowned worldwide for its quality, is plentiful here and can be found at numerous restaurants.

🔍 Did you know?

Lucky cow?
The Tokachi *wagyu* process of cultivating beef consists of a high-quality diet for the cows, including delicious pasture grass and straw produced in Tokachi. The farms also add expensive vitamin C to fatten the meat of the cows.

Key dates
mid-August -
Hokkaido Balloon Festival

We say
" If you have a car, the area is wonderful to explore. Splendid scenery and delicious food make a relaxing visit during the summer. People are very laid-back in the area and always willing to help when asked. "

Recommended for
Nature lovers

Leisurely driving

📖 Further information
www.100hiddentowns.jp/hokkaido/kamishihoro.html

Hokkaido

South Hokkaido — ESASHI 江差町

Esashi, one of the oldest towns in Hokkaido, is located on the western coast of the island's southern tip. The origins of the name Esashi are ambiguous. Some claim it derives from the Ainu word meaning *konbu* (Japanese kelp seaweed), while others say it comes from their word for cape.

Culture Spot - Inishie Kaido Shopping Street

This is a beautifully maintained street, lined with historical houses and shops, including the local branch of the Hokkaido prefectural newspaper, and a number of eateries selling local delicacies.

Nature Spot - Kamomejima

The name translates as 'Seagull Island', but it should more accurately be described as a peninsula, as it is attached to the port of Esashi. Kamomejima is part of Hiyama Prefectural Natural Park, and has long since been an important herring fishing spot. There is also a campsite in the centre of the peninsula.

An unusually shaped rock, called Heishi Rock, stands in the waters between Kamomejima and the Esashi mainland. One legend has it that this rock was dropped in the ocean by an ancient god. Every July it is adorned at the Kamomejima Matsuri Festival with a traditional decoration made from rope.

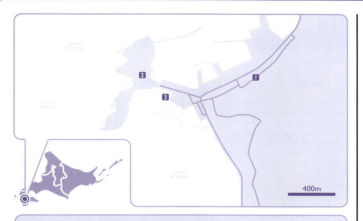

 Did you know?

For the good folk
Esashi oiwake, a type of Japanese folk music, originally came from Esashi. A typical song consists of three sections.

Key dates
first weekend of July - Kamomejima Festival
August 9-11 - Ubagami Daijingu Togyosai Festival

We say
" The short time I spent in Esashi gave me a fresh insight into Japanese life. I encountered a friendly population, fully invested not only in upholding the history of the town, and its tourist profile, but also in the town itself. I saw locals at work and at play - youngsters practising *taiko* drumming in the street, families enjoying the warm weather at the beach, plus young and elderly couples out for dinner at local restaurants. A fascinating town with a rich history. "

Recommended for
Those looking to relax

Japanese culture and history enthusiasts

Must do! Ubagami Daijingu Togyosai

This is the oldest festival in Hokkaido, and it takes place every year over the course of three days just before the Japanese summer holiday of *obon* (mid-August).

Locals pull floats sporting large portable shrines through the streets of the town. The festival celebrates the traditional end of the herring fishing season.

Culture Spot - Kaiyomaru

Kaiyomaru (see main photo) is a replica of an old Japanese warship which was wrecked in 1868 and finally salvaged between 1970 and 1990. The Kaiyomaru was the flagship of a rebel fleet led by Admiral Takeaki Enomoto, who sought to establish the Ezo Republic in Hokkaido.

Food and Drink

The area is famous for *maitake* mushrooms, herring, and the highly prized *iwanori* seaweed. This seaweed can only be harvested from the ocean in the winter months, and is considered to be a rare delicacy of the region, selling for over ten times the standard price of other seaweed. Try the herring *soba* while you are here too.

Getting there and around

Esashi is an 80-kilometre drive from Hakodate Airport. Everywhere in Esashi Town is accessible on foot, although there are also occasional buses to take you from the coast road up to the town centre. There is also a ferry link to Okushiri Island, to the northwest of Esashi.

 Further information
www.100hiddentowns.jp/hokkaido/esashi.html

33

HOKKAIDO
北海道
OTHER TOWNS

North Hokkaido
HIGASHIKAGURA

Higashikagura is a small, predominantly rural town, tucked into the skirts of the Daisetsuzan National Park. It markets itself as a flower town and has a variety of events during the summer including two flower festivals. The main resort is Hotel Hanakagura, which has a large park adjacent to a hot spring.

Culture Spots Clover Ice Cream
Nature Spots Yoshitsune Park, Hotel Hanakagura, Higashi Kagura Forest Park
We say Quiet, but worth visiting for the flowers if you are at Asahikawa or Furano.

Central Hokkaido
MAKKARI

Makkari is a pretty village located at the foot of Mount Yotei, known as 'the Fuji of Hokkaido'. The town has an arboretum, hot springs, and produces local delicacies such as *tofu* and tiger-lily bulbs, as well as drinking water from the Yotei-no-wakimizu springs.

Nature Spots Yotei-no-wakimizu springs, Makkari Arboretum, Makkari Flower Centre
We say Makkari is a great spot to stop off at as part of your drive around this region of Hokkaido.

Central Hokkaido
KUROMATSUNAI

Kuromatsunai, a small town in a vast rural area dominated by farms and forestland, is located about 140 kilometres south-west of Sapporo. The area is full of Japanese beech forests, and is renowned for hiking and trekking. The farming culture in the area means that meat and dairy products are especially popular.

Culture Spots Kuromatsunaicho Buna Centre
We say The vast expanse of space in every direction gives Kuromatsunai a real feeling of peace and tranquility. The drive here from Sapporo goes via the stunning mountain scenery of the Nakayama Toge (mountain pass).

Central Hokkaido
SHAKOTAN

Home to some of Japan's most magnificent views, the Shakotan Peninsula has three scenic capes (Ogon, Kamui and Shakoton).

Nature Spots Misaki-no-Yu (hot spring), Shimamui Kaigan Viewpoint
We say Come to enjoy the fresh air, the stunning clear, blue sea views, hot springs, local seafood and Shakotan Blue - a creamy, mint-flavoured ice cream.

Central Hokkaido
SHINHIDAKA

Shinhidaka, on the south coast of Hokkaido, is a hidden gem in one of the remotest parts of Japan. The area is famous for its seafood, *konbu* (dried seaweed) and asparagus. Speciality meat products include venison, Mitsuishi beef and whey pork.

Nature Spots Nijukken Doro Sakura Namiki (a seven-kilometre-long road, lined with over 2,000 Hokkaido Mountain Cherry Trees)
We say The tranquility, blue sea, green countryside, numerous horses and the food, all combine to make Shinhidaka a wonderful place to visit.

Central Hokkaido
YUBARI

Yubari is a popular ski resort, conveniently located just an hour's drive from New Chitose Airport. It is famous throughout Japan as the home of the delicious Yubari melon. Its memorials to the town's industrial heyday, and its place in Japanese cinema history make the town an interesting diversion on a trip to Hokkaido.

Culture Spots Coal Mining Museum, Cinema Road
We say The spectre of Yubari's abandoned theme park, and the unchecked regrowth of its surrounding vegetation makes for an unconventional but fascinating attraction. Winter continues to attract snow sports enthusiasts to Yubari's ski slopes, while in summer, its delicious melons bring a steady stream of tourists through the town.

Central Hokkaido
YOICHI

About a 100-minute drive from New Chitose Airport and also accessible by train, Yoichi is famous as the birthplace of Mamoru Mori, an early Japanese astronaut, and as the home of Nikka Whisky, whose distillery is open to the public. The nearby Hiyamizutouge viewpoint is a renowned scenic spot overlooking the little hamlet of Akaigawa.

Culture Spots Nikka Whisky Distillery, Fukuhara Fishery
Nature Spots Fugoppe petroglyphs (cave carvings), Yamamoto Sightseeing Orchard
We say A lovely area. When conditions are right, the valley in which the hamlet of Akaigawa nestles fills with a sea of cloud from which the hills protrude like small islands.

Central Hokkaido
YUNI

Yuni sits on a huge plain of farmland, criss-crossed with rod-straight access roads, pretty farmhouses and colourful silos. The farms, overseen by Mount Yubaridake, produce sunflowers, rice, barley, fruit and dairy products.

Culture Spot Yumekkukan (local history museum)
Nature Spot Fushimidai (park with scenic views)
We say A relaxing, back-to-nature area of farms and delicious local produce.

East Hokkaido
SHINTOKU

Shintoku is a vast, rolling district of fields, forests and mountains. In the north there is Mount Tomuraushi at the edge of Daisetsuzan National Park, while further south there are the famed stud farms of Shintoku, which then give way to a vast expanse of buckwheat fields.

Culture Spots Village 432 Horse Riding Club, Ecotorokko
Nature Spots Sahoro Resort Bear Mountain, Mt Tomuraushi
We say A vast district that really feels like the heart of untamed Hokkaido. Sahoro Resort Bear Mountain offers an unmissable opportunity to see Hokkaido bears in a semi-natural setting.

TOHOKU

東北地方

The Tohoku Region

Comprising six large prefectures, the Tohoku region is best known for its cold winters, gorgeous mountainscapes, hot springs, and the towering figures of the warlord Masamune Date and the *haiku* poet Basho Matsuo.

The region is slowly but steadily recovering from the effects of the tsunami and nuclear disaster that it suffered in 2011.

Whether you are looking for spectacular countryside, outdoor activities, unique festivals or just an interest in deep, rural Japan, the Tohoku region has plenty to offer.

AKITA PREFECTURE

Hot springs, lakes, festivals and rice wine - there is much to enjoy in the remote areas of Akita.

Aside from the natural beauty of Akita's mountains and coastline, visitors can also enjoy the rich historical legacy of its castles, preserved samurai districts, and Meiji-era architecture.

Why not experience the frightening but hilarious *namahage* festival in Oga, sample the various hot spring *onsen* of the area, or hike around the unspoilt lake of Towada?

Prefectural Capital
Akita City
✈ Airports
Akita Airport
Odate-Noshiro Airport
🚆 Main Train Stations
Akita Station

Other Tourist Attractions
Shirakami Mountain Range
The beech forest, variety of wildlife, and lush steep slopes of Shirakami have earned the area its designation as a World Heritage Site.
Lake Tazawa
Lake Tazawa is a caldera lake in Semboku. It is the deepest lake in Japan, and a popular vacation area thanks to its abundance of hot spring resorts and proximity to the Tazawa Ski Area - Akita's largest.
Nyuto Onsen
Nyuto Onsen Hot Spring Village is blessed with natural hot spring waters. Even now, visitors can rest up at inns that date back to the Edo era.
Tamagawa Onsen
Rejuvenative, acidic hot spring baths and hiking trails are characteristic attractions of this delightful *onsen* area.
Akita Kanto Festival (Akita City)
Aside from the *namahage* festival of Oga (see page 46), the prefecture has a variety of local-flavoured celebrations including the Akita Kanto Festival, which involves participants using their palms, shoulders and even heads, to carry huge bamboo poles bearing lanterns through the streets of the city.
Date: August 3-6

Extreme Seasonal Conditions Cold in winter.

Nyuto Onsen

AOMORI PREFECTURE

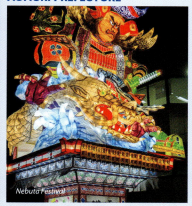
Nebuta Festival

Aomori is blessed with volcanic mountain ranges, Towada-Hachimantai National Park, hot springs, spectacular autumn foliage in Oirase Gorge, and skiing at Mount Hakkoda. Aomori also shares the vast Lake Towada and the Shirakami Mountain forests with the adjacent prefecture of Akita. Check out the unique geological features of Mutsu, and the local festival of Hachinohe.

Prefectural Capital
Aomori City
✈ Airports
Aomori Airport
Misawa Airport
🚆 Main Train Stations
Shin-Aomori Station
Hachinohe Station

Other Tourist Attractions
Shirakami Mountain Range (see *Akita Prefecture*)
Lake Tazawa (see *Akita Prefecture*)
Mount Osore
Mount Osore (the Mountain of Dread), is near Mutsu, on the Shimokita Peninsula. Some Japanese Buddhists believe the souls of the dead reside here. Many visitors make their way to this mountain during the summer and autumn festivals.
Aomori Nebuta Festival (Aomori City)
This summer festival is one of the three largest festivals in the Tohoku region. Nebuta refers to the float depicting a warrior, which is carried through the centre of the city while performers wearing unique costumes dance around and chant.
Date: August 2-7

Extreme Seasonal Conditions Heavy snow in winter.

FUKUSHIMA PREFECTURE

Japan's third largest prefecture, Fukushima is famous for its magnificent scenery, hot springs and long history. This vast area provides a variety of attractive spots from the Pacific coast of the east and the mountain regions to the west. Skiing in winter, seasonal fruits, a trip to Spa Resort Hawaiians, and the much-loved cherry blossoms of Koriyama and Miharu are all highly recommended for a visit, plus the better-known spot of Aizuwakamatsu and the hiking destination of Azuma Kofuji.

Prefectural Capital
Fukushima City
✈ Airports
Fukushima Airport
🚆 Main Train Stations
Fukushima Station

Other Tourist Attractions
Aizuwakamatsu
Located in western Fukushima, Aizuwakamatsu is blessed not only with natural delights, but also a strong historical legacy, with the well-preserved, fascinating sights of the former castle town of the Aizu domain.
Abukuma Cave
Created over millions of years, Abukuma Cave boasts remarkable stalactites, displaying their eerie beauty. The lighting system ensures visitors can see these spectacular formations in all their glory.
Bandai-Azuma Skyline
This is a sightseeing road that runs from Fukushima City and commands panoramic views of the Fukushima landscape.
Iizaka Fighting Festival (Iizaka, Fukushima City)
One of the three major fighting festivals in Japan, Iizaka's has a 300-year tradition. To a backbeat of drums, visitors can enjoy witnessing huge floats crash together in battle.
Date: early October

Extreme Seasonal Conditions Heavy snow in winter.

Aizuwakamatsu Castle

37

TOHOKU

東北地方

IWATE PREFECTURE

Iwate has a fabulous mixture of countryside, and cosmopolitan culture. The prefecture includes the former cultural and political capital of Hiraizumi, the rugged coastline of Sanriku, and the mountains of Hachimantai.

Off the beaten track, visitors can experience the fascinating folk history of Tono, or be inspired by the cooperative recovery efforts of Rikuzentakata - still being rebuilt in the wake of the devastating 2011 tsunami.

Prefectural Capital
Morioka City
✈ Airports
Hanamaki Airport
🚆 Main Train Stations
Morioka Station

Other Tourist Attractions
Hiraizumi
The city of Hiraizumi was the political centre of the northern realm of Japan in the 11th and 12th century, rivalling Kyoto, before its rapid fall. Surviving gardens and temples are a testament to its cultural legacy.

Jodogahama Beach
Take a boat cruise, or relax on the beach to enjoy views of the gorgeous white sands and jutting rocks of this section of coastline.

Ryusendo
Ryusendo are famous limestone caves. Enjoy the underground lakes and bats that make the caves their home.

Iwate Snow Festival (Koiwai Farm, Shizukuishi)
Snow sculptures, play areas, and dining facilities make this festival a great family day out.
Date: late January or early February

Extreme Seasonal Conditions Heavy snow in winter.

Hiraizumi

MIYAGI PREFECTURE

Miyagi is located on the Pacific coast in the southern Tohoku Region. Like much of Tohoku, the area was heavily affected by the 2011 earthquake and tsunami, but recovery continues apace and the area has many cultural and natural sights that remain intact. Enjoy the convenience and history of the Miyagi hub of Sendai, take a seaside stroll and a boat cruise in Matsushima - one of Japan's three most scenic views - or enjoy the historical castle town of Shiroishi.

Prefectural Capital
Sendai City
✈ Airports
Sendai Airport
🚆 Main Train Stations
Sendai Station

Other Tourist Attractions
Aoba (Sendai) Castle
Combine a trip to the Miyagi Prefectural Museum of Art with a trip to the former site of Sendai Castle. While nothing remains of the castle, spectacular views of Sendai City and beyond await those reaching the top of the hill.

Zao
Winter sports, lakes, marshes and cultural experiences greet visitors to the winter wonderland of Zao. Spring and autumn also offer wonderful vistas and trekking opportunities.

Naruko Onsen
A cluster of five villages with hot spring facilities, nearby ski resorts and a museum dedicated to the local tradition of *kokeshi* dolls.

Aoba Festival (Sendai City)
Traditional *suzume odori* dancing, floats and samurai-costumed processions welcome spring to the Miyagi area with this long-established festival. The name *suzume odori*, meaning 'sparrow dance', is derived from its resemblance to sparrows pecking the ground for food.
Date: May

Extreme Seasonal Conditions Cold in winter.

Aoba Festival

38

YAMAGATA PREFECTURE

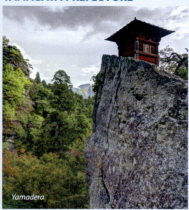
Yamadera

Yamagata is known for mountains, hot springs, agricultural products and temples. Enjoy seasonal activities such as winter sports and hiking in the spectacular countryside. Immerse yourself in the history of Sakata's still-functioning, Meiji-era rice storehouses, and enjoy a taste of the cherry culture in Sagae. Yamagata is also well-known for its traditional arts and crafts, such as lacquerware.

Prefectural Capital
Yamagata City
✈ Airports
Shonai Airport
Yamagata Airport
🚉 Main Train Stations
Shinjo Station
Yamagata Station
Other Tourist Attractions
Yamagata City
Experience cherry blossoms in Kajo Park and visit the ancient mountain temple of Risshaku-ji at Yamadera, just outside the city.
Shirabu Onsen
Set on a high plateau, Shirabu is great for fishing, and skiing, and walks in the hotter months.
Zao (see *Miyagi Prefecture*)
Hanagasa Festival (Yamagata City)
Though relatively new, this festival is one of the most popular in the Tohoku region. Its name translates as 'flower-adorned hat'. Here, large groups of performers move through the streets, wearing their floral headgear and performing their unique dances.
Date: August 5-7

Extreme Seasonal Conditions Heavy snow in winter.

NATIONAL PARKS

Towada-Hachimantai National Park (Michi-noku's Mountain Range)
Area: 85,534 ha
Features: lakes, virgin forests, active volcanoes and hot spring resorts
Did you know? Lake Towada has been shaped by volcanic activity that began approximately 200,000 years ago.

Sanriku Reconstruction National Park
Area: 28,537 ha
Features: beautiful coastlines
Did you know? Formerly known as Rikuchu Kaigan National Park, the Sanriku *Fukko* (Reconstruction) Park's name was changed to encourage visitors to return after the devastating 2011 tsunami that hit the area.

Bandai-Asahi National Park
Area: 186,389 ha
Features: volcanic mountain chains, hiking, winter sports
Did you know? The park is known for its large black bears. Villages by Mount Iide have festivals devoted to (and traditional hunting of) these bears.

Towada Hachimantai National Park

39

TOHOKU

東北地方

HIDDEN TOWNS

AKITA
- 42 Kosaka
- 46 Oga
- 50 Semboku

AOMORI
- 54 Hachinohe
- 58 Mutsu

FUKUSHIMA
- 62 Iwaki
- 66 Nihonmatsu

IWATE
- 68 Rikuzentakata
- 70 Tono

MIYAGI
- 74 Matsushima
- 78 Shiroishi

YAMAGATA
- 82 Sagae
- 84 Sakata

CLIMATE (monthly average temperatures)

MUTSU (north Tohoku)

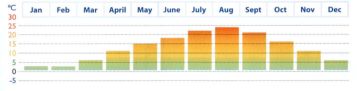

IWAKI (south Tohoku)

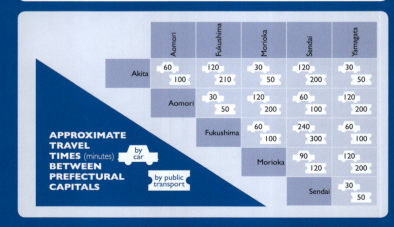

APPROXIMATE TRAVEL TIMES (minutes) BETWEEN PREFECTURAL CAPITALS — by car / by public transport

40

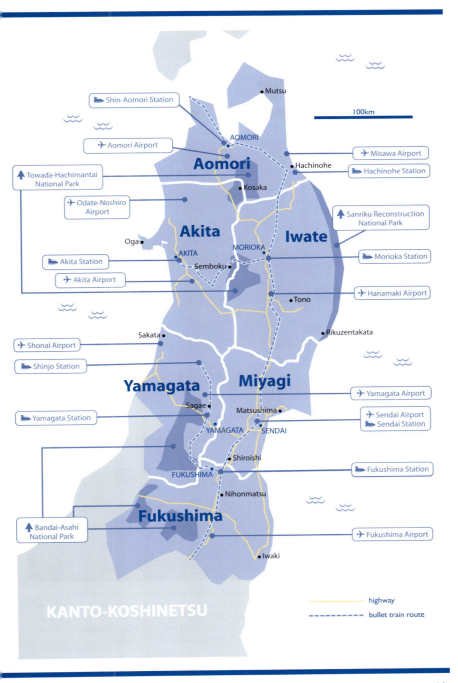

Tohoku

小坂町

Akita

KOSAKA

On the surface, Kosaka may seem like a sleepy, old mining town, but there are a variety of attractions for visitors to the area. The town has diligently preserved its Meiji-era elegance.

The centre is defined by the Meiji 100-Year Road - a pretty, tree-lined thoroughfare which includes the Mine Museum, Tenshikan (a pioneering school in the town) and the elegant Korakukan theatre. For a quieter, out of town experience, the vast Lake Towada (20 kilometres away) is a gorgeous, tranquil spot for enjoying nature through the seasons.

🌳 Nature Spot - Lake Towada

Lake Towada provides a delightful focus for nature lovers, hikers or those seeking a location for a leisurely drive. Paths crossing forded streams that trickle into the lake's tranquil waters ensure a safe, gentle hike for walkers. Visitors can see to the bottom of the lake from jetties that jut out from the shore. An observation deck in the hills to the west affords gorgeous vistas of the whole area.

👍 Must see! Korakukan

Kosaka's rapid population growth through its mining success in the Taisho era led to huge demand from the townspeople for an entertainment venue. Financed by the mine owners, the Korakukan theatre was constructed as a venue for *kabuki* performances.

As the mine's activities slowed over the years, coupled with the rise of other entertainments after the war (notably TV), the popularity of such stage performances waned. The facility was eventually closed in the 1970s with the intention of using it as a location for firefighting practice. However, thanks to the efforts of local activists wishing to preserve their history, the theatre was designated as an important national cultural property, and is now protected from destruction.

The building is unique in that its exterior has a typical Taisho-era, western facade, whereas the interior is in traditional, Edo-era style. Visitors to the theatre can have a guided tour of the building (in Japanese only) in which

the staff explain the workings and traditions of a typical *kabuki* theatre. Of note are the trapdoor and basement wheel mechanics for the revolving stage — impressively, both are operated manually, despite the weight of the sets and actors above. The dressing room is another highlight, with the walls adorned by graffiti from actors of the past.

Historically, *kabuki* performances were lit by candlelight, but from its very beginning, Korakukan used electricity, which was rare at the time. Another snippet of note is the fact that the audience are welcome to consume meals and snacks during the performances. Performers even greet

the audience outside the building after the shows, adding to the intimate ambience. At certain times in the year, notably July, famous Tokyo-based performers visit Kosaka for a short stint.

A special seat called the *rinkanseki* is also preserved at Korakukan. It was the exclusive seat of a censor during the febrile early Showa years. The officer would put a stop to any performance that he (it was always a 'he') deemed to be dangerous or had inappropriate content - usually any hint of criticism of the nation's militarism.

Did you know?

Santa?
Curt Netto (see *Kosaka Mine Office*) also introduced the tradition of Christmas to the town of Kosaka - a fitting festival for an area blanketed with snow in winter.

Whiter than light
The faces of *kabuki* performers were painted white because Edo-era actors performed in candlelight. Now, of course, there are electric spotlights, but the traditional make-up techniques are still used to this day.

Tohoku

Akita — 小坂町 KOSAKA

🏠 Culture Spot - Kosaka Museum ❸

A short walk from the Meiji 100-Year Road, the local museum houses various artefacts related to the mining history of the town. Signs in English describe the science of mining and explain the geology of the area.

🏠 Culture Spot - Kosaka Mine Office ❹

This museum beside Korakukan is a plush facility, showcasing pictures, videos and artefacts which bring to life the history of this copper mining town.

There is plenty of information on Curt Netto, the German mining expert who brought modern techniques to the town, enabling the mines of Kosaka to dramatically increase their output. Netto quickly became a Japanophile, and was well known for painting and sketching local scenes and people, with some of his works on display here.

In large part due to Netto's advice, by 1907 the Kosaka mine had become the most profitable mine in Japan. Its success ensured a population explosion in the area and the necessary development of nearby facilities for entertainment (see Korakukan).

🏠 Culture Spot - Kosaka Tetsudo Railpark ❺

The old Kosaka railway line ran to the now-defunct Kosaka Station. Rather than remove the building and track, the area has been renovated into the Railpark Museum. There are plenty of activities and sights for visitors, including an operational diesel locomotive that runs along the former passenger line.

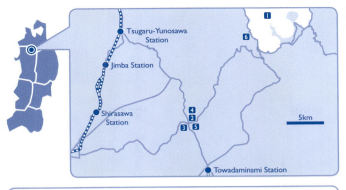

Key dates

second weekend of June - Acacia Festival (includes stage events)

We say

" Nature and a rich slab of early-industrial Japanese history make Kosaka a great place to visit. October is especially recommended for the gorgeous autumn leaves and smells around the wonderfully tranquil Lake Towada. A hike along the shore offers plenty to enjoy. I could even see woodpeckers hard at work on the lakeside tree trunks.

The Korakukan is also a fun visit for a performance and a tour of the fascinating building. "

Recommended for

Nature lovers

Kabuki fans

Accommodation - Towada Hotel 6

Towada Hotel was opened in 1939 on a wooded hill overlooking Lake Towada. The main building is made of Akita cedar, and its entrance and exterior showcase the remarkable craftsmanship of its carpenters.

Food and Drink

The Kosaka area produces its own honey and wine. Both products can be purchased at the souvenir shop of Korakukan.

Getting there and around

⊕ Odate-Noshiro Airport. Hiring a car is recommended for travelling to Kosaka. Alternatively, travel by local train services to Towadaminami Station and then by taxi to Kosaka.

⊖ Morioka Station or Shin-Aomori Station. Travel by local train services to Towadaminami Station and then by taxi to Kosaka.

⊙ Once in Kosaka, the sights are all centred in one area, and are easy to cover in a short time. Travel by rental car or taxi to Lake Towada.

Further information

www.100hiddentowns.jp/akita/kosaka.html

Tohoku

男鹿市

Akita

OGA

The Oga Peninsula boasts a beautifully carved coastline with beaches and strange rock formations.

Far removed from the hustle and bustle of Japanese cities, Oga's hot spring baths, stunning sea views, ancient shrines, folk museums and well-known *Namahage* (demonic ogre - shown above) make it an engaging place to enjoy at your own pace, discovering all it has to offer.

 Nature Spot - Hachibodai [1]

Hidden away amongst the hilltops overlooking the sea are three large, freshwater lakes which were formed following volcanic activity, around 60-80 thousand years ago. From the observation deck high above, the lakes provide great views.

Hachibodai is accessible in spring, summer and autumn, but can be cut off in winter by heavy snowfall.

 Culture Spot - Oga Shinzan Folklore Museum [2]

Here you can watch a live re-enactment of *Namahage* making their demands of children and young wives at a traditional Japanese house. The performance is all in Japanese, but is very entertaining, even for those with limited Japanese language skills. Note that the museum is only open at certain times of the year, so check opening times and the performance schedule in advance.

Must see! - Namahage Museum

Here you can explore the tradition of the *Namahage*. This interactive museum offers a short film (translated via an app) explaining the history of the *Namahage*, opportunities to observe a craftsperson making a *Namahage* mask, and even a chance to dress up in the traditional costume yourself. The Namahage Museum, the Shinzan Folklore Museum, and Shinzan Shrine are all located within five to ten minutes' walk of each other, so you should plan to visit them all as part of the same trip.

Culture Spot - Godzilla rock

Situated off the southern part of the Oga Peninsula, the Godzilla rock is at its best at sunset and can be seen as a fiery silhouette roaring out to sea as the last light of day disappears over the horizon.

Be aware that reaching this spot will mean a five to ten minute walk across rocks heading out to sea, and waterproof clothing is a must in this area, which is usually inhabited by fishers in waders.

Nature Spot - Nyudozaki

This cape is the northernmost part of the peninsula, offering a location to enjoy the fresh sea air and beautiful views of the Sea of Japan. Visitors can take a leisurely walk along the rocky coastline to the sundial and standing stones that mark its 40° northern latitude, and then on to the cape's famous striped lighthouse.

Kids - Oga Aquarium GAO

Located on the west side of the peninsula, Oga Aquarium GAO has beautiful sea views, penguins, polar bears, and a large tank that recreates the sea waters surrounding Oga, plus its own restaurant. It is definitely a must for kids.

 Did you know?

Pooled resources
The freshwater lakes formed from volcanic craters at Hachibodai act as reservoirs for the surrounding area.

Bachelor party?
Traditionally, only single men were allowed to become *Namahage*, but these days, due to a lack of young people living in the area, there is some flexibility.

Masters of rock!
There are very few people who can find the special volcanic rocks used for cooking the famous Ishiyaki hotpot (see *Food and Drink*). If incorrect rocks are used, they simply explode when cold water is poured over them as part of the cooking process!

47

Tohoku

男鹿市

Akita

OGA

🏠 Culture Spot - Namahage Sedo Festival - Shinzan Shrine 7

This ancient shrine is famous for the *Namahage* tradition that happens throughout Oga on New Year's Eve. Traditionally, the *Namahage* are young men in demonic masks and straw costumes who are blessed by local monks. They bang on the doors of village houses, screaming for young children and young wives to study or work hard. Other members of the household fend the *Namahage* off with stories of how good their relatives have been during the year, and placate the noisy intruders with food and *sake*.

In February, the Namahage Festival takes place at Shinzan Shrine. The *Namahage*, bearing flaming torches, wander amongst the crowd, searching for young children to scare into being good for the rest of the year. Many events follow, including traditional drumming, a special dance routine, and the distribution of rice cakes roasted over a large bonfire.

You can take a scheduled bus to the event, either freely laid on by your hotel, or the local public service.

Accommodation - Oga Hot Springs 8

Oga's hot spring hotels, clustered in a quiet area towards the northern tip of the peninsula, have Western and Japanese rooms with breakfast and dinner as a package. The breakfasts are usually a buffet of Western and Japanese foods. The dinners are generally cooked using locally sourced produce in a variety of traditional ways, so the choice and quality is good.

Hotels can help you with booking transport, including taxi tours, for the duration of your stay. Restaurants for lunch are few and far between in this area, so be prepared to travel (by car or taxi) to find somewhere to eat. There are no convenience stores in the area, so you may want to stock up on supplies before you arrive.

Key dates

second Friday, Saturday and Sunday in February - Namahage Festival (Shinzan Shrine)

We say

" Oga is a great place to visit, but there is limited travel assistance available in English, so it's best to organise as much as you can via a tour operator or tourist office before you arrive."

Recommended for

Nature lovers

Aficionados of traditional Japanese culture

Parents of naughty children!

 Food and Drink

Ishiyaki hotpot

This is a dish of fish, fresh vegetables, and seaweed, in a *miso* broth. Special volcanic rocks, heated to around 300°C, are added to a cedar pot together with the ingredients. This method of cooking mimics the way fishers used to heat their meals on the beach after a trip out to sea. A delicious, traditional blend of local tastes, prepared at your table.

Bouanago (conger eel)

Bouanago is grilled, dried eel best served with lemon, ground Japanese radish and a little soy sauce. Eel is well known for giving extra stamina, so if you're in need of an energy boost, look no further.

Oga Shottsuru Yakisoba

A meal of *soba* noodles fried in *shottsuru* sauce combined with seaweed and local seafood. *Shottsuru* sauce is made from the locally caught sailfin sandfish, a famous produce of the Akita region.

Getting there and around

✈ Akita Airport. Travel to Oga by taxi or rental car, or take a bus to Akita Station.

🚆 Akita Station. Take the Oga Line to Oga Station. You can make your way either by local bus or taxi to your chosen destination.

🚕 Taxis are available to hire for tours that can last for one to four hours. Hotels can help arrange this with some notice. The taxi drivers act as tour guides and kindly explain about the local area and the history behind its traditions and heritage. This service is only available in Japanese.

 Further information
www.100hiddentowns.jp/akita/oga.html

49

Tohoku

Akita

SEMBOKU
仙北市

Semboku encompasses a large and diverse area in Akita. From the graceful, Edo-era streets of Kakunodate, to the heights of Mount Komagatake and the hidden depths of Lake Tazawa, Semboku has something for everyone, and is the jewel in the crown of the Tohoku region.

Nature Spot - Dakigaeri Valley

The literal meaning of Dakigaeri is to hug and turn, coming from the fact that the path along the valley used to be so narrow that two travellers meeting would have to embrace each other in order to pass by.

The old path is now replaced with a well-made track that runs along the side of the valley.

From the red suspension bridge that marks its entrance, the path clings to the gorge, drawing you deeper in. There are beautiful views throughout the valley, with blue mountain water running along its bottom. The path ends at the Mikaeri waterfall, which is famous for the silk-like strings of water that run down the rock face - a fitting climax to the walk. The valley is best viewed in spring or autumn.

50

👍 Must see! Kakunodate ②

Kakunodate is an old samurai castle town, which in its current form dates back to 1620. The castle itself was abandoned at the start of the Edo period, as the central government looked to solidify its control of the country. The samurai houses standing in the *Bukeyashiki* district are possibly some of the best-preserved examples in Japan. A pleasant walk down a wide boulevard, with the houses, fences and gate houses stretched out in front of you, allows you to almost slip back into a bygone era.

There are two main streets that make up the *Bukeyashiki*. Along these you will find a mixture of historical residences, storehouses and craft shops - all preserved in period style. Enjoy walking around the area and experiencing this 'Little Kyoto', with many of the residences open to the public.

🤔 Did you know?

Deep, deep down
Tazawa is the deepest lake in Japan, and the 17th deepest lake in the world. The lake's surface is at an altitude of 249m, but the bottom of the lake is 175m below sea level. Despite the surrounding area being blanketed in snow in winter, the lake's surface never freezes.

🏠 Culture Spot - Aoyagi House ③

The largest of the residences, this rambling complex of buildings houses more than you would expect from a samurai accommodation. There are collections of swords and armour, and also some more unusual items, including a set of arquebuses from the 16th century - a rare find, as shortly after, all firearms were banned and destroyed in Japan until the Meiji era. In other buildings there are a set of prints and uniforms from the turn of the 20th century, marking Japan's move into the modern era, and also a set of gramophones and early vinyl, showcasing one of the previous owner's passions during the turbulent 1920s and 1930s. All in all, an interesting collection that gives insight into more than just the samurai heyday.

Tohoku

Akita — SEMBOKU 仙北市

🍶 Food and Drink - Morokoshi [4]

Morokoshi - a popular souvenir of Kakunodate - is a traditional type of sweet made from *azuki* beans. Available in a number of different forms, you can get these at several places in the town, including the Bukeyashiki branch of Morokoshian. *Morokoshi* goes well with a cup of green tea.

🌳 Nature Spot
Mount Furushiro [5]

At the end of the *Bukeyashiki* is a low, tree-lined hill, where Kakunodate Castle used to stand. The castle is now gone, but the walk to the top is worth it for views of the river and hills beyond.

🌳 Nature Spot - Lake Tazawa [6]

Lake Tazawa is actually one of the deeper lakes in the world, reaching a depth of 425m. Local legends claim that a dragon lurks in the sunken depths, protecting the lake. The dragon was originally a local girl, Tatsuko, who was searching for a holy spring so that her beautiful looks would last forever. Instead, as these things often seem to turn out, she was cursed and turned into the form of a dragon. The legend is well known in Japan and is commemorated by a gold statue of Tatsuko in the lake's waters. The lake's volcanic origins are indicated by its circular shape. Its sapphire blue waters are surrounded by mountains and, intriguingly, it has no inflows or outflows.

You can cruise on the lake by boat or rent a bicycle to cycle the perimeter.

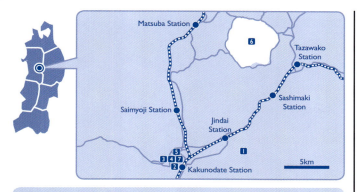

🌳 Nature Spot - Hinokinai Riverbank 7

If you are here for the cherry blossom, just a couple of minutes from the *Bukeyashiki* is the cherry-tree-lined Hinokinai River. Designated one of the best cherry blossom spots in Japan, even out of season it is a pleasant walk.

⇌ Getting there and around

- ✈ Akita Airport. Travel by bus and train services to Tazawako Station.
- 🚋 Tazawako Station. Travel by local train services to Kakunodate Station.
- 🚶 The main town of Kakunodate is wonderfully compact and can all be covered on foot. Tazawako has regular bus services from Tazawako Station.

🌿 Further information
www.100hiddentowns.jp/akita/semboku.html

Key dates

Feb 10 - Kamihinokinai Paper Balloon Festival (around 100 hand-made, paper hot-air balloons, some as large as eight metres tall, are released into the night sky)

April - Someiyoshino cherry blossoms in Kakunodate

Sep 7, 8, 9 - Kakunodate Festivals (listed as cultural assets, the festival sees the town take to the streets with floats, dancing and music)

We say

" Semboku should be high on anyone's list to visit. There is so much to see and do, and none of it disappoints. The only surprise being why more people aren't here. "

Recommended for
Everyone

Tohoku

Aomori

HACHINOHE
八戸市

Hachinohe has much to recommend it. Visitors come for its famously beautiful coastline, notable sites of historical significance and its festivals. One such celebration is the Sansha Taisai - a breathtaking five-day festival of floats that the whole town seems to stop for. With more time, you can explore the region, which has been described as 'a ceilingless museum'.

🏠 Culture Spot - Kushihiki Hachimangu Shrine

This shrine, whose origins go back to the Kamakura period, is a ten-minute taxi ride from the centre of Hachinohe. The main hall was built in 1648 and is set in a densely wooded forest of extremely tall, ancient Japanese cedars that can be strolled through in the grounds.

The jewel of this shrine is the National Treasure Room in the adjacent building. Here, amongst other exhibits of the period, are two sets of priceless samurai armour. The displays are all supplemented with an English audio commentary.

54

👍 Must see! Hachinohe Sansha Taisai Festival (31st July–4th August)

This largest float festival in Japan dates back almost 300 years. The parade of 27 floats with *mikoshi* (portable shrines) can stretch out to over two kilometres long from end to end. Everyone in the whole town seems to help out, with countless people dressed up in traditional costumes of maidens and warriors, dancing, playing flutes and *taiko* drums, and chanting in exhilarating, ritualistic rhythms. The traditionally decorated floats, pulled by long ropes, start off the size of a large lorry and then open outwards and upwards, more than doubling in size to the height of a three or four-storey building. The floats carry scenes of mythological and *kabuki* characters - leering demons, giant tigers, floating queens, flying gods, demon lords, and other strange creatures, as well as dragons, some spouting bursts of smoke from their jaws. One parade is not enough - if possible watch the daytime, dusk and night parades (when the floats are illuminated) as each has a different atmosphere. A truly world-class festival.

❓ Did you know?

Pomp and splendour

Arguably Japan's most beautiful and best preserved samurai armour rests in Hachinohe at Kushihiki Hachimangu Shrine. It was made for the lord of the region in the late Kamakura period. It has elaborate gold chrysanthemum decorations that still shine brightly, and the deep red of its lace is a testament to the skill of the dyers of the period.

55

Tohoku

Aomori

HACHINOHE
八戸市

🏠 Culture Spot - Kagami-Style Kiba Dakyu (traditional Japanese polo) Chojasan Shinra Shrine [2]

If you come for the festival, why not supplement your visit with a completely unique experience on August 2nd, and see some Japanese polo? The event began in 1827 as a means to improve the riding skills of Hachinohe soldiers. Riders are divided into two teams (red and white) and compete on horseback to catch a ball using a pole with a net, to throw it into the goal. The games last two hours - some quite competitive, with horses braying upon collision. This traditional sport now only exists in three places in Japan: the Imperial Household, Yamagata City and Hachinohe. For this reason, it is more than worth attending and is free to the general public, so come early to secure the best viewing position.

🍶 Food and Drink

There is a Hachinohe culture of backstreet eating and drinking that goes back many years. There are eight alleys and small roads in the centre with all manner of intimate bars and eateries to investigate. The red lanterns at the alley entrances welcome visitors to try Hachinohe *ramen* or the local dish of Senbei Jiru, where the *senbei* takes on a firm but sticky texture in the soup stock.

🏠 Culture Spot - Hachinohe Portal Museum (Hacchi) [3]

The Hachinohe Portal Museum is one of the newest tourist sites in Hachinohe. There are many small exhibition booths over three floors, for local foods, festivals, history and culture. There are also cafes, and a shop selling original local arts and crafts. A highlight is the handmade, wooden clock on the first floor, beneath which a large display of Japanese lions' heads announces the hour with rhythmic jaw clapping.

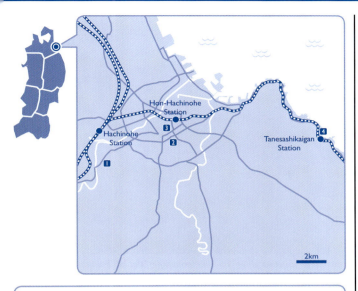

Key dates

July 31 - August 4 - Hachinohe Sansha Taisai Festival

February 17 - 20 - Hachinohe Emburi Festival

We say

"The Hachinohe Sansha Taisai Festival completely surprised me with its scale and pure entertainment value. I am sure it could give the Rio Carnival a run for its money!"

Recommended for

A stand-alone holiday with a rental car

Festival enthusiasts

Nature Spot - Tanesashi Coast

A short, 20-minute train ride and walk bring you to this nationally designated place of scenic beauty in Hachinohe. The Tanesashi Coast runs for about 12 kilometres and has long trails, an observatory, a pretty beach, and a stretch of coastal lawn where natural grass spreads to the water's edge – a rare phenomenon.

Kids

Children will love the Sansha Taisai Festival, with its colour and music, not to mention the exciting atmosphere and abundance of food and toys sold by street vendors.

Accommodation

There is no shortage of hotels in Hachinohe. The Daiwa Roynet Hotel is moderately priced and has a restaurant and shop. Most importantly, the Daiwa is in an excellent position from which to enjoy the festival parade passing outside.

Getting there and around

- Misawa Airport. Travel by bus and train services to Hachinohe Station.
- Hachinohe Station.
- The centre of Hachinohe is easily navigated on foot, but for many sights a bus, taxi or rental car is needed.

Further information

www.100hiddentowns.jp/aomori/hachinohe.html

Tohoku

Aomori

MUTSU むつ市

Mutsu is located near to the northern tip of Honshu, where the Shimokita Peninsula snakes away from the main island, ending in a remote enclave of mountains, forests and rivers. The area feels like the last outpost of the mainland, offering glimpses back to an older Japan of pilgrimages to the mouth of hell, and imps hiding out in brooks and valleys.

🌳 Nature Spot - Yagen Valley

There are two versions of how the hot waters of the Yagen Valley were discovered.

One claims that forces retreating from defeat at the Siege of Osaka, which cemented the power of the Tokugawa shogunate, found the springs in 1615.

An older tale dates their discovery back to the strangely specific 862AD, when the monk En'nin, of Mount Osore fame, was injured after getting lost in the area. He was then discovered by a *kappa* - a traditionally mischievous water imp - who bathed him in the hot springs to heal him.

There are a number of paths snaking their way up and around the wooded valley of Yagen. Perhaps the main attractions of the area are the riverside hot springs in which you can bathe and admire the beautiful countryside.

👍 Must see! Mount Osore ②

Following his return to Japan after studying in China, a ninth-century monk named Ennin (also known as Jikaku Daishi) discovered Mount Osore in the northernmost extremes of Honshu. He designated the volcanic site a sacred place.

Worshippers have prayed for over a thousand years that the souls of the deceased would return to the mountain. Mount Osore continues to offer hope for souls that wish for peace in this life and in the afterlife.

Visitors to Mount Osore today can see first-hand why Ennin was so taken by the area. The rocky landscape and bubbling sulphur pits create a mesmerising atmosphere that is said to resemble hell - while the white-sand beach around the lake has been likened to paradise.

 Did you know?

Two Mutsus
Mutsu was the first Japanese city to write its name in the more simplified Hiragana script, rather than Chinese characters. This was done to avoid confusion with the ancient kingdom of Mutsu that once encompassed almost all of the Tohoku region.

59

Tohoku

Aomori

MUTSU 市むつ

🏠 Culture Spot - Ominato Nebuta Festival

At the Ominato Nebuta Festival, large, illuminated floats depicting warriors and folk heroes roam the streets. Aomori City also hosts a renowned Nebuta Festival, but a stop off at Mutsu in early August will coincide with their local version of this festival, dating back over a hundred years. Enjoy the music and soak up the carnival atmosphere.

🌳 Nature Spot - Mount Kamabuse ③

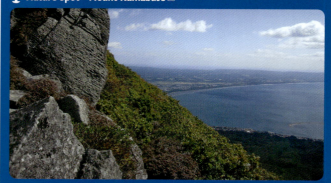

Mount Kamabuse looms large over the main town of Shimokita, and marks the head of the bay. It is also the location of Honshu's most northerly snow resort. Winter visitors should check out its compact snow course, where the slopes almost seem to lead into the sea. At other times it's possible to hike up to the top of the mountain. To do this, follow the ski lifts to the last of the huts, from where the course is signposted. After an hour or so of hacking your way through the slightly overgrown paths, you get to the top of the mountain and can take in the genuinely breathtaking views of the whole peninsula opening up in front of you. On a good day you can see Hokkaido just across the channel to the north.

Key dates

July - Osorezan Taisai Festival (Osorezan Shrine festival including the mysterious Itako-no-kuchiyose – an event where the spirits of the dead are summoned to speak with the living)

We say

" Mutsu may be a bit of a one-horse town, but what a horse! The smoking gateway to hell at Mount Osore is unmissable, and there are some wonderful areas of nature to enjoy. Also take the opportunity to enjoy the riverside *onsen* in the open air. "

Recommended for

Lovers of unspoilt nature and ancient Japanese culture

🏠 Culture Spot - Hokuyo-kan (Maritime Museum) 4

Ominato is the most northerly naval port on the main island of Japan. Due to its strategically vital location, guarding the north of Japan, the Japanese navy has kept a base here since the Imperial Fleet first sailed. There is still a naval base just outside the main town, and attached to this is the Maritime Museum. Sitting in a quaint stone building, this museum contains exhibits and photos of Japanese naval history, mainly focused on the Mutsu area.

The museum is not large, but the photos are interesting and include English captions, so it's worth checking out if you are in the area.

🚆 Getting there and around

✈ Misawa Airport or Aomori Airport. Travel by rental car or bus and train services to Shimokita Station or Ominato Station.

🚅 Shin-Aomori Station or Hachinohe Station. Travel by local train services to Shimokita Station or Ominato Station.

🚌 Most of the attractions are fairly spaced out, but there is an efficient public transport system in the area. Be careful to check timetables before going to Mount Osore.

📖 Further information
www.100hiddentowns.jp/aomori/mutsu.html

Tohoku

Fukushima
IWAKI
いわき市

The area in and around Iwaki is a testament to innovation and to the resilience of its residents.

Situated near the east coast of Fukushima Prefecture, it was part of Japan's largest coal field until oil replaced coal as Japan's main source of power in the 1960s. The local economy faced ruin, before the owner of the Joban Tanko coal mine had the idea of using the area's hot springs as one of the main attractions of a new Hawaiian-themed spa resort.

As well as Iwaki's many family-themed attractions, it is also the home to beautiful rolling hills, and shrines (including the nearby Ogawasuwa Shrine – see main picture).

👍 Must see!
Spa Resort Hawaiians ❶

As its name suggests, Spa Resort Hawaiians is a Polynesian-themed tourist attraction with four hotels, five spa-themed leisure areas, swimming pools with water slides, a golf course, restaurants and twice-daily stage shows of live hula dancing and fire juggling. It is a hugely popular family retreat which caters for all ages. The resort is a 15-minute bus ride from Yumoto Station.

👨‍👩‍👧 Kids

There is so much to do in Iwaki with kids. As well as Spa Resort Hawaiians, Aquamarine Fukushima, and Iwaki Coal and Fossil Museum, you can go to the seafront to visit Lalamew, a visitors' centre that sells a variety of local seafood, sweets, pickles and farm produce. It also has restaurants and a play facility. Upstairs, there is a small museum which commemorates the events and aftermath of the 2011 earthquake and tsunami.

🏠 Culture Spot
Iwaki Yumoto Onsen [2]

There is a cluster of local businesses housing hot spring baths located a short walk from the Iwaki Coal and Fossil Museum. The renowned restorative and healing properties of the Iwaki Yumoto Springs have been popular for over one thousand years. Enjoy this quiet, inexpensive chance to unwind and relax.

🏠 Culture Spot - Shiramizu Amidado (or Ganjo-ji) [3]

This temple, which originally dates back to the 12th century, is arrived at through its beautiful garden (called Jodo Teien) by crossing a picturesque red bridge that spans the surrounding pond, where lotus flowers bloom throughout the summer.

❓ Did you know?

Hula Girls
The story of the beginnings of Spa Resort Hawaiians (at that time called 'Joban Hawaiian Centre'), set against the closure of the Joban Tanko coal mine, was dramatised in 2006's award-winning Japanese movie, 'Hula Girls'. The actresses spent three months studying hula dancing in preparation for the film.

Real-life Hula Girls from Iwaki toured eastern Japan, performing at earthquake refugee shelters in the aftermath of the 2011 disaster.

63

Tohoku

Fukushima — いわき市 IWAKI

🏠 Culture Spot
Iwaki Coal and Fossil Museum (Horuru Iwaki-shi Sekitan Kaseki-kan) 4

This museum, situated a few minutes' walk from Yumoto Station, is home to two very distinct sets of exhibits.

When you arrive in the main hall of the ground floor, you are immediately face-to-face with the skeletons and fossils of a menagerie of prehistoric and contemporary beasts. The items on display (including the Mamenchisaurus - the largest complete dinosaur fossil found in Asia) originate from various excavations around the world. A 6.5-metre-long Elasmosaurus, discovered in Iwaki, is also here. Upstairs there is a collection of fossils and minerals, with a large window overlooking the bones below.

Walk a little further to the next elevator, and brace yourself for a descent into the recreated tunnels and scenes that illustrate the daily lives of the men and women of Iwaki who mined the Joban coal field until its demise in the 1970s. These displays provide a fascinating insight into local human history.

There is an English-language handout available that explains some of the museum's highlights.

⇌ Getting there and around

✈ Fukushima Airport. Travel to Iwaki Station by bus, then to Yumoto Station by JR Joban Line.

🚆 Fukushima Station. Travel to Yumoto Station by local train services.

You can also travel to Yumoto Station by a direct JR Joban Line train service from Tokyo Station (two-hour limited express train service).

Several bus companies operate highway bus services between Tokyo Station and Iwaki Station. Spa Resort Hawaiians runs daily, free bus services for staying guests to and from the Tokyo area.

🚶 Most of the attractions in Iwaki are located near Yumoto Station and the Onahama port area, rather than in the city centre around Iwaki Station. Spa Resort Hawaiians is accessible from Yumoto Station by local buses and their own free shuttle bus. Local buses run between the Onahama area and both Yumoto Station and Izumi Station.

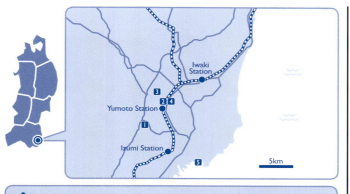

🏠 Culture Spot - Aquamarine Fukushima 5

This enormous aquarium and museum houses a wide variety of marine creatures and plants that thrive where Fukushima's ocean currents collide with the area's rivers. There is a botanical garden on the fourth floor, from which visitors can see into the aquarium's centrepiece, the Shiome Sea twin tanks, which contain a miscellany of colourful fish. These can also be observed from a triangular tunnel that runs below.

Aquamarine Fukushima has plenty of play spaces and equipment (inside and outside) and creative activities for kids. It is a superbly designed, modern and spacious facility.

English-language brochures are available.

🍶 Food and Drink

Some of the delicacies Iwaki is known for producing are *ikameshi* (squid cooked with rice inside), figs, scallions, *yanagi* (dried flatfish), bonito, red snow crabs, yams, *uni* (sea urchins), and delicious *sanma* (Pacific saury).

🛏 Accommodation

As well as Spa Resort Hawaiians, there are several impressive hotels and *ryokan* within a short walk from Yumoto Station.

📷 Further information
www.100hiddentowns.jp/fukushima/iwaki.html

Key dates

mid-January - Konpira-sama Festival (Kotohira Shrine, Yumoto)
early April - Sakura Light Up (Ogawasuwa Shrine)
mid-April - Spring Festival (Iwaki City Flower Center, Taira)
early August - Iwaki Fireworks Festival (Aquamarine Park, Onahama) and Iwaki Odori (Iwaki Station)
early August - Taira Tanabata Festival, including *jangara*, Iwaki's traditional folk dance (Taira Shopping District)
mid-August - Kaiten Yagura Bon Odori Festival (Uchigo Station)
mid-September - Yabusame (Horseback Archery) (Iino Hachimanguu Shrine, Taira)
mid-November - Autumn Leaves Light Up (Shiramizu Amidado)

We say

" If you want a quick family getaway from Tokyo, Iwaki is a great all-weather solution. If the weather is fine, include a trip to the countryside and the local shrines. If not, take shelter indoors at the family-themed attractions of Spa Resort Hawaiians or Aquamarine Fukushima. Be sure to find the time to unwind in one of the many hot spas. "

Recommended for

Families with kids of all ages

65

Tohoku

Fukushima

NIHONMATSU
二本松市

Known as a gateway for routes to several local attractions (including winter sport resorts, the nearby Ebisu Circuit race complex, and Tohoku Safari Park), Nihonmatsu itself deserves a visit for its mix of nature, history and local craftsmanship. Certainly it has enough charms for a one or two-day stay.

👍 Must see! Nihonmatsu Castle ❶

Nihonmatsu Castle originally dates from 1341, but was fully constructed in the 17th century by the Niwa clan as a major castle along the route to Edo. Later, it was also one of the strategic points of the Tokugawa shogunate forces that fought and lost the Boshin War against the Imperial Army. Today, only the stone walls remain of the castle ruins, but the whole area is a wonderful park. The location is quite a climb, suggesting that in its heyday it must have been a formidable fortress, before its destruction through modern firepower. It is a perfect spot for hiking or mountain biking, with the leafy hills and, in season, cherry blossom backdrop delivering a nature-packed day out. The paths are sturdy, but you do need to be quite fit. Reaching the peak is rewarded with panoramic views of surrounding villages and mountains, including Mount Adatara.

Culture Spot - Chieko Memorial Museum ❷

Chieko Takamura was an artist during the Taisho era. She was involved in the publication of the magazine *Seito*, which covered the women's liberation movement, and she is regarded as a pioneer of Japan's 'new woman' movement. The museum is set in the former home of her family, who used to produce rice wine. You can see the typical early 20th-century furniture and decor, as well as some of her works. A lengthy English explanation describes her life and strong marriage, as well as her sad descent into schizophrenia, which was precipitated by the decline of her father's business.

66

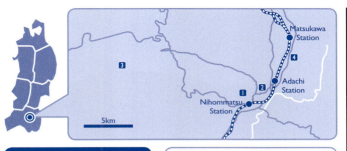

 Did you know?

Heart of stone

Just outside the town, Kanzeji Temple has a rock formation that inspired an *Onibaba* legend (a traditional Japanese horror story in which an old woman feasts on human passersby). The *Onibaba* is said to have lived among the rocks. Aside from such tales, it is thought the rocks provided a human abode during Japan's early history in the Jomon period.

Devastating

It only took a day for Nihonmatsu Castle to fall to the superior firepower of the Imperial Army forces. Hundreds of samurai died, and the castle was destroyed, never again to be rebuilt. The death of several boy fighters mirrors the much better-known tragedy of the *Byakkotai* young fighters, who perished in the larger castle town of Aizuwakamatsu, nearby.

Nature Spot
Mount Adatara [3]

You can reach halfway up the mountain via ropeway. The mountain is especially recommended in either autumn for its gorgeous sea of red leaves, or in spring for the ubiquitous *sakura* cherry blossoms. Hiking to the peak takes a couple of hours of solid effort, but is a safe, rewarding day out for mountain lovers. The ropeway also offers a spectacular view of the mountain slopes lit up during summer.

Culture Spot
Washi Denshoukan (Japanese Paper Museum) [4]

Nihonmatsu has a long tradition of paper-making. Located in a motorway service stop to the north of the town, the Denshoukan offers visitors an opportunity to purchase crafts made from traditional Japanese paper, as well as having a hands-on go at making a postcard themselves. The staff will patiently explain the process, and demonstrate how the paper is sourced from the Kozo Tree and converted into

paper through a process involving shaving, soaking and drying.

Key dates

May 3–5 - Grand Annual Festival at Mannin Komori-jizosan (festival to pray for the healthy growth of children)

October 4-6 - Lantern Festival

mid-October to mid-November - Chrysanthemum Festival

Getting there and around

Fukushima Airport. Travel to Koriyama Station by limousine bus, then to Nihonmatsu Station by local train services on the Tohoku Line.

Koriyama Station or Fukushima Station. Travel to Nihonmatsu Station by local train services on the Tohoku Line.

Once in the town, be prepared to walk quite a lot to see the best sights, or hire a taxi if you wish to visit the museums mentioned. English guidebooks can be picked up from the station.

Food and Drink

The traditional local dish is known as *Zakuzaku* - a healthy stew of carrot, radish and other root crops. Locally made sweets known as *Tamayokan* are a real treat. You can get them in traditional, maple syrup or peach flavour. Several local shops selling such sweets are still located in their Edo-era buildings. Nihonmatsu also has many breweries of its local *sake*.

We say

"Nihonmatsu's castle grounds offer a double delight of history coupled with nature."

Recommended for

Hikers / Nature lovers / History lovers

 Further information
www.100hiddentowns.jp/fukushima/nihonmatsu.html

67

Tohoku

RIKUZENTAKATA
陸前高田市
Iwate

Arguably an unorthodox tourist destination (it is most famous for being almost wiped off the map by the devastating 2011 tsunami), Rikuzentakata is one of the most forward-thinking, resilient places in Japan. This coastal town continues to rebuild and regenerate itself towards being an attractive, tsunami-proof hub for visitors.

Culture Spot - Kesen Carpentry and Folklore Museum

This museum showcases the excellent carpentry skills of Kesen carpenters. The main building is made from Kesen cedar and was built in 1992. Interestingly, its elaborate construction, which relies on the wood fitting perfectly in notches rather than using metal bolts, ensured that the building withstood the 2011 earthquake.

The building is a reconstruction of ancient, rustic homes of the area. The entrance has a statue to ward off fires, and the vast, airy living quarters are centred around an *irori* - a traditional hearth which has pots and kettles held over the fire by ropes attached to the ceiling. On a clear day, you can enjoy a gorgeous view of the sea from this hilltop museum.

Must do! Oyster Fishing Tour

As one of Rikuzentakata's regenerative tourism projects, visitors can take a boat with a local fisherman to speedily skip upon the waves and admire the town from the sea. The fresh air, bracing winds and scenic views make for a fun trip. Passengers are taken to the oyster beds and then, once back on land, the fishermen demonstrate how the oysters are farmed. In autumn and winter, you can even get a taste of the fresh oysters.

Other similar projects in the town focus on craftspeople, farmers, and producers of *yuzu* and apple.

👍 Must see! The Miracle Pine

Take a guided tour around the reconstruction zone to witness Rikuzentakata's rapid regrowth. The famous Miracle Pine - the sole survivor of the 70,000-odd pines that graced the coast - strikingly conveys the power of the tsunami. There was some controversy about spending so much money to maintain the shape of the tree after it died, poisoned by the excess of salt water at its roots, but as a symbol of defiance, hope and regrowth, it is a key spot to visit. The town has an ongoing project of replanting pine saplings in order to return the area to its former beauty.

🍴 Food and Drink
Rikuzentakata Hota-Waka Gozen (scallop and seaweed shabu-shabu set)

This specially designed delicacy - a three-tiered tower of deep-fried, raw, and grilled scallops accompanied by a *wakame* seaweed *shabu-shabu* dish (dipping food in simmering water) and rice - was commissioned to encourage local tourism. The seaweed changes colour from black to green and then is dipped in sauce and eaten. The dish is served at several restaurants outside the reconstruction zone including Wai-wai in the temporary shopping centre to the north of its former location.

Another local delicacy is the soy sauce-flavoured ice cream. Sounds disgusting? Actually, it's just the right amount of soy sauce, and resembles the flavour of vanilla with a sprinkle of salt. It is made by the local soy sauce company, Yagisawa Shoten, which, despite its factory being destroyed by the tsunami, encouragingly kept all of its staff in employment and refused to make redundancies.

🏨 Accommodation

A temple or farm stay is an option to get great home cooking and an insight into rural life and culture.

🚆 Getting there and around

✈ Hanamaki Airport. Travel by local trains and buses to Rikuzentakata.

🚆 Ichinoseki Station. From there, travel by local trains and buses. The town used to be served by trains, but after the tsunami, the line from Kesennuma to Rikuzentakata was replaced by a bus service, so plan your journey carefully.

🚌 It is strongly recommended for travellers without their own transport to contact the local authorities in advance so that a tour can be arranged.

📖 Further information
www.100hiddentowns.jp/iwate/rikuzentakata.html

💡 Did you know?

A long journey
The Kamome, a fishing boat belonging to the town's Takata High School, drifted across the Pacific Ocean for two years after it was washed away in the tsunami. It eventually made landfall at Crescent City on the northwestern coast of California. Since then, the two towns have established international, cross-cultural projects and exchange programmes which show that, through tragedy, opportunity can blossom.

Key dates

early autumn - Tour de Sanriku (bicycle race)

August 7 - Kenka Tanabata Star Festival (festival with giant decorated floats and a 900-year history)

We say

" On the surface, Rikuzentakata looks like a building site, but spend some time there, chat to the locals, and you will realise it is now one of the most dynamic and forward-thinking towns in the country. I came away thinking that Rikuzentakata can be a model for other towns in Japan, with its focus on regrowth, team spirit and positive thinking. Well worth repeated visits to see how the redevelopment takes shape. "

Recommended for

Volunteer-minded

Those interested in small town regrowth

69

Tohoku

Iwate

遠野市

TONO

Tono, situated in the centre of Iwate Prefecture, is a small town surrounded by rice fields and forest-covered mountains.

Immortalised in Japanese folklore history through its many captivating stories of mythical characters, a walk around Tono's back streets and into the surrounding countryside can feel as though you are venturing into a time long forgotten.

 Culture Spot - Tono Festival

This celebration of dance and local performing arts takes place on the third weekend of September. During the festival, the town is awash with people in traditional costumes, dancing and parading through the streets.

👍 Must see! Tono Furusato Village

A beautifully preserved Edo-period farming village of traditional, thatched-roof buildings surrounded by rice fields and ponds, Tono Furusato is a window into the past. Here you can try your hand at traditional crafts, take part in demonstrations of seasonal farming techniques and, in June, even make your own *miso* paste.

You enter the village via a visitor centre, which promotes the various Japanese films and dramas that have been made here, and sells local souvenirs, crafts, food and drink. It also has a restaurant that serves a good range of Japanese food including specialities from the local area. Be prepared to spend a few hours here, as it is a large complex with many buildings.

Food and Drink

Hittsumi

Hittsumi is a dish of large, flattened, dough-based pieces, cooked in a soy-sauce-based soup with vegetables and chicken. This tasty dish is usually served in autumn and winter to warm diners up.

Keiran

Keiran is a traditional Japanese sweet consisting of a sticky rice paste (*mochi*) containing a sweet bean paste. It is served in a bowl of steaming water and is traditionally eaten in winter. Excellent to round off a meal.

Tono Doburoku sake

Doburoku is an unrefined *sake* made after the autumn harvest, with a milky-white colour. It is only available in certain places in Tono, one of which is Furasato Village. Well worth trying or picking up as a souvenir.

Craft beer

Tono produces the Zumona brand of craft beer. They offer a Pale Ale, Golden Pilsner, Weizen and a Strong IPA amongst others. These are available at different times of the year, and bottles are available from all souvenir shops, museum shops and on the menus of most hotels and local restaurants.

Did you know?

Fancy a Kappa?
The Kappa, one of the most famous mythical creatures from Japanese folklore, is said to live in rivers and pools around Tono. The story of the Kappa is used to warn children of the dangers of playing near water, as the creatures are said to try and pull the youngsters in.

Tohoku

Iwate — TONO — 遠野市

🏠 Culture Spot - Tono Municipal Museum ❷

Situated on the third and fourth floors of Tono library, opposite the Folktale and Storytelling Centre, the Municipal Museum contains new and fascinating exhibits about how Tono has evolved over the past few hundred years. Extremely well designed and maintained, this museum paints a realistic picture of how life was for the local farming community before modernisation took place. It creates a vivid image of the importance that folklore played in the community, with many costumes and descriptions of festivals on display.

There are some English summaries at the start of each exhibit in the museum, and there is a comprehensive English guide available from the reception area.

🔁 Getting there and around

✈ Hanamaki Airport. Take a taxi to Shin-Hanamaki Station and then local train services to Tono Station.

🚆 Shin-Hanamaki Station. Take local train services to Tono Station. This picturesque journey through a valley of rice fields will take about an hour.

🚗 Getting around by rental car
You can pick up pre-ordered rental cars around the stations and many companies now offer full booking services in English and other languages. If you are coming by bullet train, you can pick up a rental car close to Shin-Hanamaki Station and make your own way to and from Tono.

Getting around by taxi
This may be a fairly expensive option if you plan on going to several places outside Tono, but if money is no object, talk to your hotel or guesthouse about options that may be available to rent a taxi for a few hours.

Culture Spot - Folktale and Storytelling Centre 3

These buildings, that date from the Edo period, have been perfectly preserved inside and out. They include the house of Kunio Yanagita, the author of 'Tono Monogatari' - a celebrated work that brings together 119 folk tales from in and around Tono. The house was brought to Tono from Tokyo so that Yanagita could spend time in the area.

The museum has basic English descriptions in all the rooms and an interactive area - that is aimed at kids - which brings to life several of the folk stories from the area. The museum has a theatre with performances (in Japanese) at set times, and also a restaurant.

Key dates

May 3 - Tono City Parade (a festival that dates back 400 years)

mid-September - Japan's Furusato Tono Festival

We say

" This is a beautifully scenic area where the farmland and countryside blend into one. I definitely recommend getting a rental car and spending up to three days exploring the town and the surrounding area. It is easy to park and walk, or hike, to the many temples and shrines hidden in the fields and mountains. "

Recommended for

History lovers

Further information
www.100hiddentowns.jp/iwate/tono.html

Tohoku

Miyagi

松島町

MATSUSHIMA

Though Matsushima is a small town, the view of its pine-wooded islands is known to all Japanese as being one of the three most celebrated beauty spots in Japan (along with the *torii* gate of Miyajima in Hiroshima Prefecture, and the sandbar of Amanohashidate in Kyoto).

These pine (*matsu*) islands have long been lauded by poets and historical figures. Take a boat tour to get up close and really appreciate their curious shapes and geology.

The town itself is beautifully set in a bay and is easily accessed from Sendai.

Nature Spot - The Seafront

Unsurprisingly, considering its famed views, the seafront of Matsushima Town is very popular with tourists and bus tours. Souvenir shops and restaurants vie for your custom with a surfeit of choice. The townspeople are used to foreigners, so expect a friendly welcome and few problems with communication. Lunch and a cruise is the typical day-trip agenda, but an overnight stay affords more leisure time to visit less crowded spots.

Just off the main drag is the Matsushimajo viewing point. Tastefully designed as a traditional three-storey building, the 360° balcony is a great place to enjoy a cool breeze, with scenic views of the lush forest canopies and the island-dotted bay.

One of the more crowded areas is the Godaido Temple, situated on an islet just a few metres from the seafront. A pair of small bridges provide access to the temple, though be careful of the spaces between the planks!

👍 Must do! Boat tour

Hourly cruises, either returning to your point of embarkation or sailing to the nearby Shiogama area, are run from the seafront. Friendly guides will help you choose the most suitable one depending on your preference and time. The tours take you around and up close to the various-sized islands, with explanations broadcasted in Japanese and English. As you cruise past certain islands, the names are explained and historical tidbits are mentioned.

Notable outcrops are the twin islands of Kamejima (turtle island) and Kujirajima (whale island), as well as various uniquely eroded rocks that years of sea and wind have sculpted into bizarre shapes. The geology of the islands fascinate with their shale underbelly resembling layered cake. Some of the islands look almost too good to be real.

The tours also take you past the oyster farms that are a source of local industry.

All in all, a fun and relaxing way to spend 50 minutes of a trip to Matsushima.

🌳 Nature Spot
Oshima Island 2

Very close to the Matsushimakaigan Station is the tiny island of Oshima, which offers pleasant strolls, caves, a pretty little red bridge and gently lapping waves. Its location away from the main drag guarantees tranquility.

❓ Did you know?

Pining poet

The famous haiku poet, Basho, was bewitched by the beauty of Matsushima. In 1689, he wrote:

'*morning and evening,*

as if someone waits for me at Matsushima

my unfulfilled love'

This is a play on words as, in Japanese, *matsu* can mean 'wait' as well as 'pine'. It seems Basho equates Matsushima with a beautiful lover waiting for him.

Tohoku

Miyagi
MATSUSHIMA
松島町

🏠 Culture Spot
Fukuurabashi Bridge and Fukuurajima Island 3

For a small fee, tourists can walk across the bay to Fukuurajima Island via the Fukuurabashi Bridge. Constructed in 1967, this pretty red bridge is evocative of similar structures built in earlier times. The bridge itself is a stand-out landmark of Matsushima Bay thanks to its length and colour, and can be seen from most viewing points on the mainland.

Once on the island, visitors can enjoy a break away from the seafront tourist hubbub. This serene island is home to a variety of flowers, insects, birds and trees, and has several promontories from which to enjoy alternative views of the bay.

🏠 Culture Spot
Shiogama Shrine

If time permits, take the boat tour from Matsushima to Shiogama. From the port, visitors can walk to the Shiogama Shrine to witness its pretty gardens and surrounding woodland. The whole complex is spacious, pleasant and intricately designed. The shrine itself is perhaps most famous for the many steps leading to its entrance, which afford exceptional photo opportunities.

It is recommended to approach the shrine via the gentle hilly back route and then descend via the steps.

🏠 Culture Spot
Kanrantei Tea House 4

The unassuming Kanrantei Tea House was a gift to the feudal lord Masamune Date from national warlord Hideyoshi Toyotomi. From here, visitors can enjoy views of the bay and the other tourist spots of Fukuurabashi Bridge and Godaido Temple. For a small fee, sip the green tea that Kanrantei serves, and imagine a world gone by.

🏠 Culture Spot
Zuiganji Temple 5

The approach to this famous ancient temple has many astonishing caves, with Buddhist carvings cut deep inside. It was founded in the ninth century, but later rebuilt by Masamune Date as his family temple.

Key dates

first Sunday in February - Oyster Festival

late October to mid-November - Autumn Light-up (various locations in Matsushima)

We say

"Matsushima is a well-known tourist spot, but don't let that put you off! The easy access from Sendai, excellent restaurants, relaxing boat cruises, and strolls that guarantee gorgeous views, make this destination a must-do for any visitor to the Sendai area. A thoroughly enjoyable trip."

Recommended for

All ages

🌱 Nature Spot - Saigyo Modoshi-no-Matsu Park 6

Just a 20-minute hike up from the station, this park provides visitors with a spectacular view of Matsushima Bay, its islands and oyster farms. A pristine, modern cafe also offers views and a chance to take the weight off your feet. The cherry blossom season augments the panorama with a foreground of pink.

Food and Drink

Matsushima is famous for several local delicacies, including oysters in winter, and conger eel during the summer months.

As well as seafood, the area is well known for its *gyutan* (beef tongue). *Gyutan* is commonly served as part of *yakiniku* sets, but the Miyagi Prefecture variety is much larger and juicier.

Matsushima also has its own *sake* and craft beer products.

For the beer, there are several delicious flavours to choose from.

Accommodation

Though more commonly known as a day-trip destination, Matsushima also has a number of quality seafront hotels. The hotel Komatsukan Kofutei, a few minutes from Fukuurabashi Bridge, provides spacious, functional rooms, *onsen*, and seafood fare alongside traditional Japanese hospitality.

Getting there and around

✈ Sendai Airport. Travel by direct bus services to the Matsushima area, or use local train services via Sendai Station to Matsushimakaigan Station.

🚆 Sendai Station. 40 minutes on the local JR Line to Matsushimakaigan Station.

🚶 Most of the spots mentioned are within walking distance of Matsushimakaigan Station, thus making Matsushima an ideal day trip if you are based in Sendai.

Kids

A trip involving lunch and a boat cruise is highly satisfying for all ages. The manageable size of the town makes it unlikely that the little ones will get too tired.

  Further information
www.100hiddentowns.jp/miyagi/matsushima.html

Tohoku

Miyagi — 白石市 SHIROISHI

Shiroishi is a historical castle town located in the south of Miyagi Prefecture. Its castle was the site of a ferocious battle during the Boshin War of the Meiji Restoration.

As well as being a draw for history buffs, Shiroishi is also renowned for its traditions of Yajiro Kokeshi Dolls and *umen* noodles. The mountains of Zao provide a stunning backdrop to everyday life in the town.

🌳 Nature Spot - Zao Fox Village

Located 20 minutes by car or bus from Shiroishi Town, Zao Fox Village is a spacious, rambling menagerie that houses a wide variety of foxes, as well as some ponies, goats and rabbits. After the initially confusing welcome from a giant plaster gorilla, you can wander amongst the foxes as they lounge, play and roam together outdoors. Visitors are advised not to touch the foxes, but are welcome to feed them from certain spots with food purchased from the visitor centre. Visit in the colder months if you want to see the foxes at their fluffiest, or in April or May if you want to see the newly born fox cubs. A visit in August will show the parents of the cubs stubbornly shutting out and even attacking their own imploring offspring, forcing them to learn how to thrive independently of their elders.

👍 Must see! Shiroishi Castle

The site of Shiroishi Castle was originally established during the Kamakura era (1185-1333), while the three-storey structure was first built in the late 16th century.

From 1600 onward, Shiroishi Castle was ruled by the Katakura clan. During the Tokugawa shogunate it was exempted from the one-castle rule, which prevented any warlords from possessing or building more than one castle in one domain.

The castle was, however, destroyed in the 1860s, after the Boshin War.

The faithfully reconstructed building that you can visit today - with its white outer walls, timber interior, scenic balconies and natural stone foundations - was completed in 1995.

Inside the castle there is a small museum that displays the history of the town, and of the castle and its reconstruction. The upper floors provide great views of the surrounding area. Also within the castle walls, there is an expanse of trees and lush grass, which is ideal for picnics.

On key dates during the year, the castle and its grounds are used for re-enactments of samurai battles, performed by locals dressed in replica armour and carrying swords, rifles and other historical weaponry.

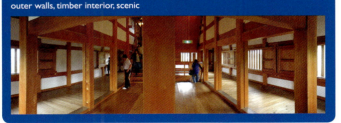

Did you know?

Noodles of compassion

Local tradition has it that Shiroishi's *umen* noodles were originally created over 400 years ago by a son who wanted to feed his father something that would not aggravate his gastric disorder. The word *umen*, written with the characters for 'warm' and 'noodles', was chosen by the feudal lord of Shiroishi castle, Kojuro Katakura, to convey the idea that the 'noodles are warmly welcoming and made with compassion for others'.

Kids

If you have access to a car, a trip to Yajiro Kokeshi Village and its workshop, and Zao Fox Village are an ideal way to spend the day with children.

Tohoku — Miyagi — 白石市 SHIROISHI

🏠 Culture Spot - Yajiro Kokeshi Village ❸

Situated out of town, near Kamasaki Onsen, en route to the mountains of Zao, this museum and its outlying studios are home to a community of craftsmen and artists keeping alive the tradition of Yajiro Kokeshi Dolls that the area is synonymous with.

Kokeshi dolls are made from hand-turned wood – just a slender, limbless, cylindrical body with a round head and beautifully hand-painted features.

The attractive main building in Yajiro Kokeshi Village is home to a museum of the history of the craft, a gift shop, and a hands-on workshop room, where visitors can paint their own *kokeshi* dolls.

🏠 Culture Spot - Samurai House ❹

At a short distance from Shiroishi Castle, the Sawabata River splits into a stream that quietly gurgles past a tasteful reconstruction of one of the area's former samurai residences. Each building in the neighbourhood is accessed by its own small, wooden bridge over the stream.

The samurai house, whose origins date back to the mid-18th century, is situated in a simple, beautiful garden. Visitors enter directly into a kitchen courtyard which leads into a dark, wooden-floored room with a hearth, and then to a *tatami* room where the head of the household would sleep. The scent of the warm hearth, combined with the sights of the garden and the traditional architecture mingle to create a very peaceful, evocative experience.

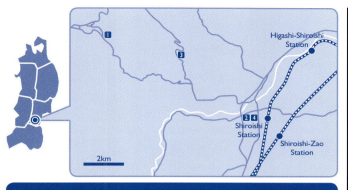

Food and Drink

The area of Shiroishi is famous for its local speciality noodles, called *umen*. Dating back over 400 years, these thin, short, simple noodles contain no oil and are famously gentle on the stomach. Many restaurants in the area, such as Adachiya and the renowned Umen Bansho, serve a variety of delicious *umen* dishes.

Accommodation

There are few places to stay in Shiroishi town centre, and a visit may require travelling in the direction of the Zao area, where there are a number of large hotels (some served by shuttle buses from the two train stations) which cater for the ski crowd during the winter months, and several of which have their own hot spring baths.

Getting there and around

Sendai Airport. Travel by local train services via Natori Station to Shiroishi Station or Shiroishi-Zao Station.

Shiroishi-Zao Station. A direct bullet train service from Tokyo to Shiroishi-Zao Station takes two hours.

The town can also be reached by trains on the Tohoku Main Line to Shiroishi Station.

Shiroishi itself is small enough to take in on foot, but access to attractions further afield and the area of the Zao mountains requires travel by bus or car.

Further information

www.100hiddentowns.jp/miyagi/shiroishi.html

Key dates

January 2 - Kokeshi Hatsubiki (Kokeshi Shrine, Yajiro Kokeshi Village)

early April - Mizubasho flowering (Doudan-no-mori)

May 3 - Shiroishi City Citizen Spring Festival (Shiroishi City centre)

May 3-5 - Japan National Kokeshi Doll Competition / Shiroishi City Local Products Festival (Shiroishi Cultural Gymnasium Activity Center)

late May/early June - Minamizao Natsu Yamabiraki Hiking Event (Shiroishi Ski Resort or Suzuriishi to Katta pass Course)

August 9 - Shiroishi Summer Festival (Shiroishi city centre)

October, first Saturday - Onikojuro Festival and Battle Reenactments (Shiroishi Castle)

We say

"With its easy access by bullet train, Shiroishi is a great place for a day trip for samurai and castle aficionados. If you are interested in seeing the *kokeshi* dolls and want to enjoy a hot spring, stay overnight in a hotel in the Zao area."

Recommended for

History enthusiasts
Traditional crafts fans

81

Tohoku

Yamagata SAGAE
寒河江市

Sagae is a small town situated in the middle of Yamagata Prefecture, and is most famous for its delicious, homegrown cherries.

Wherever you go in the town, you will find pictures of cherries in every shape and size. These fruits originated from Turkey and were exported to Europe and the Americas, before finally hitting the Sagae area of Japan. To commemorate this, the streets are filled with Turkish and Japanese flags aligned side by side. The locals are very proud of their 'Cherry Culture', and you are bound to be blown away by how tasty their cherry products are.

Culture Spot - Mogamigawa Furusato Park

Visitors to this activity, recreational, and cultural centre of Sagae are greeted by the elegantly designed glass exterior of the park's centre house. Inside, handicrafts of local artists are displayed, and there is also a cafe.

In the warmer months, the large park's flowers provide colourful scenery for those who want to enjoy a leisurely amble around the grounds, play park golf, clamber on the kids' playground, or tackle the formidable BMX/skate park.

Culture Spot - Cherry Land

The flourishing cherry culture of Sagae gave birth to Cherry Land, a large orchard where paying visitors are free to roam around and pick and eat as many cherries as they like during the cherry season (from early June to mid-July). The cherries are, of course, delicious, although you aren't allowed to take any away with you, so it's worth going there on an empty stomach and having your fill at the orchard. Don't forget to check out their varied range of souvenirs and delicious homemade gelato.

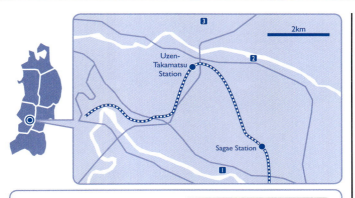

Must see! - Jionji

The most well-known temple in Sagae is Jionji. The temple itself is extremely old, but still sports a beautiful, thatched roof. There is also a three-tiered tower that looks especially lovely against the background of the green countryside.

Getting there and around

Yamagata Airport. A taxi ride is recommended from the airport. Alternatively, there are local bus and train services.

Yamagata Station. Travel by local train services to Sagae Station.

Trains are quite infrequent, running once per hour. Taxis are readily available and not too expensive. Buses are very scarce.

Some hotels will have a rental bike service, and all the attactions in the area can be reached by cycle rides. Walking to the sites is possible, but will depend on how much time you have.

Further information

www.100hiddentowns.jp/yamagata/sagae.html

Did you know?

Cherished cherries

Yamagata Prefecture is the biggest producer of cherries in all of Japan. With its cherries originally coming from Turkey, the two countries have developed a special relationship with each other. Indeed, Sagae's sister town is the Turkish town of Giresun.

To further emphasise the importance of cherries to Sagae, the official mascot of the town wears a cherry hat!

Key dates

mid to end of April - Cherry Blossom Festival

mid June - Cherry Festival

We say

" Sagae is small and tranquil. It's a great location to get away from anything commercial, and surround oneself in traditional Japanese culture. While travelling in the north of Japan, it is definitely worth stopping there for an afternoon of cherry picking during the June-July season. Just remember to check the weather, as it can be quite rainy during this period. "

Recommended for

Cherry lovers

Nature lovers

Tohoku

酒田市

Yamagata — SAKATA

During the Edo period, this unassuming town on the Sea of Japan rivalled Osaka, and even Edo, in terms of culture, wealth and influence.

A key port of the coastal trade route, its leading merchant family, the Honma clan, were the largest, richest landowners in Japan, and were able to bring the very best of Kyoto culture into the town. Visitors can still see traces of this past everywhere in Sakata.

🏠 Culture Spot - Kuromori Kabuki (February 15 and 17)

Part amateur dramatics, part village fete - this extraordinary annual event is a highlight. For almost 300 years, the farmers in this tiny hamlet on the outskirts of Sakata have performed *kabuki* in the open air of midwinter as an offering to the gods. It is a local affair, but if you go, you'll be welcomed with cups of steaming soup and hot, sweet *amazake*. Wrap up well and, unless you are extremely hardy, you may not want to stay for the whole event. Consider catching the children's performance on one morning, then heading back into town for lunch - though keep an eye on the bus times as they operate infrequently.

84

👍 Must see! Ken Domon Museum of Photography [2]

This gallery is well worth a visit for the atmospheric building alone, the work of award-winning designer Yoshio Taniguchi. It houses the entire photographic collection of Ken Domon, a native of Sakata, whose groundbreaking work made him the best-known photojournalist in Japan. It is an easy taxi or bus ride from town.

🏠 Culture Spot Maiko at the Soma-ro Ryotei [3]

This beautifully restored *ryotei* (traditional Japanese restaurant) keeps alive the tradition of Maiko entertainment which flourished in Sakata during the Edo period, when the rich merchants of the town could import the very best of Kyoto culture for their own pleasure. Here you can enjoy a close up performance of polished elegance and studied charm (see main picture) at a fraction of the price you would pay in Kyoto.

🍜 Food and Drink

Sakata ramen

Every region of Japan has its own take on *ramen*, but the Sakata variety is rather special. One reason is the quality of the noodles – most of the small, family run shops here make their own on the premises. The soul of any bowl of *ramen* is the broth, and in Sakata this is clear, clean-tasting and strong. From the first slurp you know that seafood is the key ingredient – typically kelp and dried sardine or flying fish.

💡 Did you know?

The Honmas

Everywhere you look in Sakata, you can see the patronage and influence of the Honmas. One member of that family, Munehisa Honma (1724-1803), became one of the richest men in the country through his trading acumen. He invented the candlestick graph, a tool still used to analyse market movements, and is credited with writing the first ever book on market psychology. Even today, futures traders around the world study his work and methods, hoping to emulate his success.

Scandalous!

In its heyday, Soma-ro was the centre of a national scandal. In the Meiji period, patrons of this establishment enjoyed putting on lavish feasts and, in an early form of cosplay, liked to dress up in the style of the imperial court - going so far as to select people to play the roles of emperor and empress during the proceedings. Somehow this leaked out to the press, and everyone involved was arrested for showing disrespect.

85

Tohoku

Yamagata — SAKATA   酒田市

🏠 Culture Spot - Sankyo Soko [4]

No trip to Sakata would be complete without a visit to these historical warehouses, which have become a symbol of the town. Built in 1893, they housed the rice that was exported along the coast to Japan's major cities, making Sakata one of the richest towns in the land. Sections of these buildings are still working warehouses today. Others have been converted into tourist facilities, with free exhibitions on the history and culture of the town, and souvenir shops selling local produce.

🏠 Culture Spot - Honma Museum of Art [5]

The museum itself is a newer, purpose-built building that houses pieces from the private collection of the Honma family. Explanations are all in Japanese, but visitors are still able to appreciate the exquisite charcoal ink paintings and other works on display. The real draw, though, is next door – the Japanese villa where this family used to live, surrounded by a breathtakingly beautiful garden.

🌙 Accommodation - Wakaba Ryokan [6]

Sakata remains an important business destination – the region is still a very important rice-producing area – so the town is served by a great number of reasonable business hotels. Alternatively, you could stay in a traditional *ryokan*, such as the Wakaba Ryokan, where a cat helps out in reception, and every spare ledge is populated by traditional, *kokeshi* wooden dolls.

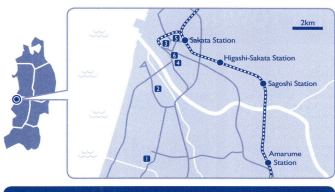

Key dates

February 15 and 17 - Kuromori Kabuki (Hie Shrine)

We say

" I was surprised at how much there was to experience in this likeable little town. There's nothing particularly flashy here, but it's a place with a strongly independent, sometimes quirky, local culture that really grew on me. Give it time to get the most out of it - a two-day trip at least, preferably three. "

Recommended for

Kabuki buffs
Art admirers

Food and Drink

As you would expect for a location on the Japan Sea, the seafood here is excellent. If you visit in winter, try the seasonal speciality, Dongara Jiru – a hearty soup made with cod, *tofu*, leeks, sea vegetables and *miso*. If you go for sushi, make a point of ordering Gasa Ebi. This delicately flavoured local prawn is too fragile to be sent south to the fish markets of Tokyo, and thus can only be consumed locally.

There has been a strong tradition of French cuisine in Sakata since 1967, when local entrepreneur and civic-minded showman, Kyuichi Sato, opened a restaurant called Keyaki. By encouraging his chefs to combine French techniques with Japanese ingredients, he was something of a pioneer in what came to be known as nouvelle cuisine. Keyaki still exists, and it now has a number of rivals, including le Pot Au Feu and L'Oasis (established by one of Sato's ex-chefs), where you can get an excellent, reasonably priced lunch.

Getting there and around

- Shonai Airport. Travel to Sakata by bus.
- Niigata Station. Travel to Sakata by the Inaho 'Limited Express' service (passengers can spend the two hours enjoying views of the rugged Japan Sea coastline).
- The town centre is small enough to walk around comfortably. Buses or taxis are necessary for getting to some of the less central museums. Outside winter, visitors are welcome to use the free bicycles provided by the town.

Further information

www.100hiddentowns.jp/yamagata/sakata.html

87

TOHOKU
OTHER TOWNS

Akita
AKITA

Akita City is home to the Kanto Festival, one of Japan's most famous summer festivals. It's a great place to enjoy local food and to visit sights located mostly within walking distance of the main train and bus station.

Culture Spots Akita City Folklore and Performing Arts Centre (Neburi Nagashi Kan), Old Kaneko Family House, Senshu Park, Akita Museum of Art, Akita Shimin Ichiba Market

We say You will probably only need one or two days to see Akita's museums and galleries, and everything is located in or around the station. Take an extra day if you want to go further afield and see some of the temples and shrines.

Akita
ODATE

Odate, surrounded by forests and mountains, is in the cultural and geographical heart of Tohoku. Human settlement here actually dates back thousands of years, although the town's main growth came later with forestry and mining. Its remote location explains the development of a number of unique local traits and crafts.

Culture Spots Odate City Museum, Oro-kan, Akita Dog Museum
Nature Spots Nagabashiri Air Hole
Must do Onsen
We say A nice city break with some local flavour, Odate is perhaps best visited in winter, when Tohoku shows its true colours - a blanket of snow giving the town a festive charm.

Fukushima
KAWAMATA

If you are looking for fresh air and a slice of small town life, consider paying a visit to Kawamata. The centre of the town, which is bisected by a pretty river, is nice for a stroll, while there are hiking opportunities in the surrounding hills.

Culture Spots Orimono Gallery (textile gallery), Hayama-no-Mori Museum
Nature Spots Akiyama-no-Koma Zakura Park
We say Kawamata is recommended as a leisurely day trip from Fukushima City. The town itself, with its narrow paths and streams, is great for strolling around. Enjoy a relaxing walk along Kawamata's peaceful river, where you can see carp, ducks and birds, or clamber the surrounding hills for a fine view of the town.

Fukushima
MIHARU

Miharu literally means 'three springs'. Its name refers to the simultaneous blossoming of the plum, peach and cherry trees there. By far its most famous landmark is the Takizakura tree, which attracts a huge number of visitors in the spring. Miharu also has other, less well-known, charms that make it an interesting town to visit throughout the year.

Culture Spots Edo-era Warehouses (town centre)
Nature Spots Takizakura Tree, Yawaragi Radium Onsen
We say A very slow, relaxing destination, except when the hordes descend on the town to view Takizakura at full bloom. If you intend to go at that time, it is strongly recommended to hike or ride a bike unless you are particularly fond of traffic jams. The locals were friendly, welcoming and clearly eager to encourage more visitors!

Iwate
HANAMAKI

Hanamaki is best known for its *onsen* and literature. This birthplace of nationally revered author Kenji Miyazawa resonates with his legacy. A walk around the small town centre is a rewarding experience in itself.

Culture Spots Miyazawa Kenji Memorial Museum, Takamura Kotaro Museum
Nature Spots Igirisu Kaigan ('England Coast'), Kuzumaru Gorge, Mount Hayachine
Must do Onsen
We say Hanamaki's airport and bullet train links make it easily accessible.

Iwate
SHIZUKUISHI

Shizukuishi lies in a basin encircled by mountains. Famed for its winter sports and the produce from the nationally famous Koiwai Farm, Shizukuishi is a vast area of countryside within the sparsely populated prefecture of Iwate.

Culture Spots Daijingu Shrine
Nature Spots Mount Iwate, Koiwai Farm, Nanatsumori Forest Park
We say Shizukuishi is especially recommended for those who want to explore the possibilities provided by the mountains in the area, whether it be climbing or winter sports.

Miyagi
ISHINOMAKI

Beautifully nestled beside the Pacific, Ishinomaki earned worldwide attention when it was severely damaged by the 2011 tsunami. However, large areas remain intact and the outskirts of the city area reveal wonderful rural retreats and sightseeing spots that are well worth visiting.

Culture Spots Ishinomori Manga Museum, Miyagi Sant Juan Bautista Museum
Must do Hiyoriyama Park
We say Ishinomaki is a fine place to venture to, with easy access from Sendai and the tourist spot of Matsushima. There are plenty of delicious eateries and pleasant views to enjoy.

関東甲信越地方

KANTO-KOSHINETSU

The Kanto-Koshinetsu Region
Probably the best-known of all areas in Japan, due to the presence of Tokyo and its metropolitan surrounds, Kanto-Koshinetsu comprises ten prefectures offering a variety of sights and activities including skiing, beach holidays, places of worship and an abundance of nature. The proximity to the major travel hubs of Tokyo and Yokohama, plus two international airports, ensure relatively easy access to attractions throughout the entire region.

CHIBA PREFECTURE

Ostensibly known as a commuter zone for Tokyo, deeper parts of Chiba's Boso Peninsula offer up a range of sights for the traveller, whereby its proximity to two international airports (including Narita Airport, which is actually in Chiba) and major train stations of Tokyo, make it perfect for day trips and convenient for jaunts. Aside from its shopping centres and amusement parks (including Disney), the prefecture also has more sedate countryside retreats and beach facilities.

Kamogawa is a great spot for a weekend's retreat, with boat trips and views of Boso Peninsula, and the hills, coves and beaches of Tateyama make for fine excursions.

Prefectural Capital
Chiba City
✈ Airports
Narita Airport
🚆 Main Train Stations
Chiba Station

Other Tourist Attractions
Narita
Home to not just an airport, but also to the breathtaking Naritasan Shinshoji Temple, which dates back to the tenth century.
Tokyo Disney Resort
Chiba's most famed attraction, in the town of Urayasu, needs no introduction here. If you plan on a visit, expect lengthy queues!
Kujukuri Beach
This beach on the Pacific coast stretches for 60 kilometres, north to south.
Mount Nokogiri
Accessed via ropeway, there are great views from the top of this mountain.

Naritasan Shinshoji Temple

90

GUNMA PREFECTURE

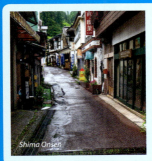
Shima Onsen

The landlocked, mountainous prefecture of Gunma is known for its hot springs and ski resorts. The small town of Kusatsu has more than 100 hot springs, the most famous of which is a large pool in the town centre with steaming mineral water gushing down a wooden chute. Ikaho Onsen in Shibukawaikaho is a hot spring resort too - this time famous for its steep stone stairs.

Prefectural Capital
Maebashi
Main Train Stations
Maebashi Station
Takasaki Station

Other Tourist Attractions
Shima Onsen
A calm hot spring town ideally positioned in a mountain valley.

IBARAKI PREFECTURE

Bordering the Pacific Ocean, Ibaraki has a diverse mixture of traditional culture, popular beaches and nature. Take a trip to the city of Kasama and its famed Inari Shrine, decorated with all manner of sculptures in the shapes of flowers and creatures, and the outstanding collection of the Nichido Museum of Art. Alternatively, a journey to the popular flower festival and the waterways of Itako is recommended.

Prefectural Capital
Mito City
✈ Airports
Ibaraki Airport
Main Train Stations
Mito Station

Other Tourist Attractions
Mount Tsukuba
Mount Tsukuba is an 877-metre-high mountain, well known for its double peaks, and very popular with climbers.
Hananuki Gorge
Especially beautiful in autumn, this gorge provides excellent hiking opportunities. The scenery of coloured leaves with the tree's branches arching over the river is a popular sight.
Surfing Beaches
The coast of Ibaraki is a surfer's paradise, easily accessible from Tokyo. The surf ranges from the larger waves in the Oarai district for preening experts, to the beginner-level waters of Kashima's Hirai district.
Plum Festival (Kairakuen Park, Mito City)
Dating from the end of the Edo era, Kairakuen Park in Mito City is considered one of the most beautiful gardens in Japan. Come in late February or early March to catch the plum trees, numbering over 3,000, in full bloom.

Hananuki Gorge

KANAGAWA PREFECTURE

Yokohama Chinatown

Often regarded as just an extension of Tokyo, there is much to do in Kanagawa. Visitors can experience the historical attractions of Yokohama (the prefectural capital), the coastal vistas and hot springs that abound at Yugawara, and the fish market in Misaki, which offers a quieter alternative to the more famous Tsukiji market - all located within a short journey from Tokyo.

Prefectural Capital
Yokohama
Main Train Stations
Shin-Yokohama Station

Other Tourist Attractions
Kamakura
The former capital is a wonderful draw, with its temples, Giant Buddha, and hiking opportunities.
Yokohama
Whether it's shopping, sport, art or history, Yokohama City proves a rewarding visit. The legacy of its Meiji-era boom years, when foreign luminaries made the city their home, is still apparent, with preserved buildings dotting the city. Chinatown is a must-visit for its fabulous restaurants.

Extreme Seasonal Conditions
Humid in summer.

KANTO-KOSHINETSU

関東甲信越地方

NAGANO PREFECTURE

Stunning scenery and warm hospitality abound in Nagano. Well-known for its hot springs and ski resorts, there are also many hidden gems to recommend the prefecture. Check out the numerous hot springs of Nozawaonsen, the ski heaven of Hakuba, the remarkable history, pretty accommodation and natural sights of Komoro, the lake and shrines of Shimosuwa, or the bucolic restfulness of Ogawa.

Prefectural Capital
Nagano City
✈ Airports
Matsumoto Airport
🚆 Main Train Stations
Nagano Station

Other Tourist Attractions
Nagano
The prefectural capital was originally built around its seventh-century Zenkoji Temple, which houses a 'hidden Buddha' statue, shown publicly only once every six years. The temple also contains a statue of Binzuru, a physician who followed Buddha. Worshippers touch the statue to pray for a cure for their ailments.

Jigokudani

Jigokudani
Monkeys in a hot spring? These blithe, relaxed simians are a charming sight, and are so used to human visitors that they barely notice us.

Nagano Lantern Festival
Centred around Zenkoji Temple, this annual commemoration of Nagano's 1998 Winter Olympic Games combines lanterns and colourful illuminations with live music and *sake*-tasting.

Extreme Seasonal Conditions Heavy snow in winter.

NIIGATA PREFECTURE

Bordering the Sea of Japan, Niigata Prefecture has hot springs, delicious local food and nature aplenty. The climatic variations between its seasons ensure the prefecture can be visited for summer beach holidays, and then winter ski tours within a matter of months. Stop by the wonderful town of Tokamachi for a great blend of art and countryside, and sample the diverse local culture and traditions of Sado Island.

Prefectural Capital
Niigata City
✈ Airports
Niigata Airport
🚆 Main Train Stations
Niigata Station

Other Tourist Attractions
Niigata
Pay a visit to the prefectural capital for delicious seafood and the huge aquarium of Marinepia.

Yuzawa
The hot spring and ski resort of Yuzawa also has a literary claim to fame as the basis of the setting of Yasunari Kawabata's classic novel, 'Snow Country'.

Murakami
A trip to this town offers a chance to visit plenty of museums and then enjoy a hike up to the castle remains of Murakami, to be rewarded with spectacular panoramic views.

Extreme Seasonal Conditions Heavy snow in winter.

Yuzawa

SAITAMA PREFECTURE

Regarded by some as a mere suburban feeder of Tokyo, Saitama has much to recommend it. The northern region of the prefecture boasts some of the most gorgeous, and easily accessible, natural features in Japan. The small town of Kawagoe has Edo-era remnants, and Nagatoro is great for hiking and river-rafting.

Prefectural Capital
Saitama City
Main Train Stations
Omiya Station

Other Tourist Attractions
Chichibu National Park
Great area for hiking (see *National Parks* section).
Urawa
Time your visit to see a match at the Saitama Stadium watching Japan's most feverishly supported football team, Urawa Reds.

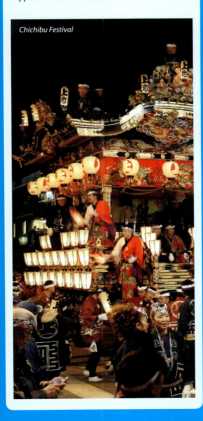
Chichibu Festival

TOCHIGI PREFECTURE

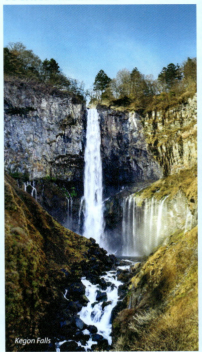
Kegon Falls

Tochigi Prefecture is dominated by the forests, breathtaking lakes, and waterfalls of Nikko National Park. Nikko itself is a tourist draw, with its elaborate Toshogu Shrine, honouring the famous shogun, Ieyasu Tokugawa. The town of Tochigi is a pleasant location, with canal boat tours, traditional sweets and historical architecture. Ashikaga, home to Japan's oldest school, is another good spot to visit.

Prefectural Capital
Utsunomiya
Main Train Stations
Utsunomiya Station

Other Tourist Attractions
Nikko Edo Mura (Edo Wonderland)
Fun, historical and cultural theme park with Edo-era reconstructed buildings, foods and performances.
Kegon Falls
Spectacular 97-metre falls in Nikko National Park.
Nasu
Hot springs, *sake* and ski resorts make up a fine triumvirate here.

KANTO-KOSHINETSU

関東甲信越地方

TOKYO PREFECTURE

A huge metropolis of uber-modernity, jam-packed trains full of hurried and harried commuters, more shops and restaurants than can ever be visited - what is there to say about Tokyo that hasn't been written about already? Well, this book aims to introduce a few quieter areas off the beaten track, that even the locals may have overlooked. Crystal clear waters for diving, and relaxing cliff-top hot springs with a spectacular sunset view? Tokyo has that at Oshima Island. Unique biodiversity and tropical wildlife? Ogasawara Island. Day-trip hiking and gorgeous autumn views? Head out to Takao mountain to the west of the city. A restful spot right in the centre? Katsushika. To paraphrase - if you're tired of Tokyo, you're tired of life. Transportation links make Tokyo's size surmountable, and trips criss-crossing the city the norm.

Prefectural Capital
Tokyo

✈ Airports
Haneda Airport
Chofu Airport

🚆 Main Train Stations
Shinagawa Station
Tokyo Station

Shibuya scramble

Other Tourist Attractions
Shibuya
The scramble crossing of Shibuya is one of the best known sights in Japan, exhibiting Tokyo's neon-lit modernity and determined crowds, all squeezed into one place.

Meiji Shrine
The vast grounds of this shrine are a popular spot as part of a jaunt to nearby Yoyogi Park, the classy shopping boulevard of Omotesando, and the teen paradise of Takeshita Street in Harajuku.

Ueno
Ueno is steeped in modern history and culture. A day in the park can be augmented with trips to Ueno Zoo, the National Museum, and the Metropolitan Museum of Art. Sample the nearby shops of Ameyoko Street for a taste of bygone market hustle.

Extreme Seasonal Conditions Humid in summer. Snow rare in winter.

YAMANASHI PREFECTURE

To the west of Tokyo, Yamanashi encompasses the northern part of Mount Fuji, where hundreds of thousands of visitors climb to the summit every year. In the Fuji Five Lakes area, resort towns surround the lakes long-ago formed by the mountain's volcanic eruptions. The region is renowned for climbing, fishing and skiing, and a more recent claim to fame is as a wine-producing region. Koshu grapes have produced international award-winning wines, which can be sampled at several different wineries and shops. The whisky producing region of Hokuto is also gathering attention for its excellent produce.

Prefectural Capital
Kofu City

🚆 Main Train Stations
Kofu Station

Other Tourist Attractions
Kofu
The prefectural capital of Yamanashi is a beautifully set, old town surrounded by mountains. The countryside is spectacular, and there are still a few remnants of its castle town past.

Otsuki
Mountains and gorges provide a great area for hiking.

Fuji Yoshida
Often a starting point for the climb, this small town at the foot of Mount Fuji has an amusement park and a popular fire festival.

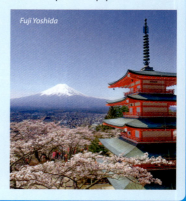
Fuji Yoshida

94

NATIONAL PARKS

Nikko National Park
Area: 114,908 ha
Features: active volcanoes, long-worshipped mountains, lakes, spectacular waterfalls
Did you know? Nikko is perhaps most famous for the autumn foliage of its wide valleys, and the gorgeous forests that merge with its world heritage cultural shrines and temples.

Oze National Park
Area: 37,200 ha
Features: mountains and plateaus
Did you know? Formerly part of Nikko National Park, Oze became a separate entity in 2007. Conservation efforts have helped keep the park safe from the threat of encroaching development.

Chichibu-Tama-Kai National Park
Area: 126,259 ha
Features: vast mountain ranges, forests, climbing, camping, fishing
Did you know? The vast forests of Chichibu-Tama-Kai are home to a diverse range of animals, including serow, bears, monkeys, deer and frogs.

Ogasawara National Park
Area: 6,629 ha
Features: unique ecosystems, karst landforms, tropical fish
Did you know? The islands boast a high proportion of Japan's indigenous species, despite being a chain of such small islands.

Minami Alps National Park
Area: 35,752 ha
Features: Mount Kitadake (the nation's second highest), forests, deep valley rivers
Did you know? Formed by ancient glacial movements, the Minami Alps are still rising even now, albeit at a rate of 3-4mm a year.

Joshin'etsukogen National Park
Area: 148,194 ha
Features: mountains, highlands, lakes and marshes
Did you know? The volcanic landscape has provided the area with a number of famous hot spring resorts, and the mountains have long been the destination for pilgrimages.

Myoko-Togakushi Renzan National Park
Area: 39,772 ha
Features: mountains, skiing, hot springs
Did you know? As well as mountain worship and various kinds of hot spring waters, the area is home to a number of legends, including the ascetic training of *shugendo* ninja.

Chubusangaku National Park
(See Chubu-Hokuriku)

Myoko-Togakushi Renzan National Park

HIDDEN TOWNS

CHIBA
98   Kamogawa
102   Tateyama

GUNMA
106   Kusatsu
110   Shibukawa

IBARAKI
114   Itako
118   Kasama

KANAGAWA
122   Miura

NAGANO
124   Hakuba
128   Komoro
132   Nozawaonsen
136   Ogawa
138   Shimosuwa

NIIGATA
142   Sado
146   Tokamachi

SAITAMA
150   Kawagoe
154   Nagatoro

TOCHIGI
156   Ashikaga
160   Tochigi

TOKYO
162   Katsushika
164   Ogasawara
168   Oshima

YAMANASHI
172   Hokuto
176   Koshu

95

KANTO-KOSHINETSU

関東甲信越地方

APPROXIMATE TRAVEL TIMES BETWEEN PREFECTURAL CAPITALS (by car / by public transport)

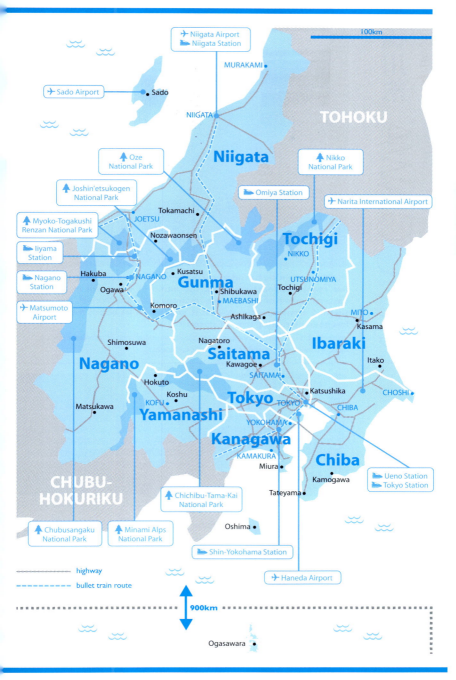

Kanto-Koshinetsu

KAMOGAWA 鴨川市
Chiba

'Hidden' might be considered a misnomer when describing Kamogawa. For many residents of Japan, the name of this town in the south-eastern corner of Chiba is synonymous with 'Sea World', the marine-themed amusement park that is located on its beach front and that has been attracting crowds since 1970.

Visitors who have time to explore Kamogawa can enjoy ancient temples, dramatic terrain, fabulous views and charming craft industries.

Culture Spot - Tai-no-Ura Boat Trip [1]

Tai-no-Ura, literally 'red sea bream bay', offers 25-minute boat excursions around the bay and nearby islands, where visitors can see shoals of red sea bream. The pleasure boats, with indoor seating for about 50 people, embark from the port directly opposite Tanjo-ji Temple. Once out at sea, a recorded narration in Japanese is broadcast (there is a free English handout available), which explains the relevance of the area to the legends of Nichiren, Kamogawa's most famous son.

Nature Spot
Fudo Daki Waterfall, Yomogi [2]

This picturesque waterfall is located in a remote, wooded spot, one kilometre from the nearest bus stop. A small shrine and a welcoming signpost directs visitors to a flight of steps that lead down to a wooden observation deck - a wonderful spot from which to admire the cascade which splits into two parts, the larger *odaki* (male waterfall) and smaller *medaki* (female waterfall).

👍 Must see! Kamogawa Sea World

Kamogawa Sea World is a large theme park with plenty of aquatic attractions inside to keep the interest of its many visitors. There are over 11,000 sea and freshwater animals, encompassing over 800 species, and three outdoor grandstand show pools. The performances by killer whales, dolphins, sea lions and belugas are a must-see, but mind where you sit – those in the front seats get drenched unless wearing a waterproof coat. Visitors can even touch the dolphins at the poolside after their performance. There are also many exhibitions that can be viewed both indoors and outdoors.

Sea World has several restaurants, including the modern Restaurant Ocean, from where diners can watch killer whales through the glass sides of their pool as they swim past. There is also a waterfront hotel, Kamogawa Sea World Hotel, located beside the park.

🔎 Did you know?

Three is a magic number

Kamogawa was the birthplace in 1222 of the renowned priest Nichiren, the founder of Nichiren Buddhism.

It is said that three prophecies occurred when Nichiren was born: pure water sprang spontaneously from his family garden, lotus flowers bloomed on the nearby shore, and an unprecedented number of red sea bream suddenly appeared in the bay.

👨‍👩‍👧 Kids - Hanami Yui

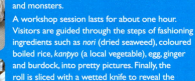

Hanami Yui is a small business that provides local outlets with hand-crafted sushi rolls that each have a cute, colourful design running through them. The staff who make the sushi also hold workshops where visitors are shown the different stages of the process and given the opportunity to make a sushi roll from their range of about 30 different designs - including pictures of pandas, butterflies, flowers and monsters.

A workshop session lasts for about one hour. Visitors are guided through the steps of fashioning ingredients such as *nori* (dried seaweed), coloured boiled rice, *kanpyo* (a local vegetable), egg, ginger and burdock, into pretty pictures. Finally, the roll is sliced with a wetted knife to reveal the masterpiece.

Workshops at Hanami Yui operate from Thursday to Sunday, and require booking one week in advance.

Kanto-Koshinetsu

Chiba

KAMOGAWA 鴨川市

🏠 Culture Spot
Places of Worship
Tanjo-Ji [S]

Tanjo-ji temple was originally built in 1276 to commemorate the birthplace of the famed holy priest Nichiren, who was born nearby in 1222. It still serves as the head temple for the Nichiren sect of Buddhism. The absence of large crowds around the temple precinct, which sits at the foot of a lush, green escarpment, allows for an unhurried opportunity to enjoy the architecture and serene atmosphere.

Seicho-Ji [6]

The sacred temple compound of Seicho-ji has a 1,200-year history. From Asahigamori, the highest point within the grounds, visitors can see miles of mountains and hilltops stretching across the Boso Peninsula. Legend says that the earliest sunrise of each day in eastern Kanto is seen from here. The holy priest Nichiren, who is commemorated with a statue at the summit, is said to have achieved enlightenment here, when facing the sunrise.

🏠 Culture Spot
Kamogawa Godosai Festival

Kamogawa Godosai Festival takes place over two days, when locals from seven nearby shrines brave the elements to chant, play their flutes and drums, and carry their *mikoshi* (portable shrines), *dashi* (floats) and *yatai* (stalls) around town. The event reaches its climax on the second day, when all the participants congregate in the evening at Awa-Kamogawa Station. There are so many locals taking part in the festival, that it's surprising there is anyone left to cheer them on.

🌳 Nature Spot
Oyama Rice Paddies [7]

The view of Oyama's 375 rice paddies, terraced and winding around the mountainside, is a wonderful sight to behold. Throughout the seasons, the colours on display transform as the rice goes through its life cycle.

In early September, groups of friends, neighbours and families gather to harvest the rice. At this time, one can see the tethered stalks drying over bamboo racks. This charming spectacle is obviously a poorly kept secret, as evidenced by the large number of photographers and other visitors. Later in the autumn, there is a special evening event when the paddies are illuminated by candlelight.

Key dates

January to late April - flower picking (Michi-no-eki Ocean Park and Farmer's Shop Kamogawa)

January to early May - strawberry picking (Minnami-no-Sato and Tamura Farms)

late March to early April - cherry blossom viewing (Uomizuka Issemba Park and Uchiurayama Kenmin-no-mori)

early September - Kamogawa Godosai Festival (around Awa-Kamogawa Station)

late November to early December - autumn leaves viewing (Yomogi)

We say

" Kamogawa is a great spot for a weekend's retreat - lots of high-brow and low-brow things to do and see. My visit in early September was frustrated slightly by drizzly conditions which denied me the view over Boso from Asahigamori. Instead, I was treated to the slightly unusual experience of being joined at the statue of Nichiren by a solitary, drum-beating, chanting monk.

If you are short on time, the Tai-no-Ura boat trip is not indispensable - I sensed a wave of relief amongst my fellow sightseers when we saw that there really were red sea bream still living in the bay. "

Recommended for

Families

Accommodation
Kamogawa Grand Hotel 8

There is no shortage of beachfront hotels near the centre of Kamogawa. The Kamogawa Grand Hotel is a fine option. As well as its regular, communal bathing facilities (which are also available to passing customers), guests can reserve a 45-minute slot in the luxurious private family bath.

A superb buffet breakfast is served in Gunjo, the hotel restaurant, which also opens for dinner. Alternatively, guests can enjoy a delicious Japanese-style course meal in the comfort of their own room. The hotel also has a coffee shop with a garden terrace, where guests can enjoy drinks to the suck and blow of the Pacific tide, just a stone's throw away.

Food and Drink

Minnami-no-Sato 9

This is an out-of-town outlet where visitors can bathe their tired feet, buy local goods and eat in the cafeteria or at an outside table, serenaded by frogs in the neighbouring rice fields. Delicacies on sale include a kind of mackerel burger called *sangayaki*, and *tai senbei* – a red snapper-shaped rice cracker.

Oraga-Don

The most famous local delicacy in Kamogawa is *oraga-don*. Different restaurants serve their own variations, but they all have in common healthy, seasonal, local sea produce served on a bowl of *nagasa-mai* rice.

Getting there and around

Narita Airport. Travel to Awa-Kamogawa Station via Chiba Station using local train services.

Tokyo Station. Travel to Awa-Kamogawa Station using local train services. You can travel directly by express train, or via Chiba Station or Soga Station.

The attractions in Kamogawa are scattered far enough from Awa-Kamogawa Station to necessitate four-wheeled transport. Bus services go to within about 20 minutes' walk from Fudo Daki Waterfall and Oyama Rice Paddies.

 Further information
www.100hiddentowns.jp/chiba/kamogawa.html

101

Kanto-Koshinetsu

TATEYAMA
館山市
Chiba

Tateyama is a seaside town on the south-western tip of the Boso Peninsula in Chiba Prefecture.

During the summer months, the area's beaches are popular with the sun-seeking set, but its miles of coastline, cliffs, sparsely inhabited coves and steep hills provide plenty of other diversions throughout the year, including fabulous boat-fresh seafood, historical religious sites, a castle, and views of Mount Fuji.

👍 Must see! Okinoshima Island [1]

Tucked behind Tateyama's naval air base, from which the comings and goings of helicopters can at times be an entertainment in itself, Okinoshima is a picturesque, tiny, uninhabited outcrop covered in woodland. It is reached by a strip of sand, and can be circumnavigated in 15 minutes.

The island's waters, rock strata and coral are popular in the summer with families, paddlers, swimmers and snorkellers, as the large number of RVs in the car park attests.

🏠 Culture Spot
Sunosaki Lighthouse [2]

The Sunosaki Lighthouse has operated since 1919 as a beacon for ships, to indicate the entry point of Tokyo Bay. The view from here is popular with visitors, some of whom pitch tents in the blustery, nearby campsite at the foot of the promontory.

Culture Spot - Shiroyama Park and Tateyama Castle

At the highest point of Shiroyama Park sits a four-storey reconstruction of Tateyama Castle, that was originally built here in the 16th century, and was the final stronghold of the Satomi clan, that ruled the area for 170 years until the Tokugawa shogunate cemented their control in the early 17th century.

Inside the building is the Hakkenden Museum, which contains a collection of exhibits relating to the series of novels, 'Nanso Satomi Hakkenden', written by the Edo-period author Kyokutei Bakin. The saga has since inspired *kabuki* plays, artworks, TV adaptations and manga comics.

Tateyama City Museum

Nearer to street level, at one end of the park's pretty walkway of sculptures and cherry trees, is the Tateyama City Museum.

Among its exhibits are artefacts relating to the religious past of the area, paintings, ancient pottery, samurai armour, and recreations of the rustic dwellings and farming tools used by the town's ancestors. The explanatory labels are in Japanese only, but an English-language supplement to the main pamphlet is available.

Nature Spot
Tateyama Wild Bird Sanctuary

This quiet woodland area is a migratory point for many species of birds, and has a choice of suggested walking courses, taking between 90 to 150 minutes to complete. These consist of steep, winding paths and the occasional resting area with tremendous views over the southern coastline. For inexperienced twitchers, the bird life may be elusive, but there are plenty of enormous butterflies and dragonflies fluttering for attention.

Strong calf muscles and a pair of binoculars may help to make your chosen trail, which you are likely to tackle mostly in solitude, more enjoyable.

There is a picnic area, and the entrance building houses a small museum.

The sanctuary shares the same approach road as the Awa Shrine.

Kids

Sunset Pier and Nagisa-no-Eki

Children are free to run amok between the absorbed amateur fishermen who line the 500-metre-long Sunset Pier, which juts out into Kagami-ga-ura bay. Beside the entrance to the pier is Nagisa-no-Eki, a building which contains the Nagisa Museum, with exhibitions of the lives, tools and boats of the local fishermen, and a shop selling local produce.

Aloha Garden Tateyama

Aloha Garden Tateyama, on the Boso Flower Line coastal road, is a large establishment which incorporates a zoo, pleasure gardens, several eateries and a souvenir shop.

Blinded by the write

Kyokutei Bakin, the author of *Nanso Satomi Hakkenden*, spent 28 years completing this vast novel, which is a romantic, fictional tale based on the family of Lord Satomi, who ruled over the Boso region during Japan's Warring States era. The first instalment was published in 1814, when the author was 47, but by the time he had finished all 106 volumes in 1841, he was 74 years old and had lost his sight.

103

Kanto-Koshinetsu

Chiba

TATEYAMA 館山市

🏠 Culture Spot - Temples And Shrines

Gakekannon (Daifuku-ji Temple) 8

Perhaps one of the most photogenic spots in Tateyama is the red and white cliffside temple of Gakekannon, near Nakofunakata Station. As well as the impressive decoration and goddess statue carved into its rock wall, the temple's stage-like platform, which is approached via a choice of several steep flights of stairs, offers a fantastic view of the bay.

Nago-ji Temple 9

Nago-ji is a cherry tree-lined area containing a beautiful pagoda, statue, and temple. Investigate a little further (and climb quite a lot higher), to follow a set of concrete steps that lead up to another observation deck overlooking the ocean. Nago-ji is located a short distance from Daifuku-ji.

Jyourakuzann Mantoku-ji Temple 10

This 30-ton, 16-metre long, bronze statue of a reclining Buddha was built in 1982. Visitors to its serene location are thoughtfully provided with a bamboo walking stick to help climb the winding approach road. Once there, a disciple explains (with the assistance of an English-language pamphlet, if requested) the method of worship, which involves circling the statue three times in a clockwise direction as you ascend with hands clasped towards the point of prayer.

Awa Shrine 11

Legend has it that this peaceful enclave of shrines and affiliated out-buildings originated over 2,600 years ago.

Tsurugaya Hachimangu Yawata Shrine 12

This head shrine of the former province of Awa also serves as the central location of the Yawatan-machi Festival of vibrant *mikoshi* parades each September.

Sunosaki Shrine 13

Climb the long staircase to this small shrine near Sunosaki Lighthouse, for a giddying view down to the sea.

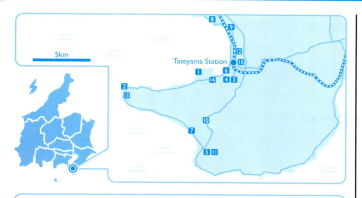

Key dates

mid-January - Yudate Shinji ceremony - praying for good health and a good fishing season (Itsukushima Shrine)

April - cherry blossom season (Awa Shrine, Shiroyama Park)

August 8 - fireworks display (Hojo Beach in Tateyama Bay)

mid-September - Yawatan-machi Festival (Tsurugaya Hachimangu Yawata Shrine Saturday, Tateyama Station Sunday)

mid-October - Nanso Satomi festival - including samurai battle reenactments

Culture Spot - Akayama Underground Tunnels

This grid of perpendicularly arranged air-raid tunnels was created to house a hospital and communications centre for the local military during the Second World War. Visitors are given a helmet and a torch before making their way into the cool, quiet, dark paths burrowed into the hillside's rough sandstone strata.

We say

" I'd envisaged a Pacific Ocean-styled, Beach Boys-themed weekend trip to Tateyama, but due to unseasonably inclement September conditions, my mood was changed to something more introspective. Despite the lack of sunshine, I had a wonderful time cycling around the hills, valleys, coves, stretches of beach and the many points of interest in the area, and I hope to return - ideally on a sunny day next time. The Sunday evening *matsuri* festivities outside the train station were an excellent finale to a great trip. "

Getting there and around

Haneda Airport. Travel to Tateyama Station by express bus.

Narita Airport. Travel via Chiba Station to Tateyama Station using local train services.

Tokyo Station. Travel via Chiba Station or Soga Station to Tateyama Station, using local train services.

To enjoy every attraction in Tateyama mentioned here is not possible on foot, but they can all be accessed by local bus services. Alternatively, battery-assisted rental cycles are available for hire from near the tourist information centre at Tateyama Station. Having your own transport also allows you time to enjoy the views of the Boso Flower Line road on the southern coast.

Food and Drink
Sushi Jinkichi

Sushi Jinkichi is apparently the oldest sushi restaurant in Tateyama town centre. No doubt its longevity is a tribute to its welcoming atmosphere and the delicious fresh fare that they serve.

Accommodation

There is a large number of seafront accommodation options in Tateyama, ranging from budget *ryokan* to swanky golfing hotels. Book early to stay during the weekend of the Yawatan-machi Festival in September.

Recommended for

Families
Snorkellers
Golfers

Further information
www.100hiddentowns.jp/chiba/tateyama.html

105

Kanto-Koshinetsu

草津町

Gunma

KUSATSU

The spa town of Kusatsu is considered one of the very best places to experience hot springs in Japan, and the area is geared almost exclusively to relaxing and bathing in volcanic baths.

Located near the active volcano of Mount Shirane, the town is like a scene from a film, where hot steam rises from the grates in the streets, and visitors can relax their feet in one of many free-to-use foot baths. Every other building is a bathhouse, either old or new. Kusatsu is surrounded by beautiful countryside and boasts an impressive ski resort, open throughout the winter months.

🏠 Culture Spot

Yubatake [1]

Yubatake is the source of the water flowing through Kusatsu, and is situated in the middle of the town. These engineered wooden channels carry hot water through the town and into a large pool to create the town centrepiece - a unique spot for photography enthusiasts and an opportunity to recharge your feet in the free public foot spas. Arrive either at sunrise or sunset to see the area bathed in spectacular sunlight.

Sainokawara Street [2]

This street leads up to Yubatake. It's a great place to find traditional restaurants, cafes, and shops where you can pick up locally produced souvenirs. You can even get some Kusatsu sulphurous *onsen* deposits to recreate a hot spring in your own home.

👍 Must see! Sainokawara Park 3

This is a beautiful park, situated about ten minutes on foot from the centre of Kusatsu. Within the park are many wells from which steaming hot water pours into free-flowing rivers, giving it the feel of a land that time forgot.

The park also houses Sainokawara Rotenburo (open-air hot springs), so after your walk, you can relax in a bath before making your way back into town.

💡 Did you know?

A tart response
The hot spring water in Kusatsu is highly acidic - so much so that if you left a one yen coin in a spa, it would dissolve in a week.

🍶 Food and Drink

Soba (buckwheat noodles)

Kusatsu has several famous *soba* restaurants, and they don't disappoint.

Maitake tempura

This is a local speciality, and usually comes as part of a set meal including *soba*. It is great as a stamina boost to keep going between the bathhouses.

Okkirikomi

This is a dish of flat, wide *udon* noodles served in either a *miso* or soy sauce broth, with many locally produced, seasonal vegetables.

Amanatto

These are traditional Japanese bean sweets coated in sugar. The beans are boiled in a sugar water to create a jelly-type consistency. These are available all around Kusatsu, and many places sell sweets made on the premises.

Onsen manju

These are small steamed cakes filled with sweet bean paste. You can buy them fresh and warm at many shops in and around Kusatsu.

107

Kanto-Koshinetsu

Gunma — KUSATSU
草津町

🏠 Culture Spot - Yumomi Performance

The water at Kusatsu is actually too hot for bathing, so it needs to be cooled. This process is called *yumomi*, and is traditionally done by stirring the water using large planks of wood.

A performance of this custom can be viewed several times a day at the Netsunoyu 4 building in the centre of Kusatsu, and you can even join in. Arrive early if you want a good view.

🏠 Culture Spot - Baths and Spas

Sainokawara Rotenburo 5

Situated in the Sainokawara Park, this is the largest outdoor bath in Kusatsu, and is surrounded by views of the mountains. Depending on the season, the mountains can be lush green or snow-covered, but the view is always perfect for relaxing in the water, or cooling off on one of the many large rocks.

Gozanoyu 6

Situated opposite Yubatake, this spa has been rebuilt in its original 19th-century style, and houses two large baths. It has a resting room and a great view of the centre of town from the second floor, best enjoyed at sunset.

108

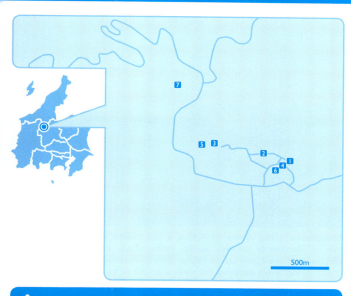

Key dates

August 1-2 - Kusatsu Onsen Thanksgiving Festival (lively festival with performances and large crowds)

mid-late August - Kusatsu International Summer Music Academy and Festival (music lessons, performances and discussions)

We say

" This is the perfect place to relax. There's no beating the laid-back atmosphere of a town that allows you to walk, bathe, eat and drink to unwind. "

Recommended for

Onsen lovers

A relaxing break

🏠 Culture Spot - Kusatsu International Ski ⑦

A very popular destination for winter sports, Kusatsu International Ski boasts an 8,000-metre-long ski run. The ski lift which runs to the summit is also in operation during the hiking season. It offers great views, and has a small restaurant at the bottom if you feel peckish after your journey.

🚆 Getting there and around

✈ Haneda Airport. Take local train and bus services to Kusatsu Onsen.

🚄 Karuizawa Station. Take a bus to Kusatsu Onsen.

🚌 The 'Kusatsu Round Bus' travels around the area and can be used to access most of the hot springs.

As the town is fairly compact, it is easy to walk to most of the main attractions. Planning a route is a good idea if you want to venture away from the bathhouses in the town centre, and be aware there are some very steep paths away from Yubatake.

 Further information
www.100hiddentowns.jp/gunma/kusatsu.html

109

Kanto-Koshinetsu

渋川市 SHIBUKAWA

Gunma

Shibukawa is the home of Ikaho, a spa resort situated halfway up Mount Haruna in Gunma. Steep, stone steps wind their way from the base of the town up to Ikaho Shrine, making for a magical walk that visitors have enjoyed for over a hundred years. You can take in beautiful views of the surrounding snow-capped mountain ranges as you stroll through Ikaho's narrow streets – browsing the many cafes and gift shops set between the hot spring spas and guesthouses.

The surrounding area is great for enjoying outdoor activities, exploring shrines and temples, or just simply relaxing in one of the many, many hot spring spas. Ikaho is famous for its welcoming atmosphere and hospitality.

Culture Spot - Kajika Bridge [1]

The Kajika Bridge is situated ten to fifteen-minutes' walk away from Ikaho Shrine. This traditionally designed wooden bridge is painted in a bright red lacquer, and spans a flowing stream rich in minerals spewing forth from the volcanic springs close by. About 50 metres from the bridge is a famous spring water source where you can sit and fill up your water bottle with iron-rich water from the left pipe, or regular water from the right.

Culture Spot - Ikaho Rotenburo (hot spring bath) [2]

Located a couple of minutes along from Kajika Bridge, this outdoor hot spring bath is the closest to the water source that supplies all the baths at the Ikaho resort, and is said to have the richest iron content. It's a very calming, natural setting which has two baths of different temperatures set amongst trees and rocks. Be sure to check out the dome outside this famous spa, as through it you can see the water source itself.

🏠 Culture Spot - Hara Museum ARC 3

This satellite of the famous Tokyo-based Hara Museum consists of a complex of galleries featuring changing exhibitions of contemporary and traditional art by world-famous artists. The museum is surrounded by several grass-covered spaces where a host of sculptures and installations may be found. Aim to spend a whole day at this attraction as there is plenty to do and see.

👍 Must see! Ikaho Green Bokujo (Farm) 4

Situated less than ten minutes' drive from Ikaho Onsen, this is the perfect place to go with a family. Ikaho Green Bokujo is a farm-themed park that allows visitors to get up close to a variety of farm animals. You can take sheep for a walk, enjoy horse-drawn carriage rides, feed the goats, pet the rabbits and even milk the cows. There are also opportunities to pick strawberries and watch a sheep dog show.

The farm includes barbecue facilities and a restaurant, as well as a gift shop selling produce of the farm, such as cheese, jam, milk and sausages.

The best time to visit is during cherry blossom season as the park is surrounded by cherry trees that make for a spectacular setting.

❓ Did you know?

Spring in the heir
During the Edo period, Ikaho hot springs were said to be famous for increasing fertility rates.

Kanto-Koshinetsu

渋川市

Gunma

SHIBUKAWA

 Culture Spot
Ikaho Onsen Stone Steps 5

These steps wind 300 metres through the centre of Ikaho Onsen to Ikaho Shrine. When following them, you can stop off at souvenir shops selling locally made goods, go into cafes and bars to imbibe much-welcomed refreshments, or just enjoy the view of the mountains in the background.

 **Food and Drink**

Mizusawa Udon

Mizusawa Udon is one of the three most famous types of *udon* noodles in Japan - its smooth and chewy texture make for a delicious meal. Typically served cold with two sauces for dipping — one sesame, and one soy sauce-based — and often combined with *tempura*.

Yu no hana manju (onsen manju)

Yu no hana manju are small, steamed cakes filled with sweet bean paste. To get them hot and fresh, it's best to buy them from specialist shops just off the stone step path on your walk through the centre of Ikaho Onsen.

Sukiyaki (beef hot pot)

A hot pot made up of fresh vegetables and beef from the local area, in a sweet, soy sauce-based broth, this is a must for anyone who enjoys comfort food of the highest order. This area is famous for its beef production, so make sure when you order that it contains Gunma beef.

Sake (rice wine)

The Ikaho area is particularly famous for *jizake* - locally produced *sake*. There are also several locally brewed craft beers available.

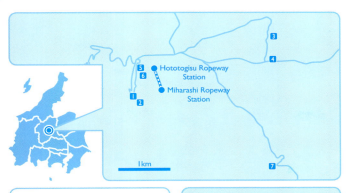

Key dates

mid-June to mid-July - Hydrangea Festival (enjoy 8,000 shrubs in bloom, and also illuminated night-time viewing is available)

late July - Shibukawa Belly Button Festival (unique dancing, with performers bearing faces painted onto their torsos)

We say

" This is a fantastic place to spend a long weekend relaxing in the hot springs, enjoying the area's hospitality and exploring the surrounding mountains. Aim to stay for a couple of days and book into a hotel or Japanese-style guesthouse close to the stone steps. This will mean everything you need to visit is within walking distance. "

Recommended for

Food lovers

Nature lovers

Hot spring lovers

Culture Spot - Ikaho Shrine

This beautiful shrine - located at the top of the stone steps - is said to be over a thousand years old, and creates a peaceful setting overlooking the town. There is a viewing platform above the shrine, offering a breathtaking view of the surrounding countryside.

Culture Spot Mizusawa Kannon

Located a short walk from the popular Mizusawa Udon Town, about a ten-minute drive from Ikaho Onsen, Mizusawa Kannon is a busy temple that buzzes with activity, as the smell of incense hangs in the air.

This ornately painted temple has several buildings, including a hexagon-shaped pagoda which houses a central column you should turn clockwise three times for good luck.

It takes about an hour to walk around the complex and stalls.

Getting there and around

✈ Haneda Airport. Take local bus and train services to Ikaho Onsen.

🚆 Takasaki Station. Take local train services to Shibukawa Station and then a bus to Ikaho Onsen.

🚶 All places of interest around Ikaho Onsen are within a 20-minute drive, and have parking available, so renting a car is the best option. Alternatively, local buses serve the tourist spots. The area around Ikaho Onsen Station is delightful for a relaxed stroll.

 Further information
www.100hiddentowns.jp/gunma/shibukawa.html

Kanto-Koshinetsu

潮来市

Ibaraki — ITAKO

Itako is approached from the west via a huge, flat expanse of paddy fields, punctuated only by walkways, irrigation trenches and white, pecking herons. As you cross the Maekawa River, the purple, blooming iris gardens of Itako Town come into view.

Until the 1950s, when a major land reclamation project transformed the area, there were no roads and almost everybody in Itako journeyed in their own punt through the waterways between their homes and the rice fields.

These days, the town is home to roads and four-wheeled traffic, but the rivers and canals are still used for transportation of commercial goods, as well as for tourist boats and punts.

Culture Spot - Kaiunzan Choshou-ji Temple

Kaiunzan Choushou-ji Temple, famous for its old hanging bell and beautiful thatched roof, was originally built on the orders of Minamoto-no-Yoritomo (the first shogun of the Kamakura era) in 1185, then restored between 1688 and 1704. The approach is through a gate that dates back to 1700, which is connected to the temple by a perfectly straight path beneath a canopy of trees.

🏠 Culture Spot
Aiyu Sake Brewery 2

Since 1804, the master brewers of Aiyu Sake Brewery in Itako have been combining local skills, rice, and spring water from the neighbouring Oou Shrine, to produce its renowned *sake* (rice wine).

Visitors are welcome to take a guided tour around the various presses and vats that reside inside the 200-year-old brewery's distinctive white walls, and sample a range of their wines in the shop area. Although the guided tours are only available in Japanese, the tasting transcends language.

👍 Must see! Suigo Itako Ayame (Iris) Garden 3

Every year, between late May and late June, Suigo Itako Ayame Garden becomes a magnet for day-trippers who come to see Itako's iris festival, where roughly 500 varieties of iris (over one million flowers) reach full bloom in the warmth of the late spring/early summer weather.

The festival has evolved since it started in 1952, when locals would exhibit their blooms in beer bottles in the park.

During the daytime, visitors can wander amongst the rows of flowers and the pretty bridges that overlook the park gardens and the waterway that runs beside it.

During the evenings, the whole park is illuminated, and it becomes a romantic setting for the *yomeiribune* – boats steered by boatmen and boatwomen carrying traditionally dressed brides-to-be to their grooms. This custom, which died out for many years, has been revived since the 1980s and is now one of the iconic sights of the iris festival. As well as the bridal boats, local performers entertain visitors with traditional songs and dances during the festival.

The garden is also a departure point for the hand-steered punts, and some of the many boat tours in Itako, including the 12 Bridges Tour.

❓ Did you know?

Splash hit

In 1973, the Japanese female singer Yukiko Noji had a hit song titled 'Yomeiribune', about Itako's bridal boats.

115

Kanto-Koshinetsu

Ibaraki — ITAKO 潮来市

👫 Kids - Itako Roadside Station *(michi-no-eki)* [4]

Itako's *michi-no-eki*, located a short distance from Itako Interchange at the end of the Higashikanto Highway, is a great place to taste, and stock up on, local delicacies such as rice crackers, pickled vegetables, fresh vegetables and cookies.

As well as restaurants, greengrocers and stalls offering free samples, this stop-off point offers activities such as pottery making and mini-golf – great for keeping youngsters amused while you agonise over which variation of *tsukudani* (fish and shellfish cooked in sweetened soy sauce) to purchase as a souvenir.

🌳 Nature Spot - Suigo Sawara Aquatic Botanical Garden [5]

Located on the west side of the Maekawa river (so technically just outside of Itako Town) is another large garden devoted to glorifying the iris. Suigo Sawara Aquatic Botanical Garden is a beautifully designed collection of paths and small bridges that afford visitors an assortment of pretty vantage points from which to admire the interplay between the flowers, the water, and the boatmen and women steering punts throughout the gardens.

Although admission is not free, the large number of day trippers that come here are a testament to the charming sights on display.

116

Key dates

early April - Cherry Blossom Festival (Gongen-yama Park)

late May to late June - Iris Festival (Suigo Itako Ayame (Iris) Garden)

early August - Itako Gion Festival (town centre)

August 13-16 - Buddhist Lantern Festival (Cho-on-ji Temple)

mid-October - Moon Festival (Suigo Itako Ayame (Iris) Garden)

November 23 - Shishi-mai (Lion Dance of Uwado) (Kunigami Shrine)

We say

❝ Itako is a very pretty town to visit while the irises bloom during May and June. The large numbers of visitors that come at this time, rather than spoiling the spectacle, actually add to its charm. ❞

Recommended for

Enthusiasts of irises and freshwater eels

Food and Drink

Teppo-zuke (gun pickles) are a local treat made from a relative of the cucumber - flattened, stuffed and pickled in chili, soy sauce and cooking rice wine. Their name comes from their resemblance to a loaded gun barrel. Tsukamoto is a cosy shop (ten minutes walk from Itako Roadside Station) which makes and sells delicious, hand-made *senbei* (rice crackers).

There are many *unagi* (freshwater eel) restaurants in Itako Town, such as the pricey but delicious Kinsui, near Itako Station. The exalted *koi* (carp) is also a popular local delicacy - perhaps owing to Itako's historical abundance of waterways. For noodle fans, Tsukamoto Soba serves delicious *soba* noodles, made inside the restaurant, from Ibaraki buckwheat flour.

Getting there and around

🛬 Narita Airport or Ibaraki Airport. Travel by local train services to Itako Station.

🚆 Tokyo Station (but nearby main stations are JR Narita Station and JR Chiba Station). Take the train from JR Narita Station to Itako Station (change at Sahara Station).

🚲 Rental cycles are available from the tourist information centre directly outside the train station, but from here, most of Itako's attractions are actually within walking distance.

🏨 Accommodation - Kanpo-no-Yado

Kanpo-no-Yado Inn is the best-known hotel in the area. Located a short taxi ride from Nobukata Station, the hotel restaurant serves a phenomenal dinner set consisting of countless courses of beautifully prepared food.

The hot spring baths on the top floor offer a fabulous, tranquil view over Lake Kitaura below.

 Further information
www.100hiddentowns.jp/ibaraki/itako.html

Kanto-Koshinetsu

KASAMA
Ibaraki
笠間市

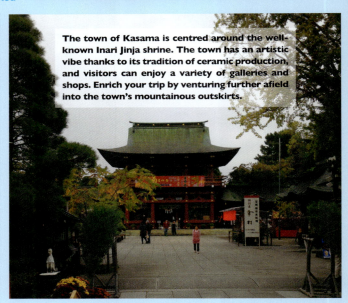

The town of Kasama is centred around the well-known Inari Jinja shrine. The town has an artistic vibe thanks to its tradition of ceramic production, and visitors can enjoy a variety of galleries and shops. Enrich your trip by venturing further afield into the town's mountainous outskirts.

🏠 Culture Spot - Kasama Geijutsu-no-Mori

Historically, the proximity of Kasama to Edo ensured that its pottery industry had a large, willing market, and consequently could flourish. The Geijutsu-no-Mori park is a large area mainly focused on the town's connection to ceramics, with several facilities to peruse and enjoy. Visitors can participate in workshops at Crafthills Kasama, as well as shop for pottery souvenirs and enjoy exhibitions by local potters.

The pottery workshops include a chance to make your own wares with a potter's wheel. Instructors are on hand to guide you through the process and ensure the end product is of excellent quality, so the workshop is suitable even for complete beginners. There are also workshops where participants can paint pottery in decorations of their choice, or make their own pottery wares by hand without the use of the wheel.

The park also incorporates a large gallery with displays of impressive, colourful ceramics, and a large exhibit devoted to local, pioneering ceramic artist, Kosei Matsui, whose work often involved small pieces of clay meticulously added to each other to form the final artwork.

There is an adventure playground for kids, with a long slide and a jungle gym, plus plenty of open space for picnics.

👍 Must see! Kasama Nichido Museum of Art ❷

Just east of the main thoroughfare of Monzen Street, visitors can find the Nichido Museum, an impressively large gallery with a variety of displays. As well as galleries devoted to local artists, there is an excellent collection of western art including works by Van Gogh, Renoir, Matisse, Picasso and Warhol. The garden also houses several impressive sculptures.

🌳 Nature Spot - Mount Atago ❸ and Mount Sashiro ❹

There are several spots for relatively easy hikes around Kasama, including ascending to the shrine atop Mount Atago, or the park at the peak of Mount Sashiro, where a Kamakura-era castle was once located.

The climb to Mount Sashiro passes a large, black stone which has a small hole in its centre. Throw three stones towards the hole and if one rests there you will be granted good luck.

❓ Did you know?

Rare wrap

Kasama has its own special take on *inarizushi* (sushi rice wrapped in fried *tofu*). A choice of fillings can include noodles or walnuts. Classes and contests are often held in the town.

Kanto-Koshinetsu

Ibaraki

笠間市

KASAMA

🏠 Culture Spot - Aiki Shrine and Aikido Dojo 5

During the 1940s, the founder of Aikido, Morihei Ueshiba, undertook intense training in Kasama (formerly Iwama Town), and established the Aiki Shrine and Aikido Dojo here. Today, Aikido has spread to 130 countries around the world, and this location is a popular attraction for members of the Aikido community.

🏠 Culture Spot - Kasama Inari Jinja 6

Many visitors come to pray to the deity of this popular shrine, who is said to grant wishes to worshippers from a variety of industries - from fishing to commerce.

While the main building is similar to other shrines, the grounds have plenty of diversions for the curious, including giant wisteria trees and statues of so-called 'divine horses'. The shrine also hosts a variety of festivals throughout the year.

There is a small gallery beside the shrine, with displays of ancient ceramics and hanging scrolls depicting scenes of nature.

Approach the shrine via Inari Monzen Street - the main street for tourists - which incorporates several tasty eateries selling confectionery, *sake* and local snacks.

Key dates

mid-April to mid-May - Azalea Festival

Golden Week - Pottery Festival (displays of Kasama-yaki)

mid-October - Kasama Roman (food and craft fair)

mid-October to mid-November - Chrysanthemum Festival

We say

" Kasama has much to offer and is doable as a day trip from Tokyo or Saitama. I was delighted by the sculptures at the Nichido Museum and surprised by the quality of their western art collection. The hospitality experienced at Shiroyama Ryokan also deserves a special mention. "

Recommended for

Pottery lovers

Day trippers from Tokyo

 Food and Drink

The Inari Jinja road, or Monzen Street, that runs through the town has plenty of little outlets to snack at, or restaurants to dine in. Try the *inarizushi*, the chestnuts and the Japanese sweets.

On the outskirts of the town is the Sudohonke *sake* brewery, which was founded during the Heian era, making it one of the longest-running breweries in the country. It produces a variety of brands which visitors can enjoy tasting.

 Accommodation

Constructed in the pre-war Showa era, Shiroyama Ryokan is a conveniently located, comfortable place to stay. The homely service and serene decor make it a highly recommended accommodation.

On Mount Atago, visitors can stay at Atago Tengu-no-Mori Sky Lodge, which provides self-catering guests with the necessary kitchenware, utensils and bathing facilities.

Getting there and around

- Ibaraki Airport. Take express buses and local train services to Kasama Station.
- Omiya Station. Travel by local train services to Kasama Station.
- The town itself is compact enough to enjoy on foot, and very pleasant to stroll around. A car or taxi will be necessary if venturing to Mount Atago.

 Further information
www.100hiddentowns.jp/ibaraki/kasama.html

Kanto-Koshinetsu

Kanagawa
MIURA
三浦市

Miura's port town of Misaki, at the tip of the Miura Peninsula, is a picturesque area best known for its tuna fish market. Across a 575-metre-long bridge from Miura is the wonderful island of Jogashima, a peaceful getaway from Kanagawa's suburban commuter belt.

🌳 Nature Spot - Kawazu Sakura [1]

Between the stations of Miura-kaigan and Misakiguchi, a treat awaits. During February and March, Kawazu cherry blossoms come into bloom along the train tracks, providing an early taste of spring. Coinciding with the blossoming of the Kawazu *sakura* trees, rape weed blossoms are also in their full glory, providing a pretty contrast between the pink of the cherry blossoms and the yellow of the rape weed.

🏠 Culture Spot - Misaki Port [2]

Misaki Port is where much of the fresh catch from Japan's southern sea waters is unloaded. The port is famed for its tuna, and the early morning auction is a must-see. The atmosphere is quieter and more studied than the better-known Tsukiji market in Tokyo, but no less interesting.

The wharf of Misaki Port, known as Urari, is filled with vendors selling fresh fish and other local produce, and the market teems with visitors as well as local residents. A trip to Misaki isn't complete without tasting some of the catch at one of the port's eateries.

👍 Must see! Jogashima Island 3

Jogashima Island, located at the southernmost tip of Miura Peninsula, is a gorgeous spot. Having crossed the bridge from the mainland, venture off the road to the clifftop trails for a short hike to enjoy coastal views that rival any in Japan. The stunning rock formations and cliffs beside the Pacific's waves are an impressive sight, especially at sunrise and sunset. To the east, Chiba's Boso Peninsula can be clearly seen, and on brighter days Izu Oshima Island and the Izu Peninsula are visible to the west. The key spot for visitors is a spectacular arched rock formation whose aperture offers views of the Pacific. The arch is two metres thick, and is clear evidence of the erosive power of the ocean.

If possible, visit on a quiet weekday, and you may get the island to yourself. Jogashima can also be reached by boat from Misaki Port.

🚆 Getting there and around

- ✈ Haneda Airport. Take local trains to Misakiguchi Station.
- 🚄 Shin-Yokohama Station. Travel by local train to Misakiguchi Station.
- 🚌 From Misakiguchi Station, take a bus, taxi or battery-powered rental bicycle to Misaki Port and Jogashima Island. Travelling by car is highly recommended, especially for day-trippers.

📱 Further information
www.100hiddentowns.jp/kanagawa/miura.html

❓ Did you know?

Fine-tuned tuna
The Misaki fish market sells up to 1,000 tuna a day. After being transferred from the fishing boats and having their organs removed, each tuna is weighed, numbered, and displayed to the bidders. The traders write down their bids on memo pads and the highest bidder wins. Compared to the boisterous auctioneering at Tsukiji in Tokyo, Misaki fish market is a more solemn, considered affair.

Key dates

mid-January - Chakkirako Festival (girls aged from five to twelve dance to a capella music while holding fans and *chakkiriko*, which are a kind of bamboo stick. The festival has taken place since the Edo era to appeal to the gods for bountiful catches of fish.)

We say

❝ For people coming from Yokohama, Tokyo and other surrounding municipalities, Misaki and Jogashima Island are well worth a one-day visit. Plan on an early start to catch the fish market auctioneering in all its studied seriousness. After a delicious early lunch of local seafood from one of the eateries that line the harbour, head off to Jogashima Island for short hikes amid breathtaking scenery. ❞

Recommended for
Nature lovers

Seafood fans

123

Kanto-Koshinetsu

白馬村

Nagano — HAKUBA

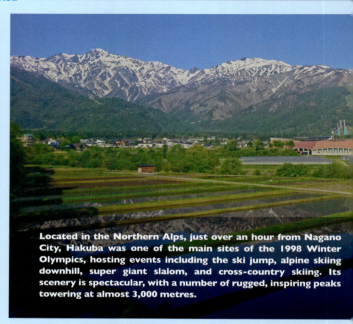

Located in the Northern Alps, just over an hour from Nagano City, Hakuba was one of the main sites of the 1998 Winter Olympics, hosting events including the ski jump, alpine skiing downhill, super giant slalom, and cross-country skiing. Its scenery is spectacular, with a number of rugged, inspiring peaks towering at almost 3,000 metres.

👍 Must do! Outdoor Sports

Winter

The Hakuba valley consists of 11 ski resorts that offer huge expanses of pistes, 135 lifts and five gondolas. Most of the resorts are not interconnected (with the exceptions of Hakuba 47 with Goryu, and Cortina with Norikura). However, there are frequent buses that enable visitors to travel between the different ski areas. Some hotels also offer courtesy buses to each of the areas at peak times. Skiers and snowboarders should choose their slopes wisely - some of the resorts have long, perfectly groomed runs more suited for beginners, while a few have steep runs and moguls aimed at experts. Off-piste terrain can also be found, especially at Hakuba Cortina.

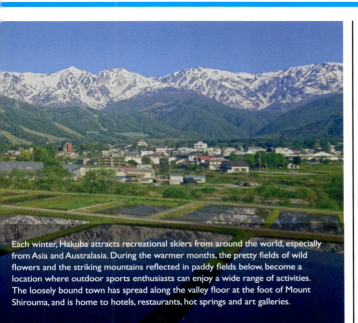

Each winter, Hakuba attracts recreational skiers from around the world, especially from Asia and Australasia. During the warmer months, the pretty fields of wild flowers and the striking mountains reflected in paddy fields below, become a location where outdoor sports enthusiasts can enjoy a wide range of activities. The loosely bound town has spread along the valley floor at the foot of Mount Shirouma, and is home to hotels, restaurants, hot springs and art galleries.

 Did you know?

Downhill uproar

In the lead-up to the 1998 Nagano Winter Olympics, there were complaints that the 1,680-metre men's downhill course was too short. An ensuing brouhaha almost resulted in the cancellation of the event for the Games, but eventually the issue was resolved by the addition of an extra 85 metres to the run.

Spring-Summer

From the springtime onwards, the humidity-free mountain air, clear rivers and lakes, dramatic mountainous terrain and lush valley floor of Hakuba are ideal for a broad range of outdoor activities, including hiking, mountain biking, mountain climbing, rafting, canyoning, canoeing, paragliding and hot air ballooning. Hakuba is home to several businesses that provide guided experiences such as these during the warmer months. Pre-booking online or by phone at least a few days in advance is advised.

Kanto-Koshinetsu

白馬村
Nagano
HAKUBA

🌳 Nature Spot - Hakuba Daisekkei [1]

Daisekkei ('great snow field') is a popular trekking destination during the spring and summer.

The trail begins from the Sarukura-Sou Lodge, and is a popular way to reach the summit of Mount Shirouma - the highest peak in the Hakuba section of the Northern Alps, and one of the few peaks in Japan with year-round snow fields. The area above the snow field is a mountaineering route where full-scale climbing equipment is necessary.

A trip up to Daisekkei is not to be undertaken lightly, as avalanches and rockfalls are common. You must check conditions in advance, and at the huts on the way, as sometimes the route will be closed because of hazards. You'll be hiking in the snow for most of the way, so dress accordingly. Note that you will need crampons and that helmets are also commonly worn.

This hike is most popular from June to October, although it is possible to go earlier if you've got an ice axe.

The views are outstanding when the weather is good, so another option is to arrange to stay overnight in one of the huts at the top, in order to see the sunrise.

🌳 Nature Spot - Hakuba Happo-One and Happo-Ike Pond [2]

Happo-One derives its name from the eight ridges that converge close to this pond, which is located at an altitude of 2,060 metres. When the clouds clear, this spot offers spectacular views of the peaks of Yaridake, Shakushidake, Mount Shirouma and the Hakuba basin. The pond's surface, when not covered in ice, mirrors the surrounding scenery beautifully.

Access from the town below is provided by the Adam Gondola, followed by two chair lifts. The remainder of the ascent is made on foot and takes about 60-90 minutes, via a pathway of wooden steps and some sections of slightly precarious stones and loose rocks - so take extra care when in slippery conditions.

The walk is not strenuous and is well within the abilities of most visitors, young and old. The pond itself is 4.4 metres deep and surrounded by alpine flowers. It remains frozen well into late spring. Ropes are employed to deter over-enthusiastic yompers from crushing underfoot the blooms of unique, indigenous flora such as *happo-takanesenburi* (gentian family) and *happo-waremokoh* (burnet).

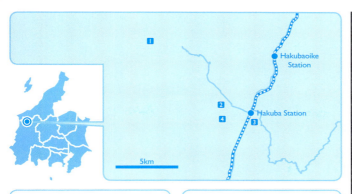

Key dates

May 3, 4, 5 - Hakuba Salt Road Festival (historical walking event - Kenshin Uesugi sent salt to Shingen Takeda during the Warring States era)

July and August - Hanazanmai (a vast variety of alpine plants in bloom at twelve venues in the village)

December 31 - Hakuba Countdown Event (annual New Year countdown event with drinking, revelry and fireworks)

We say

" Hakuba is a perfect location to enjoy wonderful outdoor activities at almost any time of the year. Bathing in a hot spring after a day in the Alps leaves one feeling rejuvenated and in eager anticipation of the next day. "

Recommended for

Visitors wishing to enjoy outdoor sports with a Japanese flavour

Accommodation
Hakuba Highland Hotel

Guests of this large but homely hotel have the option of two hot springs (one of which is also open to the public during restricted hours of the day) that each offer fabulous views of the snow-capped, jagged Northern Alps. Guests staying in the west-facing rooms can also enjoy a similar view. Breakfast and dinner are both large, buffet-style affairs.

Culture Spot
Hakuba Museum of Art

Cosseted away in a glade of rich foliage, visitors to this small gallery can enjoy a collection of small pieces created by Marc Chagall, exhibited in a roomy, airy outbuilding. The museum offers a cool and sophisticated respite from Hakuba's more strenuous attractions, and is located near to a neighbourhood of upmarket restaurants and bars. (NB closed during winter.)

Getting there and around

Most visitors from overseas fly to Narita Airport, then travel via Tokyo Station to Nagano Station, and on to Hakuba Station by Limited Express bus services (60 minutes).

Nagano Station. Travel to Hakuba Station by Limited Express bus services (60 minutes).

Affordable, frequent buses run between each resort in the Hakuba Valley throughout the day.

Further information
www.100hiddentowns.jp/nagano/hakuba.html

127

Kanto-Koshinetsu

小諸市 KOMORO
Nagano

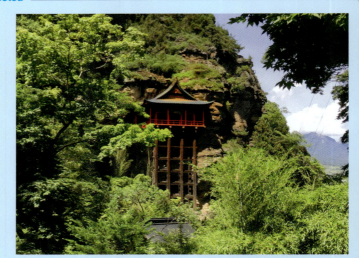

Komoro is situated a 20-minute, local train journey from Karuizawa - one of Japan's most famous rural summer retreats. As well as enjoying the same refreshing climate as its scene-stealing neighbour, Komoro's absence of bustling shopping crowds and busy bus tours allows visitors the space and time to really enjoy soaking up its beautiful mountain views, historical castle remains, hot spring baths and the mesmerising cliff face temple of Nunobiki. During the winter months, the upper slopes of the area become covered in snow and local trade shifts gear for the ski season.

Nature Spot - Takamine Kougen

The mountains to the north of Komoro are a popular attraction for hikers, skiers and snowboarders. A trip to the volcanic Mount Asama is quite an undertaking, requiring an 80-minute drive to the trails that lead from there. Closer to Komoro is Takamine Kougen.

After a 40-minute bus ride from Komoro Station, visitors old and young can enjoy the narrow, winding trail up the mountain which ends abruptly at a pile of rocks at the peak, that provides a breathtaking viewpoint of the neighbouring highlands.

🏠 Culture Spot - Nakadanasou

Although the Japanese inns are usually discussed in the accommodation sections of this book, this fabulous lodging warrants a special mention as a cultural attraction.

Nakadanasou *ryokan* is comprised of a series of wooden buildings dating back to 1898, created with a level of craftsmanship and attention to detail that harks back to more extravagant times. A corridor that crosses over the road leads on to a covered walkway up to the inn's serene hot spring.

The rooms and the corridors are all decorated with elegant simplicity, from the hand-crafted writing desks and floor lamps, to the tasteful prints on the walls.

The inn's restaurant, Harikoshitei, also boasts charming vintage architecture, where you can enjoy traditional Japanese cuisine.

The renowned Japanese author Toson Shimazaki wrote some of his famous works while visiting Nakadanasou.

If you want to explore further, take a few minutes to wander outside, around the paths that weave between the inn's outbuildings and garden.

💡 Did you know?

Major Meiji master

Toson Shimazaki (the pen-name of Haruki Shimazaki), was a Japanese author who lived and taught in Komoro (from 1899 until 1905), where he began several of his works, including 'Chikuma River Sketches' and 'The Broken Commandment'. Born in 1872, he began his career as a romantic poet, later becoming a major voice in Japanese fiction - his writing reflecting the upheavals in Japanese society during the Meiji era.

👍 Must see! Kaikoen Park

Ensure that you allow at least a couple of hours to wander around Komoro's Kaikoen Park. Here you will find over 400 years of history and culture, all in a beautiful setting just a few minutes' walk from the train station.

This is the site of the remains of Komoro Castle, which was commissioned in the early 1600s by the daimyo Hidehisa Sengoku. You can still see the walls of the castle and two of its gates - Otemon and Sannomon.

Further exploration of the park reveals how the local topography was exploited to provide the unique moat around the castle grounds.

Also within the park, there is an art museum, a memorial museum to the writer Toson Shimazaki, an amusement park for children, and a zoo, all complemented by luscious trees renowned for their beauty during the cherry blossom and autumn leaf seasons.

Kanto-Koshinetsu

Nagano
小諸市
KOMORO

🍶 Food and Drink - Manns Wine Komoro Winery [4]

A 2.5-kilometre excursion from Komoro Station will take you to this winery. Here you can sample and buy a wide range of the wines produced by Manns, many of which are made from the grapes picked from the fertile region around Komoro. Visitors can also take a tour around the premises to see the wine vats and barrels, one of the vineyards, and also stroll around the beautiful garden, beneath which is the cellar where some of the most valuable bottles are stored.

🏠 Culture Spot - Nunobiki Temple [5]

After a 15-minute climb up a shaded set of mountain steps, a steamy path arrives at the foot of a sheer rock face. Look up to see the beautiful Nunobiki Temple perching directly overhead. Continue up a little further and follow the path which takes you through a short tunnel and onto the platform of the temple itself, which was originally built in the eighth century, and where non-sufferers of vertigo can marvel at the view of Komoro Town and the mountains beyond, as well as wondering at the technical feat of building this wonderful vantage point over a thousand years ago.

Key dates

mid-April - Cherry Blossom Festival (Kaikoen)

late May - Kurumazaka Hill Climb (bicycle race on Mount Asama and Takamine Kougen)

mid-July - Citizen's Festival (town centre) and Tatehaya Shrine Gion Festival

We say

" Komoro is a wonderfully charming place to visit. The combination of indoor and outdoor attractions, and beautiful scenery ensures that a visit at almost any time of the year, in almost any weather, will be a treat. "

Recommended for

History buffs

Hikers

Those in need of a quiet break

🛏 Accommodation
Takamine Kougen Hotel 6

For visitors who wish to stay in the mountains to the north of Komoro, Takamine Kougen Hotel offers traditional-style Japanese rooms, fabulous mountain views, a restaurant serving Japanese and French cuisine, an observatory/telescope, and an ideal starting point for several mountain trails, all located at an altitude of 2,000m. The hotel caters for the ski crowd during the winter months.

👪 Kids - Kaikoen Park

Treat the youngsters to a few hours at the zoo and the amusement park in Kaikoen Park, just a few minutes' walk from Komoro Station.

🏠 Culture Spot
Aguri-no-yu Komoro 7

This hot spring centre, located about four kilometres from Komoro Station, provides visitors with an ideal respite from the elements, perfect for unwinding and enjoying the panoramic view of Komoro and Mount Asama. As well as the baths, the building also houses eateries and a shop selling local farm produce. Whether the weather is hot sunshine, misty rain or winter snow, this is a great spot to relax.

🚆 Getting there and around

✈ Matsumoto Airport. It is about 75 kilometres by rental car to Komoro.

🚉 Karuizawa Station. Travel by local train services to Komoro.

🚶 Many of the main attractions in Komoro are within an easy walk from Komoro Station. However, to get the most out of your visit, especially if you wish to visit the mountains, local buses or a hire car will be necessary. Another recommendation is to hire a bicycle from the excellently equipped tourist information centre, directly outside Komoro Station.

🔍 Further information
www.100hiddentowns.jp/nagano/komoro.html

Kanto-Koshinetsu

野沢温泉村

Nagano

NOZAWAONSEN

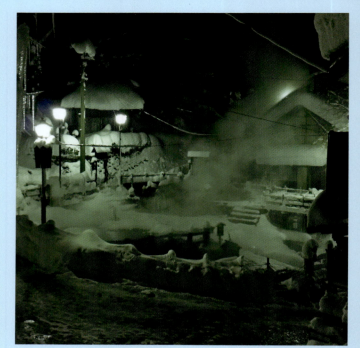

During the winter months, Nozawaonsen is one of Japan's most iconic winter sports resorts, combining a bustling, village atmosphere with competition-level ski slopes.

During the off-season, the tempo slows down and it becomes a perfect place to relax and amble leisurely between the hotels, restaurants, shops, shrines and 13 public hot spring baths that line the village's narrow, winding roads.

Culture Spot - Japan Ski Museum

Located beside the Hikage Gondola Station, the Japan Ski Museum is an excellent place to spend an hour or two learning about the history of skiing - in Japan and elsewhere - and to see paraphernalia relating to the Winter Olympics, up to and including Nagano 1998.

132

👍 Must see!
13 Public Hot Spring Baths

Nozawaonsen has been renowned for its hot springs and traditional inns since the Edo period. Legend has it that the first hot spring here was shown to a hunter by a wounded bear.

Throughout the village, there are many different types of hot springs, including 13 public hot spring baths where villagers and visitors can share a conversation and a relaxing soak.

The most well known of these baths, O Yu, is located at the centre of the village - its distinctive architecture makes it a useful landmark for navigating the many twisting roads in the area.

Entrance to the baths is free of charge, but there is a box outside each one for visitors to provide a donation for upkeep. Each bath also has an illustrated guide of the etiquette and rules to follow for *onsen* novices. Visitors should bring their own towel and soap. Be warned that the water in most of the baths is very hot. The baths are open until 11pm every day.

As well as the public baths, there are also several outdoor footbaths where you can sit back and take the weight off your feet for a few minutes. Some of these have a vat in which you can boil eggs while you luxuriate and watch the world go by.

You can even see villagers cooking vegetables outdoors in Ogama (see main photo) - the hottest spring in Nozawaonsen - which is used as a communal kitchen bath.

💡 Did you know?

Olympic links
Nozawaonsen hosted the Biathlon competition in the 1998 Nagano Winter Olympics. It is also the birthplace of several renowned athletes, including Olympic medallists Jinya Nishikata (ski jumper) and Takanori Kono (Nordic combined skier).

Kanto-Koshinetsu

野沢温泉村

Nagano

NOZAWAONSEN

🏠 Culture Spot - Nozawaonsen Snow Resort

Nozawaonsen is regarded by many as Japan's most iconic ski resort - the pretty town providing access to slopes that rank among the best in Japan in terms of size, history and snow quality. Skiing was introduced to Nozawaonsen in 1912 by an Austrian, and Nozawa is considered by some to be the birthplace of skiing in Japan. Its reputation is well known, and the town attracts many skiers from overseas. The runs are conveniently concentrated in one ski area, but the 297 hectares of terrain caters for skiers and snowboarders of all levels.

Accommodation

The popularity of Nozawaonsen during the ski season means that the village has dozens of places to stay – traditional inns, ski lodges, large and small hotels – most within a short walk of the village centre, the hot spring baths and the gondolas to the ski slopes. Many of these establishments are well used to looking after guests from overseas as well as from Japan, and wi-fi service is the norm.

🏠 Culture Spot - Dosojin Fire Festival

Celebrated on January 15th, for one day during the ski season every year the winter sports take a back seat to Nozawaonsen's flaming festivities. As evening settles, revellers converge in the centre of the village and make their way to the festival site, taking care not to have their expensive skiwear torched by stray embers from the huge, smouldering bales of twigs being recklessly swung around by the participants. Ensure that you keep your wits about you, because the element of showmanship tends to win out over standard health and safety considerations.

At the festival proper, the town's inhabitants gather to build a large tower. The tradition is for a team of aggressors to charge the tower armed with flaming bales of tethered twigs. It is the job of the other team to repel and extinguish their attacks.

Although the event does have an element of pantomime - all attacks are successfully repelled until the tower finally goes up in flames at ten o'clock - the revellers' consumption of rice wine provides a charmingly unpredictable element of mayhem to the proceedings.

Key dates

January 15 - Dosojin Fire Festival (Banbanohara)
early March - Winter Holy Light Night Festival (Hikage slope)
mid-March - Nozawaonsen Hatoguruma Ski and Snowboard Cup (Nozawaonsen Snow Resort)
mid-March - Naski Cup Athletic Snow Contest (Hikage slope)
late March - Spring Mountain Festival (Yamabiko slope)
early June - Tsutsuji Azalea Festival (O Yu street, Tsutsujiyama Park)
mid-June - Takenoko (Nemagaridake bamboo shoot) Festival (Soto-yu, Kawahara-yu)
mid-August - Summer Night Bon Dance Festival (the precincts of Yuzawa Jinja shrine)
early September - Yuzawa Jinja shrine Annual Festival (the whole village)
early November - Nozawana Festival (Nozawaonsen Sparena)

 Food and Drink

There are a large number of small restaurants and snack bars in Nozawaonsen, but many are closed outside of the winter season. Nonetheless, the places that are open offer a wide range of delicious meals and local delicacies.

Atarashiya 4

Atarashiya is a guesthouse renowned for its delicious *unagi don* (eel on rice), and *yakitori* (skewered, grilled chicken pieces) that are served in its attractive restaurant.

Nappa (78) Cafe 5

You can enjoy excellent coffees and snack meals in this charming, nostalgia-decorated cafe that looks out onto the footbaths beside Ogama.

AJB Brewery 6

A recent addition to the many eateries and watering holes in Nozawaonsen, AJB (Anglo-Japanese Brewing Co.) serves home-made, gourmet beers that have been brewed on site.

Nozawana

Pickled *nozawana* is one of the most famous local foods of Nagano Prefecture. According to legend, in the 18th century, the master of a Buddhist temple from Nozawa found this Japanese leaf vegetable in the mountains of Kyoto and replanted it in Nozawaonsen.

Onsen Manju

Onsen manju are small dumplings filled with sweet, red *anko* paste and steamed over hot spring water.

We say

"A fabulous place to visit during the ski season. Outside of the ski season, Nozawaonsen is not a destination for 'doing' things, but is instead a lovely place to unwind and take it easy for a day or two, enjoying the local food, drink and restorative powers of its hot springs. Allow yourself plenty of time to wander around the village. The interplay between the steamy hot springs and the mountain streams, temples, shrines, and local architecture, provides an abundance of delightful views."

Getting there and around

✈ Matsumoto Airport. Travel to Matsumoto Station by bus, then to Iiyama Station by local train services. (Note - most visitors arrive via Narita Airport or Haneda Airport.)

🚌 Iiyama Station. Travel to Nozawaonsen by bus (25 minutes).

🚶 When you have arrived in the village, most places of interest are a short walk from each other, so taxis and buses are mostly unnecessary. There are two gondola courses that run from the village up to the ski slopes during the ski season.

Recommended for

Skiers and snowboarders
Onsen fans

 Further information
www.100hiddentowns.jp/nagano/nozawaonsen.html

Kanto-Koshinetsu

小川村

Nagano

OGAWA

The quiet village of Ogawa is nestled deep in the heart of Nagano Prefecture's mountainous Kamiminochi District.

From its upper slopes, visitors to Ogawa are treated to one of Japan's most breathtaking views — an unspoiled panorama of the northern Alps, from Mount Kitakuzu in the south as far as Mount Korenge in the north. Winding mountain roads connect local farms and orchards to the village in the valley below. The area is snow-covered during the winter, but its farms and fields glow with colour from spring to autumn.

👍 Must see! Views of the Northern Alps

The biggest draw for visitors to Ogawa is its stunning views of the Northern Alps.

There are several vantage points in the area that provide vast, unbroken vistas, with little interference from the electric pylons, cables and other eyesores that so commonly taint similar spectacles elsewhere in Japan.

From dawn to dusk (and, on a clear, moonlit night, until even later), you can watch the shades and colours of the panorama slowly transform.

Two of the best-known places to enjoy the views from are the **Ogawa Observatory** [1] and the Rinrinkan guest house.

Rinrinkan is also famed for its views of the local cherry blossom trees, which bloom in mid-to-late April, attracting photo enthusiasts from all over Japan.

🛏 Accommodation - Rinrinkan [2]

Rinrinkan's scenic *tatami* rooms are spacious enough to accommodate families and large groups. The restaurant opens out onto a deck with an amazing view, and serves delicious, freshly prepared local fare. Rinrinkan also has a fire-lit, outdoor barrel bath which, with prior notification, guests can use.

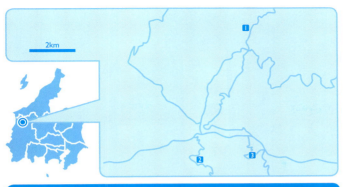

:bulb: Did you know?

No horsing around

Ogawa is the family home of a dynasty of Japanese equestrians and Buddhist priests.

Most members of Ogawa's Sato family are internationally competing horse riders. Kenki Sato and Eiken Sato are both Olympians, while their sister, Tae Sato, has regularly been national champion.

Their father, Shodo Sato, heads the 460-year-old Myosho-ji Buddhist temple compound, and also the neighbouring horse-riding club. Sato Senior was a member of Japan's equestrian team before the 1980 Olympics in Moscow - but was unable to compete because Japan boycotted the Games.

Key dates

mid to late April - cherry blossom at Rinrinkan

second Saturday of October - Autumn festival - ending at Takebu Hachimangu Shrine

We say

" Unless you are coming to tackle Ogawa's scenic cycle trails, this is a place to slow down, unwind and enjoy the flavours and the views of the Northern Alps of Japan. "

Recommended for

Photography enthusiasts

:rice: Food and Drink

Oyaki Mura 3

The stuffed dumplings of Nagano Prefecture, called *oyaki*, are renowned throughout Japan. Ogawa is considered by some to be the birthplace of *oyaki*, but most of the villages in the area have their own varieties, depending on the season and local vegetation.

The dough of *oyaki* dumplings is made from whatever flour is readily available (wheat in the case of Ogawa), while the various fillings are made of seasonal vegetables such as aubergine, squash, *aona* (local leafy vegetables), and pickled *nozawana* (one of northern Nagano's most famous vegetables), all diced up and mixed with *miso* paste and soy sauce. The stuffed ball of dough is then seared

on a large skillet that is heated over an *irori* (a traditional Japanese hearth). Oyaki Mura is a shop and restaurant up in the hills above the village, where visitors can sit in a cosy den and see the dumplings prepared and cooked before them. The oyaki are served with complimentary *miso* soup and *soba* tea. If you want to get even more out of your visit, you can contact Oyaki Mura in advance and make a reservation to learn how to make the *oyaki* yourself.

:arrows: Getting there and around

:airplane: Matsumoto Airport. Travel to Matsumoto Station by bus, then to Nagano Station by local train services. (Note - most visitors arrive via Narita Airport or Haneda Airport and travel to Nagano Station from there.)

:bus: Nagano Station. Travel to Ogawa Shinden by a 40-minute bus journey.

:car: When you have arrived in Ogawa, local transit is not straightforward. If you have booked to stay at Rinrinkan, their staff will pick you up from, and return you to, Ogawa Shinden bus stop.

Being such a mountainous, rural spot, a car is the best way to get around. However, Rinrinkan is connected to several cycle trails and has mountain bikes that visitors can borrow. Be warned – the slopes can be quite steep.

:info: Further information

www.100hiddentowns.jp/nagano/ogawa.html

137

Kanto-Koshinetsu

SHIMOSUWA
下諏訪町
Nagano

Shimosuwa, historically a resting station for travellers on the key Edo-era mountain highway of Nakasendo, is most famous for its colourful and exhilarating Onbashira Festival which is held every six years. If your visit doesn't coincide with the festival, there is still much to be enjoyed, including museums, shrines, and the scenery around Lake Suwa, and the rivers that run into it.

Culture Spot - Nidec Sankyo Musical Box Museum

Musical boxes are known as *orgel* in Japan, derived from the Dutch word for organ. First introduced by the Portuguese missionaries of the 16th century, these devices developed from being just a foreign curiosity into instruments that are still popular in Japan today.

The Nidec Sankyo Musical Box Museum explains the history of musical box production in the town, from when its factories opened there in the 1960s. There are displays of musical boxes on the first floor, with touch-screen devices that provide a selection of songs to choose from. The real attractions are on the second floor, where gorgeous, giant, 19th-century antique musical boxes made from wonderfully intricate components are displayed. Visitors can also enjoy regular demonstrations of how the boxes work, with live-action performers accompanied by an animated backdrop - which children are sure to enjoy, although explanations are only in Japanese.

For souvenir hunters, the ground-floor shop has a variety of musical boxes on sale.

👍 Must see! Onbashirakan Yoisa (Onbashira Festival Museum) 2

The pillars of Harumiya and Akimiya shrines are symbolically replaced every six years, in the Chinese years of the tiger and the monkey. During the Onbashira Festival in April and May of the designated year, huge trees are cut down in a Shinto ceremony, and the logs are dragged and ridden down the mountains to the shrines, via sometimes incredibly steep hills. The Onbashira Festival museum, which opened in 2016, brings this festival to life for those who are unable to see it in person. Videos and touch-screen displays explain the routes of the logs, and the communal effort required for such a huge project. The highlight is a model log which visitors can ride whilst watching a participating rider's view of the slide down a mountain. Such an experience really clarifies the derring-do required to ride one of the logs for real.

🏠 Culture Spot - Stone Buddha Manji-no-Sekibutsu 4

Located just across a narrow, shallow river from the Harumiya Shrine, this stone statue is a popular spot for tourists. Dating from 1660, the statue appears to be simultaneously angry and calm - a nice attraction, especially thanks to its woodland setting on the bank of the Togawa River.

🏠 Culture Spot - Suwa Taisha 3

Shimosha Harumiya and Shimosha Akimiya - two of the shrines in Suwa Taisha - share a lot in common in their design and surroundings, however there are subtle differences which can provide a fun spot-the-difference game for visitors. While best known for the mind-blowing Onbashira Festival, the shrines also host parades and music on the last day of July and first day of August each year. Even on a non-festival day, the shrines are worth visiting just for their peaceful surroundings and intricate architecture. While there, make sure to see the famous pillars (called *Onbashira*) that are replaced in the festival every six years. *Onbashira* are smooth to the touch and absolutely massive.

💡 Did you know?

A pillar of the community

In the Shinto religion, constant renewal is necessary to purify the spirit, which explains why the Onbashira Festival has been held for over 1200 years.

139

Kanto-Koshinetsu

Nagano — SHIMOSUWA — 下諏訪町

🌳 Nature Spot - Lake Suwa 5

With a circumference of 16 kilometres, Lake Suwa is a popular draw for cyclists and joggers, and has dedicated lanes for both. A clear day provides splendid views of the distant Mount Fuji.

🏠 Culture Spot - Folklore and History Museum 6

Close to the entrance of Akimiya Shrine, this museum is free to enter, and displays photos of festivals and townsfolk through the ages, plus other paraphernalia, all housed in a charmingly rickety wooden building.

🏠 Culture Spot - Gishodo Watch and Clock Museum 7

Along the Nakasendo is the Gishodo Watch and Clock Museum, which has a plethora of fun, hands-on displays that help explain the science of clocks. The constant background sounds of pendulums and whirring cogs contribute to an engaging experience for visitors of all ages.

In the courtyard, there is a reconstruction of a huge Chinese water clock from about 1,000 years ago, with life-size animatronic models of Chinese scientists from the time, providing explanations of the workings of this fascinating device.

Perhaps of even more interest to Japanophiles are the antique Edo clocks on display. The Edo era employed a different system for measuring time, with the hours calculated in different sets for day and night. The clocks and displays help explain this complex system, and are a fascinating insight into the world of Edo-era Japan.

Explanations in English are available.

Key dates

every 6 years in early April and early May (2022, 2028, etc.) - Onbashira Festival

July 31-August 1 - Shrine festivals with parades, stalls and musical performances

We say

" Shimosuwa is a lovely place to visit. There is plenty to see and do, and it is particularly recommended for families. Easy access from Tokyo and Nagoya means that it is worth a visit, even if you cannot time it to coincide with one of Shimosuwa's festivals. "

Recommended for

Families

Fans of unique festivals

 Kids

Shimosuwa is great for youngsters. The area has lots of attractions that will keep kids interested, including the Stone Buddha statue. The musical box and clock museums have enough fun, hands-on displays to satisfy young, curious minds, and to top it all, a short walk down to Lake Suwa can be augmented by a stop off at Mizube Park where, on a clear day, views of Mount Fuji provide a dramatic backdrop to the slides, swings and ball game areas. The park can also be used for barbecues, and hosts a fireworks display every evening throughout the summer.

Food and Drink - Basashi

The horse *sashimi* of Shimosuwa, known as *basashi*, has its roots in the days of horse breeding in the area. Though not to everyone's taste, it is surprisingly succulent.

Accommodation
Onyado Maruya 8

Just a 12-minute walk from Shimo-Suwa Station, Onyado Maruya is a gorgeous traditional guesthouse on the Nakasendo. The rooms are huge and comfortable, and dinner, served in the room, is a multiple course affair including the local speciality of horse *sashimi*.

Its location is perfect for visiting all the recommended sights, being just a matter of steps away from Akimiya Shrine and several museums.

Getting there and around

- Matsumoto Airport. Make use of the limousine bus and local trains to Shimosuwa.
- Nagano Station. Travel by local train to Shimo-Suwa Station.
- All sights are within walking distance of Shimo-Suwa Station, but there are also bicycle rental providers supplying battery-assisted bikes for visitors who want to explore further afield.

 Further information

www.100hiddentowns.jp/nagano/shimosuwa.html

Kanto-Koshinetsu

佐渡市

Niigata — SADO

One of the largest islands in Japan, Sado's isolated location has led to the development of robust and diverse local cultures and traditions, and offers visitors a range of activities in a beautiful setting.

Culture Spot - Seisuiji Temple

According to legend, Emperor Kammu was much enamoured of Kiyomizudera Temple in Kyoto, and felt sorry that so few Sado residents were able to travel to Kyoto to experience the temple's beauty. Searching for a suitable location in which to build their own temple, a monk saw something shining in a river and declared that place to be the perfect site. Founded in 808, Seisuiji Temple shares the same Chinese characters as the more famous temple in Kyoto, and was built in its image. The buildings are rebuilt every 200 years, and the current ones seem to be going through a process of slow decay as they merge into the forest and the mountain. The stone-staired approach, guarded by solemn cedars, leads out onto the slightly eerie, deserted temple. Brushing aside the greenery to climb the stairs up to the temple, and then stepping out on to the raised platform, you can almost hear the echoes of the past. Seisuiji Temple is a little out of the way, but it is a beautiful, undisturbed den of tranquility.

👍 Must see!
Sado Kinzan Gold Mine ❷

Sado Kinzan Gold Mine was in operation for nearly 400 years from the 17th century. Its importance to the economy - producing a total of 78 tons of gold - meant that it was taken under the direct control of the government. Visual evidence of its importance can be seen in the mountain itself, which has been literally cut in half by miners trying to access the precious ore. The number of residents of the nearby gold rush town of Aikawa peaked at 50,000 - almost the same as the present-day population of the entire island. Continuing production until as recently as 1989, the mine is now the main tourist attraction on the island. The mines are lit and paved so visitors can experience the cramped and dirty conditions in which the miners had to work (and their animatronic descendants still toil).

🌳 Nature Spot
Tokinomori Park ❸

Sado was a breeding ground for the Japanese crested ibis until the last one died in 2003. A regeneration programme has now been implemented to rebuild the domestic ibis population using birds brought in from China. Tokinomori Park is the main centre for this project, and visitors have the opportunity to see some of the birds in the closed environment of the park.

💡 Did you know?

Pretty prison
Sado was traditionally a place to exile dissidents or problematic public figures, ranging from holy men to emperors. The first exile was in the year 700, and the last a millennium later in 1700. Emperor Juntoku spent so much time exiled here that posthumously he became known as 'Sado-no-In', after his place of incarceration.

🏠 Culture Spot - Kitazawa Flotation Plant ❹

At one time, this was the largest flotation plant in Asia, with the capacity to process up to 50,000 tons of gold ore each month. After being abandoned, and then restored, the overgrown buildings now resemble a lost city being reclaimed by nature.

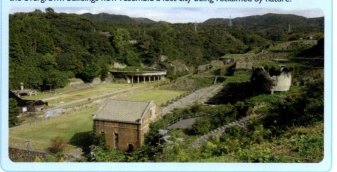

Kanto-Koshinetsu

Niigata — SADO　佐渡市

🏠 Culture Spot
Sado Historical Legends Museum [5]

The Sado Historical Legends Museum offers a glimpse into the origin of some of the folk tales associated with the island. Due to its location, Sado has often been either a site of banishment or sanctuary. Brought to life by robots and intricate moving stage scenes, the museum covers some of the main stories in its history. Though predominantly in Japanese, the displays are quite impressive, and views of its garden with the valley in the background contribute to the museum's charm.

🌳 Nature Spot - Senkaku Bay [6]

The forces of nature have worked away at the Senkaku Bay coastline over time to produce its dramatic, rocky features. A walk along the coast takes in steep-sided cliffs, looming over sharpened rock promontories and foam-specked waves. Senkaku Bay has a lighthouse and a viewing platform that look over the coastline. There are also boat tours from spring to autumn.

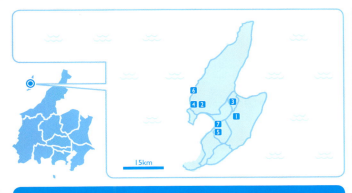

Key dates

August - Ryotsu Festival (a celebration of both the children's Star Festival, and the opening of Ryotsu Port, with parades and fireworks)

mid-August - Earth Celebration (Sado's biggest draw, hosted by the *taiko* group, the Kodo Drummers)

We say

" A beautiful combination of history, culture and nature makes Sado a perfect island to explore. There are so many things to do here that a long trip is recommended to fully appreciate the island. "

Recommended for

Everyone

🕊 Food and Drink - Obata Sake Brewery 7

One of a number of famous breweries on the island, Obata has won awards both nationally and internationally for its velvety smooth *sake*. Visitors can explore the factory and watch an informative video (an English-language version is available). Enjoy the variety of brews on offer at the tasting area, and nod sagely as the staff regale you with explanations of the complex range of flavours.

🚆 Getting there and around

✈ Niigata Airport. Take a taxi to the port and then a jetfoil or ferry to Sado Island.
🚊 Niigata Station. Take a bus to the port and then a jetfoil or ferry to Sado Island.
⛴ Sado can only be reached by boat. Ferry services run all year round from Niigata to Ryotsu.
Seasonal services also run from Naoetsu to Ogi, and Teradomari to Akadomari.
There are no trains on Sado, so you will need to either rent a car or use buses and taxis. The island is very large and some of the attractions are far apart, so plan transportation carefully.

 📖 **Further information**
 www.100hiddentowns.jp/niigata/sado.html

145

Kanto-Koshinetsu

TOKAMACHI 十日町市

Niigata

An intriguing blend of the prehistoric and historical, the natural and the modern, visiting Tokamachi is like walking into a David Lynch film. At first it seems fairly straightforward, but once you peel beneath the surface, there is so much more than you expected.

🌳 Nature Spot - Tanada Rice Fields

Tokamachi is famous as one of the best sites to see rice fields terraced to mould and blend into the surrounding hills - *tanada* in Japanese. With a striking appearance in all seasons, the fields fit seamlessly into the landscape and work their way up and down the slopes. Hoshitoge, literally 'star pass', is one of the best spots to view this locally.

🏠 Culture Spot - Tokamachi City Museum

A pleasant footpath lined with sculptures leads to the Tokamachi City Museum from Tokamachi Station. The museum takes you through the story of one of the more historical areas of Japan. As possibly one of the snowiest towns on Earth (with an average snow depth of about two metres), the people have both shaped and been shaped by the conditions. You can see recreations of

how residents lived throughout the different periods. Perhaps most interesting are the Kaengata Doki - flame-shaped earthenware vessels. Looking like the crowns of fantasy kings, these vessels are at least 4,500 years old, but seem ageless.

👍 Must see!
Echigo-Tsumari Art Triennale 3

The Echigo-Tsumari Art Triennale is a little hard to pin down and define. In many ways this will be either its greatest appeal or turn off. Since 2000, it has taken place every three years. It consists of numerous fixed facilities (open every year) scattered around the city, as well as various events that are held during the Art Triennale years. The entire list of exhibits is distributed between dozens of different locations. It can be a little hit-and-miss, but its seemingly random nature adds somewhat to its appeal. There are installations, temporary exhibitions and also chances to stay the night in some of the art locations, which are exhibits themselves. Perhaps intentionally, one of the charms of exploring around the disparate locations of the exhibits is that you also get to see a lot of the countryside of Tokamachi.

Culture Spot - Kimono Festival

Tokamachi is one of the main areas of textile production and manufacture in Japan, so appropriately enough it has a kimono festival. Every spring, the main road in town is sealed off for a couple of hours whilst stalls and awnings are rapidly thrown up. Local girls, dressed in kimonos, then stroll around the town after the Coming of Age Ceremony.

🌳 Nature Spot - Bijinbayashi 4

Following extensive clearing of the area to feed the charcoal industry at the start of the Showa era, a large beech forest sprung up on the cleared ground. The trees were so attractive that the area was named Bijinbayashi - literally 'beautiful lady wood'. More reminiscent of the rolling hills of Britain than the mountains of Japan, it is best visited in spring when the new leaves come through.

Culture Spot
Echigo-Tsumari Satoyama Museum of Contemporary Art, KINARE 5

This gallery offers a series of installations and exhibits from various artists. There's also a pleasant coffee shop and *onsen* at the facility.

🔎 Did you know?

It's snow joke
Tokamachi is one of the heaviest snowfall regions in Japan. The greatest amount of snow recorded was 425cm in 1945. There is a tale from the time that there were a number of injuries from people falling off the road and onto the roofs of the houses to the side. Although it seems an unlikely tale, it is supported by a number of photographs in the museum, showing people walking on huge snowy roads, clearly looking down on the tops of the neighbouring houses.

Kanto-Koshinetsu

Niigata — TOKAMACHI 十日町市

🏠 Culture Spot
Matsudai Nohbutai 6

Looking not unlike a crushed concrete spider, navigating the building itself is part of the mystique of this centre, which exhibits and promotes 'local exchange'. Displays include a classroom entirely made up of blackboards, on which you can write and thus participate in the exhibit yourself, as well as explore the mysteries contained in the numerous drawers. Also watch out for the toilets, which are perhaps not as easy to exit as you might think!

🌳 Nature Spot - Kiyotsukyo Gorge 7

Hidden away to the south of the town, Kiyotsukyo Gorge is one of the best-known gorges in Japan. At its exit, where the river's waters calm, you can find shops and cafes. The gorge itself is so steep it can only be viewed via a tunnel constructed into the side of the cliffs. This cool passageway breaks out onto viewpoints looking directly onto the gorge. A small exhibition at the end has some photos of the inundation of snow that can occur in winter. Allow about an hour to go up and down the gorge.

Culture Spot
Tokamachi Snow Festival

Tokamachi is host to one of the largest snow festivals in Japan. Running for three days on the third weekend in February, you can enjoy a number of events and sculptures in the town.

Nature Spot - Rafting on the Shinano River

The Shinano River is the longest and largest in Japan. Each year, after the huge snowfalls in the area have melted, the river becomes one of the best spots for rafting in Japan. Enjoy the fast-paced action as you hurtle downstream.

Kids - Kyororo Museum

Just next door to the beech forest is the Kyororo Museum. Its striking rusted iron facade, with a large tower attached, looks more like a furnace than a venue for displaying artefacts. The  insides are devoted to the local flora and fauna. Extensive exhibitions take you through the plants and trees, and animals and insects you can find in the area. More hands-on than most places, it is a very kid-friendly space.

Food and Drink - Hegi Soba

These seaweed-infused noodles, served in wooden boxes called *hegi*, are spun into bite-sized pieces to make this local delicacy easier to eat. Best enjoyed with crunchy *tempura*.

Getting there and around

- Niigata Airport. Take local train services to Tokamachi Station.
- Echigo Yuzawa Station. Local train services to Tokamachi Station or Matsudai Station.
- There are a couple of attractions in the town itself, but a lot of things, especially the art exhibition, are scattered around the area. Public transport is limited so access to a car is advisable.

Further information
www.100hiddentowns.jp/niigata/tokamachi.html

Key dates

third weekend in February - Tokamachi Snow Festival (the first of the modern wave of snow festivals in Japan. There are a series of events leading up to the Snow Carnival, which offers fireworks and performances.)

May 3 - Tokamachi Kimono Festival (celebrating the town's status as one of the main centres of kimono production)

August 25-27 - Tokamachi Summer Festival (traditional summer festival featuring floats, stalls and dancing)

We say

" A great town - the fusion of nature, tradition, and the modern, means there is something for everyone. Transport will be an issue, especially for the art exhibition, so plan carefully in advance. "

Recommended for

People who like to explore off the beaten track

Families

Kanto-Koshinetsu

Saitama

川越市

KAWAGOE

Kawagoe, in Saitama prefecture, is a satellite town of Tokyo that still retains charming pockets of history and beauty, hidden in plain sight of the capital's suburbs.

Culture Spot
Kawagoe City Museum ❶ and Kawagoe City Art Museum ❷

For some quiet, highbrow respite from the Kurazukuri Zone (see *Must see!*), the elegant, modern Kawagoe City Museum contains exhibits and informative videos that shed some light on the history and traditions of the area. Next door, at Kawagoe City Art Museum, the spacious, hushed galleries host a range of works exhibiting a variety of creative techniques mastered by Japanese artists over the years. As well as these permanent displays, the museum also has temporary exhibitions.

150

Must see! Kurazukuri Zone

Wander for 20 minutes northwards from any of the town's central train stations, and the aluminium, plastic and neon ugliness fall away to reveal the old centre of commerce that is the home to a range of historical architectural styles, and sites of interest.

Taisho-Roman Street 3

By pedestrianising some of the streets, and also removing the eyesore of overhead cables, Kawagoe has created a lovely setting for visitors to properly admire the distinctive black and brown, solid architecture of its Taisho-era stores.

Toki-no-Kane (Bell Tower) 4

This formidable wooden structure, housing a clock bell, is Kawagoe's most iconic sight. Dating back to the Edo era, it was first erected in the 1600s, but being prone to local fires, it has been rebuilt many times over the years - most recently in 1893. The bell, which is rung four times a day, is revered for its rich timbre.

Kashiya Yokocho (Penny Candy Alley) 5

On a short, cobbled lane inlaid with small, coloured glass squares, several wooden stores have been selling a miscellany of traditional Japanese sweets since the end   of the 19th century. You may see a few fellow sweet-toothed shoppers eating ornate creations that have been handmade on site. The seductive aroma of warm sugar, evoking images of scenes from a Far-Eastern Chitty Chitty Bang Bang, draws many nostalgic shoppers to this quiet corner of the town.

Kawagoe Festival Museum 6

Kawagoe is famed for its huge festival held every October. For those who visit the town at other times of the year, this museum serves to provide a taste of the sights and sounds of this major event. Various exhibits and a large-screen video installation outline the long history of the festival, which dates back to the 17th century.

On display is the skeleton of an undecorated float, plus two (of the 29) eight-metre-tall portable shrines used in the festival, fully bedecked in the ornate handiwork and vivid colours of the various traditional motifs featured on each float. The theatrics, masks and costumes of the festival are a glimpse into the wonders and horrors of Japanese folklore. There is a listening station where you can experience many variations of the *hayashi* music that is performed on each float during the festival, and an exhibition of wonderful photos of the festival taken over the years.

 Did you know?

Rub a Rakan
Among the 538 Statues of Rakan (see next page), there are 12 holding an animal - each one of the 12 Buddhist zodiac signs. If you find the one that corresponds with your own year of birth, you can rub its head and make a wish.

Kanto-Koshinetsu

Saitama — KAWAGOE — 川越市

🍶 Food and Drink - Eel and Sweet Potato

Kawagoe is famed for delicious *unagi* (eel) and *imo* (sweet potato), and you can taste them in combination in a dish called *imo unajyu* at several restaurants in the town, including the pretty Imozen Unagi Senmonten Unakko, near Kashiya Yokocho.

🏠 Culture Spot - Kita-in Temple 7

Although the Kita-in Temple's origins date back to the Heian period in 830, the buildings in the temple area you see today were established during the Edo period. The open spaces and greenery make a pleasant location for a gentle stroll.

Paid access to the main building allows visitors to roam between the rooms via *tatami*-covered walkways, and to look out onto the pretty grounds which include a zen garden and an area, adjacent to the temple, containing the '500 Statues of Rakan' (actually 538). These make for an entertaining diversion, with the statues' expressions ranging from frivolous to studious to outright menacing.

152

Key dates

January 1-7 - Koedo Kawagoe Shichifukujin (Seven Gods of Good Fortune) Tour (Kawagoe Station)

January 3 - Hatsudaishi (first homage of the new year at temples dedicated to great religious leaders)

late July - Kawagoe Million Lights Summer Festival (around Kawagoe Station)

late-August - Koedo Kawagoe Fireworks Display (Isanuma Park or Aina Water Park)

3rd Saturday and Sunday of October - Kawagoe Festival (Kawagoe City area)

We say

" Kawagoe is very conveniently located for a day trip from Tokyo. When you exit from the station, you're faced with the uninspiring sight of another typical satellite town of the capital. However, despite still being in the bosom of suburbia, Kawagoe contains many charming pockets of history and beauty. The whole town is excellently signposted for English speakers, and my visit, blessed with sunny spring weather, was an enlightening pleasure. "

Recommended for

Day trippers from Tokyo

🏠 Culture Spot
Honmaru Goten (Kawagoe Castle) 8 and Kawagoe Hikawa Shrine 9

There are still some remains of Kawagoe Castle, which stood from the 15th century until the Meiji Restoration, enclosed by Honmaru Goten, an elegant construction dating back to 1848.

Another historical attraction is Kawagoe Hikawa Shrine, located less than one kilometre from the Kurazukuri Zone. Approached via an imposing *torii* gate, visitors to the small temple complex are greeted by an array of cute, fish-themed *omikuji* (lucky charms). Beside the main temple, there is a covered walkway where handwritten wishes are suspended.

🚊 Getting there and around

✈ Narita Airport or Haneda Airport. Buses travel directly to Kawagoe.

🚆 Ueno Station / Tokyo Station / Omiya Station. Travel by local train services to Kawagoe Station / Hon-Kawagoe Station / Kawagoeshi Station.

There are also direct trains to Kawagoe from Ikebukuro Station and Seibu-Shinjuku Station.

🚶 All of the attractions mentioned can be visited in a day, on a leisurely looping stroll beginning and ending at any of the town's three train stations.

📖 Further information
www.100hiddentowns.jp/saitama/kawagoe.html

153

Kanto-Koshinetsu

長瀞町

Saitama
NAGATORO

Nagatoro is only two to three hours from Tokyo, but it feels like a trip to a different era.

Set in a beautiful valley, this small town delights visitors with its red leaves in autumn, its amber wintersweet plants in winter, and its cherry blossoms in spring.

Nagatoro provides visitors with a range of activities including river boating, riding a cable car to Mount Hodo, and walking scenic hiking trails. Nagatoro's sights can be easily covered in a day trip, but an extra day is recommended for hikers.

👍 Must see!
Nagatoro Iwadatami ❶

Iwadatami means rock *tatami*. The rock formation, by the Arakawa River - just 100 metres south of the station - resembles *tatami* mats. You can hop along the rocks, enjoy the views, or sit and picnic as the water flows past.

🌳 Nature Spot - Mount Hodo ❷

Visitors can take the cable car or hike up Mount Hodo. At an elevation of just 497 metres, it is a leisurely climb for most. From the top, there are great views of the surrounding mountains, cloaked in different colours depending on the season. There are many pleasant hiking trails you can take from here, or alternatively descend the mountain via the picturesque Hodosan Shrine.

154

Did you know?

Tatami rocks!

The rock *tatami* of Iwadatami are overlapping layers of crystalline schist rock. Nagatoro is known as the birthplace of the study of geology in Japan, and has been visited by many researchers and students since the end of the 19th century.

Meiji changes

Historically, Nagatoro was a centre of agriculture that opened up to increased tourism with railway access gained in 1911. The railway building is a classic example of Meiji-era architecture.

Key dates

first Sunday of March - Himatsuri (Fire Festival)

August 15 - Funadama Festival

We say

" Nagatoro is a nice day trip if you are based in the Kanto area - a relaxing rural break from the urban sprawl of Greater Tokyo's suburbs. "

Recommended for

Young families

Hikers

Culture Spot
Hodosan Shrine 3

Hodosan Shrine, which sits quietly among the wooded hills, was first built in 110 AD. The shrine building and its grounds blend in beautifully with the surrounding countryside. As well as Hodosan, Nagatoro offers a range of small temples known as 'The Seven Flower Temples of Nagatoro', which can be easily reached on foot or by bicycle. Each temple displays a different flower featured in Japanese literature.

Culture Spot
Arai Silkworm House 4

Conveniently located between the station and the foot of Mount Hodo is the Arai Silkworm House - a pretty Edo-era facility, with a distinctive shingle roof, that was built for raising silkworms.

Kids - Arakawa River 5

River boating and whitewater rafting along the Arakawa River are great fun and popular in summer. For longer stays, there are riverside campsites with barbecue facilities.

Getting there and around

✈ Haneda Airport. Travel to Tokyo Station by train. From there, travel to Nagatoro by local train services.

🚆 Tokyo Station. Travel to Nagatoro by local train services.

🚶 The centre of town is great for a stroll. If you wish to hit the hills or ride beside the river, rental bicycles are available from the tourist information centre by the station.

Further information

www.100hiddentowns.jp/saitama/nagatoro.html

155

Kanto-Koshinetsu

ASHIKAGA
足利市
Tochigi

The small town of Ashikaga is well-known amongst the Japanese, as it lends its name to an era of Japanese history - the Ashikaga shogunate of 1336-1573.

The roots of the name come from the fact that the shogunate was formed from a clan that originated in Ashikaga. Now, the town enjoys plenty of visitors thanks to several temples and buildings of interest and its proximity to Tokyo. The town is surrounded by mountains, and is popular with hikers.

Culture Spot - Nagusaitsukushima Shrine

Several kilometres north of the town lies Nagusaitsukushima Shrine. Approach by road before taking one of the hiking routes to the shrine. The hike can be quite tough, but the reward is this gorgeously tranquil location. The shrine is distinguished by the huge stones that form its base. A pretty bridge links the shrine to one of these stones, which has a cave beneath.

🏠 Culture Spot
Banna-ji Temple ❷

Banna-ji dates from the 12th century and was originally the site of a fortified residence of the Ashikaga clan, and to this day the temple is still surrounded by a moat. Bridges cross the moat on all four sides of the temple, and the grounds provide a tranquil location to stroll in, with several pretty buildings scattered around the temple complex.

👍 Must see!
Coco Farm and Winery ❸

Coco Farm and Winery is a lovely place to taste the wines of Ashikaga. Sample a few of their products at the tasting counter, then enjoy a delicious lunch with a bottle of your choice. The wine shop and cafe sit at the bottom of an extremely steep hill with rows of grapevines leading to its summit.

💡 Did you know?

Edo-era engineering
The Watarase River runs through Ashikaga and is recommended for picnics, strolls, riverside sports and bike rides. The river eventually empties into the Tone River, but originally it fed into the Edogawa River and on to Tokyo Bay. However, in the 17th century, the Tokugawa shogunate rerouted the river to reduce the risk of flood damage to the area.

157

Kanto-Koshinetsu

足利市

Tochigi

ASHIKAGA

🏠 Culture Spot - Orihime Shrine 4

Northwest of the town centre, built on a hillside, lies Orihime Shrine. Though a fairly recent construction (the shrine dates from the Meiji era), it is worth climbing its 229 steps for the excellent views and striking, bright red exterior.

🌳 Nature Spot - Ashikaga Flower Park 5

Open all year round, this park is best-known as the largest wisteria garden in Japan. From mid-April to mid-May, visitors can marvel at the park's laburnum and colourful wisteria. There are illuminations to enhance the scenery during the evenings of this period, and in the winter.

🏠 Culture Spot - Ashikaga School 6

The Ashikaga School is known as the oldest school in Japan, and is designated as a national historic site. Though there are competing theories as to the original purpose of the school, it is thought that its first pupils were the offspring of provincial government officers. The school is known to have taught, among other things, Confucianism, the art  of warfare, and medical science. At the beginning of the 16th century, Christian missionary Francis Xavier introduced the school abroad as 'the most famous academy in Japan'. The current gates and buildings are delightful to meander around, and it is all tastefully surrounded by carefully designed Japanese gardens.

158

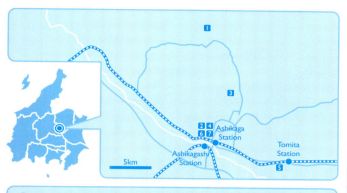

Key dates

first Saturday of August - Ashikaga Fireworks Festival

first Sunday of November - Ashikaga Takauji-ko Marathon

We say

" Ashikaga is great to visit if you are Tokyo-based and fancy a day trip or a weekend stay. Being used to tourists, the town has good facilities, but is also pleasantly sedate. Why not take a hike in the nearby hills and then reward yourself with a trip to the Coco Farm and Winery for lunch and souvenir shopping? "

Recommended for

Hikers

Wine lovers

Accommodation - Guest house Shokoan

Conveniently located near the Ashikaga School, Guest house Shokoan is a very reasonably priced place to stay, with all necessary amenities, including a fully equipped kitchen. Sleeping up to five people, this is an ideal family accommodation. The building itself dates from the Meiji era, and a number of eateries and shops are within short walking distance.

Getting there and around

Ashikaga is easily accessible from Narita Airport and Haneda Airport. Take local train services to Ashikaga Station or Ashikagashi Station.

Oyama Station. Travel by local train services to Ashikaga Station.

Getting around is easy in the town, with all the historical sights mentioned being in close proximity to each other. Transportation will be needed to reach the Coco Farm and Winery. A battery-powered bicycle, hired from either Ashikagashi Station or the tourist information centre opposite Ashikaga School, is especially recommended as the ride is enjoyable and traffic is sparse. Venturing up to Nagusaitsukushima Shrine will require a taxi or rental car, and a lengthy hike.

Further information

www.100hiddentowns.jp/tochigi/ashikaga.html

Kanto-Koshinetsu

栃木市

Tochigi — TOCHIGI

Tochigi City has had a prosperous history thanks to its convenient location between Nikko and Edo (now Tokyo). Visitors can share in this illustrious past, as the city avoided damage in World War II and thus still retains much of its historical character. It bears the moniker 'Storehouse Town' thanks to the large number of distinctive Edo-era buildings that have survived to this day.

👍 Must see!
Japanese Sweet-Making Experience (at Yamamoto So-Honten ❶)

At this traditional Japanese confectionery shop by the river, with a prior booking, visitors can experience the craftsmanship behind traditional Japanese sweets. The attraction of these colourful, handmade sweets - the dough mimics the colours of seasonal flowers - is more artistic than culinary, with the key being the presentation. The hour-long experience really helps to bring home the skills involved in Japanese cuisine. The art lies in the shaping of the sweets through a gentle rolling and prodding with one's digits. Once finished and decorated, the sweets are ready to eat, usually served with green tea.

🏠 Culture Spot - Tochigi Dashi Kaikan (Tochigi Doll Float Museum) ❷

In the autumn of alternate years, there is a spectacular festival featuring beautifully handcrafted and embroidered doll floats. For visitors unable to time their visit to Tochigi with the festival, the Doll Float Museum shows highlights of the festival on a large screen, as well as providing displays in English and Japanese of paraphernalia related to the celebration. The museum houses several of the floats, which, seen up close, are impressively tall and intricately decorated.

160

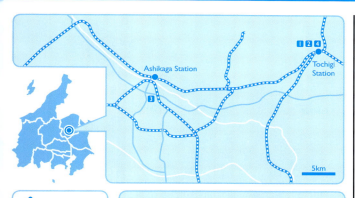

🏠 Culture Spot
Tochigi City Centre and Reiheishi Road 3

In 1617, the casket of the supreme shogun Ieyasu Tokugawa was transferred to Nikko through Tochigi.

Religious pilgrimages were then made through the town's central Reiheishi Road.

The narrow, winding street still boasts Edo-era shops and warehouses with their distinctive exterior and roofs.

🌳 Nature Spot - River Cruise 4

The Uzuma River was the lifeblood of Tochigi, thanks to the income derived from shipments of goods to Edo. Visitors can enjoy a round trip of about 150 metres, as the boatman punts them along at a gentle pace. He will even sing a traditional folk song to enhance the experience. Drifting along the river provides a unique view of the traditional buildings that line its banks, and passengers can also feed the ducks and carp. This is about as close to a Venice gondola ride as it is possible to experience in modern Tochigi Prefecture.

Did you know?

The frog chorus
In 1996, as part of its efforts to combat noise pollution and to protect and promote the environment, the sound of the tree frogs on Mount Ohira in Tochigi was designated as one of the 100 Soundscapes of Japan by the Ministry of the Environment.

Key dates

mid-June - late June - Mount Ohira Hydrangea Festival

mid-November - Tochigi Autumn Festival (doll float festival held every other year)

We say

" Tochigi is a great place to spend a few hours absorbing its historical atmosphere. Its location close to Nikko makes it a recommended stop on a tour of Tochigi Prefecture. "

Recommended for

History lovers

Day trippers from nearby prefectures

⇌ Getting there and around

- ✈ Tochigi City is easily accessible from Narita Airport and Haneda Airport.
- 🚆 Oyama Station. Travel by local train services to Tochigi Station.
- 🚶 Getting around Tochigi City is remarkably easy, with the major sights all within walking distance of the railway station.

 Further information
www.100hiddentowns.jp/tochigi/tochigi.html

Kanto-Koshinetsu

Tokyo — KATSUSHIKA 葛飾区

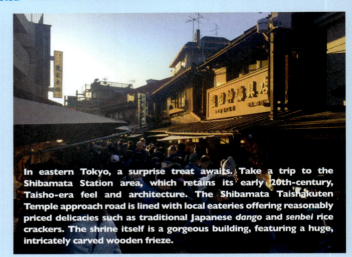

In eastern Tokyo, a surprise treat awaits. Take a trip to the Shibamata Station area, which retains its early 20th-century, Taisho-era feel and architecture. The Shibamata Taishakuten Temple approach road is lined with local eateries offering reasonably priced delicacies such as traditional Japanese *dango* and *senbei* rice crackers. The shrine itself is a gorgeous building, featuring a huge, intricately carved wooden frieze.

👍 Must see! Shibamata Taishakuten Temple

This Nichiren Buddhist temple is the main focus of the area, and gets crowded on weekends and holidays. Enter via the ornate gate to the right of the pretty bell tower, and climb the steps to the altar. A walkway connects you to the entrance from which you can circumnavigate the temple and enjoy the main attraction - the wooden frieze, which is carved to depict tales from Buddhist scripture. The wooden carvings date from the Showa and Taisho eras and are remarkably detailed, down to the characters' facial expressions and clothing. Behind the temple is a garden which can be enjoyed from its perimeter walkway. It's a delightful spot, with a carp-filled pond and pretty trees.

🍶 Food and Drink

Shibamata is known for eel dishes, traditional Japanese *dango* (small rice dumplings covered with a generous helping of sweet red bean paste or other flavours), and rice crackers of various textures and flavours. The street leading to the temple also hosts a fascinating traditional sweet shop decked out with Showa-era posters, pinball machines, and vintage space invader games.

Did you know?

Ferry good
The nearby Edogawa River can still be traversed by a small boat steered by a ferryman. These ferries date back to the Edo era, and the Yagiri-no-watashi ferry landing is the only one of its kind remaining in Tokyo.

Key dates

early April - Shibamata Sakura Festival

late August - Tora-san Festival (*bon odori* dancing at Taishakuten)

We say

" A pretty retreat within the urban chaos of Tokyo, I found the Shibamata area to be wonderful, with the tree-lined banks of the Edogawa River evocative of a bygone age. A weekday visit is highly recommended to avoid the crowds. "

Recommended for

Day trippers

Japanese film cinephiles

 Culture Spot - Yamamoto-Tei

A stone's throw from the Taishakuten Temple is the Yamamoto-Tei. Constructed at the end of the Taisho era, the building was the former home of the Yamamoto family, who made their wealth from camera components. Now owned by Katsushika Ward, the house is a wonderful mix of traditional Japanese and early 20th-century western architecture, with a series of rooms opening out onto a garden. Enjoy green tea and snacks in one of the most restful spots in the city.

 Culture Spot - Tora-san Museum and Yoji Yamada Museum

Fans of Japanese cinema will be well aware of Tora-san, the hero of over 40 films directed by Yoji Yamada. The film series was set in Katsushika Ward, and the Tora-san Museum has a reconstruction of a set that was used for many of the films, plus other artefacts and information related to the series.

Adjacent to the museum is another building with photos and exhibits of further works by Yoji Yamada, including his early 21st-century samurai trilogy, which garnered wide international recognition, and his remakes of Japanese classics.

Getting there and around

- Haneda Airport or Narita Airport. Take local train services to Shibamata Station.
- Tokyo Station. Take local train services to Shibamata Station.
- Shibamata Station is easy to reach from anywhere in Tokyo. Once there, visitors can stroll around the sites at their leisure as a half-day or day trip.

 Further information
www.100hiddentowns.jp/tokyo/katsushika.html

163

Kanto-Koshinetsu

小笠原村

Tokyo

Ogasawara Islands OGASAWARA

Officially part of Tokyo, but approximately a one-thousand-kilometre, 24-hour boat ride away from the metropolis, Chichijima of the Ogasawara island chain is a paradise of exquisite white beaches, steep cliffs, unique sea life, and tropical fruits.

Despite these features, Chichijima is far from comparable to a luxury subtropical resort, and that is where its charm lies. The island used to be uninhabited, and even now it retains a sense of cultural isolation which the villagers are keen to maintain.

164

Must see! Outdoor Activities

With a variety of activities available on the island, it is worthwhile taking a tour - hiking and whale watching are some of the popular ones. There is also dolphin watching, which is possible all-year-round and offers the opportunity to even swim with these elegant marine mammals. Stand-up paddle boarding (SUP) is popular too, and provides an alternative method of getting close to the whales and other marine life. For hiking, amazing views can be enjoyed from the various observation points that dot the mountainous interior of the island. You may also be lucky enough to spot some of the unique land-based wildlife of Chichijima.

Culture Spot
Takonohazaiku

A traditional craft activity to supplement your time on the island is *takonohazaiku*. Items are made from leaves of the *tako* tree, such as bags, boxes and charms.

Did you know?

Glorious isolation

The Ogasawara Islands are also called the Bonin Islands. The word *bonin* comes from the Japanese word *mujin*, meaning 'no people'. The islands are nicknamed 'The Galapagos of the Orient', thanks to the abundance of natural plant life and indigenous species. Chichijima was largely uninhabited until 1860, when the Tokugawa shogunate began settling there. Over subsequent years, American whalers visited, and the island was even used as a stop-off point for the epoch-changing, mainland-bound black steamers of Commodore Perry in his push to open up Japan to western trade.

Nature Spot - Minamijima ■

Minamijima is an uninhabited island located to the southwest of Chichijima. A guide is required, as visitors need to be aware of the rules of the island in order to help protect its unique and valuable ecosystem. The island is gorgeous and has amazing lagoons and rock formations.

Nature Spot
Hahajima ■

Hahajima is approximately two hours by ferry from its sister island, Chichijima (or should that be spouse island? Hahajima literally means 'mother island' to Chichijima's 'father island').

Here visitors can tour the wartime defences of the island as well as enjoy similar activities to those on Chichijima, such as whale watching and jungle trekking.

Nature Spot - Chichijima Beaches ■

Everywhere you go on Chichijima there are beaches that are just breathtaking. Each of them has different characteristics - some are great for snorkelling and others for swimming. Depending on the season and climate, you may be able to see the incredible sunset that gives the sense of exclusiveness, knowing that you are isolated from everything else. Warm all year round, there is little to stop you enjoying the beaches and sea activities on offer. Diving and surfing, among other exploits, are popular.

Some of the beaches can only be reached by boat, such is their inaccessibility, but the less remote include Miyanohama and Kominato beaches.

Kanto-Koshinetsu

Tokyo
小笠原村
OGASAWARA
Ogasawara Islands

Food and Drink

As you can imagine, the tropical climate of the island helps to cultivate a range of fruit, such as starfruit, passion fruit, mangoes, papayas, bananas and lemons. From late spring to summer is the ideal season to visit to enjoy the tropical selection at its ripest. Even out of season, you can still taste the fruit in a variety of ways. At most of the restaurants, you can order desserts such as lemon cheesecake, passion fruit chiffon cake, as well as pies, jams and candy, which make great souvenirs. The Shima (island) honey is also quite popular - a deep rich amber honey with a distinctive flavour. Try yoghurt with a drop of Shima honey to start your day.

Culture Spot
Sakaiura Beach [4]

Reflect on a poignant slice of modern history by snorkelling around the wreckage of a Japanese warship at Sakaiura Beach. The Hinko-maru was sunk by a torpedo during the war, and now rests, and rusts, in shallow waters off this beach.

Though the US island-hopping amphibious assaults of the Pacific War didn't involve Chichijima, the island's proximity to Iwojima made it a key strategic point in those dark times, as Japan's primary long-range radio station site. There are numerous reminders of the war. Near downtown, visitors can find a small tunnel that was created during World War II, which residents still use as a short cut. If you are interested in the history of the island, taking a tour of the wartime curios is strongly recommended, where the guide will explain the details of Chichijima's role in the war.

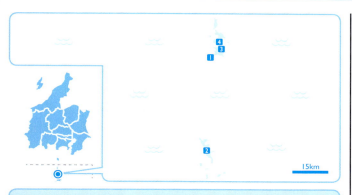

Getting there and around

The only way to get to Chichijima from the Japanese mainland is the day-long Ogasawara Maru liner from Tokyo port. It is clean and colourful inside with facilities to sleep, either private or shared, though motion sickness pills are recommended. Be aware that the time of the trip by boat depends on the weather. The choppier the sea, the longer the journey, so plan accordingly.

Shuttle buses run by private companies provide access to many of the island's attractions. There are also some public buses. Renting a battery-powered bicycle is possible. Some movement on the island is restricted in order to protect its biodiversity.

Further information
www.100hiddentowns.jp/tokyo/ogasawara.html

Key dates

July 26 - Ogasawara Sadayori Shrine Festival (kayak races and the delicacy of stewed tortoise)

August - Summer Festival (fireworks, *bon odori*, music and beach volleyball)

We say

" Be sure to stay on the deck of Ogasawara Maru when departing from the islands. There will be a series of extraordinary performances by the villagers on the port, and even some somersaulting into the ocean as they see you off. It's rather touching to imagine the relationship between the islanders and the visitors. I heard them call the main island *naichi* (inside land), which emphasises the pride they have in their isolation. Ogasawara Maru is the only connection to the world, and while it stays in port (bringing about 600 tourists), the town becomes festive. Most stores in town are closed when the tourists depart and the Ogasawara Maru returns to Tokyo Port. "

Recommended for

Nature lovers

Mountain climbers

Divers

167

Kanto-Koshinetsu

大島町
Tokyo
OSHIMA
Izu Oshima Island

Izu Oshima (Oshima for short, literally 'big island') is the largest and northernmost of the Izu Shoto group of islands, about 120km from the port of Tokyo. Oshima is dominated by its active volcano, Mount Mihara, but there are plenty of other natural delights for visitors to enjoy on this sparsely populated island, just a short jetfoil boat trip or flight from Tokyo. Its location gives excellent views of the Izu Peninsula and Mount Fuji on a clear day, especially as evening approaches and the golden-red sun slips beneath the Pacific.

🌳 Nature Spot
Tsubaki Hana Garden [1]

This beautiful camellia garden has been cultivated by its friendly staff since it opened in 1970. Wander around the many and varied colourful trees and plants, taking in the views across the ocean towards Mount Fuji.

Camellia is a key product for the islanders - its oil finding an eager market throughout Japan. It is used as a beauty product for both young and old. In fact, since the Edo era, Oshima islanders have been lauded for their lustrous black hair, thanks to the flower's oil.

🏠 Culture Spot
Oshima Park Zoo [2]

See red pandas, camels, and an array of other animals for free at Oshima Park Zoo, part of the Oshima Park complex.

🏠 Culture Spot
Oshima Furusato Taikenkan [3]

Visitors can come here to experience traditional cultural activities such as Japanese *taiko* drumming and even make their own cold-pressed camellia oil.

Nature Spot - Beaches

There are excellent family beaches near both the ports of Okata and Motomachi. There are also multiple diving and snorkelling services with which to sample the crystal-clear waters lapping the coasts of the island.

Culture Spot - Habu [4]

If visiting the southern tip of the island, make sure to stop by the winding lanes of Habu. There are excellent eateries tucked away amid these back streets, views of sleepy harbours and ageing buildings unchanged over the decades.

 Did you know?

Scary silver screen superstars

Izu Oshima has cult movie status - the island being the inspiration behind the 1989 *Godzilla* film, in which the monster is reborn from the crater at the centre of Mount Mihara. Izu Oshima also features in the 1998 classic Japanese horror movie, *Ring*.

Prison island

Not every visitor to the island has come voluntarily. During the Edo era, the island was used as a prison for hardened criminals. A tough sentence indeed, but a prettier spot than Alcatraz.

Must see! Mount Mihara Volcano [5]

This active volcano dominates the Oshima skyline.

Its last significant eruption in 1986 led to a mass evacuation of the island, as the lava hurtled down the mountain's slopes, reshaping the landscape.

Visitors can drive to the rest area halfway up the mountain and then walk to the edge of the crater for breathtaking views, both inside the crater itself, and across to Shizuoka's Izu Peninsula.

As well as the gentle climb up to the crater's edge, seasoned hikers can take the longer route which more or less follows the circumference of the crater and back down the other side towards the *urasabaku* (back desert), a dark wasteland formed out of the volcanic ash from past eruptions. On this barren expanse, it is difficult to believe that one is still technically in Tokyo.

Kanto-Koshinetsu

Tokyo
Izu Oshima Island OSHIMA
大島町

👍 Must do! Oshima Isshudoro (one-lap road)

One of the best and simplest ways to experience Oshima is to drive right around the circumference of the island. It takes just under two hours to make a full circle following the *isshudoro* - an experience which is enhanced by spectacular sea views from one window, and mountain views out of the other.

🌳 Nature Spot - Hot Springs

What are the benefits of living on the slope of a volcano? Hot springs. Oshima's residents channel the waters to various spots on the island, notably the Gojinka and Hama-no-yu facilities in Motomachi. The latter is an outdoor spa in which bathers of both genders can bathe together, providing they are wearing swimming costumes. Time your visit to enjoy a spectacular sunset from this cliff-top *onsen*. If venturing further up Mihara, the Oshima Onsen Hotel offers excellent facilities and astounding views of the volcano.

🌳 Nature Spot - Senba Stratum Section 6

This astonishing snapshot of history was revealed during the construction of the road to the south of the island, and shows more than 90 layers of rock formed over 20,000 years, from the many eruptions of Mount Mihara. The clarity of the layers, in lighter and darker shades of brown, make this impressive geological sight a must see.

🍶 Food and Drink

Oshima, being an island, is of course famed for its seafood. Traditional island divers hit the seabed to gather shellfish. Another common local speciality is *bekko* (a raw fish marinated in soy sauce with green chillies), which has a distinctive flavour, copper colour and succulent texture.

There are also other distinctive local delicacies such as *ashitaba* and *kusaya*. The former is a wild plant which has a tangy taste, great as a supplement to soup or egg dishes. *Kusaya* is the epitome of an acquired taste - and it may take you a lifetime to acquire it. This dried fish is arguably the smelliest foodstuff in the land, hence the word *kusai* (stinky) in its name. Approach with caution.

Toriton 7

Close to the port of Motomachi, this ice-cream shop and small cafe offers a spectacular range of home-made flavours. Ask the friendly staff for local recommendations.

🚆 Getting there and around

High-speed jet ferries and overnight boats from Takeshiba Pier (in Tokyo bay), Atami (in Shizuoka) and Tateyama (in Chiba) embark to Oshima Island. Depending on weather conditions, the boats either land at Motomachi on the west coast of the island or, more often, the sheltered harbour of Okata on the north coast.

✈ There are flights to and from Oshima from the small Chofu Airport in western Tokyo.
🚗 Once on the island, the best way to see Oshima is to rent a car, although there are also regular bus services around the island.

🏞 Further information
www.100hiddentowns.jp/tokyo/oshima.html

Key dates

spring - Oshima Tsubaki Matsuri (Camellia Festival)

We say

❝ Climbing the volcano, learning a little about the local culture and sampling the island cuisine - there is so much to do on this small but fascinating island. It seems bizarre that there are so few visitors, considering Oshima's proximity to Tokyo. A great spot for a couple of days, Oshima truly is a hidden gem. ❞

Recommended for

Hikers

Nature lovers

Kanto-Koshinetsu

北杜市
Yamanashi
HOKUTO

Hokuto springs from where three great mountain ranges meet. Since the South Alps, Yatsugatake and Okuchichibu ranges converge here, it means that you will have dramatic mountain vistas as the backdrop to everything you do. Close enough from Tokyo to be convenient, but far enough away to feel apart, Hokuto has grown up as a sanctuary from the urban jungle.

172

🏠 Culture Spot Kiyosato ❶

Kiyosato is a highland resort which has the look and feel of a playground for those escaping Tokyo. At an altitude of over 1,000m, it can provide a cool escape from the heat of the lowlands. The resort offers a variety of options, from chic boutiques and trendy cafes, to horseback riding and ski slopes.

 Did you know?

Sunny climes
Hokuto - and more specifically, Akeno - reputedly gets the most hours of sunlight of any place in Japan. Whether this is the reason for the many sunflower fields in the area, or just serendipity, we may never know.

Nature Spot - Verdant Garden Verga ❷

Verdant Garden Verga is a large holiday site aimed at families, offering the chance to play and relax in the countryside. A variety of zones, encompassing forests and rivers, provide numerous facilities including camping and chalet rooms, hot spring baths, and shops. The staff also offer workshops for kids in forest and nature crafts.

🏠 Culture Spot - Misogi Shrine ❸

Misogi Shrine is a relatively new shrine, built in 1985, but belonging to one of the oldest Shinto sects, Misogikyo. The shrine is for the worship of the God of the Sun, and is designed to purify the soul. As you would expect, the shrine has a tranquil air - it follows the more simplistic lines of older shrines like Ise Jingu in Mie Prefecture. Enjoy the grounds and shrine, but also look out for the dramatically situated *noh* theatre. Regarded as one of the best in Japan, it sits in a small lake with a rise on the opposite shore for the audience. On the third of August every year, they hold a performance of Yatsugatake-Noh, which takes place at night, illuminated only by flaming torches.

173

Kanto-Koshinetsu

Yamanashi — HOKUTO 北杜市

🏠 Culture Spot
Higashizawa Ohashi 4

Although its function is just to carry the road around the mountain, this bridge now also acts as the emblematic image of Kiyosato. The red iron structure cuts across the line of the mountains and is a popular photo spot.

🏠 Culture Spot
Yatsugatake 5

The Yatsugatake mountain range is said to be one of the oldest mountain chains in Japan, and its highest peaks used to rise higher than Mount Fuji. Legend says that the Goddess of Fuji herself tore down Yatsugatake out of jealousy. Whether due to the simple passage of time or to the wanton actions of a jealous deity, the peaks are now carved into dramatic plunging shapes. Yatsugatake is just a few metres too short to be classified as an Alp, but it has long been a popular mountain retreat. Aka Dake, literally 'red mountain', is the most impressive of the peaks, and is serviced by a number of huts around its base. It is also one of the few areas which stays open all year round. Yatsugatake provides some challenging but very rewarding hiking and is well worth the effort.

👍 Must see!
Suntory Hakushu Distillery 6

Suntory, the founders of the first malt whisky distillery in Japan, has been producing whisky since 1923. In 1973, Suntory established its second malt whisky distillery, 'Hakushu'. Tucked into the skirts of the Southern Japanese Alps, the facility is surrounded by broad forests trailing off to snow-capped summits. The location provides clear underground water ideal for whisky making. There are tours of both the bottled water plant and the whisky distillery. Guides take visitors round the sites and describe the production process (an English audio guide is also available). The distillery tour is concluded with a tasting session in the main hall. A small tower offers clear views of the surrounding countryside from the top, and there is a museum below that houses some nice period artefacts from the history of Suntory distilling.

Chateraise Hakushu Factory

A tour of an ice cream factory is always an appealing option. Visitors to Chateraise Hakushu Factory can walk around the edge of the building, looking into the production line, where the ice cream and *anko* (bean paste) are produced using the local natural water.

Key dates

July to August - Akeno Sunflower Festival

mid-October - Paul Rusch Festival (a harvest festival meets American county fair, with stalls, animals, ice cream, etc.)

We say

" Hokuto is a dramatic location that offers a lot of options. There is some tourist infrastructure here so you will not be short of somewhere to go. The area is huge though, and public transport very limited, so plan carefully in advance. "

Recommended for

Families

Those escaping from city life

🏠 Culture Spot - Paul Rusch Centre 7 and Seisen Ryo 8

The very existence of Kiyosato is partly due to the assiduous work of one man, the American Paul Rusch. Rusch made his home in the area and spearheaded a redevelopment program called KEEP, a combination of agricultural, economic and religious activities. His home and visitor centre are open to the public, an incongruous mixture of 1950s Americana in a Japanese town. The highlights of the museum are the agricultural and missionary displays, which unabashedly lead onto the Japan American Football Hall of Fame.

Seisen Ryo is the main centre for KEEP activities now. There is a hotel and shops, and a local nature centre. Perhaps most appealing, however, is the Dormouse Museum. This suitably sized museum offers a small number of items relating to the titular rodent.

🚆 Getting there and around

✈ Haneda Airport or Matsumoto Airport in Nagano, and then travel by local train services to Kobuchizawa Station.

🚄 Kofu Station. From there, travel by local train services to Kobuchizawa Station.

🚗 Hokuto is a vast area, and public transport is very limited. Even in the Kiyosato area you will probably need a car.

📘 Further information

www.100hiddentowns.jp/yamanashi/hokuto.html

175

Kanto-Koshinetsu

Yamanashi — KOSHU
甲州市

If there is any need for further evidence that Japan can adopt, adapt and arguably even surpass western techniques and tastes, it is the Koshu area of Yamanashi. Not long ago, Japanese wines were known for their sweet flavour and domestic-only market. Following improvements in the winemaking process, and making full use of the ideal Yamanashi topography and climate, the grapes of the area have prospered, and now Koshu wines are internationally renowned, exported all over the world, and winning awards.

In 2005, Enzan, along with the town of Katsunuma and the village of Yamato, merged to create the city of Koshu. The area is dotted with vineyards, and the surrounding mountains, plus the looming glory of Mount Fuji, provide a gorgeous backdrop to a wine-tasting and shopping visit.

👍 Must see!
Katsunuma Budo Hill ①

This hilltop complex has a hotel and a hot spring bath for visitors planning a longer stay in the town. The facility also boasts a restaurant with a wine cellar of approximately 180 kinds of locally produced wine, with tasting opportunities offered.

🌳 Nature Spot - Miyakoen ②

This is the collective name for the area where the vineyards have their wine shops and tasting counters. A short walk from winery to winery provides a smooth, easy visit and, more importantly, a chance to sample a delicious range of local wines in a short space of time.

There is also a museum which shows objects and tools related to the winemaking process, as well as photos of past winemakers from Koshu, helping illustrate the history of wine production in the area.

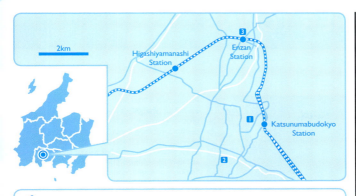

 Did you know?

Develop a thick skin

The Koshu grape is a hybrid unique to Japan, that has a thick skin which helps it withstand the relentless humidity of the Japanese summer.

Key dates

first Saturday in October - Katsunuma Grape Festival (grape and wine tasting service)

We say

" Doable as a day trip from Tokyo, the Koshu area is fantastic for wine lovers. Tuck into the various types of wine and get shopping. A trip here will provide clear evidence that the area deserves its high reputation for producing excellent wines. "

Recommended for

Wine lovers

Hikers

Culture Spot - Former Takano Residence (Liquorice Mansion)

Worth a visit prior to getting stuck into all those wines or hitting the slopes for a hike, is the huge country residence of the Takano family, purveyors of herbal medicine. Liquorice was cultivated for the domestic market as it had long been used as a medicine for various ailments, especially the common cold. The house is known as the Liquorice Mansion for this reason, and its proximity to Enzan Station makes it a recommended spot to drop by and see how a typical residence of a rich farming family of the Edo era would look. The Doll Festival in March is a recommended time to visit, with an outstanding display in the house.

Getting there and around

Haneda Airport. Travel to Kofu Station.

Kofu Station. From there, take local train services to Enzan Station or Katsunumabudokyo Station.

From the main conurbation of Kofu Station, both Enzan Station and Katsunumabudokyo Station are short journeys away. If without a rental car, a short taxi ride can be taken from either of those stations to the main Miyakoen area for wine tasting. Bus tours to the area are also frequent - a relaxing way to enjoy a trip.

Food and Drink - Wine

The journey of the Koshu grape is said to have begun a thousand years ago, as it travelled along the Silk Road and found its Japanese home in Yamanashi. The distinctive characteristics of Koshu grapes are the delicateness and freshness of their flavour - considered a good match for the subtleties of Japanese cuisine. There are now more than 80 wineries in Yamanashi Prefecture, providing about 40% of Japan's domestic wine production.

 Further information

www.100hiddentowns.jp/yamanashi/koshu.html

KANTO-KOSHINETSU
関東甲信越地方

OTHER TOWNS

Kanagawa
MANAZURU

Manazuru is a little fishing port town set on a small jut of land, just ahead of its bigger brother peninsula, Izu. It's an easily reachable destination, taking about 90 minutes from Tokyo (considerably less if you take the bullet train) and is nestled among other tourist spots such as Atami and Hakone. The walk from Manazuru Station is a recommended first course of action. Visitors can follow its steep, meandering road past local shops and houses, to be finally greeted by the port, the sea and the surrounding forest.

Culture Spot Nakagawa Kazumasa Museum
Nature Spot Manazuru Iwa Beach
Must do Kibune Festival
We say The Kibune festival, on July 27 and 28 every year, is one of the big three boat festivals in Japan, along with similar events in Hiroshima and Sendai, and has a fantastic atmosphere. There are beautifully decorated boats, *mikoshi* portable shrines, songs and dances. The festival climaxes with the *mikoshi* being carried by hand and walked into the water, as the ultimate gift to the sea.

Nagano
MATSUKAWA

Matsukawa is a predominantly agricultural area, famous for its fruit production. Orchards line the low slopes, skirting the towering heights of the Central Alps.

Culture Spot Daijo Park
Nature Spot Nakahira Farm
Must do Forest Adventure Matsukawa
We say A great town for fruit lovers and outdoor activities enthusiasts, Matsukawa is a pretty spot for a short visit.

178

Nagano
SAKAKI

Sakaki is a town very much unused to foreign tourists, but ironically, it was once a booming way-point of inns and brothels in the Edo era, due to its location on the Hokkoku Kaido Road, linking the Sea of Japan with the capital. Sakaki still retains touches of that history, but its true delights lie in the surrounding nature of rivers and prominent, sharp-peaked hills.

Culture Spot Sakaki History Museum
Nature Spot Chikuma River
Must see The Museum of Tetsu (sword museum)
We say Sakaki is a pleasant spot for an easy day trip from Nagano or Karuizawa. It's great to cycle along the Chikuma River and enjoy the curious juxtaposition of industrial activity (represented by the factories on the west bank) and slow-paced bucolic lifestyles (epitomised by the vegetable smallholdings on the east bank).

Saitama
KAMIKAWA

Venture into deeper countryside, and Saitama offers up a plethora of natural treats. The town of Kamikawa covers a vast area including mountains, parks and *onsen* resorts. Time your visit with the autumn colours, winter *sakura* or spring cherry blossoms.

Nature Spot Jomine Park
Must see Kanasana Shrine
We say An autumn visit is highly recommended to enjoy hikes in the cool weather, and the patchwork quilt of autumn hues on display. Kanasana Shrine is a particular delight, thanks to its surrounding forest and streams.

Tokyo
HACHIOJI

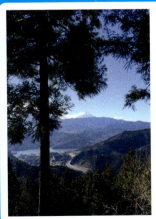

The town of Hachioji is situated in the foothills of the Okutama Mountains in western Tokyo, and is home to several popular hiking attractions, including Mount Jinba and Mount Takao. Mount Takao is one of the most popular day trips from the nation's capital, its summit accessible by cable car and several hiking routes of varying lengths, that are manageable by most people in good health.

Culture Spot Yakuoin Temple, Takao 599 Museum
Nature Spot Monkey Park and Wildflower Garden
Must do Mount Takao
We say At less than an hour's journey from the centre of Tokyo, Hachioji is a great place to escape the metropolis, stretch your legs and breathe some fresh air. On a clear day, the viewpoint at its summit provides great photo opportunities for climbers to be pictured in front of Mount Fuji. At its foot, there is a small town with restaurants, a lovely museum and a hot spring located adjacent to Takaosanguchi Station.

179

CHUBU-HOKURIKU

中部北陸地方

The Chubu-Hokuriku Region
Spread out over a large area of the country, Chubu-Hokuriku includes the Pacific-bordering prefectures of Shizuoka, Aichi and Mie. In its centre is the landlocked prefecture of Gifu. This area is historically significant as the location of the ancient Tokaido road that linked Edo (modern-day Tokyo) to Kyoto.

The Sea of Japan coastline is known as the Hokuriku region, including Toyama, Fukui and Ishikawa, and is renowned for its heavy snowfall in winter and spectacular all-year-round vistas and seafood cuisine.

AICHI PREFECTURE

By turns, flat, hilly, and mountainous, Aichi is a much-visited area, thanks to the industrial hub of Nagoya and the historical ceramics and textile industries of the prefecture. The riverside castle of Inuyama and the impressive pottery and craftsmanship of Tokoname are recommended.

Prefectural Capital
Nagoya City

✈ Airports
Chubu Centrair International Airport

🚆 Main Train Stations
Nagoya Station

Other Tourist Attractions

Nagoya
Japan's fourth most populated city is less of a draw than the celebrated metropolises of Osaka, Kyoto and Tokyo, but is still worth dropping by for its reconstructed castle, museums and vibrant nightlife.

Korankei Valley
Gorgeous autumn hues attract tourists to this valley just outside Nagoya.

Minamichita
A popular hot spring resort with romantic inns and swimming beaches.

Konomiya Hadaka (Naked) Festival
(Inazawa City)
Dating back over 1,200 years, this raucous festival in freezing February involves loincloth-clad males being sprayed with cold water as they pray for good luck. The so-called 'Lucky Man' is chased around the shrine, utterly naked, as the participants aim to touch him to get good luck.

Korankei Valley

FUKUI PREFECTURE

Fukui Prefecture has it all - spectacular coasts, lakes, history, and culture preserved in museums and heritage sites. Fukui prides itself on its artisanal legacy, with a history of products from pottery to spectacles. Gorgeous seafood dishes served at traditional Japanese inns by the famously welcoming locals complement the countryside and culture perfectly. Away from the better-known sights, the prefecture has even more to recommend it, whether it's the hot spring resorts of Awara, the famous 'castle in the clouds' of Ono, the wonderful history and lakes of Wakasa, or Katsuyama's renowned dinosaur museum.

Prefectural Capital
Fukui City
✈ Airports
-

🚂 Main Train Stations
Fukui Station
Tsuruga Station

Other Tourist Attractions
Tojinbo Cliffs
These amazing rock formations, carved out by the Sea of Japan, are a fantastic sight. Visitors can clamber over these pillar-shaped rocks and, bravely, peer down at the churning waves below. Pleasure boat cruises can also be booked to enjoy the rocks from a sea-level perspective.

Tojinbo Cliffs

Maruoka Castle
Dating back to 1576, Maruoka Castle still boasts its original keep. The steep walk up to the castle grounds is rewarded with spectacular views.

Ichijodani Asakura Clan Historic Ruins
These are partially reconstructed ruins of Ichijodani Castle Town, in the centre of the prefecture. The castle was the base of the Asakura clan during the Muromachi period until Nobunaga Oda burnt the town to the ground in 1573. Recent excavations have helped reveal how the town looked in its heyday, and there are now reconstructions to showcase the layout and architecture of the era.

Mikuni Festival
Six floats bearing warrior dolls parade through the streets of Mikuni Town, which is lined with hundreds of stalls.

GIFU PREFECTURE

Home to traditional mountain villages and popular skiing resorts, Gifu is also famous as the location of the epoch-defining Battle of Sekigahara of 1600, which triggered the unification of the country under the rule of the Tokugawa shogunate. Hiking and hot springs abound throughout the prefecture, and Gero is one such spot, worthy of a few days' break.

Prefectural Capital
Gifu City

🚂 Main Train Stations
Gifu-Hashima Station

Other Tourist Attractions
Shirakawa-go
A hugely popular draw - there are breathtaking views throughout this village of preserved, traditional triangular thatched-roofed farmhouses.

Takayama
A historical town well known for its excellent spring and autumn festivals, Takayama also has popular skiing facilities nearby.

Okuhida
Gorgeous outdoor baths, surrounded by mountains, characterise this remote spot. The town also boasts a double-decker ropeway into the Northern Alps, and great hiking opportunities.

Gujo Hachiman
Pristine canals, a summer dance festival, and Japan's leading producer of replica food are all claims to fame for Gujo.

Gifu City
The city of Gifu is famous for cormorant fishing. The Nagara River Ukai Museum explains the history and methods of this ancient tradition.

Furukawa
A small mountain town, Furukawa gained wealth and fame for its timber, which is still utilised by the local carpenters.

Hirayu Waterfall

181

CHUBU-HOKURIKU

中部北陸地方

ISHIKAWA PREFECTURE

Thanks partly to the wonderful, historical city of Kanazawa, Ishikawa attracts a large number of tourists all year round. Nature lovers also hit Ishikawa for its mountains and coastal areas. For lighter crowds and staggering views from the sacred white mountain to the sea, go to Hakusan, where visitors can also take the challenge of tasting blowfish ovaries. Wajima has a morning market dedicated to local delicacies and the town's signature lacquerware, which can also be enjoyed at two museums there.

Prefectural Capital
Kanazawa City
✈ Airports
Komatsu Airport
Noto Airport
🚄 Main Train Stations
Kanazawa Station
Other Tourist Attractions
Kanazawa

Kanazawa City

Kanazawa is a popular draw, thanks to its parks, castle and Edo-era teahouses. The sprawling, beautiful Kenrokuen Garden is internationally renowned, drawing visitors from all over the world.
Noto Peninsula
The Noto area is famous for its rocky shoreline, spectacular cliffs and tranquil farming villages.
Kaga Onsen
Incorporating four ancient hot spring resorts, Kaga Onsen is a popular destination for a relaxing soak. A characteristic of the town is its communal public bathing, where tourists and locals can mix.
Abare Festival (Noto)
This July festival has giant lanterns paraded through the streets. The revellers dance around the flames to the rhythm of *taiko* drumming. The following day, *mikoshi* portable shrines are flung into the sea.
Extreme Seasonal Conditions Heavy snow in winter.

MIE PREFECTURE

A lengthy coastline with fascinating rock formations, plus nationally protected natural areas - Mie has much to offer. Arguably Japan's most sacred region, Mie's lengthy Shinto history is represented by Japan's oldest shrine, the wonderful Ise Grand Shrine. Further south, Kumano is a coastal treat with rugged rocks, religious treasures, and pilgrimage routes.

Prefectural Capital
Tsu City

✈ Airports
-

🚆 Main Train Stations
Tsu Station

Other Tourist Attractions

Ago Bay
A pretty, island-dotted bay, famous for pearl cultivation, with a large number of oyster rafts floating in the sea.

Iga
The Ninja Museum of Igaryu in Iga is a popular draw for lovers of these skilled mercenaries.

Shima
A good spot with beaches, coastal walks, and an amusement park.

Tado Festival (Kuwana City)
This celebration at Tado Shrine during May features young men on horses attempting to jump over a two-metre high wall. There are also traditional archery performances.

Ago Bay

SHIZUOKA PREFECTURE

Fujinomiya

Shizuoka is known for its tea, coastal vistas, mountain ranges and waterfalls. Sample the Showa-era chic of the famous hot spring destination of Atami, the history-laced coastal town of Shimoda, or the fantastic temples and views of Mount Fuji from Matsuzaki.

Prefectural Capital
Shizuoka City

✈ Airports
Shizuoka Airport (also known as Mt. Fuji Shizuoka Airport)

🚆 Main Train Stations
Shizuoka Station
Mishima Station

Other Tourist Attractions

Fujinomiya
The city is located on the southwestern slopes of Mount Fuji, and centred around its Sengen Shrine - considered the most important shrine in the region, and a common starting point for a climb up the mountain.

Lake Hamanako
A 15th-century earthquake conjoined this large lake with the Pacific Ocean, and made the water brackish. Now the main draw is its Kanzanji hot spring resort.

Fujinomiya Autumn Festival (Fujinomiya City)
Floats loaded with performers and dolls, and portable shrines parade through the town with Mount Fuji providing a resplendent backdrop.

183

CHUBU-HOKURIKU

中部北陸地方

TOYAMA PREFECTURE

Tateyama Kurobe Alpine Route

Clinging to the Sea of Japan, Toyama is well known for its variety of seafood. Inland, the Tateyama Kurobe Alpine Route runs through the Northern Japan Alps. The Hida mountains offer hot springs and plenty of skiing opportunities. Off the beaten path, why not try the festivals and seafood of Himi, and the spectacular rice paddies, shrines and mountains of Kamiichi?

Prefectural Capital
Toyama City

✈ Airports
Toyama Airport

🚆 Main Train Stations
Shin-Takaoka Station

Toyama Station

Other Tourist Attractions
Takaoka
Takaoka is known for its tulip fair, pretty castle park, and the awe-inspiring Zuiryuji Temple. The nearby roads and architecture are also pleasant for strolling around.

Tateyama Kurobe Alpine Route
Connecting Nagano to Toyama, this Northern Alps route offers spectacular views all year round. Especially well known are the 20-metre-high snow walls of the 'snow corridor' part of the route at the height of winter.

Kurobe Gorge
Take a ride on the sightseeing railway through this gorgeous forested gorge to appreciate its steep cliffs, and then rest up at a hot spring.

Toyama Festival (Toyama City)
Street dancing and performances in this huge, popular summer festival.

Extreme Seasonal Conditions Heavy snow in winter.

NATIONAL PARKS

Chubusangaku National Park
Area: 174,323 ha
Features: mountains, cliffs, valleys, lakes
Did you know? The park is extremely popular among visitors (especially climbers) for the variety of its mountain landscapes and its easy accessibility.

Hakusan National Park
Area: 49,900 ha
Features: mountains, forests
Did you know? Mount Hakusan has long been one of the most revered mountains in Japan, thanks to its distinctive snow-capped, isolated appearance - standing out due to the lack of other high mountains around it.

Ise-Shima National Park
Area: 55,544 ha
Features: woodland, coastal areas
Did you know? This national park of Mie differs from others in Japan because the area is mostly known for its shrines and temples, and is thus as much lauded for its cultural heritage as its natural history.

Fuji-Hakone-Izu National Park
Area: 121,695 ha
Features: Mount Fuji, hot springs, lakes, coastlines
Did you know? The past volcanic activity of the area has meant that, as well as lakes, there are lava tunnels and caves dotting the park.

Yoshino-Kumano National Park
(See Kansai)

Chubusangaku National Park

CHUBU-HOKURIKU

中部北陸地方

HIDDEN TOWNS

AICHI
- 188 Inuyama
- 192 Tokoname

FUKUI
- 196 Awara
- 198 Katsuyama
- 202 Ono
- 204 Wakasa

GIFU
- 208 Gero

ISHIKAWA
- 210 Hakusan
- 212 Wajima

MIE
- 214 Ise
- 218 Kumano

SHIZUOKA
- 222 Atami
- 224 Shimoda

TOYAMA
- 226 Himi
- 228 Kamiichi

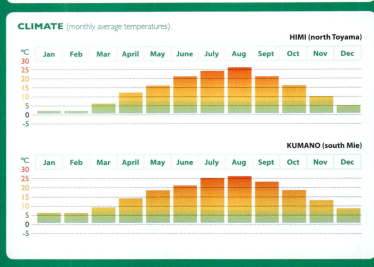

CLIMATE (monthly average temperatures)

HIMI (north Toyama)

KUMANO (south Mie)

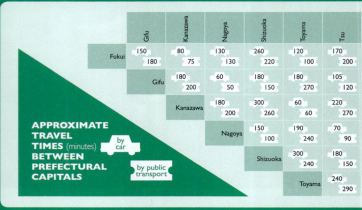

APPROXIMATE TRAVEL TIMES (minutes) **BETWEEN PREFECTURAL CAPITALS**

by car / by public transport

	Gifu	Kanazawa	Nagoya	Shizuoka	Toyama	Tsu
Fukui	150 / 180	80 / 75	130 / 130	260 / 220	120 / 100	170 / 200
Gifu		180 / 200	60 / 50	180 / 150	180 / 270	105 / 120
Kanazawa			180 / 200	300 / 260	60 / 60	220 / 270
Nagoya				150 / 100	190 / 240	70 / 90
Shizuoka					300 / 240	180 / 150
Toyama						240 / 290

186

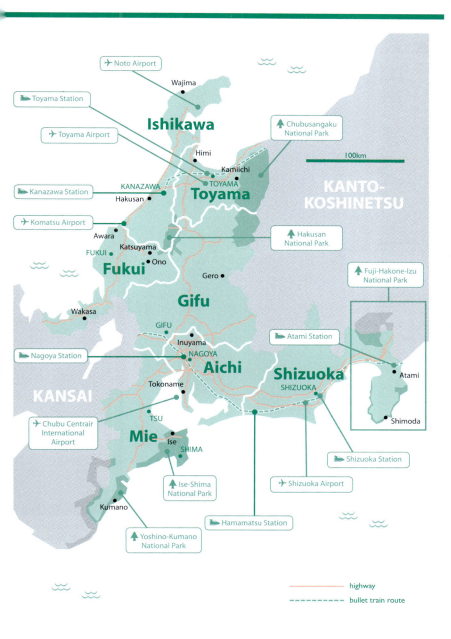

Chubu-Hokuriku

Aichi

INUYAMA
犬山市

Inuyama, literally meaning 'dog mountain', is in Aichi Prefecture and works well as a wonderful day trip from Nagoya. It is most famous for its small but beautiful castle - said to be the oldest surviving one in Japan - and the street leading to it which has a variety of eateries and traditional shops.

Longer stays offer a chance to visit the amusement parks and museums on the outskirts, such as Meiji-mura which houses an abundance of Meiji-era architecture. The town offers other great sights, such as cormorant fishing throughout the summer and early autumn, and the wonderful garden of Urakuen. It is also host to a festival in April every year, where huge floats parade around the town transporting puppeteers and their dolls to the sounds of flutes, drums, yells and general revelry.

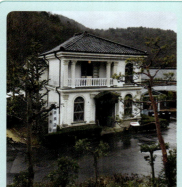

🏠 Culture Spot - Meiji-mura

Overlooking Lake Iruka, the open-air museum of Meiji-mura (Meiji Village) showcases over 60 buildings from the Meiji period (1868-1912) that have been dismantled and moved from various areas of Japan to this park where they are on permanent display. Two to three hours can easily be spent here.

Meiji-era architecture saw a huge influence from Europe, as Japan rushed to westernise, and perhaps only in Japan would an attraction devoted to late 19th and early 20th-century architecture be such a draw. It may be of more interest to non-European visitors, as the experience does feel like visiting a small European town. Nevertheless, the fact that the structures of the time were so impermanent yet so impressive makes it a meaningful visit, to witness evidence of the rapid-moving, fleeting eras that Japan has had since the end of the Edo era. Most Meiji-era constructions were torn down or destroyed due to war, earthquakes, safety issues, or simply Japan's relentless push to continuously have the most modern functional architecture.

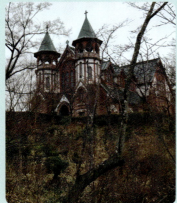

Visitors can see old schoolhouses, shops, the front entrance to the once-lauded Imperial Hotel of Tokyo, the Meiji-era emperor's own train carriage, and the desk where the Portsmouth Treaty, which formally ended the Russo-Japanese War, was signed in 1905.

The park has a thorough English explanation outside each building, but the more detailed displays within are mainly in Japanese.

Meiji-mura is fun for kids too, with a maze, quizzes and plenty of chances to rest and snack. It's a great jaunt from central Inuyama, or if you are planning a longer stay in the Nagoya area.

👁 Did you know?

A fishy business
Considered cruel by some and clearly not for everyone, there's no denying that *Ukai* cormorant fishing is a unique way to make a catch. The technique's lengthy history dates back to the early Edo era, and entails the tying of torches to the bows of small boats in order to attract smelt fish, which are then harvested for the fishermen by gobbling cormorants which skim the surface of the Kiso River.

Dogged dog mountain castle
Inuyama Castle's lengthy survival is a rarity in Japan, as many such castles suffered destruction during the blistering modernisation of the Meiji era, or from natural disasters and Second World War bombing. The castle was in fact the base for Hideyoshi Toyotomi's forces, numbering a staggering 120,000, during the Battle of Komaki Nagakute in 1584, the only time that he fought directly with Ieyasu Tokugawa before the latter pledged loyalty.

Chubu-Hokuriku

犬山市

Aichi

INUYAMA

🏠 Culture Spot - Urakuen [2]

Urakuen is a traditional Japanese garden close to the castle, which incorporates Joan, one of Japan's most celebrated teahouses - a designated national treasure. Joan was originally built in 1618 by Urakusai Oda, a younger brother of Nobunaga Oda, and an aficionado of the tea ceremony.

The design of the gardens ensures that the views are pretty throughout the seasons, displaying vivid colours throughout spring and autumn, and particular beauty during the winter snows.

🏠 Culture Spot - Castle Town [3]

The street leading to the castle is great for a stroll and a browse, with plenty of places to rest and snack at, to try traditional Japanese craft-making, or rent a kimono for the day. The road also has several museums of note.

Karakuri Ningyo Museum displays the puppet doll passengers of the tall floats that crowd the town during its annual April festival. This is a wonderful opportunity to see the intricately designed puppets up close and to manipulate their torsos and limbs.

Shirotomachi Museum showcases the town's history. There is limited English here, but a large model of the town helps visitors to visualise how the area appeared in its heyday. There is also lacquerware, colourfully illustrated Edo-era books, and artistic wall hangings on display. The museum is great for kids too, with hands-on exhibits and a chance to try on some period costumes.

Dondenkan is the museum where some of the floats for the Inuyama Festival are housed while inactive - a chance to inspect them in detail if your visit isn't timed with the festival.

Another spot of note is the former Isobe Residence, a typical late Edo-era townhouse, which visitors can enter for free.

A discount ticket that covers entrance to all the museums and the castle is available.

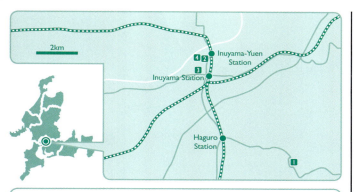

Key dates

early April - Inuyama Festival (huge decorated floats parade through the town in this internationally recognised festival)

We say

" Inuyama is wonderful. Its accessibility makes it a must-visit spot if you are based in the Nagoya area. The castle is a justifiably popular attraction, and the narrow street leading up to it retains much of its historical feel. Although lined with souvenir shops and eateries, it isn't as in-your-face pushy or as pricey as such areas tend to be in tourist hubs. "

Recommended for

History lovers

Must see! Inuyama Castle

What is remarkable about Inuyama Castle is its survival through the years. Originally built by an uncle of Nobunaga Oda in 1537, the castle changed hands many times (which was typical of the chaotic Warring States era) before ending up in the hands of the Naruse clan.

The castle stands on a hill overlooking the Kiso River. A steep but manageable sloped approach through rows of red *torii* gates leads visitors to the entrance of the main grounds and keep. The castle's interior can get very crowded with foot traffic as the steps up the four levels of the castle are narrow and steep, with low beams proving a testament to the age and authenticity of the building.

The interior is beautifully preserved, and has avoided the modern touches (such as lifts and tacky displays) that many castle reconstructions have undergone in Japan.

Getting there and around

- Chubu Centrair International Airport. Travel by local train to Inuyama Station.
- Nagoya Station. Travel by local train to Inuyama Station or Inuyama-Yuen Station.
- The castle is within walking distance from the main train stations, and the castle road is perfect for a stroll. Regular buses transport visitors to Meiji-mura and other attractions outside of town, such as Japan Monkey Center and Little World, an open-air museum devoted to the various cultures of different ethnicities of the world.

Further information

www.100hiddentowns.jp/aichi/inuyama.html

Chubu-Hokuriku

常滑市 TOKONAME
Aichi

Tokoname provides an urban getaway, where modern development fits snugly within the historical environs. Beaches and shopping malls lie next to rambling streets and cosy cafes. Check out this charming town, located less than an hour from Nagoya.

Culture Spot - Tokoname Pottery

Tokoname is famous for its pottery and ceramics, and has a history of production dating back to the Heian period, over a thousand years ago. It is one of the 'six historic kilns of Japan', and its produce is still revered worldwide. Using the distinctive red clay from the nearby fields, the industry progressed until, by the 1950s, it was the largest production centre in all of Japan, and the black smoke from the forest of chimneys was said to block out the sun. Although the scale of production is now much smaller, the spirit of the town's industrial past still seems to endure. What was once a workshop of industry, is now a myriad of pathways winding around artisanal workshops, cafes and historical sites.

Nature Spot
Ono Beach 1

This beach has apparently been visited by a variety of ruling clans of Japan over the centuries. It is a nice spot for a paddle and offers great views of the sun setting over the horizon.

Must see! Tokoname Pottery Footpath

The well-signposted Tokoname Pottery Footpath is a wonderful route to explore the town's back streets and alleyways. The route takes you through a jumble of old buildings and factories, now mainly converted into studios and workshops.

There is a short course of 1.6 kilometres and a long course of four kilometres. With the variety of things to do and see along the way, your walk may take much longer than those distances suggest.

Denden-Zaka 2

Denden-Zaka is a short, pretty street leading up a hill. The walls are lined with clay pots and *shochu* jars, whilst underfoot, broken firing stands provide the grip. This pattern of clay pots lining the sides of alleys can be seen repeated throughout the district.

Climbing Kiln Square 4

A climbing kiln is a fuel-efficient system that allows for multiple batches to be fired at the same time. The heat moves up the kiln before exiting at the top. There used to be 60 of these distinctive kilns in the area, but this is the last remaining one that can be seen.

Takita Family Residence 3

The Takita family were merchant shippers who carried Tokoname wares all around the Ise Bay area trade routes, and up east as far as the Kanto region. Their traditional house has been restored to a period piece of Edo-style living.

Workshops

Many of the workshops in the area offer the chance to make and bake your own ceramics. Master potters will lead you through the basics and help you produce your own piece of *Tokoname-yaki*, though it is wise to be realistic about the outcome and not expect to match the veterans! Booking in advance is advised.

Did you know?

Perfect pot
The signature item of the area is the Tokoname teapot. This redware pot is often seen as the best pot for brewing green tea, and its design is supposed to lead to the tea having a sweeter, mellower flavour.

Chubu-Hokuriku

Aichi — 常滑市 TOKONAME

🏠 Culture Spot - Rinku Area

Wonder Forest Curio [5]
There are a variety of different amusements available here, from go-kart racing to hot spa bathing. Quite a good spot to keep the kids entertained.

Mentai Park [6]
A whole park devoted to the small, spicy fish egg, much beloved in Japan. From the egg-shaped mascot perched on top of the building - you know what to expect inside - there is wall-to-wall tangy goodness for you to try and buy. If you need to dig deeper, try the factory tour where you can observe the colour-coded staff carrying out their *mentaiko* production duties.

Rinku Beach [7]
A small but pleasant, palm tree-lined beach with views on a clear day across the bay to the next prefecture. The main draw is the barbecue facilities.

🏠 Culture Spot - Tokoname Tounomori [8]

Tokoname Tounomori is a museum, ceramics lab and training studio rolled into one. The museum is all in Japanese, but has a series of photos and artefacts on the development of pottery production in the area. The lab and studio offer a more hands-on experience, but booking in advance is required. Also check out the woods and shrine on site.

🏠 Culture Spot - Tokoname Ceramic Mall [9]

The Tokoname Ceramic Mall is located away from the main pottery production areas, and is a one-stop shop for all your ceramic needs. Although lacking the atmosphere of the historical parts of town, it conveniently has all the main producers of *Tokoname-yaki* in one place. If you want to cut to the chase and just buy pots, this is the place for you.

🏠 Culture Spot - Onomachi [10]

Step out of the station at Onomachi, and enter into a charming flashback of older times. A historical castle town, walking the back streets here reveals a series of attractive shrines, and a lot of traditional buildings that have remained, giving the town its retro feel.

🏠 Culture Spot - Ono Town Historical Walk

There are a number of footpaths that weave through the town and offer a very pleasant afternoon stroll around the neighbourhood. The Ono Town Historical Walk is fairly well signposted and will guide you around the backstreets.

Key dates

end of March - Spring Festival (spring floats make their way around the town)

mid-October - Tokoname Pottery Festival

We say

"Tokoname is a wonderful town to explore. Its industrial background has now mainly been gentrified and offers some wonderfully atmospheric backstreets to get lost in and explore. Tokoname is a must if you are interested in Japanese crafts."

Recommended for

Pottery enthusiasts

An urban weekend escape

Families

🏠 Culture Spot
INAX Museums [11]

On a redeveloped site of the LIXIL Corporation, stand the modern and impressive INAX Museums. Predominantly a history of tile and clay manufacturing in the area, there are a number of different buildings to pass through, including a surprisingly interesting history of the toilet, ranging from vintage pottery bowls to modern gold thrones. There is also a tile museum with some lovely exhibits and a studio where you can make and design your own tile. Although the museum is mostly in Japanese, the visual aspect of the products makes it enjoyable for anyone.

🏠 Culture Spot - Maneki Neko [12]

Tokoname is the largest producer of *maneki neko*, the ubiquitous lucky cat with one paw raised, that can be seen throughout Japan. A particularly impressive specimen can be seen on the bridge just before the pottery district.

🏠 Culture Spot - Ono Castle Ruins [13]

A bit of a trek from the station and up a hill, a visit to the historical site of Ono Castle is rewarded with great views out over the town and bay. If you do make it out to the castle, be sure to check out Kedi Baskan at the base of the hill. The studied chic of this coffee shop offers a great spot to relax, surrounded by a bric-a-brac of kitsch and found items.

⇌ Getting there and around

- Chubu Centrair International Airport. Take local train services to Tokoname Station.
- Nagoya Station. Take local train services to Tokoname Station.
- All the attractions listed are within walking distance of the nearest station, making getting around very easy for visitors.

📄 Further information
www.100hiddentowns.jp/aichi/tokoname.html

195

Chubu-Hokuriku

Fukui
あわら市
AWARA

If hot springs and delicious food are essential ingredients for a quality trip, look no further than Awara Town in Fukui Prefecture. Awara-shi covers a wide area including around the station of Awara-Yunomachi - the focus of most people's visit - with a choice of hot spring *ryokan* and foot spas, enveloped in a laid-back atmosphere. Since 1883, when the hot springs in Awara were discovered, the town has been a popular resort for guests from all over Japan, reaching 1.6 million visitors a year.

👍 Must see! Yunomachi Square

The open square of Yunomachi, located opposite the train station at the centre of town, offers wonderful footbath facilities. This huge building is roofed, but is otherwise open to the elements as it faces out on to the square. This is the hub of the town, where young and old alike can relax in the water, the temperature dependent on each bather's proximity to the source.

The square is also host to a museum dedicated to Awara's most famous son, Professor Genkuro Fujino, who patiently helped the famous Chinese author Lu Xun prepare his class notes while he was studying in Sendai as a medical student in 1904. Lu later wrote an affectionate essay entitled 'Mr Fujino'. The pair's camaraderie and mutual respect remains a welcome symbol of Sino-Japanese friendship.

The museum has many artefacts from the professor's medical work. Visitors can also enter his old house next door and get a feel of Taisho-era life.

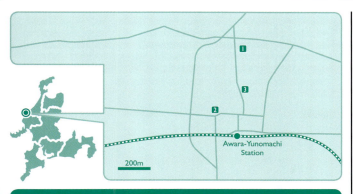

Food and Drink - Japanese Sweets

Since the town's sudden growth in 1883, the sweet shop Darumaya [2] has been serving traditional home-made confectionery. There is also a 'Sweet Walking Tour' which entails a stroll around the town while sampling the unique sweets of various stores.

Culture Spot
Santopia [3]

The Santopia facility, a short walk east of Yunomachi Square, offers a brief, free explanation of the town's history, in English and with illustrations, as well as displays of local art, and a hot spring.

While you bathe, eggs can be cooked in the hot water at the entrance. It takes about 40 minutes, so they will be ready to eat after enjoying a lengthy soak.

Culture Spot
Awara Onsen Spring Festival

On April 29th, day-long festivities take place, with food stalls, games, portable shrines, musicians, and floats sporting giant models of well-known anime characters and historical figures.

The floats circle the town and perform at various spots, before eventually converging on the main thoroughfare by Yunomachi Square, in a sea of colour and music. You may even get the chance to join the high-spirited performers on one of the floats.

Getting there and around

- Komatsu Airport. Travel by bus and train services to Awara-Yunomachi Station.
- Fukui Station. Travel by local train services to Awara-Yunomachi Station.
- The locations mentioned are all within easy walking distance of the town's train station. Taxis may be required to reach some of the hot spring *ryokan* accommodation, as many are on the outskirts of the town.

Further information
www.100hiddentowns.jp/fukui/awara.html

Did you know?

Sprung into action

The hot springs were discovered in 1883 by locals desperately digging for water to irrigate their crops after a long drought. The discovery changed local life drastically, and the town developed so quickly that the local authorities had to restrict the number of hot spring facilities that could be established.

Drunk monk

The hugely popular tourist attraction of Tojinbo is about eight kilometres away from Awara. Here you can view and walk along eroded cliffs that jut out to sea, or even take a boat ride to view them up close. Legend has it that Tojinbo was originally the name of a monk who riled his acquaintances with his bad drunken behaviour and was eventually lured to the cliffs and thrown to his death!

Key dates

first Saturday of February - Setsubun Ghost Event (participants are dressed up as ghosts)

April 29 - Awara Onsen Spring Festival

August 8-9 - Awara Hot Spring Water Splashing Festival

We say

"A lovely, slow-paced town with a fantastic social atmosphere at its open square, excellent food, and *onsen* facilities."

Recommended for

Onsen lovers
Food lovers

197

Chubu-Hokuriku

Fukui

KATSUYAMA 勝山市

Nestled in the valley basin of northeastern Fukui, Katsuyama Town's recent history is entwined with its local textile production, but in prehistoric times the area was the stomping ground for a diversity of dinosaurs.

Katsuyama is now home to a culturally rich town centre, and a large ski resort with three mountain parks, hot springs, and various activities taking place in and out of the ski season.

🏠 Culture Spot - Heisenji Hakusan Shrine ⓘ

Sumptuous, moss-carpeted grounds surround this historical shrine, dating back to the eighth century, cloaking it with a magical air of tranquility. A long, gentle path of sunlight-dappled stone steps ascend to this former home to over 6,000 Buddhist monks. Outside of religious festivals, this is a place of serenity - perfect for a stroll.

198

🏠 Culture Spot - Katsuyama Castle Museum ❷

This edifice is an impressive sight from outside, and punctuates the view of the long, wide valley beautifully.

The balcony on the sixth floor affords a 360° view over the surrounding area, including the Seidaiji Temple, pagoda and the surrounding forest.

Comparatively, the inside seems a little underwhelming, although the paucity of fascinating artefacts is offset by an abundance of space and light.

Objects on display include swords, firearms, suits of armour, and textiles from local feudal families, prints, artworks and embroidery from the Chinese Qing Dynasty, and dazzling folding golden screens and friezes.

Note that the castle museum was built at the end of the 20th century with money donated by the town's benefactor, Kiyoshi Tada, and is neither of the same design nor in the same location as the castle that historically resided in Katsuyama.

🔎 Did you know?

A home where the dinosaur roam

The number of dinosaurs discovered in Fukui is greater than anywhere else in Japan. Fossils of the Fukuiraptor (4.2 metres long), Fukuisaurus (4.7 metres long) and Fukuititan (almost ten metres long) date back to approximately 120 million years ago.

👍 Must see! Fukui Prefectural Dinosaur Museum ❸

The spaceship-like architecture of this museum, which is partly built into a hillside, is a fitting abode for this fantastic museum.

The huge, domed interior houses a multitude of exhibits, all labelled with excellent explanations in English and Japanese. Audio commentary is also available from a rented headset.

In the Dinosaur World section, there are 42 mounted dinosaur skeletons and a variety of other artefacts, including such curiosities as the fossilised remains of a velociraptor and a protoceratops, both killed mid-altercation.

In the Earth Sciences section, there are hands-on displays and glass cabinets housing row upon row of precious fossils, minerals and rocks gathered from around the planet.

The descriptions on the displays describe the history of the plant and animal life, back in the era when Japan was still conjoined with the Asia land mass. Many of the exhibits have been discovered locally since the turn of the millennium.

Naturally, the museum gives considerable focus to its own regional prehistoric paragons, the Fukuisaurus, Fukuiraptor and Fukuititan.

199

Chubu-Hokuriku

Fukui

勝山市

KATSUYAMA

🏠 Culture Spot
Seidaiji Temple [4]

The breathtaking enormity of the Echizen Daibutsu (giant Buddha) statue (over 17 metres high - larger than even the Buddha of Nara), the beautiful great hall that houses it, and the gatehouses of its approach all combine to make the Seidaiji Temple a stunning attraction.

The walls of the great hall are lined with towering galleries of small black and white Buddha statues, each contrasting in colour with the alcove in which it resides.

Also within the temple precinct is a traditional Japanese moss garden, and Japan's tallest five-storied pagoda, where an elevator takes visitors to the top floor of the 75-metre-high tower.

 Food and Drink

Katsuyama is known for the cultivation of local delicacies such as Taro Potatoes, rocket-shaped Midi Tomatoes, and sweet, soft Wakaino Melons. A signature dish of the town is Echizen Katsuyama Soba, which uses the rich-flavoured buckwheat noodles grown in the area.

 Kids - Dino Park [5]

Within the grounds of the Fukui Prefectural Dinosaur Museum there is an outdoor play area where youngsters can run around and play on dinosaur-themed slides. Kids who enjoy craft activities should visit the hand-weaving workshop area at Yume Ole Textile Factory Memorial Hall.

Key dates

last Saturday and Sunday of February - Sagicho Festival (300-year-old festival of dance, drums and fire, celebrating the arrival of spring)

end of December - an end-of-year market where locals sell traditional hand-made goods such as straw hats, snow shoes, farming tools and vegetables

We say

" The knowledge that several of the most magnificent sights in Katsuyama were only recently built might cause some visitors to experience a niggling sense of hollowness (though it should be remembered that nearly all historical castles and temples in Japan are reconstructions of the original buildings). Nevertheless, the town's textile museum is a very real slice of Japan from the recent past, and the fabulous dinosaur museum and beautiful Heisenji Hakusan Shrine are excellent reasons to arrange a visit. "

Recommended for

Dinosaur and geology enthusiasts

Skiers

🏠 Culture Spot - Yume Ole Textile Factory Memorial Hall 6

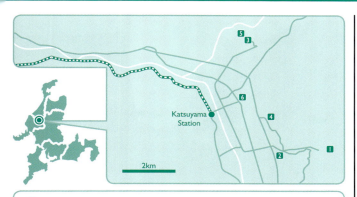

This lovely, old, wooden building, located near the town centre, is the site where local girls in the last century used to divide their time between their school studies and the weaving of thread for the manufacture of goods such as parachutes.

The upstairs of the building contains an array of fascinating and fantastically maintained looms, which can be observed as they hypnotically clatter and weave white thread into cloth. There are also video installations and vintage photos that depict the lives of the town's ancestors. Downstairs is a workshop area where visitors can learn how to weave by hand, as well as a cafeteria and shop selling local produce.

⇌ Getting there and around

✈ Komatsu Airport. Travel by bus to Fukuiekihigashiguchi Bus Stop, then by local train services to Katsuyama Station via Fukui Station.

🚆 Fukui Station. Travel by local train services to Katsuyama Station.

🚲 Bicycles are available for a small fee on request from the train station ticket office. There are also plenty of bus services to the attractions and hotels, that depart from directly outside the station.

🌿 Further information

www.100hiddentowns.jp/fukui/katsuyama.html

Chubu-Hokuriku

大野市

Fukui

ONO

Known as 'Little Kyoto' and famed for its 'Castle in the Sky', Ono has much to offer for any history-loving Japanophile. The grid-like layout of the town centre and the wonderfully located hilltop castle make for a worthy tourist destination. Ono is also renowned for its high-quality local water, used in its delicious *sake*.

🏠 Culture Spot - Samurai Houses

Ono's historical atmosphere is superbly encapsulated by two large *bukeyashiki* (samurai houses) that visitors can enter and wander around at leisure.

The buildings are located at the foot of the castle hill. One of the houses used to be that of the local Uchiyama clan, and contains an elegant garden with an excellent view of the castle above, as well as an Edo-era *miso* warehouse demonstrating architectural features unique to this region. The spacious houses provide a fascinating window into the past of this wonderful small town.

🏠 Culture Spot - Ono City History Museum ②

This history museum has interesting displays in two rooms. There are maps from various ages, showing the castle town layout, as well as samurai armour, a palanquin, folding panels and even a British-made inflatable globe dating from the early Meiji era, showing Tokyo marked as 'Yedo'.

202

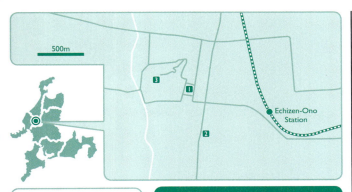

💡 Did you know?

For the sake of *sake*
There are areas dotted all over Ono Town where visitors can taste its famously refreshing water, which is essential for the cultivation of the rice from which the area's delicious *sake* is made.

Key dates

mid-August - Echizen Ono Castle Festival (fireworks and *bon odori* dancing)

end of October - Kuzuryu Autumn Leaves Festival

We say

" Ono is a wonderful town if you like history or even just enjoy gentle strolls around the smaller towns of Japan. Recommended as a day trip if based nearby or worth a stopover if your main aim is mountain climbing. "

Recommended for

Castle lovers
History lovers
Mountain climbers

🏠 Culture Spot
Ono Castle Downtown

Ono is known as 'Little Kyoto' due to its strict geometric layout, which resembles the grid pattern that Kyoto also borrowed from ancient Chinese towns. The area has several old buildings, temples and streams, and overlooking it all, the castle strikes a daunting, elevated pose. It's a great place for wandering around the narrow lanes and acquiring a genuine feel of what life in an ancient castle town was like. Conversely, the rear side of the castle hill is pure countryside, with paddy fields, a river, and barely a building in sight. All in all, a gentle bucolic atmosphere pervades, allowing visitors to enjoy a peaceful respite.

👍 Must see! Echizen Ono Castle ③

This gorgeous castle is known as the 'Castle in the Sky', as it appears to float in the air during cloudy and foggy conditions. This sight is best appreciated from one of the surrounding mountains, when low-lying fog shrouds the town below.

The uphill walk to the castle takes around 20 minutes from the bottom. The path is well-paved and it is a gentle slope. In the summer heat, the route is mercifully shaded by overhanging foliage. Once at the top, the 360° views of Ono Town and the surrounding paddies and mountains are breathtaking. The castle museum has a few artefacts such as lacquered wares, clothing, weapons and scrolls. Be aware that the castle is closed in winter, when the Fukui snows make the ascent treacherous.

🔁 Getting there and around

- ✈️ Komatsu Airport. Use the limousine bus and then local trains to Echizen-Ono Station.
- 🚄 Kanazawa Station. Take JR and local lines to Echizen-Ono Station.
- 🚶 All the sights are within walking distance from Echizen-Ono Station. Alternatively, hire a bicycle from the JR station staff. The flat, grid-like layout of the town makes it simple to navigate and easy to manage on foot - at least until you reach the castle hill.

📗 Further information
www.100hiddentowns.jp/fukui/ono.html

Chubu-Hokuriku

若狭町

Fukui

WAKASA

This tranquil town on the Sea of Japan has it all. Its local history museum proudly displays the area's archaeological finds from the Jomon era, the Five Lakes of Mikata exhibit an array of Japanese countryside at its most resplendent, and visitors can also enjoy the treat of the area's culinary delights.

🌳 Nature Spot - Uriwarinotaki waterfall

Above a pretty park with ponds and watermills, is the Uriwarinotaki waterfall. This elegant feature has long been enjoyed for its spiritual qualities and has helped slake the thirst of travellers along the Saba Road. Even now, locals come to the spot to top up containers with fresh water. The waterfall gets its name from the temperature of the water. Uri means melon. Wari means split. So, the water was once regarded as so cold that it could split a melon!

204

👍 Must do! Mikatagoko (five lakes)

The lakes of Mikata have been revered at least since the 7th century - evidenced by the famous *Manyoshu* collection of poems which includes a *waka* (a traditional 31-syllable poem) devoted to them.

Many lakeside residents make their living from the plentiful fish that inhabit the lake, including carp, eel and shrimp. Eel from the area have been supplied to Kyoto since the Edo era. A technique known as *tataki ami* (literally, beating net) is a traditional way to make a good catch.

Each of the five lakes has distinctive characteristics, with the water differing in each one, from the freshwater of the lakes further inland, through the brackish waters of the smaller lakes, that then join the sea-facing salt water of the coastal lakes.

Beside Lake Mikata, there are prominent, traditional boathouses known as *Funagoya*, which have distinctive thatched roofs. They are especially beautiful when covered with snow in the winter months.

The lakes are the natural habitat of a number of birds, and there are several spots along the shores for twitchers. For walkers, trails from the lakes head off into the adjoining woods and beside rivers where traditional farmhouses and boat sheds can be observed.

On the west shore of Lake Suigetsu, there are souvenir shops, accommodation, and tourist boats if you fancy a leisurely cruise. Nearer to Mikata Station, next to the Wakasa Mikata Jomon Museum, is a *michi-no-eki* store where visitors can stock up on local produce such as the region's ubiquitous *umeboshi* (Japanese pickled plums).

There are several ways to enjoy a trip to the lakes of Wakasa. Hiring a bicycle from one of the spots on the lake shores and circumnavigating the area is extremely pleasant, thanks to the lakeside lanes devoted to cyclists and walkers. Alternatively, take a drive along the Rainbow Line toll road in the mountains above the lakes, to get stunning views, or hop on a boat tour to see the lake from a duck's-eye view.

🔍 Did you know?

Miracle lake
Lake Suigetsu is internationally renowned among geologists for its varve sediment. This is sediment that has collected at the bottom of the lake over thousands of years (at an average of just 7cm every 100 years), and its analysis provides valuable information for radiocarbon dating.

Why is the sediment so valuable to scientists? No major river flows into the lake and there is no oxygen at its bottom, so no animal can survive there and affect the sediment. Lake Suigetsu's varves remain untouched and undisturbed, earning it the moniker of 'the miracle lake'.

205

Chubu-Hokuriku

若狭町

Fukui

WAKASA

🏠 Culture Spot - Kumagawa-Juku Historic Post Town

Located five kilometres from Kaminaka Station are the historical buildings of Kumagawa. The area prospered as a post town along the Saba Road, where *saba* (mackerel) and other fresh fish were transported all the way from Wakasa Bay down to the hungry markets of landlocked Kyoto. The narrow road has old warehouses, townhouses, shops and even a guardhouse, and is a peaceful reminder of a bygone Japan. At the end of the road is a small museum, which has a little English, explaining the history of the Saba Road, where the fish were conveyed overnight by horse or on foot. Kumagawa reached its bustling and thriving peak in the early 18th century, but conscientious preservation of the buildings ensures a real treat for visitors to this day.

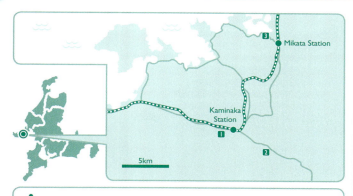

Key dates

mid-May Saturday and Sunday - Wakasa Mikatagoko Two Day March (five lakes walking event)

August - Wakasa Uriwari Water Festival

mid-September - Wakasa Mikata Jomon Festival (food, activities and nature at the Jomon Park) - also known as Wakasai.

🏠 Culture Spot - Wakasa Mikata Jomon Museum

This museum, dedicated to exhibits of the area's ancient history, is a fascinating treat. There are 9,000-year-old pots, and ancient wooden longboats reminding visitors that the Jomon period was an era of sophisticated craftsmanship - their clothes even displayed a sense of fashion. The area here, known as Torihama, has had major excavations which show that the lakes of Wakasa were a vital source of fodder for the ancient Japanese. The museum has wall friezes and models depicting life in the period, and any visitor will likely feel wistful for the seemingly peaceful, less frenetic existence on display.

Models also show the diet of the era. It wasn't just fish, but wild boar, deer, vegetables and nuts that the Jomon people of the area consumed.

Outside this excellent museum, there are full-scale replicas of Jomon-era

homes set against the backdrop of the Mikata Lake, which help visitors to more fully visualise the lifestyle of the era.

We say

"Wakasa is simply one of the most peaceful places I have been to - especially in Japan, where it can be difficult to get away from noise. When cycling around the lake, enjoying the gorgeous views of the waters against mountain backdrops, there were no sounds, save for the lake's waters lapping the shoreline, and ducks quacking beneath the circling hawks. Topped off with quality food and a bit of history at the Jomon Museum and Kumagawa, Wakasa is a real treat."

Recommended for

Nature lovers

Enthusiasts of history - both ancient and recent

Those looking for a very quiet break away from it all

⇄ Getting there and around

✈ Komatsu Airport. Travel by local bus and train services to Mikata Station.

🚆 Tsuruga Station. Travel by local train services to Mikata Station or Kaminaka Station.

🚗 A rental car or taxi is necessary for the Rainbow Line route above the lakes. Bicycles can be hired from various locations, including Mikata Station, for a 25-kilometre jaunt around the lakes. At Kaminaka Station, you can hire a taxi or rent a bicycle to see the recommended sights of Uriwari waterfall and Kumagawa-Juku.

📖 Further information

www.100hiddentowns.jp/fukui/wakasa.html

207

Chubu-Hokuriku

Gifu

GERO

下呂市

Though not well known among foreign visitors, Gero has long been a place of recuperation and relaxation for the Japanese, thanks to its hot springs - including open air baths and free foot spas that can be found dotted around the town.

Set in a striking valley, criss-crossed by two rivers, the town is perfect for strolling around, sampling local goods, and as a base for hikes further afield. Combine a soak with a visit to the nearby Gassho Village in the hills above the town, or go hiking amid the lush nature of Gandate Kyo. Gero is ideal for a two or three-day stay.

Culture Spot - Gero Onsen Gassho Village [1]

In the hills above the town centre, Gero Onsen Gassho Village contains several reconstructions of mountain village architecture, and includes buildings relocated from the better-known tourist spot of Shirakawa-go, also in Gifu.

Some of the houses have life-size models of farmers, and artefacts that help to illustrate the rural lifestyles of pre-industrial Japan.

Visitors can also try their hand at workshops, to make ceramic art or patterned Japanese *washi* paper. There are restaurants, performances of folk tales, and even a slide on which restless children can speed down on mats from the top of the hill.

Food and Drink - Tenryo Brewery [2]

Rice flourishes in the Hida region, making use of the soft water from the Japanese Northern Alps, so it is no surprise that *sake* is a renowned product of the area. With a prior booking, you can observe the brewing process up close at the Tenryo Brewery in Hida-Hagiwara - a business boasting a 300-year history. The impressive containers for the *sake* are massive at 10,000 litres, which equates to around 4,000 bottles. The alcohol is brewed in winter, undergoing a meticulous, labour-intensive production process, from rice milling to fermentation, stirring of the vats with long poles, pressing, until the final bottling stage, which is followed by aging the *sake* prior to shipping. After the tour, enjoy a tasting of their products, with the deliciously sweet 'Gin' *sake* especially recommended. A must-visit for connoisseurs of *nihonshu*.

Did you know?

Feeling sick?
The Chinese characters for Gero mean 'Lower Bath', but the pronunciation is the same as the Japanese word for vomit.

This doesn't seem to have affected the popularity of the town, and maybe helps to keep it in the public eye!

Razan-rated
In the Edo era, the poet, philosopher and advisor to the early Tokugawa shoguns, Hayashi Razan, named Gero as one of the top three *onsen* resorts in Japan. It's unlikely that he visited enough to be able to judge authoritatively, but the town's pretty situation and laid-back atmosphere are said to be unchanged since those days.

Key dates

August 1-4 - Gero Onsen Matsuri (parades, fireworks and stalls)

We say

" Gero is a great place with plenty to offer. Just a relaxing *onsen* stay will suffice, but it is definitely worth making the effort to get out to Gandate Kyo and catch the countryside at its best. I was surprised and delighted to see wild monkeys at play, and huge frogs hopping out of our path. "

Recommended for

Hikers
Relaxing breaks
Families

Must do! Gandate Kyo 3

A 40-minute drive from central Gero, or 20 minutes from nearby Hida-Osaka Station, 54,000-year-old lava from the Mount Ondake volcano forms the steep cliffs and rock formations of Gandate. Knowledgeable guides can be hired to take visitors on two or four-hour routes around this wonderful valley full of flowing waterfalls and fascinating plants and wildlife.

Chances are you will come across wild animals. Grasshoppers, monkeys, and astonishingly well-camouflaged frogs can be seen, as well as evidence of more elusive beasts such as wild boars. These dig holes in the paths to form mud baths in which they roll to rid themselves of insects clinging to their fur. There are also squirrels that strip tree bark to make high nests, beyond the reach of predators.

The courses are not too tough, and school age kids are welcome. Tours are conducted even in the rain, when the usually serene emerald waters of the rivers and streams become noisy, gushing torrents.

Getting there and around

- Chubu Centrair International Airport. Take local train services to Gero Station.
- Nagoya Station. Take local train services to Gero Station.
- Gero is prettily set and a joy to walk around, with foot spas and souvenir shops aplenty. The surrounding mountains help the town to retain its charm, despite the occasional functional eyesore.

Culture Spot
Gero Museum of Hot Spring 4

Good as a rainy day option, this *onsen* museum houses displays and artefacts explaining the history of, and science behind, hot springs. A craft area allows visitors to make a traditional print postcard, and a foot spa on the museum balcony is a nice spot to relax. A sign recommends visitors do three laps of the waters of the foot spa as an aid to blood circulation.

Further information
www.100hiddentowns.jp/gifu/gero.html

Chubu-Hokuriku

Ishikawa
HAKUSAN 白山市

The town of Hakusan stretches from the port of Mikawa on the Sea of Japan, to the inland peak of Mount Hakusan. Its blend of culture, history, nature and unique cuisine ensures that it has much to offer any keen Japanophile.

Culture Spot - Shirayama-Hime Shrine

Mount Hakusan towers over the local area, literally and figuratively. Combining both aspects, the God of Hakusan is said to actually reside here. The Hakusan *kami* is a god of water and of harmony. These facets are mirrored in the approach route to Shirayama-Hime Shrine - a tree-lined stone walkway, with a small brook gently working its way down the slope. This place of worship is the head shrine for over 3,000 Shirayama shrines across Japan. To the back of the complex, there is a pool of water from Mount Hakusan where, at certain times, it is possible to see monks immersed in its freezing embrace as part of their ascetic training.

Food and Drink - Kikusake

Four great rivers have their origins on Mount Hakusan. The icy waters of the mountain are said to give the local *sake*, Hakusan Kikusake, its distinctive taste. So proud are the town's residents of their famous beverage that they have applied to the WTO's geographical indication system, to have Hakusan Kikusake recognised in the same way as Bordeaux wines and Scottish whisky. There are a number of breweries in the area, and one of them, Manzairaku, has a shop in Tsurugi Town at their former brewing site. The building itself is over 240 years old, and inside you will see a kettle hung over a small fire, the flames of which have been constantly burning, without interruption, for as long as the building has been there. Inside, there is the chance to purchase, and try, any of their signature rice wines. Particularly recommended are some of the seasonal limited editions.

Must see!
Shiramine Snowman Festival

With such large amounts of snow every year, a snowman festival is a logical choice. The festival is held on consecutive Fridays in late January and early February, first at Kuwashima and then at Shiramine village. Like the village, the festival has a lot of local charm with an ad hoc air, as families and businesses all construct snowmen outside their houses, without a set plan - snowmen families enjoying dinner at a table set with food and drink, a giant snow Thomas the Tank Engine for children to sit in and many, many more. Keep out the cold with bowls of *miso* soup or steamed bean buns from tables the locals set up along the roads. In the centre of the village, there is a giant snow slide for children to throw themselves down.

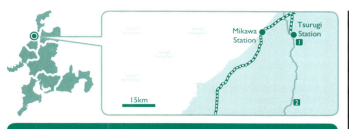

🍶 Food and Drink - Pickled blowfish ovaries

The consumption of *fugu* (blowfish) is famous worldwide due to the fact that, if prepared incorrectly, it can kill you. Enough poison is stored in the ovaries of the blowfish to kill five or six people. This accounts for why pickled blowfish ovary is sometimes referred to as a 'miracle food'. Only produced in the Mikawa area of Hakusan, the ovaries become edible through being pickled in salt, rice bran, fish oils and *sake* residue in a process that takes three years. During this time the poison is not just drawn out of the ovaries, it is actually reduced in toxicity. How this happens is still a mystery. The pickling takes place in factories on the dockside, right where the fish is unloaded. The factory certainly has a distinctive smell of pickled fish and is a fascinating insight into production of this strangest of foods. During the three year process, the ovaries are stored in barrels that are over 30 years old. The barrels turn a metallic red as the poisons leak out. The finished product has a sharp and almost spicy taste, and is a delicacy served best with rice and some of the local *sake*. Factory visits will need to be booked in advance and are best arranged by contacting the local tourist information centre.

🏠 Culture Spot - Shiramine Historical Buildings 2

Shiramine is a small village backed by mountains on the Tedori lake. Well known as the trail head for those wishing to ascend Hakusan, it maintains much of the character of towns from an earlier century, with narrow streets and cluttered wooden buildings. With the areas receiving more than four metres of snow annually, the local architecture has used a combination of timber and mud-lined walls to protect the locals from the climate.

⇌ Getting there and around

- ✈ Komatsu Airport. Travel by local bus and train services to the Hakusan area.
- 🚉 Kanazawa Station. Travel by local train services to Mikawa Station or Tsurugi Station.
- 🚗 The sights mentioned are spread out, so making use of a rental car is the most convenient way of getting around.

📖 Further information

www.100hiddentowns.jp/ishikawa/hakusan.html

❓ Did you know?

Festival for the fossil finder

The local area is referred to by some as the birthplace of geology in Japan, with many plant and dinosaur fossils having been found in the area from the early Cretaceous period. They were first discovered by a visiting Prussian geographer, Dr. Rein, on his way down from climbing Hakusan. There is a monument and even a festival named after him.

Key dates

late January - early February - Snowman Festival (one-day event)

We say

" A great spot to visit, thanks to its mixture of different attractions. Time a visit for the Snowman Festival for good family fun. "

Recommended for

Sake enthusiasts

Nature lovers

Chubu-Hokuriku

Ishikawa — WAJIMA
輪島市

The coastal town of Wajima, perched near the top of Ishikawa Prefecture's Noto area, is a tough place to access, taking two hours by bus from Kanazawa, but the effort is well-rewarded. Wajima is nationally renowned for its historical lacquerware tradition, but also attracts visitors who come to enjoy the architecture, morning market, a foot spa and the seaside views.

🌳 Nature Spot - Senmaida Rice Paddies

Ten kilometres up the coast from the town centre, visitors can relish the rare sight of paddies overlooking the ocean. Wajima's *senmaida* is a terraced hillside that descends to the waterfront. There is also an eatery here.

🏠 Culture Spot - Wajima Kiriko Art Museum [2]

This modern, crescent-shaped museum on the seafront houses more than 30 *kiriko* giant lanterns (10-15 metres tall, weighing up to two tons) used in the August Grand Festival, and also one of the huge poles of tethered bamboo that are set aflame at the climax of the actual festivities. You can inspect the intricate handiwork of the *kiriko* from ground level, or from a sloped gantry that leads up to the top of the exhibits. The third floor provides views of the town and the ocean, plus the giddying vertical drop down to the bottom of the tethered pole.

👍 Must do! - Morning Market

On each weekday*, Wajima's cobbled street market stirs into life from about 8 a.m. The vendors simply shift their wares from inside their premises out onto the road. Visitors can shop for fresh vegetables and locally caught seafood, including the eye-wateringly expensive abalone, but the main attraction is the *Wajimanuri* lacquerware. Beautifully crafted cups and bowls displaying strata of rich pigment have been made and sold in Wajima for over 600 years and command a high price to this day. A more affordable option for the casual shopper is the hand-painted chopsticks which also exhibit a formidable level of craftsmanship. Prices are coarsely divided between cheap (imported, mass-produced) and not cheap (locally hand-crafted). Be on your guard against thieves who swoop down from the sky for ice creams - Wajima has an audacious avian population. (*Wajimanuri* is also displayed at the Wajima Urushi Craft Museum, and there is a tour of craftsmen's studios available.)

* Except the second and fourth Wednesdays of each month, and Jan 1-3.

🔁 Getting there and around

- Noto Setoyama Airport. Travel to Wajima Town by taxi (this can be pre-booked).
- Kanazawa Station. Travel by express bus to Wajima Town (two hours).
- Wajima's morning market and Kiriko Art Museum are a short walk from the town's bus station. A trip to Senmaida Rice Paddies will take about 40 minutes by bicycle (available from the tourist information centre) along the hilly coastal road. Four-wheeled transport is recommended for excursions any further afield.

📗 Further information
www.100hiddentowns.jp/ishikawa/wajima.html

💡 Did you know?

Lacquer knowledge
Wajimanuri is Wajima's unique technique of applying natural lacquer mixed with *jinoko*, a finely powdered mineral, to wooden wares. The complex process can involve as many as 124 different stages, performed by an association of specialist master craftsmen.

Crafty verse
While many visitors to Japan will know of *haiku* poetry, Wajima's own *dandara* word game, developed by generations of lacquer craftsmen, might be a revelation. The poem has four phrases, consisting of five, then seven, then seven, then five syllables - but the two seven-syllable phases are homophones. *Dandara* poems are hung from the lampposts that run from Wajima's roadside station to the morning market.

Key dates
August 22-25 - Wajima Grand Festival (parade of giant *kiriko* lanterns, and *mikoshi* carried into the sea)

We say
❝ Wajima is abuzz in the morning - friendly market traders, a bustling harbour and wheeling birds of prey. The wide boulevards, uncluttered by overhead power cables, make sauntering around town whilst admiring the Meiji/Taisho-era architecture a breezy pleasure. If there is money burning a hole in your pocket, *Wajimanuri* makes for a classy keepsake of your trip. ❞

Recommended for
Coastal cycle rides
Lacquerware enthusiasts

213

Chubu-Hokuriku

伊勢市 ISE

Mie

The ancient spiritual heart of Japan beats on in this quiet, backwoods town. As the centre of pilgrimage in Japan for more than a thousand years, Ise offers the chance to slip back in time and experience the unchanging air of the shrines. With over 125 shrines in the area and a beautiful coastal locale, Ise is a must-see on any list.

Kids - Ise Azuchi Momoyama Jokamachi

During the Azuchi Momoyama period, great warlords gathered vast armies and battled their neighbours, all hoping to unite the kingdom and take up the mantle of shogun. The country was finally tamed, and the samurai took up graceful domesticity, but the Ise Azuchi Momoyama Jokamachi celebrates that great warring age. Aimed at kids, there are chances to dress up, enjoy shows, and see period-dressed performers.

Must see! Ise Jingu

In tradition, it was Yamatohime-no-Mikoto, the daughter of Emperor Suinin, who first founded this shrine at Ise, looking for a permanent location to worship the deity, Amaterasu Omikami. This was more than 2,000 years ago, and the inner (Naiku) and outer (Geku) shrines themselves may have first appeared as key places of worship in the third and fifth centuries.

What is known is that the first buildings date back to Emperor Tenmu (673-686), and that Ise is, and always has been, the main focus of worship and pilgrimage in the Shinto religion. So popular was it that an estimated one in ten Japanese people visited Ise during the Edo period, despite the travel involved.

There are over 125 shrines in the Ise area, but the two main ones are Naiku and Geku. The traditional route is to take in Geku first, before moving on to Naiku, about five kilometres away.

The main sanctuary buildings are rebuilt every 20 years, on an adjacent site, following exactly the same design - a system dating back to the first rebuilding in 690. Each one has its alternate location next to it.

This constant rebuilding is perhaps the most fascinating aspect of Ise. You are not seeing an antique building, aged and crumbling, or a modern interpretation - at Ise you get to see them in exactly the same condition as generations of pilgrims have, stretching back 1,500 years. This is a rare chance to experience real history, as you step into a place that would appear unchanged to a visitor from centuries before.

The buildings themselves are clinically simple in their lines and design.

Their architecture is considered a pure Japanese style, as they were constructed before any influence from mainland Asia arrived. Simple, unadorned wood beams hold up plain thatched roofs. The clean wood flows down into a carpet of white stones. The sanctuary buildings themselves are actually invisible, hidden away behind a white curtain that occasionally whisks aside to allow glimpses of beyond. Ise is perhaps all the more impressive because of what you cannot see. The buildings seem like they are being withdrawn from view, the sense of holiness increased as everyone has to create their own temple in the mind.

Of the grounds themselves, gravel paths wind past streams and tall trees, and over wooden bridges to lead you on to your goal.

Ise is the most sacred and perhaps the greatest of all the shrines in Japan and, as with pilgrims of the past, should be the main focus of any trip to this area.

Did you know?

Worth a second look

The august sounding Princess Yamatohime-no-Mikoto, daughter of 11th Emperor Suinin, visited the area and the coastline in mythic times, and was so struck by the coastal beauty that she looked back to view it again. In Japanese, to look twice would be *futa-mi*, and so the area got its name.

Chubu-Hokuriku

Mie

伊勢市 ISE

🏠 Culture Spot - Futami [3]

The beach at Futami, with tall elegant pines shading the wooden fronts of the hotels and stores, has something of the air of a late-19th-century European beach resort. Enjoy the period charms of a bygone age and watch the sun chase the shadows across Ise Bay to the land behind. Futami has a range of *ryokan* to stay in, and is a good base for exploring the area.

👪 Kids - Ise Meotoiwa Interactive Aquarium [4]

Billed as a somewhat intriguing 'petting aquarium', this marine-themed amusement park has perhaps seen better days.

There are regular shows from the walruses, dolphins and seals that populate the aquarium and allow you to get up close and have your photo taken with them. Hopefully one day the slightly incongruous guinea pigs will also don swimwear and take the plunge too.

🏠 Culture Spot - Oharaimachi [5] Okage Yokocho [6]

Oharaimachi is the one-kilometre-long traditional approach to the inner shrine. The road has lost none of its hustle and bustle from Edo times, when around 400,000 pilgrims a year used to proceed down here en route to their final destination. Shops and vendors offer refreshments and souvenirs, especially the traditional *akafuku* (red bean sweets). Just off to one side of the main road is Okage Yokocho. This recently constructed area features Edo-period-style shops, buildings and entertainers, offering another chance to dip briefly into the past. After the serenity of the shrine, Oharaimachi offers a chance to reacquaint yourself with the pleasures of the physical world.

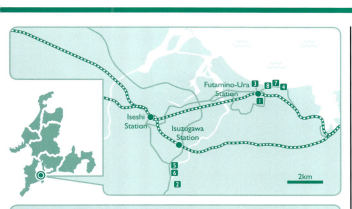

Key dates

May, September & December - Meotoiwa Rock Festival (the symbolic rope connecting the two rocks at Meotoiwa is replaced three times a year in a special event)

early October - Ise Festival (this two-day event is a traditional festival featuring parades, markets, and refreshment stalls)

We say

" For those with an interest in ancient Japan and especially the shrines and temples, Ise is a must. Some of the best shrines in Japan are preserved here in a wonderful state. Futami makes a pleasant side trip, and a chance to enjoy an old-style beach resort. "

Recommended for

History lovers

Relaxing weekends away

Families

🌳 Nature Spot - Meoto Iwa 7

Sitting in the waters just off the coastline of Futami are the Meoto Iwa, literally 'wedded rocks'. The larger represents the husband and the smaller represents the wife, symbolically linked by a sacred *shimenawa* rope. Best viewed at sunrise where, if you are fortunate, you can see the sun ascending between them, with Mount Fuji floating in the background.

🏠 Culture Spot - Hinjitsukan 8

First constructed in 1887 as an inn to accommodate visitors to Ise Jingu, Hinjitsukan remained in service until 1999, and has received a number of important guests over the years, including the Taisho Emperor. Now it is a museum, and gives a glimpse of how the well-heeled would have stayed and travelled in the Meiji period. Evocative wooden passageways and courtyards lead to the impressive grand hall.

🔁 Getting there and around

- ✈ Chubu Centrair International Airport. Travel by local train services to Iseshi Station.
- 🚄 Nagoya Station. Travel by local train services to Iseshi Station.
- 🚌 The two main sanctuary buildings are quite far apart, but there are regular tourist bus services between the two. Futami is a short train ride from central Ise.

📖 Further information

www.100hiddentowns.jp/mie/ise.html

Chubu-Hokuriku

熊野市

Mie

KUMANO

Kumano is famous among the Japanese as part of the ancient pilgrimage trail of the Mie area. The route was registered in 2004 as a World Heritage Site and, visiting here, it is easy to see why.

Aside from the Matsumoto Toge mountain trail of the area, there are plenty of other natural delights to enjoy, making an extended stay in the town worthwhile. Taxi tours and boat rides can be booked, to ensure visitors get the most out of the sights located away from the centre.

218

Food and Drink

Sanma (Pacific saury) sushi is presented with the whole fish on a bed of rice, cut up into mouthful-sized chunks - a method of preparation unique to the area.

Another regional dish is *mehari sushi* - a rice ball wrapped in the local pickled mustard leaf known as *takana*. The name allegedly derives from the need to open your eyes wide (*mehari*) as you chow down on the rice ball.

The area is also known for its vegetables. Drive along any road from the town centre, and you will soon find rows of unmanned miniature stalls stocked with fresh vegetables of all varieties, supplied directly from the farm. Just pop coins in the 'honesty box' and help yourself!

Culture Spot - Akagijo Castle Ruins ❶

Combine a trip to the Maruyama Senmaida rice terraces (see next page) with a climb to the top of the ruins of Akagijo. The castle walls are still intact and the ruins are surrounded by hills and forests. A wonderfully peaceful spot.

Must do! World Heritage Kumano Kodo Matsumoto Pass

A gentle hike along this mossy, cobblestoned path allows visitors to visualise the journeys of pilgrims from ancient times. Walkers can enjoy the tranquil woodland, but should always keep an eye on the path, as it is quite uneven and the moss makes it slippery, especially after rain, so take the opportunity to enjoy the trail at a leisurely pace rather than seeing it as a chance for exercise. The roots intertwine with the stones, and mountain crabs creep between the gaps, while gentle streams also contribute to the serene atmosphere.

The route ends at Odomari Beach ❷, which boasts golden sand and a great view. The trail is only about one kilometre in length, and rises to approximately 135 metres, taking about an hour at the recommended, gentle pace.

More energetic hikers have the option of continuing along further trails beyond Odomari Beach, returning via the same path to Kumano Town or by catching a train from Odomari Station back into town.

Did you know?

Don't shoot!
At the top of the Matsumoto Toge trail, visitors can see a *jizo* stone statue as the peak marker at an elevation of around 100 metres. The statue has a scar on its right cheek, which legend says was caused by a pilgrim shooting it, having mistaken it for a forest spirit.

The path to righteousness
Mie has long been a focus for pilgrimages, and the trails of the area were not just seen as a means of getting between the shrines of the region, but as holy experiences in themselves, by enabling worshippers to commune with the spirits via the wonderful countryside, or by struggling through the sometimes dangerous routes.

Chubu-Hokuriku

Mie — KUMANO — 熊野市

🌳 Nature Spot - Maruyama Senmaida

Hire a taxi or rent a car to head out of town and enjoy the remarkable terraced rice fields of Maruyama Senmaida. On the approach, the road narrows and starts winding uphill before striking upon a gorgeous valley filled with colours and smells.
Take a walk through the fields along the snaking path down to the valley, and don't forget to greet the scarecrows as you pass.

🏠 Culture Spot - Hananoiwaya Shrine

About a kilometre south of Kumano's town centre stands Hananoiwaya Shrine. At the end of a beautiful tree-lined approach, the shrine grounds open out. There, visitors hit upon a massive, sacred rock of approximately 45 metres in height. This rock has been an object of worship for hundreds of years, giving credence to the claim that Hananoiwaya is Japan's oldest shrine – it is said to have been visited since prehistoric times. Twice a year, in early February and October, a giant rope is pulled from the shrine grounds to the nearby beach by local worshippers, marking a festival considered unique, even for a country where distinctive festivals are commonplace.

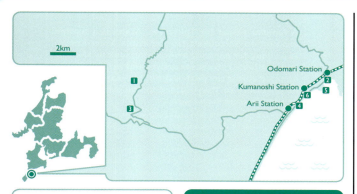

Key dates

February 2 - Hananoiwaya Spring Festival

early summer - Mushi Okuri (torch procession at Maruyama)

We say

" Kumano is a fantastic spot for hikers and nature lovers. The Matsumoto trail is a wonderful, tranquil hike that harks back to the slower days of ancient times. The rugged coastal cliff formations confirm that nature is truly the greatest artist, and Mie Prefecture is one of its canvases. "

Recommended for

Walkers

Nature lovers

🌳 Nature Spot - Onigajo 5

This coastal spot, translated as 'devil's castle,' is made up of astonishing cliff face formations shaped by erosion over the millennia. The wide area offers a variety of photo opportunities of both the formations themselves, and the peninsula across the bay, with waves crashing at the base of the promontory. It is a fantastic spot.

👨‍👩‍👧 Kids

Kids can enjoy Kumano's natural attractions as much as adults, with the rock formations and eroded cliffs providing a thrilling backdrop for coastal exploration. The challenge of the Matsumoto Toge trail is possible for any child above toddler age, with the reward of the Odomari Beach as the destination.

🌳 Nature Spot - Shishiiwa 6

Along the coast, just south of Onigajo and within walking distance from Kumanoshi Station, Shishiiwa ('lion rock') is another remarkable, eroded precipice. It acquired its name from its resemblance to a lion roaring out to the Pacific. In late spring, its jaws appear to grab the sun and, in November, the full moon.

🚉 Getting there and around

✈ Chubu Centrair International Airport or Kansai International Airport. Take local train services to Kumanoshi Station.

🚆 Nagoya Station. Travel by local rapid train down the coast to Kumanoshi Station.

🚶 The town itself is small and a pleasant setting for a stroll. The Matsumoto Toge trail is within walking distance of the station, but to reach the other recommended natural sites mentioned here, a car or taxi is necessary.

Various taxi sightseeing courses are offered by the tourist information centre directly opposite the station. These courses range in length from one to three hours.

📋 Further information

www.100hiddentowns.jp/mie/kumano.html

Chubu-Hokuriku

Shizuoka
ATAMI
熱海市

A familiar resort for Tokyoites, Atami is a seaside location on Shizuoka's Izu Peninsula. Long-known as a venue for enjoying a hot spring soak by the sea, and a notable retreat for artists and writers, Atami boomed during the post-war bubble years thanks to its proximity to Tokyo, aided by the establishment of a bullet train stop there.

Although those halcyon days are long over, Atami still attracts a large number of visitors, and its buildings and shops retain a certain Showa-era charm. The coastline is pretty, and ascending to the hills above the town, either by car, ropeway or on foot, affords rewarding views of the town, its hilly backdrop, the sea, as well as the tiny island of Hatsushima and the larger Oshima to the southeast.

👍 Must see! MOA Museum of Art

Originally established to display the art collection of an eccentric multimillionaire, the MOA Museum of Art is more than just a vanity project. This plush building up in the hills to the west of the station is a popular draw. The museum houses a range of works including Henry Moore sculptures, Heian-era decorative sutras, 14th-century painted scrolls, Edo-period calligraphy, and gorgeous folding screens.

The collection has extensive English explanations which provide detailed context on the artists and the subjects. Non-flash photography is allowed in the museum, and there are bamboo and teahouse gardens to stroll in.

The collection is small, especially in the context of the museum's vast size, but it's worth taking your time here and enjoying the gardens and sea views.

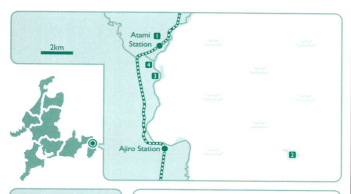

🌳 Nature Spot Hatsushima [2]

Regular boats ferry visitors to Hatsushima - a small island which is great for strolling around and that offers excellent views of Atami, set against its hilly backdrop. Enjoy the variety of flowers on the island, dip in a hot spring, and stop off at one of the seafront restaurants for a seafood dish.

🏠 Culture Spot - Trick Art Museum [3]

Adjacent to the kitschy Atami Castle is the much more rewarding Trick Art Museum. Each display is hands-on, with a chance to have your photo taken interacting with the art, or to enjoy the quizzes about the art as they play tricks on your eyes. It is a kaleidoscope of ideas and visual joy for all the family.

🏠 Culture Spot - Kiunkaku [4]

In the centre of Atami is a museum that was once the luxurious retreat of some of Japan's most domestically famous authors, such as Osamu Dazai and Yukio Mishima. The tranquil garden and private *onsen* evidently provided inspiration for the artists that frequented there.

⇌ Getting there and around

✈ Haneda Airport. Take local train services and bullet trains to Atami Station.
🚆 Atami Station.
🚶 The town clings to the coastline, and all the sights are within walking distance of the station, though be aware that the town is very hilly. There is also a local bus service which provides an all-day pass.

📖 Further information
www.100hiddentowns.jp/shizuoka/atami.html

👀 Did you know?

Hot sea

The *kanji* characters for Atami literally mean 'hot sea', and the town made its name through its many hot springs. Atami features in the classic Yasujiro Ozu 1950s film 'Tokyo Story', where the busy Tokyo-based adult offspring of the main elderly characters send them away to Atami for a break, rather than actually spending time with them themselves.

Key dates

mid-July - Atami Kogashi Festival (a parade of floats through the town)

every month - seaside fireworks displays

We say

"Atami is prettily located, and its Showa kitsch and general need of a lick of paint are actually quite charming. What once looked dated and sad, now looks nostalgic and even of historical interest!"

Recommended for

Day trippers from the Tokyo area

Family vacations

Chubu-Hokuriku

Shizuoka
SHIMODA
下田市

If you are looking for white sand beaches, crystal blue waters and hot springs where you can relax and unwind, then Shimoda is the place for you. Situated a few hours from Tokyo in the south of the Izu peninsula, it's the perfect place for a short break.

The historical importance of Shimoda is visible all over town as the port where Commodore Perry landed his 'black ships' from the US, and ended Japan's international isolation.

Must do! Museums and Sightseeing

The Museum of Black Ships ❶
This museum is dedicated to the arrival of the famous Black Ships that heralded the end of Japan's lengthy isolation from the rest of the world. The museum has two floors of exhibits that show the arrival of American, British, Russian and Dutch sailors and dignitaries. There are many items from the time, including letters, prints, clothing and weapons.

Perry Road ❷
Named after Commodore Perry, and apparently the road he took to Ryosenji Temple, this is a beautifully preserved street that runs each side of a river down to the sea. Its picturesque red bridges, and mix of small, old and new houses, cafes, restaurants and shops make for a lovely short walk.

Shimoda History Museum ❸
This museum focuses on Shimoda's role in Japanese history. There are many interesting exhibits (with English explanations) showing Perry's visits, and the establishment of Japan's relations with the US and Russia.

Shimoda Harbour Boat Tour ❹
Visitors can take a 20-minute tour of Shimoda Harbour in a replica of a Black Ship. The tour takes in the cliffs and small islands around the harbour, and its port of departure offers the opportunity to observe the local fish traders buy and sell the day's catch.

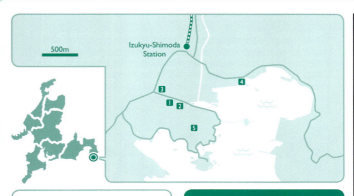

:question: Did you know?

Hordes of hydrangea

There are around three million hydrangea blossoms lining the route through the park and hillsides where June's Hydrangea Festival takes place.

Key dates

mid-May - Black Ship Festival (fireworks, parades and US/Japan cultural exchanges)

We say

" Shimoda and its surrounding beaches are a great spot to take things slowly and relax. You can visit the small museums and sights in Shimoda in one day, as they are all very close together. Although the local buses are frequent, if you're travelling to the beaches, I definitely recommend going by bicycle or car to allow more time to enjoy the surrounding countryside. "

Recommended for

History lovers

🏠 Culture Spot - Hydrangea Festival (throughout June)

This festival is a must for all flower enthusiasts to enjoy the full bloom of around 150,000 plants throughout the picturesque Shiroyama Park **5**. The park itself is built on the remains of a castle, and contains countless winding paths lined with flowers, and numerous spots to stop to rest, or even purchase Hydrangea plants from vendors located throughout the park. The course is steep in places and can be covered in one to three hours, depending on your pace.

🍽 Food and Drink

Seafood is a key draw for visitors to Izu. Popular dishes include *ise ebi* (king prawn). Measuring over 30 centimetres long, *ise ebi* is indeed the king! Eaten raw as *sashimi*, it has a delicate and slightly sweet taste.

⇌ Getting there and around

- ✈ Haneda Airport. Take local train services to Izukyu-Shimoda Station.
- 🚆 Atami Station. Travel by local train services to Izukyu-Shimoda Station.
- 🚶 The sights in Shimoda are within walking distance from each other, or there is the option to rent bicycles. Travelling by rental car is another great way to get around at your own pace. Rental cars can be picked up in Atami and then driven along the beautiful coastal roads and highways all the way to Shimoda. Great for travelling at leisure around the nearby beaches.

 Further information
www.100hiddentowns.jp/shizuoka/shimoda.html

Chubu-Hokuriku

氷見市

Toyama

HIMI

The sleepy, pleasant town of Himi is recommended to visit either as a day trip from nearby Takaoka, or as a more relaxing two-day stay. Coastal views and river walks abound, but the main reason to go is for its delicious food. Himi has its own speciality beef, *udon*, and curry, but the sheer variety of its seafood is the big sell for the town. Great for foodies.

🌳 Nature Spot - Asahiyama Park ⓘ

Just west of the town centre is Asahiyama Park. Stop by the beautifully set, creaking, wooden Jonichiji Temple and its tranquil pond, then clamber up the winding paths to enjoy panoramas of the town from the hilltop park. A clear day will allow excellent views of the surrounding peninsula. The observation tower, though an eyesore, is worth a climb for even further views.

A kids' park helps make Asahiyama a good day out for the family.

The more energetic can go on even further, up to the Fureainomori forest area for short hiking trails.

 Did you know?

Manga mania
Famous manga artist Motoo Abiko, better known as Fujiko Fujio Ⓐ, was born in Himi in 1934. His best-known works include Ninja Hattori-kun and Kaibutsu-kun.

As well as the Manga Road, there is a small museum of his work in the centre of the town.

Key dates
April 17 - Marumage Festival
April 17-18 - Gon-gon Festival
end of May - Nagasaka Rice Terrace tourist event (designated one of the 100 best rice terraces in Japan)

We say
" Combined with a trip to nearby Takaoka, Himi is a great visit for a bit of fresh air and for lovers of Japanese seafood. A big meal and a stroll round the town is a superb way to spend a few hours. Bring a big appetite! "

Recommended for
Food lovers

 Must see! Marumage Festival (April 17)

Historically in Japan, *marumage* is the round, knotted hairstyle that was traditionally worn to signify a betrothed female. The origins of Himi's Marumage Festival date back to when *geisha*, wishing for a happy marriage, would have their hair done in the *marumage* style and would pray at Senjuji Temple ❷ in the city. Nowadays, any women are free to participate in the festivities.

The festival involves a colourful parade of *mikoshi* portable shrines and musicians, children wearing decorative hats, followed by women with *marumage* hairstyles. It is a lively, fun festival, forming a highlight of the town's year.

Also on the 17th and the 18th is the Gon-gon Festival at Jonichiji Temple ❸ at the foot of Asahiyama Park, where you can hear, and indeed have a try yourself at, the ringing of a huge bell with a choice of two long logs. The festival has its roots in farmers striking the bell as a prayer for rain.

 Kids The centre of the town has a street known as Manga Road, which has a tie up with the Himi-born manga artist Fujiko Fujio Ⓐ. Statues of his characters line the streets to welcome locals and visitors alike. The street culminates at the Ninja Hattori-kun Automaton Clock on a bridge crossing the Minato River. There are regular performances here from spring to autumn, where statues of manga characters on the bridge spray out water.

Culture Spot - Himi Banya-gai ❹

Banya-gai is the name of the mall of souvenir shops and restaurants located a short walk to the north of the town. Local food can be sampled here and all your souvenir needs can be covered. The food court is a great place to try local snacks such as beef sushi, spicy beef croquettes, ice cream and Himi's own curry recipe. Next to the shopping area is an *ashi-yu*, where you can dip your toes in the cloudy hot spring water for free.

 Getting there and around

- Toyama Airport. Travel by limousine bus and local train to Himi Station.
- Shin-Takaoka Station. Travel by local train services to Himi Station.
Toyama Station. Slightly longer alternative, serviced by trains and buses.
- Getting around Himi is quite manageable on foot or by bicycle. Bicycles can be rented between 9am and 4pm from Himi Station or the Himi Banya-gai shopping area.

 Further information
www.100hiddentowns.jp/toyama/himi.html

Chubu-Hokuriku

KAMIICHI 上市町

Toyama

Kamiichi lies sandwiched between the mountains and the sea. The town feels dominated by the overwhelming nature surrounding it, and has the feel of a country town from 50 years ago. Relax in its easy charms and enjoy the temples, baths and mountains.

🏠 Culture Spot - Downtown Tours

The tourist information centre at Kamiichi Station offers mountain bike rental. Those with the necessary energy and fitness levels can try to make it out to the more further-flung parts of Kamiichi, although beware of the hills once out of town. For easier options, visitors can try some of the model cycling courses around the town. Kamiichi has rice fields, houses, and shrines stitched together against the backdrop of the Northern Alps. Some sights in the vicinity include:

Otori Shrine [1]
Otori Shrine is hidden in the grounds of a high school. It is a small and slightly overgrown shrine - however its main highlight is the preserved roots of a giant cedar tree. Originally there were three huge cedar trees in Kamiichi, dating back hundreds of years, and they were symbols of the town. However, two of them perished during the war and were lost to the town. When the last remaining cedar also came down, the locals preserved its massive base and set it on display in a small building just off the main shrine.

Kitajima Shrine [2] Zenshoji Temple [3]
A small shrine, just back from the river, Kitajima is a fine example of a functional, local shrine. Zenshoji Temple is also of a similar character.

228

👍 Must see! Oiwasan Nissekiji Temple 4

Built in 725, Oiwasan Nissekiji is the head temple for the Shingon Mishu sect. It is a pleasant shrine, but its main attraction may be the opportunity to try out various traditional Buddhist rituals such as Takigyo and Shabutsu. Takigyo is the purifying ritual of standing under a waterfall, and there is a choice of six spots from which the water pours onto you. Shabutsu involves the copying of Buddhist images, and to speed up the process, the staff will put an outline of the image onto the paper provided. You will need to book in advance if you wish to take part. There is also a series of traditional shops on the road beside the temple, which provide a good opportunity to try some Japanese sweets and the local speciality, Oiwa Somen noodles.

🤔 Did you know?

Holy crab!
The most famous spots on Mount Tsurugi are Kani-no-tatebai and Kani-no-yokobai. The names literally mean the place where you have to scuttle up or sideways like a crab. The first involves climbing a rock face, and the second involves having to take a blind step onto, hopefully, a foothold beneath you. Enjoy!

🏠 Culture Spot
Ryusenji Temple 5

Ryusenji Temple was built in 1370, and is on a small rise, a short drive out of the main town. The temple is approached via a tree-lined avenue dating back several hundred years. Follow this through the woods to the main temple precinct, built in a quadrangle style with the main shrine on the opposite side to the entrance. Other paths lead either to the top of the hill or else flow down to the riverside. Relax and enjoy 'forest therapy' in the countryside environs.

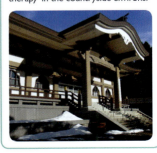

🏠 Culture Spot
Nishida Museum 6

Opened in 1993 by, and named after, the founder of the Fuji Chemical Industry Company, the Nishida Museum is a somewhat eclectic mixture of styles and artefacts. The works on show represent a personal collection and are said to symbolise the flow of the Eurasian continent from the ancient to the modern. As such, you can find Byzantine and Greek pottery, Russian icons, and Egyptian reliefs occupying adjacent displays. The museum also features several mandala paintings, and has a pleasant garden at the front.

229

Chubu-Hokuriku

Toyama
KAMIICHI 町市上

🌳 Nature Spot - Mount Tsurugi

Rejoicing in the catchphrase 'the most dangerous mountain climbable', Mount Tsurugi certainly has the power to quicken the pulse of even experienced hikers, and this does set it apart as one of the most sought-after peaks to climb in Japan. Tsurugi had been considered unconquered until 1907, but when the summit was finally reached, a number of small metal items were found. They turned out to be religious items dating back to the Heian period, over a thousand years prior. As you use fixed chains to scramble up the sheer sides of the mountain, it does make you wonder about a monk scaling Tsurugi all those years ago, with perhaps just a stick and wooden shoes. Ascending the mountain is a wonderful experience, but don't go anywhere near it unless you know what you are doing, as it is only recommended for experienced climbers.

🌳 Nature Spot
Anantan Miraculous Water 7

Designated one of the 100 best spring water locales in Japan, Anantan is a slightly Heath-Robinson-esque hybrid of a traditional shrine coupled with the pipe and scaffolding of a small scale, bottling factory. The water is free if you want to just top up your bottle. There are also a number of walks into the surrounding countryside from here.

🏠 Culture Spot
Tsurugi-no-Ajikura 8

Set in the middle of swaying rice fields, Tsurugi-no-Ajikura sells local produce and is a good place to get your hands on some local rice. They also do an array of other local fare including teas, jams and curry.

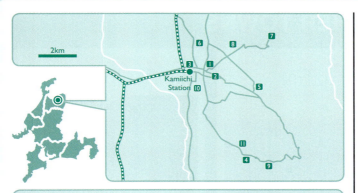

🏠 Culture Spot - Ookami Wolf House [9]

Located an ambitious 25-minute cycle uphill from Nissekiji Temple is the Ookami Wolf House. It's a very atmospheric example of a Japanese country house. Its fame comes from featuring in the anime hit, Wolf Children, and is run by a group of friendly local residents.

🌳 Nature Spot
Alps-no-yu [10]

Stretch out and relax in the hot water piped down from the Northern Alps and watch the locals chat and gossip whilst lounging in the open air. There are a variety of baths for men and women, and a restaurant on site.

🌳 Nature Spot
Oiwa Fudo Onsen [11]

Oiwa Fudo is a small, local bath, somewhat hidden away. Its secluded nature is a great chance to experience a more ascetic, country *onsen*.

⇌ Getting there and around

- ✈ Toyama Airport. Take local bus and train services to Kamiichi Station.
- 🚆 Toyama Station. Take local trains to Kamiichi Station.
- 🚴 Most of the attractions listed are a little spread out and probably preclude walking. However, most are reachable by bicycle.

📖 Further information
www.100hiddentowns.jp/toyama/kamiichi.html

Key dates

mid-February - Mount Tsurugi Snow Festival (food, drinks and stalls in the town centre)

June 1 - Opening of Mount Tsurugi (a small religious ceremony at the base of the mountain to offer prayers for the coming climbing season)

August 13 - Kamiichi Hometown Festival (traditional summer festival featuring food, dancing and fireworks)

We say

" Kamiichi is a nice example of a local country town. There is a fine mix of heritage and nature that will make exploring the town a rewarding experience. Climbers will delight in the challenge that Mount Tsurugi provides. "

Recommended for

Hikers

Nature lovers

CHUBU-HOKURIKU
OTHER TOWNS

Fukui
ECHIZEN

Aside from Echizen Town itself, the municipality also includes three other neighbouring towns - Otacho, Miyazakimura, and Asahicho. The area is relatively remote, in that it is not served by train or highway, and the buses there are infrequent. The fact that the town attracts so many visitors is testimony to the variety of attractions on offer - from tasting some of the best crab in Japan, to making your own pottery, or exploring the rocky splendour of the Sea of Japan coastline.

Culture Spot Echizen Pottery Village
Nature Spot Echizen Kaigan coast
Must do Echizen Crab Museum
We say A great place to visit for the wonderful coastline, but a car or taxi will be required.

Fukui
MINAMIECHIZEN

Minamiechizen is located on the coast of Fukui Prefecture. Summer activities include hiking and diving, while nearby ski slopes operate during the winter. The area has flat, rice-growing farmland, punctuated by mist-shrouded hills. There is a historical Korean influence on local trade, owing to the town's proximity to sea trading routes.

Culture Spots Imajo Juku, Imajo 365 Ski Area
Must see Kitamae Ship Owners' Residences (Kono)
We say Minamiechizen Town's antiquity is barely more impressive than that of many small, rural towns, but the nearby coastal spot of Kono is pretty and fascinating. Access to its fabulous, huge, old Kitamae Ship Owners' Houses is via an evocative backstreet, lined on each side with beautiful buildings dating back to the Edo period.

Ishikawa
TSUBATA

Conveniently located near the popular tourist spot of Kanazawa, Tsubata is an excellent destination for a number of reasons, depending on your tastes. The outskirts offer the vast forests of Shinrin Park, the cultural properties of Kurikara Fudoji temple, and the historical legacy of the adjacent Kurikara Battlefield. Top it all with a seafood meal in the quiet town centre to make the trip one to remember.

Culture Spot Kurikara Fudoji Temple
Nature Spot Shinrin Park
Must see Kurikara Battlefield
We say Certainly a town for Japanese history and culture buffs or those who can't get enough of locally sourced seafood. The town itself retains a certain charm harking back to its more illustrious past. Its proximity to Kanazawa marks it as an easily accessible day trip, especially if you have your own transportation.

Mie
IGA

Iga is a historical town, slightly overshadowed by its more famous neighbour, Ise. There is a pleasant castle in the centre of town that offers nice views of the surrounding low-lying hills, but Iga's two main claims to fame are its historical roots as the home of Ninjutsu martial arts, and as the birthplace of Basho, the legendary poet. Take in the castle, soak up the atmosphere of the famous bard, and then explode into action at the Ninja Museum.

Culture Spot Memorial Museum, Basho birthplace, Minomushi-an, Iga Ninja Museum
Must see Iga Castle
We say Iga has more than enough to make it a pleasant day out for those in the area, and its compact centre makes it easy to navigate around. The variety of different attractions means there should be something for everyone. Especially recommended for those with a keen interest in Japanese history.

Shizuoka
MATSUZAKI

This sleepy port town, located on the southwest of the Izu peninsula, is famous for its beautiful view of Mount Fuji looming high over the Southern Alps, across the sea from the port. Blessed with countless hot spring resorts and baths, this is a place to unwind and wander around – a fantastic retreat from urban bustle.

Culture Spot Namako Wall Street
Nature Spot Matsuzaki and Kumomi Beach
Must see Dogashima Tensodo Cave
We say Come here to explore quiet beaches and ports hidden within volcanic outcrops. The mountain roads are ideal for capturing photographs of epic scenery.

Shizuoka
MORIMACHI

Deep in the heart of Shizuoka, Morimachi has a long cultural history exemplified by its array of temples and shrines. Dating from over 1,400 years ago, Okuni Shrine is a delight to visit thanks to its distinctive thatched roofs and large grounds, with charming red bridges and tall cedar trees.

Culture Spot Daitoin Temple
Nature Spot Acty Mori
Must see Okuni Shrine
We say Certainly good for a visit if you have access to a car and are based in or around western Shizuoka. Okuni Shrine is a beautiful spot, even for a country teeming with pretty shrines, and the surrounding countryside of Shizuoka is always a treat.

233

関西地方

KANSAI

The Kansai Region
For centuries, the Kansai region has been home to some of the most historically and commercially significant spots in the country. Aside from the well-known cities of Osaka, Kyoto, Nara and Kobe, there is a huge number of natural and cultural gems throughout the region's prefectures. Wakayama's sacred sites are renowned, while castles, mountain shrines and temples, and gorgeous coastal views dot the area.

HYOGO PREFECTURE
The vast prefecture of Hyogo boasts a variety of appealing destinations, from its vibrant prefectural capital of Kobe and the fabulous castle of Himeji, through to the gorgeous spectacle of the Seto Inland Sea, with hot spring resorts further inland. Away from the famous sights, visitors can enjoy the castle ruins and seafood dishes at the coastal town of Akashi.

Himeji Castle

Prefectural Capital
Kobe City
✈ Airports
Kobe Airport
🚆 Main Train Stations
Shin-Kobe Station

Other Tourist Attractions
Himeji
Himeji is Japan's most famous and, arguably, most beautiful castle. Its white visage and huge size attract large numbers of visitors.
Kobe
This port city has a bustling Chinatown, the well-developed seafront Harborland area with shops, cinemas and museums, and interesting historical architecture up in the hills.

Kinosaki Onsen (hot spring baths)
A top hot spring destination in Kansai, Kinosaki has Japanese inns set along a charming willow-lined river.
Takeda Castle
If lucky, visitors can see these castle ruins in Asago City floating above a sea of clouds on misty autumn mornings. Originally built in the 15th century, the castle was abandoned in the early 17th century after its clan backed the wrong horse in the decisive Battle of Sekigahara.
Aioi Peron Festival (Aioi City)
In this festival, which takes place on the last weekend of May each year, dragon boat races are held in the bay.

KYOTO PREFECTURE

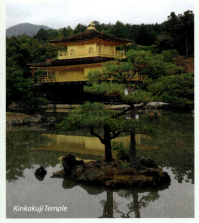
Kinkakuji Temple

One of the biggest draws in Japan for foreign visitors, Kyoto is simply a delight. The well-beaten path leading to the tourist spots of the temples of Ginkakuji, Kinkakuji and Kiyomizudera need no introduction, and are simply a must-do for any first-time visitors to the country. The rest of the city has several less-lauded temples that are still spectacular compared to those of other prefectures, making the city well worth an extended stay. Once out of the city proper, there is much to do for those with more time, or those that have already seen the famous sights. The spectacular sandbar of Amanohashidate in Miyazu is a major attraction in the area.

Prefectural Capital
Kyoto City
✈ Airports
-
🚆 Main Train Stations
Kyoto Station

Other Tourist Attractions
Uji
The smaller sibling of the mighty tourist spots of Kyoto and Nara, Uji is situated between the two. The Byodo-in Temple and Ujigami Shrine are fine historical complexes in the city, which is also well known for its green tea.

Miyama
Located in the mountains in the centre of the prefecture, Miyama has traditional, thatched-roof farmhouses throughout the town, which are still inhabited.

Gion Festival
This summer festival involves spectacular floats and thousands of revellers in the heart of Kyoto City.

NARA PREFECTURE

One of the most delightful towns in Asia, the historical and tranquil surroundings of Nara are a treat for visitors to Kansai. Further small towns in the prefecture also provide plenty of similar, though less well-known, destinations. Ikoma is home to an exceptional shrine set against a wooded backdrop high in the mountains. The remote village of Soni has a plateau with panoramic views far and wide, and Asuka is worth visiting for its cultural sights of temples and stone figures.

Todaiji Temple

Prefectural Capital
Nara City
✈ Airports
-
🚆 Main Train Stations
Nara Station
Kintetsu Nara Station

Other Tourist Attractions
Nara
Japan's ancient capital is a wonderful destination, with leafy parks and the famous Giant Buddha at Todaiji Temple. Outside the town, there are fascinating ancient *kofun* burial mounds. Hire a bike and fully enjoy this superb area.

Yoshino
Known primarily for the cherry blossoms lining the slopes of its eponymous mountain, Yoshino also has a rich, sacred cultural history.

Deer Antler Cutting Ceremony
Through October, the deer of Nara are rounded up and shorn of their antlers. This is a necessity, as they can be quite aggressive when approaching tourists for snacks.

Extreme Seasonal Conditions
Humid in summer.

KANSAI

関西地方

OSAKA PREFECTURE

Japan's second-smallest prefecture is one of its most visited, thanks to the city of Osaka. The city has been witnessing a renaissance, with a huge increase in tourists as a result of cheap flights, smoother travel visa processes, and growing interest from other Asian nations. Don't let the hordes put you off, as this vibrant area has so much to see and do.

The site of the 1970 Osaka Expo at Suita is a wonderful, family-oriented park with a host of natural features and fascinating remnants of the Expo. Izumisano has plenty to offer in natural sights, shopping and temples. Chihayaakasaka is a truly hidden treasure with pretty countryside and great hiking opportunities.

Prefectural Capital
Osaka City

✈ Airports
Kansai International Airport
Osaka International Airport

🚆 Main Train Stations
Shin-Osaka Station

Other Tourist Attractions
Osaka
Famous for its chatty, outgoing locals, Osaka has a sparkling vibe. Shopping, entertainment, and Universal Studios Japan are huge draws, but the city also has historical appeal, with its prefectural museum housing many interesting artefacts. The reconstructed castle is a definite must-see.

Tenjin Festival
Dating back over a thousand years, this festival takes place on July 24-25. There are parades on the streets and processions on Osaka's Okawa river, plus fireworks and a huge number of food stalls.

Tenjin Festival

SHIGA PREFECTURE

Dominated by the giant Lake Biwa, Shiga is somewhat overshadowed by the more famous prefectures of Nara and Kyoto. Nevertheless, there are plenty of beaches and holiday resorts for restful stays, as well as a chance to climb Mount Ibuki for extensive views over the lake's tranquil waters. Located in the centre of the prefecture, the town of Hikone hosts samurai houses and one of Japan's most iconic castles.

Prefectural Capital
Otsu City

✈ Airports
-

🚆 Main Train Stations
Maibara Station

Other Tourist Attractions
Koka
This rural spot is a popular hub for ninja lovers, that rivals Mie's Iga. Its proximity to Kyoto and rugged terrain made it the perfect hiding place for the hunted during the Warring States era. Koka includes a ninja house and a ninja village for enthusiasts.

Enryakuji Temple

Otsu
Enryakuji Temple, located on Mount Hiei, boasts a long history, having been established in the Heian era and suffering violent destruction at the hands of Nobunaga Oda during the Warring States era.

Omi Hakkei
Omi Hakkei, or 'eight scenic views of Omi', are famous vistas of Lake Biwa. Immortalised by the artist Hiroshige, similar views can still be enjoyed around the lake.

Otsu Festival
Traditional music and elaborate floats mark this autumn festival, which has a long history dating back to the early Edo era.

236

WAKAYAMA PREFECTURE

Wakayama Castle

The holy prefecture of Wakayama is home to pilgrimage routes to Shinto shrines, and mountain-top Buddhist temples. Visit Minabe to relax amongst its forests and orchards.

Prefectural Capital
Wakayama City
✈ Airports
Nanki-Shirahama Airport
🚆 Main Train Stations
Wakayama Station

Other Tourist Attractions
Koya
Enjoy the atmospheric temples of Mount Koya, some of which provide overnight lodging where guests can experience a monk's lifestyle.

Kumano
On the southern tip of Wakayama's Kii Peninsula, Kumano is focused around three shrines which make up a historical pilgrimage route. Adding to the eerie atmosphere, Kumano is known as 'The Land of the Dead', as the spirits of Shinto-worshipping ancestors are said to inhabit the area.

Shirahama
Popular as a retreat for Osakans, Shirahama has a 640-metre-long sand beach and an abundance of hot spring resort hotels.

Oto Festival (Shingu)
This long-held festival takes place in February at the town's Kamikura Shrine, involving some 2,000 revellers, dressed in white, dashing down stone steps while brandishing flaming torches.

NATIONAL PARKS
Yoshino-Kumano National Park
Area: 61,406 ha
Features: mountains, rivers, beaches, the holy areas of the Kii mountain range
Did you know? The Osugi Valley is famous for its waterfalls, both small and large, numbering around a hundred.

San'inkaigan National Park
Area: 8,783 ha
Features: sand dunes, cliffs, caves and reefs
Did you know? As well as the famous Tottori dunes, the park is known for its unique rock formations, including the pine tree-topped outcrop of Sengan Matsushima, and the Hasakari Rocks - where the rock forming the roof of the sea cave collapsed, becoming sandwiched between the two rocks that formed the cave walls.

Seto Inland Sea National Park
(see Chugoku)

Seigantoji Temple in Yoshino-Kumano National Park

KANSAI
関西地方

HIDDEN TOWNS

HYOGO
240   **Akashi**

KYOTO
244   **Miyazu**

NARA
246   **Asuka**
250   **Ikoma**
252   **Soni**

OSAKA
254   **Chihayaakasaka**
258   **Izumisano**
262   **Suita**

SHIGA
264   **Hikone**

WAKAYAMA
266   **Minabe**

CLIMATE (monthly average temperatures)

MIYAZU (north Kyoto)

MINABE (south Wakayama)

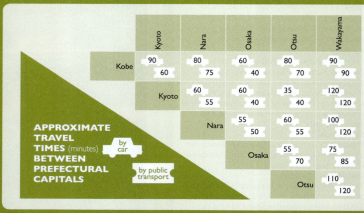

APPROXIMATE TRAVEL TIMES (minutes) **BETWEEN PREFECTURAL CAPITALS** — by car / by public transport

	Kyoto	Nara	Osaka	Otsu	Wakayama
Kobe	90 / 60	80 / 75	60 / 40	80 / 70	90 / 90
Kyoto		60 / 55	60 / 40	35 / 40	120 / 120
Nara			55 / 50	60 / 55	100 / 120
Osaka				55 / 70	75 / 85
Otsu					110 / 120

238

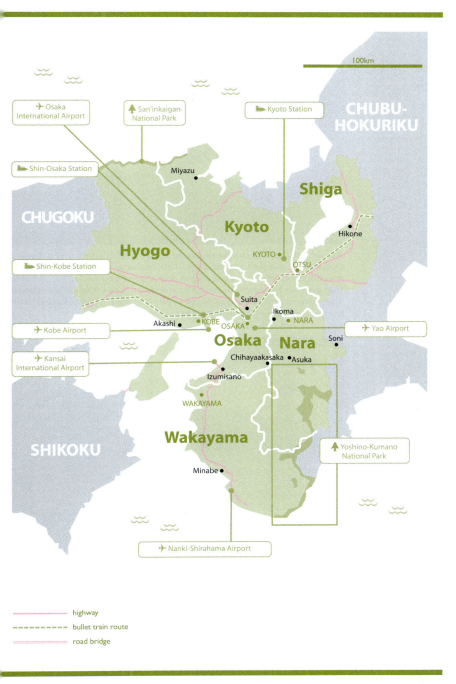

Kansai

明石市

Hyogo
AKASHI

Akashi is located at the southern tip of Hyogo Prefecture and a stone's throw from the port city of Kobe. This fishing town is centred around Akashi Park, which was created in and around impressive castle ruins that provide a throwback to the era of feudal lords. The area's relaxed atmosphere makes for a place to explore at your leisure, taking in all that a traditional Japanese port can offer.

Kids

Akashi Municipal Planetarium [1]
This is the oldest planetarium in Japan and is situated directly on top of the Meridian date line. It has a 360° viewing platform, large interactive exhibits, a special play area for toddlers, and craft areas for slightly older children. Be aware that all information and exhibits are in Japanese, but it's still well worth a visit.

Visitors are recommended to check the facility's website for when the planetarium shows start. There are usually five shows a day, starting from early morning.

Food and Drink

Akashi Brewery [2]
The Akashi Brewery is well known for its *sake*, whisky and award-winning craft beers. Visit the brewery, enjoy the restaurant, or pick up some souvenirs.

Culture Spot - Akashi Castle ruins [3]

Akashi Castle was built between 1617 and 1620 as a coastal defence against the western clans of Japan. All that remains today are the castle's stone walls and two well-preserved watchtowers. Entrance is free to watchtowers at weekends, and an English handout is available.

Culture Spot
Akashi City Museum of Culture [4]

This museum shows off all you could want to know about the natural and cultural history of the Akashi area. It even has a model skeleton of an Akashi elephant which inhabited the area about two million years ago. All information and exhibits are in Japanese only.

Culture Spot - Akashi Park [5]

Akashi Park is a large area centred around the ruins of Akashi Castle and its watchtowers. There are big open spaces, flower gardens, a large lake, a traditional Japanese garden and teahouse, and even a baseball stadium. It's a perfect place to relax with a picnic or take a stroll around. It has a very communal atmosphere created by the many families, groups of friends, and students that visit.

Must see! Akashi Kaikyo Bridge [6]

Located beside Maiko Station, or ten minutes by car or taxi from Hitomarumae Station, this suspension bridge (see main photo) is huge - the longest in the world at 3,911 metres. You can pay a small fee to go up into the special viewing platforms and walk out along the underside of the bridge itself. It's a great place to view the whole bay and Awaji Island, and also has a souvenir shop and restaurant.

Did you know?

Akashi blooming
Akashi Park has over 1,000 cherry blossom trees and is in the top 100 places in Japan for cherry blossom viewing.

Kansai

明石市

Hyogo

AKASHI

🍶 Food and Drink

Akashi-yaki
Akashi-yaki is the most famous local dish and a tasty option for lunch or an afternoon snack. It consists of steamed, chopped octopus cooked in a creamy, eggy batter which is formed into a ball. It's then dipped into a *dashi* soup and eaten whole.

Akashi-dai (bream)
The area is famous for its bream, which is available everywhere as *sashimi*, sushi, or served slightly seared. A must for any seafood lover.

Nori (dried seaweed)
Akashi *nori* is famous throughout Japan and is used in eateries throughout the city. You can pick some up as a souvenir in Uontana (the local shopping arcade).

Octopus
An adopted symbol for the town - octopus is everywhere you look, from street signs and restaurants, to markets and floor tiles. Try the local speciality as *sashimi*, *tempura*, or in the famous *Akashi-yaki*.

🏠 Culture Spot - Cherry Festival (Akashi Park)

This cherry blossom festival usually takes place over a weekend in early April. The park is bustling with people enjoying the cherry blossom, either by walking around the many hidden areas tucked away at the end of winding paths, or sitting under the trees eating, drinking and relaxing into the late evening. Inside the park are stalls selling traditional Japanese festival foods and offering face painting for the kids. This is also the only time of year when both Akashi Castle watchtowers are open all weekend, and you can even enjoy dressing up in a samurai warrior costume. It's a good idea to get to the park early in the morning to secure a prime spot under the blooming cherry trees.

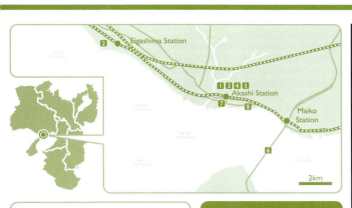

Key dates

mid-September - Akashi Food Festival

early October - Akashi Meridian Dontokoi Festival (lively event with a variety of dances in Akashi Park)

We say

"Aim to spend a couple of days here if you like to take things slowly. It's a busy working port during the day, but it does close down after five o'clock. Focus your stay around Akashi Station as there isn't much further out."

Recommended for

Families

Leisurely breaks

Food lovers

Must see! Uontana Traditional Shopping Arcade

This long arcade is situated five minutes from either Akashi Station or the local port. It is the perfect place to sample the morning's catch, or pick up a range of local produce. It's also a great spot for lunch, with numerous restaurants selling local dishes including the famous *Akashi-yaki*. Get there around two o'clock at the latest, before the food starts to run out. The restaurants and the shops all close at around five o'clock, so this is not the place for an evening meal.

Nature Spot Okura Seaside Park

This beach is a great spot for a swim in the summer, or for a barbecue in the cooler spring and autumn months. Its large open grass spaces are ideal for kids to work off any excess energy.

Accommodation

Accommodation in Akashi consists of a series of hotels ranging from small to large. They are all fairly old and in need of a bit of a facelift. The rooms are comfortable, but imagine them as a place to sleep rather than a place to relax.

Getting there and around

- Kobe Airport / Kansai International Airport / Osaka International Airport. Travel by limousine bus and local train services to Akashi Station.
- Nishi-Akashi Station. From there you can get a local train to any location in or around Akashi. Alternatively you can get a taxi from Nishi-Akashi.
- Everything is easily accessible by short taxi rides or from local trains via Akashi Station.

Further information

www.100hiddentowns.jp/hyogo/akashi.html

Kansai

Kyoto

MIYAZU
宮津市

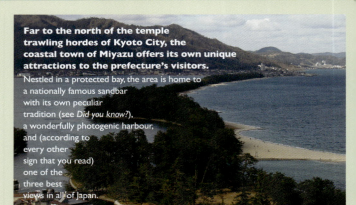

Far to the north of the temple trawling hordes of Kyoto City, the coastal town of Miyazu offers its own unique attractions to the prefecture's visitors. Nestled in a protected bay, the area is home to a nationally famous sandbar with its own peculiar tradition (see *Did you know?*), a wonderfully photogenic harbour, and (according to every other sign that you read) one of the three best views in all of Japan.

👍 Must see! Amanohashidate Beach / Shrine ❶

The main draw for most visitors to this area is Amanohashidate, a naturally occurring sandbar that runs across Miyazu Bay. The two ends are connected by a pine-tree-lined thoroughfare which visitors can either saunter or cycle across. On foot it takes about 45 minutes to traverse one way. Many visitors make use of the frequent ferry and private speedboat services that shuttle back and forth for half of their round trip. These boat companies also offer sightseeing loops of the bay. Alternatively, there are numerous outlets providing rental cycle services. The journey across the sandbar is a pretty one, with small waves lapping against the banks to either side of the avenue (one side a sandy beach, the other a stone-lined border), and a small shrine which, surprisingly, has a freshwater spring despite its saltwater surroundings. From the jetty at the same end as Amanohashidate Station, visitors can watch the occasional operation of a rotating bridge that allows access to bigger boats, while seagulls wheel above, and petite jellyfish propel themselves in the sleepy waters below.

🌳 Nature Spot - Viewpoints of Amanohashidate - Viewland ❷, Genmyoan ❸, Kasamatsu Park ❹ and Mount Nariai ❺

The full splendour of Amanohashidate is not immediately apparent when viewed from sea level, but there are several wonderful vantage points from which to take in the sight of the whole sandbar. Viewland is a family-friendly amusement park which is accessed by a funicular located a few minutes' walk from Amanohashidate Station. Halfway down the same slope, guests of the upmarket Genmyoan hotel are also privy to a slightly quieter version of the northwards vista. On the other side of Miyazu Bay, Kasamatsu Park, which has an observatory reached by cable car, lends the most famous southwards view over Amanohashidate. The park is particularly popular with sightseers during the cherry blossom and autumn seasons. An even more breathtaking view is from the summit of Mount Nariai, where the enormity and beauty of the panorama is made even sweeter by a tasteful coffee shop conveniently located there. Halfway down the road from the summit is Nariaji Temple. The somewhat austere temple is complemented by a picturesque pond and five-tiered pagoda, whose gold and vermillion colours beautifully catch the sunlight against a backdrop of the dotted islands and rugged highlands of Kyoto's north coast.

244

Culture Spot - Ine-no-Funaya Boathouses

The boathouses occupied by the fishermen of Ine Bay, located on the Tango Peninsula outside Miyazu, 25 kilometres north of Amanohashidate, are one of the most delightful sights in the area. There are over 200 of these residences and boatyards, each built to overhang a garage-like mooring. Serpentine roads follow the winding coastline, where gulls laze in the placid waters which run right up to the rickety, dark wood-panelled houses in the harbours. Boat tours of the bay are also available.

Food and Drink

The best-known delicacies of Miyazu are Matsuba crab (from November to late March) and *Buri-shabu* (yellowtail hot pot) (from November to March). The town is also home to the Amanohashidate Winery.

Getting there and around

- Osaka International Airport or Kansai International Airport. Travel to Amanohashidate Station by bus or local train services.
- Kyoto Station. Travel to Amanohashidate Station by bus or local train services.
- A car is recommended for access to the summit of Mount Nariai and to the Ine boathouses. Otherwise, visitors who wish to enjoy the ferries, funiculars and cable cars in the area can easily walk or ride a rental bicycle to these attractions from Amanohashidate Station.

Further information
www.100hiddentowns.jp/kyoto/miyazu.html

Did you know?

Behind you!
Many first-time visitors to Kasamatsu Park will be bemused by the sight of tourists bent double, with their bottoms pointing towards Amanohashidate, gazing backwards between their legs. This *matanozoki* pose is said to transform the image of the sandbar into 'a bridge to heaven'.

Key dates

mid-May - Miyazu Matsuri Festival

We say

" An extra push northwards from Kyoto City is well rewarded by a visit to Amanohashidate and Ine. The sandbar looks beautiful throughout all four seasons, and the harbours of Ine are a unique sight. As well as a great range of hotels and delicious seafood restaurants, there is a luxurious hot spring located directly outside Amanohashidate Station. "

Recommended for

Massive panoramic coastal views

Kansai

明日香村

Nara

ASUKA

Asuka Village, a short train ride away from its bigger, more illustrious neighbour, Nara, is a hidden gem.

A place of great beauty and interest, with an established tourist infrastructure - Asuka has excellent English signage at all tourist places, English leaflets readily available, rental audio guides in English and free wi-fi in many places. Though it is not yet on the main tourist routes, perhaps it soon will be, given the town's plan to register and obtain World Heritage status.

Asuka was once the political centre of Japan, from 592 to 710, before the Imperial Palace moved to present-day Nara. Thus, Asuka is filled with ancient sites of historical and cultural importance - temples, mystical stones, imperial tombs and ancient burial mounds.

246

👍 Must see! Asuka's Stone Figures

Asuka is famous for its strange granite stones in various parts of the region, the exact origins of which remain a mystery.

Kame Ishi - Tortoise Stone [1]

Kame Ishi is a huge granite stone carved to resemble a tortoise. Legend has it that should this stone ever turn to face west, the whole of Nara will sink into a sea of mud.

Saru Ishi - Monkey Stones [2]

The name for these stones comes from their simian appearance. Four of the five can be found in the grounds of the Tomb of Princess Kibihime, a seventh-century royal.

Nimen Ishi - Two-Faced Stone [3]

The faces of this stone represent good and evil. It can be found in Tachibanadera Temple, one of the main temples in Asuka, which is large, inviting, and extremely peaceful in the early morning.

🌳 Nature Spot - National Parks

The area surrounding Asuka Village has five national parks established since the 1970s, collectively named the Asuka Historical National Government Park. Walking or cycling around Asuka is a joy, as you will come upon wonderfully well-maintained parkland, copses, hills, streams and attractive terraced fields unique to the area - all with an ever-present mountain backdrop.

Takamatsuzuka Area [4]

Of all the five areas, this is the closest to Asuka Station - just 15 minutes away on foot. In the park grounds is the Asuka Historical National Government Park Hall, which serves as an introduction to Asuka. Inside, there is a large 3D model map of the whole town where you can press a button for any place to have its location lit up.

After visiting the hall, stroll around the attractive parkland to find the two tumuli (artificial earth mounds built over an ancient grave) of Takamatsuzuka and Nakaoyama. The former is a striking conical shape which once contained a priceless archaeological find, now housed in the nearby Takamatsuzuka Mural Hall.

💡 Did you know?

No meat for you!
In 672, Emperor Tenmu (the 40th Emperor of Japan) defeated Otomo-no-Oji (the son of Emperor Tenji) and built the new imperial capital in Asuka. He is perhaps best known for prohibiting the consumption of meat, due to his Buddhist beliefs. The Mausoleum of Emperor Tenmu, on a high tumulus, can easily be visited while in Asuka.

247

Kansai

明日香村

Nara

ASUKA

🏠 Culture Spot
Ishibutai Tumulus 5

This is the largest square-shaped burial mound in Japan. The tomb itself is built from 30 stones that altogether weigh over 2,300 tons. The ceiling stone alone weighs about 77 tons, and invites speculation about what technology existed at the time these huge rocks were lifted. Visitors can actually walk inside this ancient construction, to take a step back in time to a deeply superstitious age.

🏠 Culture Spot - Okadera Temple 6

After a steep approach, visitors come across a vast Buddhist complex nestled on the forest slopes.

Okadera is also known as Ryugai Temple, a name derived from a legend that its founder, Priest Gien, trapped an evil dragon (*ryu*) inside a pond with his power. This very pond is viewable in the grounds, along with the *Kannon of Wish Granting* which, at 4.6 metres, is the largest clay Buddhist statue in Japan.

Food and Drink

Asuka's remote tranquility also means that it has a paucity of eateries. The station area has a few small restaurants, but for dinner it is best to head to nearby Kashiharajingu-mae - just five minutes away by taxi or two stops on the local train - which has many more options.

Accommodation

B&B Asuka 7 provides a very central location for sightseeing (near Tachibanadera Temple) and value for money, with beautifully furnished rooms. The owner used to live in the UK, so speaks good English, and can advise guests on their stay in Asuka.

248

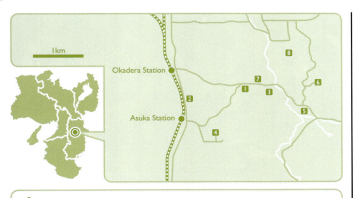

🏠 Culture Spot - Nara Prefecture Complex of Man'yo Culture 🎋

This museum celebrates 'Manyoshu', the first written collection of poetry in Japan, which dates back to the Asuka period and was published sometime around the eighth century. The museum is a modern complex that was built over the excavation site of a major archaeological find from the era. Visitors can experience the ancient culture through life-sized model figure exhibits recreating tableaux of ancient life, along with 3D movies. There is also a light and sound show in the museum's theatre to introduce you to the world of Man'yo poems and songs.

🚆 Getting there and around

- Kansai International Airport. Travel by local trains to Asuka Station.
- Kyoto Station. Travel to Kashiharajingu-mae Station using local train services.
Shin-Osaka Station. Local trains to Asuka Station.

🚶 Asuka is best explored on foot for those that don't mind walking a few kilometres in a day. Otherwise, bicycles can be easily rented from the station area. Just left of the station exit is a tourist information centre with English speaking staff, and free English maps.

👨‍👩‍👧 Kids

Although not especially a place for kids, the park areas of Asuka are great places to run around in. Also, the Man'yo Museum has many interactive exhibits - in Japanese only.

Key dates

first Sunday of February - the Onda Matsuri Festival. (Takes place at the Asukaniimasu Shrine, near Asukadera Temple. It is an ancient fertility festival to bless the planting and cultivation of rice, and includes masked actors on stage as demons performing comic sketches, with one mingling in the crowd to spank the devil out of the younger members!)

late August - Asuka Hikari-no-Kairo (candlelight festival where various spots in the village are lit up with small lanterns)

mid-September - Amaryllis Festival (in the terraced rice fields, including a scarecrow contest)

We say

" I found this to be an incredibly peaceful place, as the small town is surrounded by an abundance of green plains and rolling hills, which along with its ancient past, gives Asuka a distinct 'Tolkienesque' feel. "

Recommended for

A rural retreat

History lovers

📷 Further information
www.100hiddentowns.jp/nara/asuka.html

249

Kansai

Nara — IKOMA
生駒市

Off the beaten track, but conveniently located close to the well-known stomping grounds of Nara and Osaka, Ikoma is a wonderful destination for a one or two-day trip. Particularly recommended for hikers, the hills offer plenty of exercise, and tucked into the countryside are charming temples, each with their own unique features. Hozanji, halfway up Mount Ikoma, is worth seeing for even the most temple-weary traveller.

Culture Spot - Ikoma Shrine [1]

15 minutes from Ichibu Station on the Ikoma Line, in a peaceful wooded setting, Ikoma Shrine is well known in the area and boasts a centuries-old relationship with the Japanese Imperial family. The shrine is dedicated to the worship of seven deities - two gods of fire and five gods of war.

Culture Spot - Hozanji Temple [2]

Sometimes it is easy to be 'templed-out' by Japan, especially if you have travelled around Kyoto and Nara, but a few cases throw up surprises with their settings and architecture. One example is Hozanji - a stunning, sprawling temple facility set against a mountain backdrop. Mount Ikoma was originally an object of worship for the people in the region, so this area was selected as a location for the religious training of monks in the 17th century, and soon became one of the most popular Buddhist temples in the region. Still now, worshippers visit there to pray for prosperity.

Climb up past the pagodas and through the rows of statues to gain a bird's-eye view with the temple as a foreground to the wider Ikoma area.

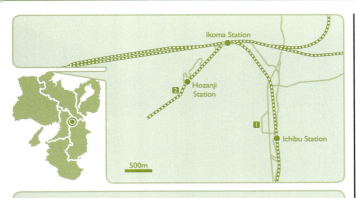

👍 Must do! Hiking the Kuragari Mountain Pass

The hike from Minami Ikoma Station to Hiraoka Station - across the famous Kuragari Mountain Pass that separates Nara and Osaka - can be completed in half a day and is extremely rewarding. The hot summer months are probably best avoided, but other times of year provide gorgeous views of paddy fields, rivers and waterfalls.

The recommended hike is along Route 308, which narrows as it ascends the mountain. The thoroughfare used to be the quickest way to reach Nara from Osaka, and so was used by traders and Edo-bound lords. Worshippers also used the trail when on pilgrimage to Hozanji Temple, halfway up Mount Ikoma.

Feel free to explore paths off the main road to experience as much of the area as time allows, but be warned that the hike is quite steep, especially if you choose to embark in the opposite direction, from Hiraoka.

The peak of the Kuragari mountain pass itself is a charming spot, with restaurants, and a cobbled street that retains the aura of an era when pilgrims would walk the route. A sign marks the border of Nara and Osaka prefectures.

⇌ Getting there and around

- ✈ Kansai International Airport. Travel by local train services to Ikoma Station.
- 🚄 Shin-Osaka Station or Kyoto Station. Travel by local train services to Ikoma Station.
- 🚋 From Ikoma Station, you can get the Taisho-era cable car up the mountain, stopping at Hozanji Station for the temple and nearby lodging. For hiking, take the Ikoma Line to Minami Ikoma Station and set off for the Kuragari mountain pass.

📖 Further information

www.100hiddentowns.jp/nara/ikoma.html

💡 Did you know?

Hiking Haiku
The famous Edo-era poet, Matsuo Basho, wrote a *haiku* poem on the way to Osaka after going over Kuragari mountain pass from Nara. In fact, it marked his final trip before succumbing to a stomach illness, aged 50.

Key dates

early August - Ikoma Dondoko Festival (a variety of booths, and performances from local entertainers including a *bon odori* dance and a fireworks display)

early October - Ikoma Shrine Fire Festival (accompanied by Shinto music, you can see various fire rituals, such as participants racing down the stone steps, wielding large flaming torches on their shoulders. The festival is said to date back to the era of Emperor Tenmu (673-686))

We say

" Ikoma has plenty to offer for hikers and non-hikers alike. Hozanji is a pretty temple set in spectacular countryside. The charming stone-stepped approach and nearby inns give it a unique feel that helps it stand out among the many temples of the area. For the energetic, there is a great choice of walking and hiking opportunities. "

Recommended for

Hill-loving hikers
Temple lovers

251

Kansai

Nara

曽爾村 SONI

Simply one of the most beautifully set villages in Japan, Soni attracts a large number of visitors for the views and hikes at its famous plateau. Lower down in the valley, the village itself is in a charming setting that provides a gentle switch to bucolic life, far away from the more manic, urban parts of Japan.

👍 Must see! Soni Plateau ⓘ

Soni Plateau is an awe-inspiring spot with gorgeous panoramic views, hiking opportunities and open nature. Its concave shape gives it a unique feel, and the steep hike to the rim of the plateau is rewarded with excellent vistas of the surrounding mountains and forests. The plateau is covered in swathes of Japanese pampas grass which the locals traditionally used as roof covering. In spring, the grass is set on fire as part of a controlled burning to help maintain the fertility of the land.

The spectacle changes with the seasons, with the lush green meadow of spring and summer followed later in the year with the silvers and golds of autumn. On bright autumn days, the grass sways in the breeze, further enhancing the spectacular view. The best time to see it during this season is just before sunset, as the grass is bathed in gold, creating a magical effect. Also, as dusk falls on a clear night, the starry sky over the plateau is an unmissable treat.

For hiking, autumn is the most popular time to come because of the pampas grass, but early spring can be just as rewarding, and there are fewer hikers.

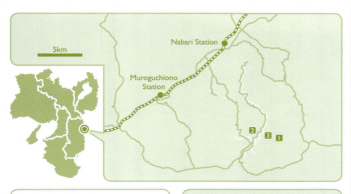

Nature Spot - Mount Yoroi

The bare, vertical rock face of Mount Yoroi looms over Soni impressively. This mountain gets its name from its resemblance to the breastplate of a suit of armour (*yoroi*).

Nature Spot - River walk

The Soni River cuts a swathe through a narrow valley, with residences set tightly against its banks. Paddy fields and a variety of wildlife make a riverside stroll a recommended part of a trip to Soni.

Culture Spot - Farm Garden

An absolute must for souvenir shopping and local products, Farm Garden was established in 2001 to showcase local goods. Especially recommended are the cheap, locally grown vegetables, and the hotcake powder made from Soni rice. Three flavours - plain, chocolate and banana - provide an excellent family-oriented souvenir. Other popular local goods are the tomato curry and the beer.

Also worth dropping by is the bakery next door, which has a variety of breads and pastries made from Soni rice.

Combine the trip with a stop off at the nearby *onsen*, to clear away the hiking aches in a restful, modern building with wooden and stone baths affording excellent views of the mountains and plateau. A great complement to your visit to Soni.

Getting there and around

- Kansai International Airport. Take local trains to Nabari Station and then a bus to Soni Village.
- Shin-Osaka Station or Kyoto Station. Travel by local trains and buses to reach Soni Village. Be aware that the buses are infrequent.
- Once in Soni, you need a taxi to reach the plateau unless you are planning to hike all the way up. In autumn, buses run directly from Nabari Station to the plateau.

 Further information
www.100hiddentowns.jp/nara/soni.html

Did you know?

Show me the way
The plateau has insects in abundance. As well as butterflies and caterpillars, you can find Japanese Tiger Beetles, which are known as *annai mushi* (literally, 'guiding insects') as they jump ahead of any walkers and seem to be showing them where to go!

A mountain turtle?
The Soni plateau reaches approximately 700 metres above sea level and covers 38 hectares. Closest to the plateau, Mount Kame is named after the Japanese word for turtle, due to its shape.

Key dates

mid - end of June - Firefly Festival
August 14 - Summer fireworks (about 1000 fireworks impressively echo through the mountains)
mid-September to late November - Yama Akari (Soni Plateau Lantern Festival)

We say

" Soni is gorgeous. An extremely pretty village in itself, but the hiking routes and joyous views once at the Soni plateau help make this town a highly recommended place to visit, and a notable entry in this book."

Recommended for

Hikers
Nature lovers

Kansai

Osaka

千早赤阪村

CHIHAYAAKASAKA

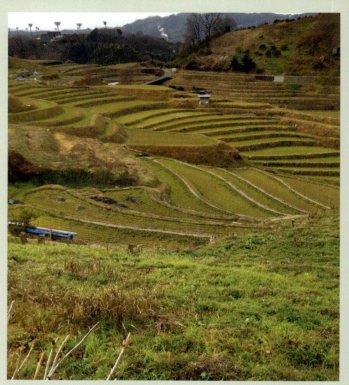

Situated about 35 kilometres from the centre of Osaka, Chihayaakasaka and Mount Kongo are historical, picturesque destinations located within the Kongo mountain range that borders Nara Prefecture.

This quiet spot - the site of legendary historic battles fought by the 14th-century samurai general Masashige Kusunoki - is home to beautiful, terraced paddy fields and the highest mountain in Osaka Prefecture. The area is popular with hikers and cyclists, providing them with breathtaking seasonal views and delicious local produce.

Nature Spot - Shimoakasaka Terraced Paddy Fields

A short walk from the Akasaka Junior High School bus stop (or a 25-minute stroll from Chihayaakasaka Village) is a quiet, lush valley that, according to the local literature, is the home to one of Japan's 100 best terraced paddy fields (see main image). The terrain offers a different view in every season, including a special candlelit illumination event during November.

While you are there, you can also see a memorial stone marking the location of the Shimo-Akasaka castle ruins, where Masashige Kusunoki battled the forces of the Kamakura shogunate. Although initially defeated, Kusunoki successfully recaptured the castle within two years.

👫 Kids - Kongozan play area and Museum of Nature and Astronomy [2]

Near the ropeway station at the top of Mount Kongo, there is a play area for children, as well as the Museum of Nature and Astronomy. This museum houses an astronomical telescope (used at night and for special monthly star gazing events), traditional toys made from natural materials, and exhibits with information about local birds and insects.

👍 Must see! Mount Kongo [3]

A cable car departs twice every hour from Chihaya Ropeway Station (last stop on the Kongo Bus route: Chihaya Ropeway-mae) to the upper reaches of Mount Kongo. After enjoying stunning views during the six-minute ascent, you can then visit the Museum of Nature and Astronomy, the beautiful Shakunage-no-michi (rhododendron path), or else gaze out towards Osaka Bay from the nearby observation platform. You can also hike to the summit of Mount Kongo, passing Katsuragi Shrine, Temporinji Temple and the ruins of Kunimi Castle.

The mountain is famous for the spring cherry blossom, summer greenery, beautiful autumnal leaves, and the sparkling winter frost that decorate its steep forest slopes.

Make sure that you don't miss the last cable car back (17:00 or 18:00, depending on the time of year), as the walk down is precipitous and potentially very dark.

If you prefer to hike, the climb takes about 60 minutes, but be warned that, although paved all the way, some sections are very steep and might be a challenge during more extreme weather conditions.

💡 Did you know?

Tough times for tofu
The Chihaya River used to be lined by nearly 60 water mills where local businesses made *tofu* by grinding soy beans and making freeze-dried bean curd. However, since the 1950s this local industry has gone into decline and now just a handful remain. One of them is Matsumasa, which is located near the start of the hiking trail of Kongozan.

Super samurai
Masashige Kusunoki was a 14th-century samurai general. During the Genko War - an attempt to transfer the governance of Japan away from the Kamakura shogunate - Kusunoki fought for Emperor Go-Daigo. Many Japanese still consider him to be the epitome of samurai loyalty, courage, and devotion to the Emperor. He even has a statue outside Tokyo's Imperial Palace.

Kansai

Osaka

千早赤阪村

CHIHAYAAKASAKA

🏠 Culture Spot - Chihayaakasaka Village Museum of Local History 4, Birthplace of Masashige Kusunoki 5, Takemikumari Shrine 6

Many of the points of local interest in Chihayaakasaka relate to its most famous inhabitant, Masashige Kusunoki (also known as Nanko-san). Within a few minutes' walk from the Chihayaakasaka Village Office bus stop, you can visit Chihayaakasaka Village Museum of Local History and the birthplace of Masashige Kusunoki.

You may want to do some background research on this famous samurai general before your visit, as most of the detailed information at these sites is provided in Japanese only.

After a short walk from here, you can also find the beautiful buildings that comprise Takemikumari Shrine (also known as Suibun Jinja).

Many of the homes and farmhouses in this area were built using traditional architecture and building materials, retaining their thatched roofs to this day.

🍚 Food and Drink

Chihayaakasaka is known for its local delicacy - Tanada Kome rice flour pudding (a local variation on the popular *purin* dessert).
Being a rural, agricultural area, Chihayaakasaka has several local market stalls (one is located near Chihayaakasaka Village Museum of Local History, another near Akasaka Junior High School) where delicious seasonal goods such as *mikan* (Japanese citrus fruit), rice, *tofu* and onions can be bought.

256

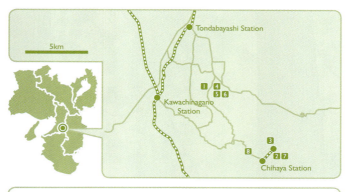

Key dates

April 25 - Nanko Festival (spring festival)

November - Chihayaakasaka terraced paddy fields candlelit illuminations

We say

" The highlight of my trip was the quiet, red lantern-lined walk from the top of the Mount Kongo Ropeway to Katsuragi Shrine. Although I really enjoyed my visit (in early February), I was caught out by unseasonably mild weather, and was only able to catch the beautiful frost on the trees of Mount Kongo by waking up at sunrise and walking from Konanso Inn to the observation platform. "

Recommended for

Seniors
Hikers

 ### Accommodation - Kongozan Konanso Inn

Near the cable car station at the top of Mount Kongo is the Kongozan Konanso Inn, which offers reasonably priced traditional rooms (albeit with wi-fi and TV), a luxurious cypress bath, and a restaurant that serves a range of delicious, filling, traditional food. In the summer months there are also camping facilities and bungalows available to rent.

Kids

Chihayagawa Masu Fishing Area

Upstream from Chihaya Village, you can go fishing for rainbow trout from a long row of pools at the Chihayagawa Masu Fishing Area. You can then take your catch to the kitchen in the main building where they will cook it for you.

 ### Getting there and around

- Itami Airport. Travel via Osaka-Abenobashi Station or Kawachinagano Station to Tondabayashi Station by local train services.
- Shin-Osaka Station. Travel via Tennoji/Osaka-Abenobashi Station to Tondabayashi Station by local train services.
- A bus ride from Tondabayashi Station will take you to Suibun Jinja (20 minutes) or to Chihaya Ropeway Station (40 minutes).

 ### Further information
www.100hiddentowns.jp/osaka/chihayaakasaka.html

257

Kansai

泉佐野市

Osaka

IZUMISANO

Quiet natural retreats, ancient temples and shrines, urban outlets and developments - all only minutes from Japan's second city - Izumisano provides a compact weekend away, with something for everyone.

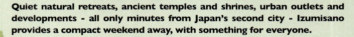

Culture Spot - Hine Shrine [1] and Oizeki Park [2]

Hine Shrine is a pleasant spot located about 30 minutes' walk from Hineno Station. A path through the back of the grounds leads to the quiet Oizeki Park, built over a small river gorge - best viewed for the cherry blossom or the autumn leaves.

Did you know?

Kansai can-do
Kansai International Airport was entirely constructed on a man-made island in Osaka Bay. This involved excavating three mountains, and the use of 10,000 workers and 80 ships - a creation that increased the size of the Osaka Prefecture area by so much that it was no longer the smallest prefecture in Japan, relegating Kagawa Prefecture to that position. Impressive enough as that is, the airport is approached by a 3.75-kilometre bridge leading out from Rinku Town. The airport was even named one of the ten 'Civil Engineering Monuments of the Millennium' by the American Society of Civil Engineers.

👍 Must see! Mount Inunaki 3

So the story goes... An old hunter was stalking a deer through the woods when his dog suddenly started barking. At this, the deer ran off and the hunter, in his rage, cut off the dog's head. The dog's head then flew off and killed a snake that was, unseen, about to kill the hunter. The hunter then felt remorse upon seeing his dog's loyalty to him. The hunter went on to become an ascetic monk, the dog, meanwhile, gave the mountain its name - Inunakisan ('Dog Howling Mountain').

This tale pretty much encapsulates the three key elements of many a Japanese legend: loyalty, old people and death.

The mountain now offers a peaceful day out. The main route is a pleasant walk along a wooded river valley with a number of waterfalls to enjoy. There are several small shrines and temples, and sacred areas along the way with some interesting stories attached to them. In one spot, a young woman cried herself to death over a man, and now if you drink from the water there every day, your wish will come true. There is also the more practical Separation Shrine, where, if there is someone you want to sever your relationship with (spouse, boss, or howling dog) you can pray here for it to come true.

🏠 Culture Spot - Shugen-do

The route is a popular pilgrimage for the Shugen-do (mountain asceticism). For a fee, visitors can stand under waterfalls or be held in place precariously over a sheer drop. Booking is required and you may need someone to help you with the Japanese.

The paths on the mountain are fairly good and should be fine with small children. Allow three hours to get there and back with stops along the way.

Kids

At the Spring Festival in April, a mass of 80kg of trout is released into the river for people to try and catch. Less ambitious anglers might consider the July Summer Festival, when a mass of goldfish are released at the same spot. Consider waders and a rod for April, and perhaps a shrimping net for July.

Kansai

Osaka — IZUMISANO
泉佐野市

🍶 Food and Drink

Izumisano Fishing Cooperative [4]

Izumisano Fishing Cooperative is a market area next to the port. It offers all the delights of a Japanese fish market, including a large number of strange looking creatures of the deep, and over-enthusiastic market folk trying to sell you the said monsters. Worth considering is the barbecue area at the back. Once you have rented a basic set, including meat, you can then also take any purchases from the fish market and grill them. On the top floor of the market are also a couple of seafood restaurants in which to consume the local catch. Local delicacies include prawns and Japanese blue crab.

Kotarina JA Market [5]

A short walk from Hineno Station, this market gives you the chance to sample some local produce. The *mizunasu* aubergine is a plump variety recommended for pickling.

Kitashoji Brewery

A relatively new entry in the world of *sake* brewing, Kitashoji has been running for 95 years and is located in an old-style wooden building. Inside, you can try their range of chilled *sake* before buying. Tours of the brewery are also available (ten people or more - in Japanese only), though you should book in advance.

🏠 Culture Spot
Rinku Town [6]

This modern seashore development offers a number of different features, including an outlet mall, a park, and its flagship draw, Rinku Tower. The tower is the third tallest building in Japan and provides spectacular views from its hotel and top-floor restaurants.

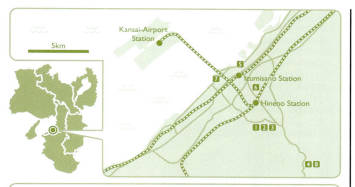

Key dates

mid-April - Inunakiyama Spring Festival (a large mass of baby trout are released into the river)

mid to late July - Inunakiyama Summer Festival (goldfish are released into the river for children to fish)

late September - Izumisano Festival (traditional local festival with floats and dancing in the streets)

We say

" A nice balance of different things to do that should suit a family. Also a compact area with good transport. Inunakisan and its places of worship are the main feature, but the town itself offers plenty of other fun options. "

Recommended for

Families or a relaxing city break

Accommodation
Fudouguchikan

Right next to the bus stop at Mount Inunaki, by the river, is the unassuming Fudouguchikan *ryokan*. Once inside, however, you can enjoy all the best of the Japanese *ryokan* experience. A low building from the front, the back opens up to five storeys as it is built on the side of the mountain valley.

Wooden passages wend and wind their way down and around into the side of the valley. Each room is tucked away in its own world, with views over the river. Of the 11 rooms - some Japanese-style and some Western-style - a few have their own private outdoor *onsen*. There is a public bath as well, which offers the chance to relax and enjoy the view. Dinner is taken in your room, with staff bringing in a variety of seasonal dishes, all in *kaiseki* style.

Getting there and around

- Kansai International Airport. Travel by local train services to Izumisano Station.
- Shin-Osaka Station. Travel by local train services to Izumisano Station.
- Most of the sights are about 15-20 minutes' walk from each other, and rental bicycles are available from the tourist office. Inunakisan has regular bus services running from Izumisano.

Further information
www.100hiddentowns.jp/osaka/izumisano.html

261

Kansai

吹田市

Osaka
SUITA

The small town of Suita, in the suburbs of Osaka, burst into international recognition when it hosted the Osaka Expo in 1970. Though the Expo pavilions have long been torn down, in their place the vast Expo '70 Commemorative Park still welcomes visitors all year round, offering a refreshing respite from the urban bustle of central Osaka.

Culture Spot - Expo '70 Commemorative Park

With the participation of 77 countries and over 64 million visitors in six months, the 1970 Japan World Exposition was a huge success. Whilst all the pavilions from the 1970 Expo are long gone, there are still a few remnants. The most famous is the Tower of the Sun (see main image), a giant sculpture which dominates the park and remains as impressive as it must have first been to its 1970 audience.

The park, though, is mainly a vast green area teeming with nature, and facilities for family activities. There are flower displays throughout the year, sculptures, water features, a barbecue area, playgrounds, pedal boats and a wide stream with stepping stones.

An observation tower affords an excellent view of the surrounding area, and throughout the park, signs with photos refer visitors to the former locations of pavilions in 1970.

Culture Spot - Expo '70 Pavilion

Fancy a trip into a 1970s time warp? If so, depending on your age, the Expo '70 Pavilion will be a bizarre or a nostalgic experience. A couple of hundred metres east of the park entrance, the museum was known as the Steel Pavilion during the Expo, and hosted live music performances. Now it houses programmes and other paraphernalia from the Expo of 1970, as well as an exhibit on the history of all international Expos. Photographic wall displays transport visitors back to an era of psychedelia and unique fashion styles. The highlight of the museum is the central arena, which plays recordings of the dissonant music of Stockhausen, whose work was performed at live concerts during the Expo.

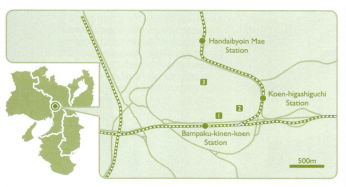

Must see! The National Museum of Ethnology ③

Opened in 1977, the National Museum of Ethnology is the highlight of a trip to the Expo '70 Commemorative Park, providing wide-ranging displays on the daily lives and cultures of peoples of the world.

Particularly of note is the Oceania section, which has displays of clothing, art, folk crafts and replicas of traditional sea vessels. The Americas section features totems and other vibrant, colourful exhibits, such as models of skeletons from Mexico, assembled to celebrate the November 2nd Day of the Dead.

Moving on to the Africa section, displays can be found on cave paintings, ancient pottery, accessories, explanations of food, and exhibits tracing the history of Africa as the cradle of humankind. Overall, it is a fun, educational treat for old and young alike, and there are digital guides available in the language of your choice.

Getting there and around

✈ Kansai International Airport or Osaka International Airport. Travel by local train or monorail to Banpaku-kinen-koen Station.

🚄 Shin-Osaka Station. Banpaku-kinen-koen Station is a short train journey away.

🚶 From the station, the entrance to the park is just a short walk away.

 Further information
www.100hiddentowns.jp/osaka/suita.html

Did you know?

See you in 6970
There is a time capsule, closed in 1970, with orders not to be opened until the year 6970. It includes objects such as tea ceremony utensils, a 'gastrocamera' (a small camera for photographing the inside of the stomach), musical scores, earrings, baby clothes, a rock sample from Mount Everest and even an artificial eye!

Key dates

late May - early June - evening fireflies
early June - late June - Hydrangea Festival
Saturdays, Sundays and holidays from early to mid-July - early morning lotus viewing and *zobihai* (drinking *sake* through a lotus stem)

We say

" As a pleasant, wholesome break from the hubbub of central Osaka, Expo '70 Commemorative Park is perfect for a family day out. I was impressed by how the city developed the vast Expo area after it closed. The park's focus on nature and our relationship to it makes it arguably a more pleasant place to visit now than in its crowded, halcyon days of 1970. "

Recommended for

Kansai day trippers
Nature lovers
Families

Kansai

彦根市

Shiga

HIKONE

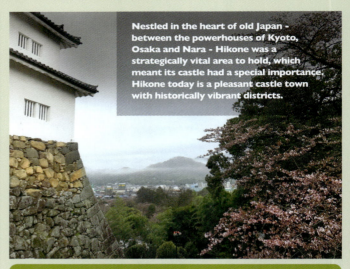

Nestled in the heart of old Japan - between the powerhouses of Kyoto, Osaka and Nara - Hikone was a strategically vital area to hold, which meant its castle had a special importance. Hikone today is a pleasant castle town with historically vibrant districts.

👍 Must see! Hikone Castle

Often regarded as one of the best-preserved castles in Japan, Hikone Castle was once actually in a state of much disrepair and was only saved from destruction when a dignitary passing through the town was moved by the dilapidated state of the once proud edifice. He then successfully petitioned the Meiji Emperor to preserve the castle and thus it was saved from being dismantled - the sad fate of most castles in that modernising period. The castle now has been beautifully preserved and allows visitors to step into the past through wandering around its grounds and building. The main keep dominates the skyline of the town and offers great views from the top, over the lake and hills.

Hikone Castle Museum has a number of interesting items and exhibits from the history of the fortification. Particularly impressive is the distinctive flame-red suit of armour worn by the castle's founder, Naomasa Ii, at the legendary Battle of Sekigahara. There are also some creepily lifelike *noh* masks with distinctive expressions.

🌳 Nature Spot - Lake Biwa

Lake Biwa is the largest lake in Japan, and hollows out all of Shiga Prefecture. Biwa is actually one of the most ancient lakes on the planet, formed four million years ago. This protracted existence has allowed the lake to develop a notably diverse ecosystem, as well as providing water for the people and industries around it.

The shores of Lake Biwa are a nice place to relax or to take a stroll. There are a couple of boat cruises that run across the lake from Hikone to some small islands, offering a gentle way to take in the scenery.

Culture Spot - Yume Kyobashi Castle Road

A main street, 350 metres in length, stretches out from the moat of the castle and runs off towards Kyoto. Described as the 'Old New Town', the street is an attempt to capture the hustle and bustle of an Edo-period castle town within a modern context. The buildings have the white walls and dark, wooden lattices that were typical of the era, and the wide street has the feel of a boulevard. A stroll here offers opportunities to relax and eat, as well as to do some shopping for local arts and crafts.

Culture Spot - Genkyuen Garden and Hoshodai Guest House

Just across from the base of the castle walls, this garden is designed around a large pond with a teahouse in the middle. The most distinguished guests of the castle lords stayed at the accompanying guesthouse and, presumably, were suitably impressed by the gardens made available for their enjoyment.

Getting there and around

✈ Chubu Centrair International Airport / Osaka International Airport / Kansai International Airport. Travel by local train services to Hikone Station.

🚆 Kyoto Station. Travel by local train services to Hikone Station.

🚶 The main attractions in Hikone are all very central and easy to cover on foot. Lake Biwa is about 25 minutes away if you are walking.

Further information
www.100hiddentowns.jp/shiga/hikone.html

Did you know?

The spoils of war
Hikone Castle came to importance when Naomasa Ii provided crucial support to the victorious Tokugawa forces at the Battle of Sekigahara in 1600. He was given permission to move the existing castle to its present location, but sadly never saw the castle that he dreamt of. Ironically, his strong performance at the Battle of Sekigahara that won him the castle and domain, also gave him a lingering bullet wound which is commonly believed to have led to his death two years later.

Key dates

early August - Hikone Manto-Nagashi, Buddhist Lantern Festival (thousands of small candles are floated down the river towards the lake)

early November - Parade of Little Edo Hikone Castle (adults and children dress up in period costume and parade through the castle grounds)

We say

" Hikone Castle, and the streets and buildings surrounding it, evoke a wonderful period feeling and are great fun to stroll around and explore. Definitely worth visiting as a day trip if you are in the area. There are also some scenic cruises on the lake for a relaxing time. "

Recommended for

History fans
Families

265

Kansai

みなべ町
Wakayama MINABE

As the express train rolls down from Osaka, feel yourself slip into an older, more remote part of Japan. Minabe is a seaside town that is traversed by an ancient pilgrimage route, with rolling *ume* (*prunus mume* – or 'Japanese apricot' to the layman) groves, and hidden beaches.

Nature Spot - Senrinohama Beach

Part of the Minabe Pilgrimage Route, Senrinohama is approached by a short tunnel that feels like an entrance to a secret garden. The beach is the largest nursery of endangered loggerhead turtles in Japan.

There are also a number of rock features in the area, including the appropriately named Camel Rock. Enjoy the beautiful location and check out the Senri-oji shrine just up the steps from the beach.

Must see! Iwashiro – Minabe Pilgrimage Route ❷

The Kumano kodo is a web of paths that fan out across the Kii Peninsula, before converging on the religious centre at Kumano. The trails - going through mountains, forests and along the coast - have carried pilgrims over rugged terrain for over 1,000 years.

A short coastal section of the network runs through Minabe. Consult the map board outside Iwashiro Station before starting out. The paths are mostly concrete on the first section, but the route twists and turns, carrying you through *ume* orchards, before a short tunnel leads out onto the nearly hidden Senrinohama beach. Across the sands lies Senri-oji, one of the 99 sub shrines housing children of the main deity at Kumano. These *oji* serve to guide and protect the

pilgrims along their road. Leave a sea shell at the shrine before heading back inland on the route back to Minabe-oji. The walk should take a couple of hours and give you glimpses of an ancient tradition.

The route is generally well signposted in English, but you will need to be careful at some junctions.

Nature Spot - Komezu Park ❸

Komezu Park is a great place for families to relax. Conveniently situated next to the Kishu-Minabe Royal Hotel, the park has a number of swings and play areas for kids. The palm trees around the park also lead down to a sandy beach where you can splash about in the Pacific waters.

👁️‍🗨️ Did you know?

White Wakayama
Minabe is the third-largest producer of *kishubinchotan* charcoal in Japan. This charcoal whitens when heated and has long been used in traditional Japanese cookery.

Kansai

みなべ町 — Wakayama MINABE

🏠 Culture Spot - Minabe Ume

Wakayama is the *ume* capital of Japan, and much of the town's production is geared towards that of *umeboshi* pickles. Ten times more are produced here than in any other region of Japan. *Ume* infuse the scenery, cuisine and atmosphere of Minabe.

Ume blossom

Orchards cover the low hills leading down to the bay. When all the *ume* trees flower in February, the hills are painted white with blossom. Like the better-known cherry, *ume* blossom viewing marks the passage out of winter. Meander up and down the slopes of the orchards, and stop to have a picnic under the boughs. During peak season, some areas are lit up to enjoy viewing into the evening. The two best sites are Minabe Bairin Ume Orchard and Iwashiro Daibairin Ume Orchard. Buses run from Minabe and Iwashiro stations respectively during peak season in February. At other times take a taxi, or enjoy an hour-long walk to the orchards from the stations.

Kishu Umeboshikan

The trees in the area produce the distinctive *nanko ume*. Its thin skin and soft flesh make it the most sought-after type for pickling. Ten minutes from Minabe Station, Kishu Umeboshikan gives you the complete *umeboshi* experience. On weekdays, you can tour the factory and see how the pickles are produced. For a small fee, you can choose to try your hand at making either pickles, juice, or *umeshu* (liquor). With stern instructions not to drink the alcohol, the staff guide you through the process. The explanation is all in Japanese, but is fairly easy to follow thanks to clear demonstrations. You can then take the fruits of your labour away to enjoy at home.

Ume Shinkokan (Ume Promotion Museum) [4]

A short drive from Minabe Station is the Ume Shinkokan. Although predominantly about the local produce, it also has some information about the local area and its history. There are a few signs in English, but it is predominantly in Japanese. However, some good pictures and displays mean that you can still get a sense of the area.

Key dates

late January through February - *Ume* blossom season

We say

"A chance to really see a rural part of Japan, with beautiful ocean views and a warm climate. Its relatively compact size makes it easy and fun to navigate around. Enjoy a simple break, where you don't have to rush about."

Recommended for

Families or a quiet break away

Food and Drink

Kaisenbou Inoyoshi

Take the steps down from the Kishuji Minabe Hotel and you arrive at the Kaisenbou Inoyoshi fish restaurant.

Split over two floors, with some views out over the bay, you have the potentially off-putting sight of seeing your dinner swimming around in pools set into the floor as you make your way to your table.

Try *shirasu* - very small fish on rice with a dash of soy sauce - or a selection of *sashimi*.

Enjoy the variety of seafood dishes and the relaxed local atmosphere, washed down with a selection of Japanese drinks.

Food and Drink

Café de Manma

When you enter this cafe, you can see a beautiful view of Minabe Bay from every seat. The restaurant is managed by an *umeboshi* farm, so the *ume* are used in a lot of the dishes, along with other local foodstuffs. It serves mainly western fare, with a seasonal *umeboshi* buffet.

Getting there and around

- Nanki-Shirahama Airport. Travel by bus, rental car or taxi to Minabe.
- Shin-Osaka Station. Travel by local train services to Minabe Station.
- The compact nature of the town makes it easy to get around on foot and enjoy the sights.

 Further information
www.100hiddentowns.jp/wakayama/minabe.html

KANSAI
OTHER TOWNS

関西地方

Hyogo
KASAI

Spread out over several kilometres, Kasai covers a large area of charming countryside, which is best visited by car to ensure that you can see all of its natural and historical sights.
Culture Spot Hokkezan Ichijoji Temple
Nature Spot Hyogo Prefectural Flower Centre
Must do Kasai Tamaoka Historic Park
We say Kasai is good for a day trip from Himeji, especially if you love hiking. A car is necessary in this area.

Kyoto
MAIZURU

Maizuru Bay looks out from the northern coast of Kyoto Prefecture onto a calm inlet of the Sea of Japan. Lush hills surround its scenic harbour, which is also home to a naval base, port and a ferry that connects the Kyoto region with Hokkaido.

Much of the culture of Maizuru today was shaped by the aftermath of World War II, when the town became the point of repatriation for many of the returnees from overseas campaigns after hostilities ended.

Culture Spots Maizuru Repatriation Memorial Museum and Park, JMSDF Vessels, Goro Sky Tower
Nature Spot Maizuru Shizen Bunka-en (Natural Culture Park)
Must do Maizuru Aka Renga (Red Brick) Park
We say Maizuru is well worth the trip if you can time your visit to combine one of its many seasonal events with a walk around the Brick Park and the harbour.

Nara
KATSURAGI

Katsuragi is a town rich in history and rugged beauty, less than ten kilometres from the mountains on the border of Osaka Prefecture.

Within a walk from the local train stations, you can visit the 'birthplace of sumo wrestling', an impressive Buddhist temple and the scenic twin peaks of Mount Nijo. Travel a little further, and you can also enjoy a ropeway ride to the summit of Mount Katsuragi.

Culture Spots Sumo-kan (sumo museum) Kehaya-za, Sekkoji Temple
Nature Spot Mount Nijo
Must do Taima-dera Temple
We say The many charms of the journey from Taimadera Station up as far as Taima-dera Temple, via a *manju* shop and sumo museum on Takenouchi Street, make Katsuragi well worth a day trip, especially if you are already in the Nara area. Stay longer if you wish to climb Mount Nijo or to combine your trip with a visit to one of the nearby towns of Chihayaakasaka, Asuka or Soni.

Osaka
HABIKINO

Habikino is most famous for its location on the Takenouchi Kaido - an ancient road that connected the area to the historical capital of Nara. Parts of the road still maintain their old appearance, and the keyhole-shaped *kofun* burial mounds that are abundant in the area are a major draw. Hire a bicycle from the tourist office and circle around the burial mounds to get a feel for the Kofun era of Japanese history that the mounds give their name to.

Culture Spot Takenouchi Kaido
Nature Spot Furuichi Kofun Tombs
We say Strictly for the history buffs, Habikino is a pleasant small town for strolling or cycling around, as a quiet diversion from the hustle of central Osaka.

271

CHUGOKU

中国地方

The Chugoku Region
Honshu island's westernmost prefectures are collectively known as Chugoku. Translated as 'middle country' despite its western location, the origin of the name is popularly thought to come from its position between Kyushu and Kansai, two of the most historically significant areas of Japan before the focus of power spread east to Edo (Tokyo).

Chugoku boasts some of the finest historical, natural and cultural spots in the country, with a wealth of feudal castles, island-dotted seas, and rocky shorelines.

HIROSHIMA PREFECTURE

Think of Hiroshima, and inevitably the atom bomb of August 6th 1945 comes to mind. While the prefectural capital city of Hiroshima rightly commemorates the bombing with its Genbaku Dome, Peace Park and Peace Memorial Museum, these draws are only a part of what awaits visitors to the area. The city itself is delightfully vibrant and prettily located on several rivers. Outside the city, a visit to Hatsukaichi's Itsukishima Island to witness the spectacular sea-located red *torii* gate of Itsukushima Shrine is a must. The gorgeous floral vistas and bright colours of Sera are also recommended. The prefecture's location makes it a great place to set off on a tour of the Seto Inland Sea. Why not take the biking route of Shimanami Kaido from Hiroshima to Ehime, to appreciate those famous sea views at a gentle pace?

Prefectural Capital
Hiroshima City
✈ Airports
Hiroshima Airport
🚆 Main Train Stations
Hiroshima Station

Other Tourist Attractions
Onomichi
Used as a starting point for the popular Shimanami Kaido cycling route across the Seto Inland Sea, Onomichi is a pretty town characterised by its narrow sloping lanes that lead visitors to a number of quaint temples.
Tomonoura
This pretty fishing village was the model for 'Ponyo', the Studio Ghibli animated film.
Hiroshima Flower Festival (Hiroshima City)
Hosted across three days during the Golden Week holiday of early May, this festival is a blast of vibrant colour, as flowers line the Peace Boulevard of the city.

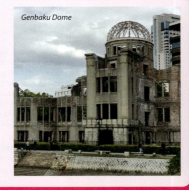

Genbaku Dome

OKAYAMA PREFECTURE

Okayama Prefecture is renowned for its rural retreats, art galleries, and castles. Great as a gateway for island hopping to Shikoku across the Seto Inland Sea, the prefecture is also home to Okayama City - the pretty prefectural capital, Kurashiki - a town of beautifully preserved canals and warehouses, and the fascinating history and splendid accommodation options of Mimasaka.

Prefectural Capital
Okayama City
✈ Airports
Okayama Airport
🚩 Main Train Stations
Okayama Station

Other Tourist Attractions

Okayama City
The city's titular castle is known as 'Raven Castle', due to its distinctive black exterior. Opposite its moat is the celebrated Koraku-en Garden, which draws large numbers of tourists throughout the year.

Bitchu-Takahashi
The small mountain city of Takahashi is best known for Matsuyama Castle - one of the oldest surviving castles in Japan - perhaps thanks to its elevated position on the mountain overlooking the town. The base of the mountain is home to temples, museums, and preserved Edo-era samurai houses.

Inujima
Venture into the Seto Inland Sea and visit Inujima, named after its dog-shaped rock, and enjoy the modern art of this small island.

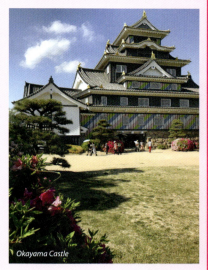

Okayama Castle

Saidaiji Temple Naked Man Festival
The stereotypical polite and shy Japanese gentleman stays at home for this one. In the bitter cold of early February, thousands of participants in skimpy loincloths battle in the main temple building, to grab a stick lowered from the ceiling, and stuff it into a wooden box to earn a year's worth of good luck.

Korakuen, Okayama

273

CHUGOKU

中国地方

SHIMANE PREFECTURE

The sparsely populated prefecture of Shimane is home to a wonderful mix of history, ancient culture and natural areas. The major prefectural hub of Matsue is a popular draw, and the ancient shrine at Izumo garners thousands of visitors a year from all over Japan and its Asian neighbours. The award-winning garden of the Adachi Museum of Art in Yasugi is another of Shimane's outstanding attractions, with other recommended spots including the theatre traditions and fantastic nature of Masuda, as well as the activity-packed island of Nishinoshima.

Prefectural Capital
Matsue City

✈ Airports
Izumo Airport
Iwami Airport

🚆 Main Train Stations
Matsue Station

Other Tourist Attractions
Matsue City
The prefectural capital is a charming city with a wonderful, long-surviving castle, and serene canal waterways on which visitors can enjoy boat trips.

Iwami Ginzan (silver mine)
Set in the mountains of Oda, silver was mined here from the early 16th century and continued for nearly 400 years. Visitors can observe the mine shafts as well as the museums and shrines of the wider area.

Tsuwano

Tsuwano
This tranquil town is home to old, white-walled samurai houses and carp-filled roadside streams. The town also includes pretty shrines and even a chapel to commemorate the persecuted Christians of the early Edo era.

The Morotabune Ritual (Mihonoseki Harbour)
This Shinto festival takes place on December 3rd every year, and involves boat races between two long canoes manned by traditionally attired crews. The festival is a reenactment of a famous episode in the ancient Kojiki text.

TOTTORI PREFECTURE

The coastal prefecture of Tottori has much to recommend it, from the unique sand dunes of Tottori Sakyu, through to the panoramic views from the Tottori Castle ruins, and on to the celebrated cherry trees of Kyusho Park. The spectacular cliff-face shrine of Sanbutsuji on Mount Mitoku in Misasa is well worth the hike, and the seaside and culture of the tranquil town of Sakaiminato provide a serene destination.

Prefectural Capital
Tottori City

✈ Airports
Tottori Airport
Yonago Airport

🚆 Main Train Stations
Tottori Station

Other Tourist Attractions
Tottori Castle Ruins
Destroyed due to the modernising zeal of the Meiji era, all that remains of Tottori Castle are the stone foundations and a single wooden gate. Nevertheless, the location itself provides stunning views of the area, and can be combined with a trip to observe the Meiji-era European-style architecture of the Jinpukaku Residence at its base.

Tottori Sakyu (Sand Dunes)
These vast sand hills along the coast are a much-loved tourist spot, and any visitor will feel they have been transported out of Japan and into an Arabian dream. Such a feeling is only enhanced by the chance to ride a camel through the dunes. The tides and coastal winds continue to constantly reshape the dunes.

Shan-shan Festival
Tottori's summer festival features street dancing with paper umbrellas, which originated as a performance, praying for deliverance from drought.

Tottori Sakyu

YAMAGUCHI PREFECTURE

Historically significant for its role, when known as Choshu, in the overthrow of the Tokugawa shogunate, Honshu island's westernmost prefecture of Yamaguchi has preserved much of this legacy. Yamaguchi City - the prefectural capital - dates back to the 14th century, when the ruling Ouchi clan lords designed it to look like 'The Kyoto of the West'. In fact, it rivalled Kyoto for influence during the Warring States era of civil war. Nowadays the city has a calmer feel and is known for its historical temples. Notable attractions are the superbly preserved castle town architecture of Hagi, and the Meiji-era industrial heritage sites on its outskirts.

Prefectural Capital
Yamaguchi City

✈ **Airports**
Yamaguchi Ube Airport

🚆 **Main Train Stations**
Shin-Yamaguchi Station

Other Tourist Attractions
Mine City
Akiyoshidai plateau and Akiyoshido caves are the major draws to Mine. The limestone rocks that dot the plateau's karst landscape are unique in Japan. The caves are similarly impressive, with underground waterfalls and cobalt blue waters.

Iwakuni
This former castle town is revered for its distinctive Kintai-kyo looping arched bridges. Time your visit with the cherry blossoms in full bloom for maximum photography opportunities.

Iwakuni

Kintai-kyo Festival (Iwakuni)
This annual festival, held in late April, includes a fully costumed reenactment of the departure of the local lord, an event that would take place under the strict Edo-era system of *sankin kotai*. This was implemented by the Tokugawa regime to keep the lords of the far-flung regions in check, by insisting they visit Edo regularly. The festival also has traditional music and performances.

Setonaikai National Park

NATIONAL PARKS

Setonaikai National Park
Area: 66,934 ha
Features: islets, hiking, cycling
Did you know? The island-dotted Setonaikai (Seto Inland Sea) National Park encompasses 11 prefectures.

Daisen-Oki National Park
Area: 35,353 ha
Features: mountains, forests, coastal areas
Did you know? The park boasts some of the most revered religious sites in Japan, including Izumo Taisha and Mount Mitoku.

CHUGOKU

中国地方

HIDDEN TOWNS

HIROSHIMA
278   Hatsukaichi
282   Sera

OKAYAMA
284   Kurashiki
288   Mimasaka

SHIMANE
292   Izumo
296   Masuda
300   Nishinoshima

TOTTORI
304   Misasa
306   Sakaiminato

YAMAGUCHI
308   Hagi

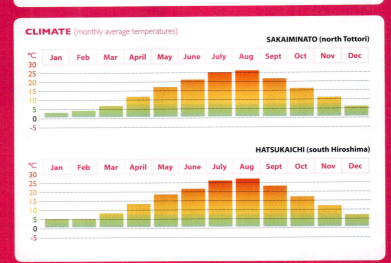

CLIMATE (monthly average temperatures)

SAKAIMINATO (north Tottori)

HATSUKAICHI (south Hiroshima)

APPROXIMATE TRAVEL TIMES (minutes) **BETWEEN PREFECTURAL CAPITALS**

by car / by public transport

	Matsue	Okayama	Tottori	Yamaguchi
Hiroshima	160 / 240	160 / 80	260 / 220	130 / 110
Matsue		180 / 200	140 / 150	240 / 310
Okayama			170 / 170	250 / 140
Tottori				330 / 300

276

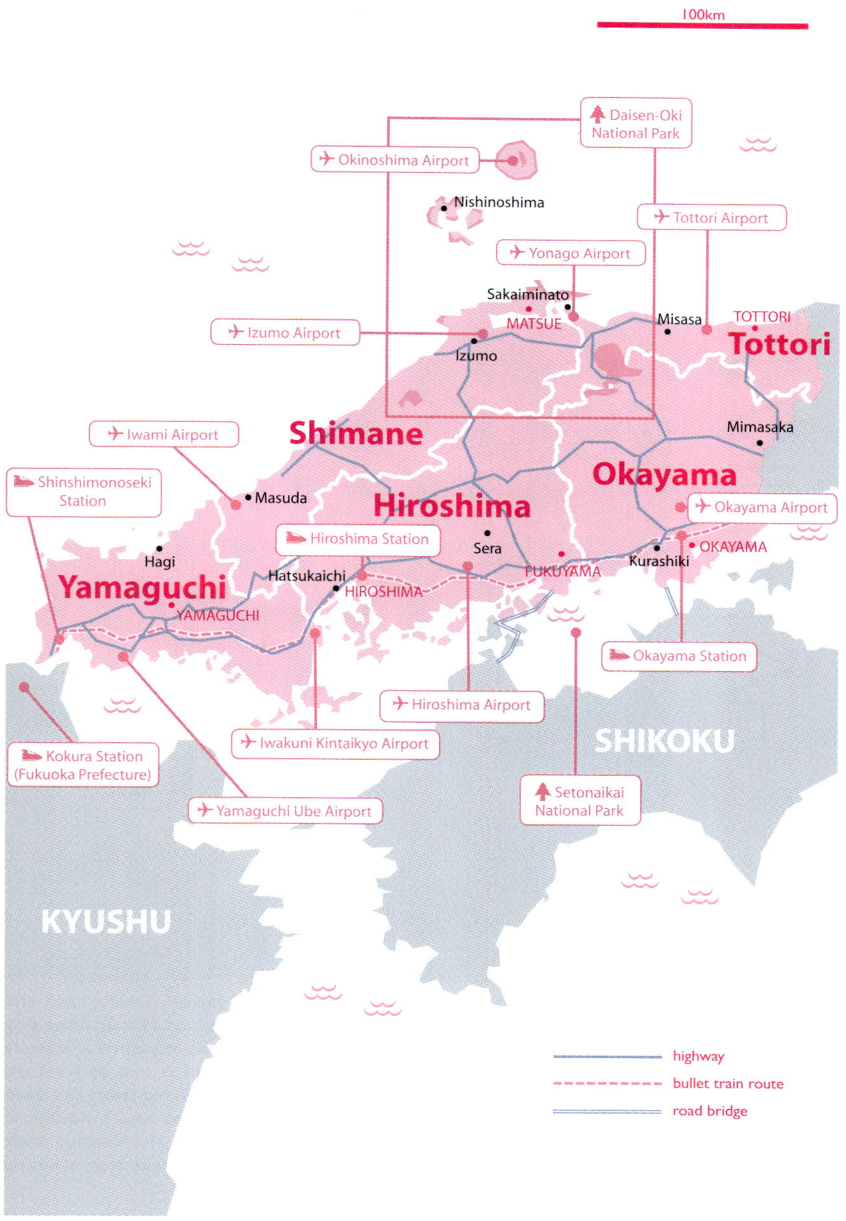

100km

✈ Daisen-Oki National Park

✈ Okinoshima Airport

• Nishinoshima

✈ Tottori Airport

✈ Yonago Airport

Sakaiminato

✈ Izumo Airport

MATSUE

• Misasa

TOTTORI

Izumo

Tottori

Mimasaka

✈ Iwami Airport

Shimane

Okayama

🚩 Shinshimonoseki Station

• Masuda

Hiroshima

✈ Okayama Airport

Sera

• OKAYAMA

Hagi

Hatsukaichi

Kurashiki

🚩 Hiroshima Station

FUKUYAMA

Yamaguchi

HIROSHIMA

YAMAGUCHI

🚩 Okayama Station

✈ Hiroshima Airport

SHIKOKU

🚩 Kokura Station (Fukuoka Prefecture)

✈ Iwakuni Kintaikyo Airport

🌲 Setonaikai National Park

✈ Yamaguchi Ube Airport

KYUSHU

——————	highway
– – – – – –	bullet train route
═══════	road bridge

277

Chugoku

Hiroshima
HATSUKAICHI 廿日市市

Housing one of the heralded 'three views of Japan', (along with the sandbar of Amanohashidate in Kyoto Prefecture, and Matsushima Bay in Miyagi) the island of Itsukushima (also known as Miyajima - literally 'shrine island') in the municipality of Hatsukaichi is one of western Japan's most revered spots. The iconic *torii* gate, rising from the Seto Inland Sea, is a staple of many a tourist snapshot and guidebook, but there is so much more to the island - explore the various back streets and temples, and climb Mount Misen for a great trip, steeped in history and nature.

👍 Must see! Itsukushima Shrine

Follow the tourist hordes from the port, along the coast, past the pesky deer, and there it is - Itsukushima's sea-anchored, red *torii* gate. Much of its beauty is derived from changes to the tide and weather. During high tide it appears to float on the sea, and is arguably at its most magnificent. Low tide offers the chance to wander close up to the gate on the damp sand. The gate is centred in a U-shaped bay, with pine-tree and stone-lantern lined paths, providing views from several angles.

The shrine was first constructed in the late sixth century, and in 1168 the site was chosen by the powerful lord, Taira-no-Kiyomori, as the venue for his family shrine. It is a vast complex, all in vibrant red, with a *noh* stage in the middle, and a chance for serene strolls along its wooden boardwalks that, though roofed, are pretty much open to the elements.

The ebb and flow of the tide is surprisingly quick. Wander away from the shrine for lunch or a hike in the hills, and when you return, the *torii* gate will be ankle or knee-deep in water.

In the evening, the romance of the location becomes even more apparent, and you will see guests walking around the island in their *ryokan yukata*, enjoying the illuminated shrine casting a rouge hue. There are also boat cruises to take in the view - especially enjoyable on warm, still summer nights.

Part of the shrine's charm is its verdant backdrop. In spring, the cherry blossoms augment the view - contrasting the shrine's copper-red with the *sakura's* resplendent pink.

🌳 Nature Spot - Momijidani Park

Just behind Itsukushima Shrine, Momijidani Park - at the foot of Mount Misen - provides a chance to enjoy some tranquility away from the tourist groups. The wooded canopy and delicate waterfalls are a lovely location for a rest. The park is especially beautiful during autumn thanks to its maple trees. From the park, visitors can access the ropeway to the top of Mount Misen.

💡 Did you know?

Shellfish survivors
Gathering shellfish near the *torii* gate is popular at low tide. After the Battle of Miyajima, some of the vanquished forces of Sue Harukata's invading army retreated into the hilly peaks of Miyajima and hid, only daring to come to the shore at night to pick shellfish, which they boiled in their helmets.

Chugoku

Hiroshima — HATSUKAICHI 廿日市市

🌳 Nature Spot - Mount Misen [3]

At a height of 535 metres, Misen is a tree-covered, easily climbable mountain. The summit grants climbers a splendid view of the Seto Inland Sea and its small islands. Visitors can either hike up one of several paths all the way to the top, or use the ropeway to take out much of the effort, before making the last push to the observatory deck at the summit.

In total, the walk from the base will take approximately 90 minutes. It is steep, but the path has stone steps all the way, providing a fun and safe climb. Just make sure to bring a small towel to mop away the sweat, and enough to drink, as there are no services at the top of the mountain.

Once at the observatory, or seated on one of the huge rocks that mark the peak, the views of the islands of the Seto Inland Sea, and to the mainland as far as the city of Hiroshima, are amazing.

Also near the top is a shrine that houses an eternal flame - one of Misen's major draws. It is said to have been constantly burning for 1,200 years, and was used as the pilot light for the Flame of Peace in Hiroshima's Peace Park.

🏠 Culture Spot Daisho-in Temple [4]

Head into the hills a little and follow the signs to this wonderful temple. It is full of nooks and crannies, with surprises behind them. A path of stone Buddhas with cute expressions runs parallel to a gushing stream and, nearby, what appears to be a cave is a softly lit, tranquil residence for more statues.

Arguably one of Japan's finest temples - it would perhaps gain more recognition if it wasn't in the shadow of the more famous Itsukushima Shrine - wandering around the grounds makes for a fairytale experience.

🏠 Culture Spot - Miyajima History and Folklore Museum [5]

Not bad as a stop off if it's rainy or too hot, this museum features artefacts from the lives of Miyajima's villagers of the past. There are a few English explanations and a subtitled video explaining the history of the island. One of the exhibition rooms has picture scrolls and dioramas explaining the Battle of Miyajima, a 16th-century conflict between an invading army of 20,000 and a defensive one of just 3,500 who, though hugely outnumbered, ultimately prevailed.

There is also a rest area where visitors can take the weight off their feet by sitting on the *tatami* mats and looking out over the museum garden.

Key dates

August - Kangen-sai Festival (the largest festival at the shrine, with decorative boats, lanterns and traditional music)

We say

" Although certainly less hidden than many of the other towns in this book, Hatsukaichi's popularity is well deserved. Seeing Itsukushima's iconic *torii* gate at close quarters is a must-do for any visitor to this part of Japan, but the island is so much more than just that. A major highlight is climbing Misen while enjoying the island's tranquil countryside, away from the other tourists. "

Recommended for

Nature lovers

Any visitor to the west of Japan

Culture Spot
Goju-no-To Pagoda 6

Dating from the early 15th century, this five-storey pagoda is one of the major landmarks of Itsukushima, dominating views when entering by boat or climbing up the mountain. At night, bathed in spotlights, the pagoda appears even more breathtaking.

Food and Drink

The approach from the port to the shrine is tastefully lined with a number of eateries and souvenir shops. *Anago* (conger eel) and *kaki* (oysters) are the key island delicacies, and definitely worth sampling when making a visit here.

Getting there and around

🛬 Hiroshima Station. Travel by local train services to Miyajimaguchi Station and then take a boat across to the island from the port right by the station.

✈ Hiroshima Airport. Take the airport limousine bus to Hiroshima Station and then follow the above directions.

🚢 The ferries to the island are frequent and the journey only takes ten minutes. Get up on deck for a great view of the island, the oyster beds floating on the sea surface, and the red gate guiding you in. The island is very easy to walk around, with the shrine just a short walk from the port.

Kids

The island has an aquarium - always fun for youngsters - and plenty of stalls and shops full of snacks and toys. Kids will also enjoy the shrine itself, avoiding the deer, and paddling up to the red *torii* gate.

Further information
www.100hiddentowns.jp/hiroshima/hatsukaichi.html

Chugoku

世羅町

Hiroshima
SERA

Near the centre of Hiroshima Prefecture, surrounded by mountains, is the town of Sera. With a population of around 16,000, it is on the surface a sleepy little location. However, what Sera offers is not situated in the middle of the town, but surrounding it on all sides. From spring to autumn the surrounding area is transformed into a sea of colours and fragrances. From cherry blossoms to tulips, sunflowers to lavender, strawberries to *nashi* (pears) - the fields around the town provide an ever-changing seasonal vista. Whether as a day or an overnight trip, Sera is a great place to visit if you want to take a break from the hustle and bustle of Hiroshima City and see a different side of Japan.

👍 Must see! Sera Kogen Farm ⓘ

Sera Kogen Farm is popular for both its Tulip Festival in spring and its Sunflower Festival in summer.

The farm is spread out over a gently sloping hill that allows easy viewing of the artistic designs in which the flowers are set out. There are plenty of areas to rest in the shade, and possibly indulge in their very tasty Sera Burgers.

 Did you know?

Sporty Sera

Sera's local high school has long been a formidable force in long distance relay running. Because of this, Sera attracts keen runners to the area, who hope to gain something by running where the locals train. To accommodate this, Sera has set up a running course along the river that cuts through the town.

Key dates

mid-April to mid-May - to see the cherry blossom and tulips

mid-July to September - to see the lilies, sunflowers and lavender

Nature Spot - Sera Yuri En

Sera Yuri En (Lily Garden) hosts flower festivals in both spring and autumn, when the flowers are in their full glory.

Kids

Most of the attractions in Sera are outdoors which, in turn, makes Sera a very kid-friendly place to visit. Along with the wide open spaces for kids to move around freely, every place visited seemed to sell ice cream.

If your kids want to play, then try Sera Yume Park (Sera Dream Park). As well as having a large play area, there is a short hiking track to the top of the mountain — useful for curbing the energy levels of hyperactive youngsters.

Food and Drink

Sera Town itself has culinary delights to satisfy everyone. You will find most of the restaurants scattered along the main road (albeit at five to ten minute intervals on foot). The pick of the local restaurants was easily the Oheso Cafe and Bakery . Situated outside of the town, near the information centre, this spot is a highlight for visitors, as it not only produces beautiful artisanal bread, but from 11am to 2pm the cafe serves delicious Spanish food.

We say

" Sera is an area I would definitely go back to in the future. My entire experience was enjoyable and allowed me to see a whole different side of Japan. Particularly refreshing was the wide open space. The highlight of my trip was the drive into Sera itself. Getting off the expressway and winding through the country roads threw up sights of an older, more rurally centred Japan. Along the route were small pockets of old-style farmhouses alongside family-owned rice fields. "

Getting there and around

✈ Hiroshima Airport. Travel by bus or car to the Sera area.

🚅 Hiroshima Station. Travel by bus or car to Sera.

🚖 Visitors without their own transportation will have to rely on taxis to take them around Sera, as bus services are limited.

Recommended for

Nature lovers

Those looking for a countryside break

 Further information
www.100hiddentowns.jp/hiroshima/sera.html

Chugoku

倉敷市

Okayama

KURASHIKI

Kurashiki is one of the oldest textile industry centres in Japan. Its beautiful historical canals and warehouses are amongst some of the most iconic in the country.

🏠 Culture Spot
Ohashi House ❶

The Ohashi House is a well-preserved samurai dwelling from the Edo period. Having picked the wrong side in a battle, the owners spent some time hiding out under a bridge (*hashi* - hence the family name Ohashi). Their fortunes were restored thanks to rice and salt trading which, in 1796, helped fund the construction of this residence. The house is a fine example of the period homes of the wealthy, and contains a number of historical artefacts.

🏠 Culture Spot - Kurashiki Museum of Folkcraft ❷

Showcasing the Folkcraft movement of the 1920s and 1930s, this museum aims to illustrate the beauty of 'hand crafted art of ordinary people'. Inside the museum are a number of antique everyday items that were traditionally used in Japan. The sprawling wooden building is of perhaps as much interest as the exhibits.

284

🏠 Culture Spot - Seto Ohashi Bridge ③

Comprising six bridges, five islands and many magnificent views - the Seto Ohashi Bridge is the longest two-tiered bridge in the world, and hops from island to island, connecting the Honshu mainland with its smaller neighbour, Shikoku. The bridge can be crossed by car or train, but may be best viewed from the cruise boats that sail beneath it.

🌳 Nature Spot - Mount Washuzan ④

Part of the Setonaikai National Park, Mount Washuzan is on a promontory leading out into the sea. There are a number of paths dotted around the hill, as well as a visitor centre and restaurant, but it is the breathtaking views of the Seto Ohashi Bridge and the innumerable islands dotting the inland sea that make the trip here memorable.

🏠 Culture Spot - Ohara Museum of Art ⑤

Founded by local industrialist Magosaburo Ohara in 1930, the museum was the first in Japan for western art. Behind its slightly incongruous neoclassical entrance, the museum maintains a collection of works from international luminaries such as Monet, Munch and Picasso. Over the years, wings showcasing more contemporary western and Asian works have been added to the gallery, which now holds a vast and imposing collection. Adjacent to the Ohara Museum of Art, the Shinkei-en Garden is a traditional-style Japanese garden built around a pond, with a teahouse and exhibition hall attached - a lovely spot to take a break and relax.

🏠 Culture Spot - Honmachi and Higashimachi Districts

Located near to the picturesque canal district, along the old route east towards Osaka and Kyoto, the streets and alleys of Honmachi and Higashimachi Districts were originally the habitats of local traders and craftsmen. These backstreets still bustle with life, and are especially evocative at night, when the streets fill with people popping into its bars and restaurants.

❓ Did you know?

Classic Kurashiki
Kurashiki actually used to be a seaside town, with the current location of the train station formerly overlooking the sea. After years of land reclamations, the station is now thoroughly landlocked a fair distance from the coast.

Chugoku

Okayama — KURASHIKI
倉敷市

👍 Must see! Bikan Historical Quarter

The heart of Kurashiki is the Bikan Historical Quarter. Dating back to Edo times, this area of merchant storehouses was the commercial heartbeat of the town. Wares would come in and out via road and canal, with boats loaded from the warehouses on the banks of the waterways. Houses and bars filled the back streets, while the magistrate's office at the end of the canal would keep a close eye over it all for the Shogun back in Edo.

The area has been carefully maintained and is arguably the best preserved merchant district in Japan. These days, the iconic black and white buildings are converted museums and shops, and the willows quietly weep while boats whisk tourists, rather than cargo, along the waterways.

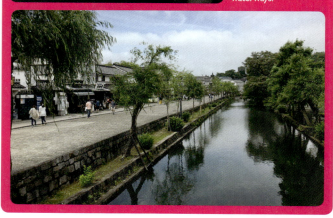

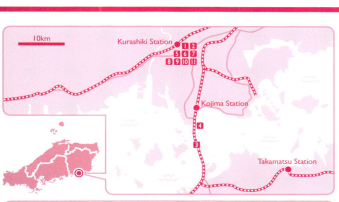

Key dates

late July - Kurashiki Tenryo Summer Festival (street festival with dancing and Tenryo Taiko drummers)

autumn - Sen'i Kojima Seto Ohashi Bridge Festival (hundreds of stalls selling different types of textiles)

mid-October - Kurashiki Byobu Festival (involves a procession through and around the town - the merchant houses open up and display their collections of *byobu* folding screens)

We say

" Kurashiki's Bikan Historical Quarter is an unmissable treat. With the high number of other sightseeing options also in the area, it is definitely worth visiting this town for its history, culture and art. "

Recommended for

Families

History enthusiasts

A relaxing break

Accommodation
Ryori Ryokan Tsurugata 8

Located literally next to the canal, you can spend the day exploring the town and then take two steps off the road and be luxuriously quartered in a traditional *ryokan* with a history going back over 250 years. The winding wood-lined corridors lead you to your private lodging. One of the highlights is the banquet of local fish served in your room.

Culture Spot - Kanryuji Temple 9 and Achi Shrine 10

On a small, rounded hill rising from the town's historical district are Kanryuji Temple and Achi Shrine. A pleasant walk up some stone steps leads to these places of worship and a quiet garden, best visited when the wisteria is in bloom. Some lovely views over the town can be seen from the top.

Culture Spot
Kake Museum 11

Opened in 2002, this museum is a collaboration between the area's local educational institutions, displaying a series of exhibitions of works by young and upcoming artists. It makes a nice counterpoint to the other more established museums in the town.

Getting there and around

🛫 Okayama Airport. Travel by bus services to Kurashiki Station.

🚆 Okayama Station. Travel by local train services to Kurashiki Station.

🚶 The historical quarter is conveniently clustered, and easy to walk around in a day. To visit the Seto Ohashi Bridge, take local train services to Kojima Station.

Further information
www.100hiddentowns.jp/okayama/kurashiki.html

Chugoku

美作市

Okayama

MIMASAKA

Mimasaka is locked into the heart of rural western Japan. This quiet backwater has notable history, and offers resort-style attractions in an *onsen* setting. Unwind at one of the spa resorts and venture out to take in some local history and crafts.

👍 Must see! Yunogo Onsen (Sagi-no-yu)

1,200 years ago, a Buddhist priest saw a heron nursing its injured leg in the hot waters of the area, and thus the name of the *onsen*, Sagi-no-yu (hot water of the heron) was established. Today there are a number of hot baths in the area, as well as an open-air foot bath in the centre of town. Yunogo Onsen is a compact resort town with a number of splendid tourist attractions.

🏠 Culture Spot - Toy Museums

Japan Museum of Contemporary Toy and Hall of Music Box 2

This museum has a number of interactive displays and a great variety of toys to look at. It is also worth checking out the music box show that runs at regular intervals. This event is surprisingly interesting, as the staff talk you through (in Japanese) the history and design of the different music boxes, before setting them to play.

Model Train Museum 3

Here, the main attractions are the large model train dioramas that visitors can set up and run, watching the trains run around the scaled mountain scenes. There is also a large display of trains and a variety of other toys to take in.

Showa Retro Museum 4

This museum is decked out as a toy shop from the 1960s, so visitors can get a glimpse into the past inside this authentic recreation.

If visiting all three museums, make sure to buy the combination tickets beforehand.

🏠 Culture Spot
Musashi Miyamoto

Musashi Miyamoto is one of the most famous samurai warriors in Japanese history. Fighting more than 60 duels from the age of 13, Musashi is credited with inventing the style of fighting with two swords. He is also the author of the legendary strategy text, 'The Book of Five Rings'. His birthplace was the quiet village that now bears his name, and there are a number of monuments and locations associated with his life in the village, including the slightly underwhelming Musashi Museum. The village has a few well-preserved buildings linked back to the great swordsman, and is a pleasant spot to stroll around. The museum, however, is little more than a dusty back room with a couple of scrolls and some blades in cases. Perhaps interesting for devotees, it does at least remind us that legendary figures often come from humble origins.

💡 Did you know?

Mimasaka soccer
Mimasaka has a surprising amount of sporting links. The Okayama Yunogo Belle Women's football team plays top-flight football and is based in the town. There is also the Okayama International Circuit, which held a couple of Formula 1 races in the mid-1990s.

Chugoku

Okayama — MIMASAKA
美作市

🏠 Culture Spot - Glass Studio TooS 5

There are a number of craft shops and factories in the area. Glass Studio TooS offers visitors the chance to try their hand at glass blowing. Take a look at the samples in the shop next to the factory, and then choose what type of glass and colours you want. Within the hot atmosphere of the actual studio, the staff will guide you carefully through the process, and actually perform most of the difficult and dangerous stages. In many ways, it's more fun just to watch them deal with the glowing red glass. All the instructions are in Japanese, but after half an hour of blowing, cutting and rolling, you will have your own personally created glass.

🌳 Nature Spot - Mount Ushiro and Dosenji Temple 6

Mount Ushiro, the highest mountain in Okayama, clocks in at 1,344 metres high. Though not as high as many other summits in Japan, this one is a more achievable climb within a day trip. Ushiro is one of the centres for the ascetic training known as *shugendo*. Though there is still a small section on the south side of the mountain on which women are not allowed (as tradition stubbornly dictates), all the main routes are open to anyone, and on clear days offer fantastic views. It can be quite steep-going in places, so plan ahead and take a map. It is also a good idea to stop by Dosenji Temple, which is closely linked to the mountain, on the way.

Key dates

second Saturday in February - Anyoji Temple Festival (this naked festival involves local men purifying their bodies in the river then fighting to grab aromatic wooden amulets dropped into the crowd)

end of March - Yunogo Dolls Festival (a number of traditional dolls are displayed throughout the town and there are also some street performances and stalls)

second Saturday and Sunday in October - Ohara Autumn Festival (a number of stalls and stands are lined up, and in the evening portable shrines are transported around the town)

We say

"Yunogo Onsen makes a convenient base, with a number of things to do in the town. A relaxing hot spring break with some historical spots in the area is what awaits visitors here to guarantee a genteel time."

Recommended for

Historians

Hikers

Onsen lovers

Arts and crafts aficionados

 Accommodation - Kifu no Sato 7

This beautiful *ryokan* offers a stylish chance to unwind. The decor is wood-lined and *tatami*-floored. The original founder was a keen flower arranger, and this tradition is maintained with *ikebana* displays positioned all around the hotel. The full course dinner offers a sophisticated evening, with Japanese *kaiseki* cuisine. If you are staying, and want to explore Yunogo Onsen, it might also be worth renting bicycles from reception.

 Nature Spot - Firefly Viewing

Just off the centre of the town, the Otani River is the place to visit on warm June evenings when the fireflies emerge. Stroll along the path next to the river and watch these magical bugs glow and flicker around the river. There is an annual firefly festival at the end of May to celebrate this most marvellous natural phenomena.

 Getting there and around

- Okayama Airport. Travel by limousine bus and local bus services to Yunogo Onsen.
- Okayama Station. Take local train services to Hayashino Station.
- Yunogo Onsen itself is quite compact, and easy to get around on foot. Travel to Mount Ushiro and Dosenji Temple requires a train to Ohara Station, and then a taxi ride.

 Further information

www.100hiddentowns.jp/okayama/mimasaka.html

Chugoku

Shimane

出雲市 IZUMO

Izumo Taisha (Grand Shrine) is famous throughout Japan and the rest of East Asia, attracting many tourists from Korea, Taiwan and mainland China. A visit to the town reveals much more besides the iconic shrine, with the Old Taisha Station's Taisho-era architecture and paraphernalia a draw for railway enthusiasts, the impressive Shimane Museum of Ancient Izumo giving a solid explanation of the lengthy human history of the area, and, in the southern outskirts, the fantastic Tachikue Gorge proving a spectacular natural highlight, with eerie statues and sharply rising cliffs.

Culture Spot - Old Taisha Station [1]

Just a short walk south of Izumo Shrine is the Old Taisha Station, which was closed in 1990 and eventually converted to a museum. Originally opened in 1924, the design of the wooden station building was inspired by, and modelled on, Izumo Shrine. Inside, railway enthusiasts can enjoy mannequins in period costumes, and other historical artefacts from the early years of Japanese rail travel.

Nature Spot - Lake Shinji [2]

Izumo's eponymous airport lies on the western shore of the vast Lake Shinji. The lake is made up of brackish water - its eastern area is connected via a sliver of water to the lagoon of Nakaumi and out onto the Sea of Japan.

Visitors can enjoy sunset cruises on the lake, as well as hot spring soaks at any one of the resort facilities on the lake's shores.

292

👍 Must see! Izumo Taisha ③

 Did you know?

Soba, so good
Izumo, and the wider Shimane area, is famous for its *soba* (buckwheat noodles). The Izumo variety is known for its dark colour and, specifically, *warigo soba* is served in a three-tier stack of lacquer bowls.

If you ever think you are 'shrined out' by parts of Japan that are ostensibly famous for their sacred history, try Izumo. Even for hardened Japanophiles, this is a delight.

Izumo's biggest attraction is the awe-inspiring Izumo Taisha - said to be the oldest shrine in Japan. Worshippers have been visiting this site for approximately 1,500 years, and the current buildings - dating from 1744 - are hugely impressive constructs, the central shrine being the largest of its kind in Japan. Izumo is a land of myths and legends, and every October the millions of Shinto gods are said to come to the shrine, a visit that is celebrated with an elaborate festival.

Any visitor is likely to notice the popularity of the shrine among young couples - a phenomenon explained by the shrine's presiding god being the deity of marriage, prompting visitors to pray for luck in love.

Outside the vast main hall are massive straw ropes known as *shimenawa*. Circumnavigate the grounds to see the impressive buildings and their roofs from all angles. By the shrine's main *torii* gate entrance, there are plenty of souvenir shops and eateries to supplement the trip. Local delicacies abound, and the road between the nearby station and the shrine is great for a wander.

🏠 Culture Spot - Izumo Yayoi-no-mori Museum ④

This museum is situated to the south of central Izumo, and displays various artefacts excavated from ancient Yayoi-era burial mounds. These include pottery, beads and bracelets that ancient luminaries took to the grave with them.

Chugoku

Shimane
IZUMO 出雲市

🌳 Nature Spot - Tachikue Gorge 5

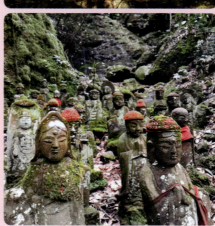

Located on the River Kando, about ten kilometres south of Izumo, is a natural treasure in the form of the dramatic cliffs and milky-green waters of the Tachikue Gorge. Two suspension bridges for walkers mark the area. A recommended circular walking course can be done in under an hour.

Cross the river on one of the pedestrian suspension bridges from the main road and walk along the well-maintained narrow path to gain great opportunities to observe the vertical cliff faces up close, backed by the sound of the gently flowing river below, and tiny trickling waterfalls from the clifftop.

Walk on a little, and Tachikue's main draw reveals itself - over 1,000 tiny stone Buddhist statues with various facial expressions, looking out onto the river in calm meditation. The statues are everywhere, in every crevice, nook and cranny of the cliff-face rock. It creates an altogether eerie atmosphere, albeit with an undeniable dash of cuteness.

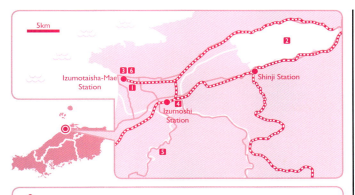

Key dates

May 14-16 - Imperial Grand Festival (Izumo Taisha)

October - Celebration of the annual coming of the Shinto gods

We say

" Izumo is a great spot for a day or two as part of a tour of the Shimane area. Why not combine it with a hot spring soak at Tamatsukurionsen, and a sample of the historical delights of the prefectural capital of Matsue? The gentle hike along the Tachikue Gorge was a particular highlight, with its impressive rocks and thousands of creepily cute miniature statues. "

Recommended for

Nature lovers

Shrine enthusiasts

🏠 Culture Spot - Shimane Museum of Ancient Izumo 6

This museum is a short walk from Izumo Taisha and a must-visit part of a trip to Izumo. It is a well-staffed, modern museum with an abundance of displays including Yayoi-era artefacts, replicas of ancient literary works and maps, plus - the museum's highlight - gorgeously designed vases and cups. Excavations of the area have also revealed a vast amount of ancient implements, especially bronze bells and spearheads dating from between the second century BC and the first century AD. There are also bizarrely shaped sixth-century pots designed and used for religious services. A fine museum that will help any visitor garner a more profound understanding of the deep cultural legacy of the area.

🚆 Getting there and around

✈ Izumo Airport. Take local buses or train services to the Izumo area.

🚅 There are no bullet train stops in Shimane, but train services run to Izumoshi Station and Izumotaisha-Mae Station via the local major stop of Matsue Station.

🚶 The shrine and museum are next to each other, but visitors will need to use wheeled transport to reach Tachikue Gorge. If taking a bus there, make sure you know the departure times, as they are infrequent.

📖 Further information

www.100hiddentowns.jp/shimane/izumo.html

Chugoku

Shimane

MASUDA 益田市

Masuda looks out from the west coast of Shimane Prefecture onto the Sea of Japan. Beyond the town centre, the land rises to a range of hills, valleys and gorges, gushing streams and tranquil paddy fields.

Within the town, a vibrant culture of art and traditional theatre thrive in both its stylish arts centre, and the more informal venues that house the area's renowned Iwami Kagura performances.

Nature Spot - Omote-Hikimi Gorge

The rainwater that gathers on the mountains of Chugoku becomes channelled into a fast-flowing stream that carves a dramatic, twisting gorge down through the valleys, through the town of Hikimi below, and then on to meet the Takatsu River.

Despite the area being a popular scenic spot during the warmer months (with some allocated areas for strolling), Masuda's revellers seem to be fastidiously tidy, so it is kept wonderfully litter-free.

Many of the beautiful spots from which to enjoy the sights and sounds of the gorge are only accessible by car or bicycle. Also, there are few landmarks or signposts in the area, so consider making use of a local taxi service to guide any excursion into the hills and valleys.

If you're not planning a picnic, ask your driver to meet you a little further down the hill and take some time to enjoy a stroll.

🏠 Culture Spot - Shimane Arts Centre ❷

Masuda boasts a fabulous arts centre called Shimane Arts Centre Grand Toit (Grantowa), that is home to several art galleries, theatre/concert halls and a cafeteria. The building is shrouded in magnificent brown tiles and lined with polished wooden floors and walls. As well as being the port of call for all major performers visiting Shimane Prefecture, the museum exhibits permanent collections alongside a regularly changing programme of exhibitions and events.

👁 Did you know?

Prominent poet
Masuda's most famous son is the poet Kakinomoto-no-Hitomaro. Born in the late seventh century, Hitomaro is considered by many to be the greatest of Japan's ancient poets. His position at the Nara Court was similar to that of poet laureate. The 'Manyoshu', the oldest anthology of Japanese poetry, contains dozens of his poems.

👍 Must see! Iwami Kagura

Every Saturday night, just a stone's throw from Masuda Station, a cross-section of Masuda town life - elderly couples, working parents with young children, indolent teens, theatre aficionados — all gather in an inconspicuous civic amenity room, to take their places on stacking chairs and *tatami* flooring, and immerse themselves for 90 minutes in ancient folk tales of magical gods and dragons, wrathful ogres, heroic warriors and tragic princesses, enacted by sword-wielding dancers to the driving rhythms of drums, cymbals and bamboo flutes. Children in the audience are at one moment terror-stricken as a beast roams the audience looking for an infant to steal away from its parents arms, a moment later scrabbling desperately to catch sweeties tossed into the spellbound gathering by a god of fishing and commerce.

Although closely related to the Japanese theatre traditions of *noh* and *kabuki*, Iwami Kagura (Iwami is the western region of Shimane Prefecture) is refreshingly free of high-brow trappings. Traditionally performed at village Shinto shrines, it now has a semi-permanent home in Masuda's town centre.

297

Chugoku

Shimane — MASUDA — 益田市

🏠 Culture Spot - Ikoji Temple [3] and Manpukuji Temple [4]

Founded in 1363, Ikoji was the family temple of the Masuda family. Toyo Sesshu, one of the most widely revered masters of ink and *washi* painting of his time, was the head priest here. Sesshu designed Ikoji's fabulous Zen garden.

Just a few minutes' walk from Ikoji is Manpukuji Temple. Built in 1374, its woodwork still contains bullet holes from a skirmish between Choshu and pro-Tokugawa forces in 1866. Manpukuji also has a beautiful, 500-year-old Zen garden.

🏠 Culture Spot
String Puppet Show

About four times a year, the puppeteers, narrators and musicians of the small but renowned Masuda String Puppets Association perform plays (*ningyo-joruri*) in the smaller of the two theatres in Masuda's Shimane Arts Centre.

The traditional string puppets used are over 100 years old, operated by a closely knit team of experts, from a gantry above the miniature stage. The performance is relayed on a large video screen above the stage for those sat further away. Tales of ancient family travails and feudal disputes are recounted by a narrator kneeling at the side of the puppet performance, to the accompaniment of live *shamisen* music. After the production ends, the audience are welcomed backstage to see the puppets at close quarters.

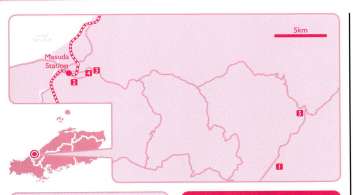

Key dates

late March / early April - cherry blossom season

second Saturday in June - Mito Fireflies Festival (short walk from Mito-onsen)

September 1st - Hassaku Festival (all-day Iwami Kagura performance at Kakinomoto Shrine and a horseback archery event at the bank of the Takatsu River near the shrine)

Autumn (Oct, Nov) - Iwami Kagura is often performed at harvest festivals at Masuda's shrines.

We say

"The rural charms of the hills behind Masuda make it a wonderful, clean, unspoilt destination, but difficult to negotiate without a car. I found the Iwami Kagura a fabulous experience - theatre by the people, for the people."

Recommended for

Fans of theatre

Those with access to a car or a budget for a taxi

Cyclists

🏠 Culture Spot - Minoji Yashiki 5

This restored farmhouse and its out-buildings house a collection of historical artefacts of local life, including farm tools, clothes, dishes, dolls and a display of sumptuous, hand-made Iwami Kagura costumes. In the main thatched building you can walk around the different rooms that housed the master's family and visiting samurai warriors.

👫 Kids

If the youngsters are tugging at your sleeve to run around and play, Manyo Koen (near Hagi Iwami Airport) is a large park with a spacious playground, a cafeteria, and pretty gardens with a great view of Masuda Town and the ocean. On a rainy day, there is the Shimane Arts Centre, while in the summer there are sandy beaches to keep the whole family happy.

🍶 Food and Drink

Being a sunny seaside town, Masuda prides itself on its range of seafood and fruit. Local specialties are *hamaguri* (clam), *ika* (squid), *ayu* (sweet fish), *wasabi* and *yuzu* (small citrus fruit), melon and grapes. There are plenty of restaurants selling the local delicacies near the town centre.

⇌ Getting there and around

- ✈ Hagi Iwami Airport. Travel to central Masuda by shuttle bus.
- 🚆 Shin-Yamaguchi Station. Travel to Masuda Station by local train services.
- 🚌 Although there are local buses, some of the more beautiful spots in the area are difficult to access without a car or a taxi. Also note that rental bicycles might not be available.

📖 Further information

www.100hiddentowns.jp/shimane/masuda.html

Chugoku

Shimane

NISHINOSHIMA
西ノ島町

An explosion of green, formed by the collapse of a massive, ancient stratovolcano, the island of Nishinoshima is one of the most beautiful and remote areas of Japan. From dramatic wave-cut shore lines, to verdant pastures patrolled by free-grazing horses, Nishinoshima is a joy to visit.

Culture Spot
Hekifu-kan Museum [1]

The museum is situated on what was once the residence of Emperor Go-Daigo during his exile on the island. The building itself consists of just a room or two, but there is a pretty shrine at the top of some steps with more views over the sea.

Culture Spot - Mount Takuhi and Shrine [2]

Mount Takuhi is the highest mountain on the island, but is actually only a short walk from the car park. Its main feature is the shrine - the oldest building on the island - that is built into an indent on the cliff face. The lights on it once operated as a lighthouse to guide errant fishermen back home.

🌳 Nature Spot - Kuniga Coast Sightseeing Boat Tour

Imperial retreat?

The Oki Islands were at one point designated 'islands of exile', and up to 2,000 nobles were sent here, including two emperors - Emperor Go-Daigo and the less fortunate Emperor Go-Toba.

Emperor Go-Toba was exiled to the islands after revolting against the shogunate government. Whether he enjoyed the scenic nature and remoteness, or pined for the metropolitan life of the court in Kyoto, we will never know, as he died here.

Emperor Go-Daigo, we can be more certain, was not impressed by the charms of the island, as he promptly escaped, raised an army, and then retook his capital - if only for a short time.

The tour embarking from Beppu Port is a wonderful way to enjoy the stunning coastline of Nishinoshima. A shorter tour is available from Urago Port (April to October).

There is also the option for sea kayaking, which provides an even closer encounter with the sea caves. Make sure to book in advance, especially during summer months.

" Starting out from Beppu Port, sightseeing boats chug through the waves, pulling in to shore to admire several bays and coves, and then back out to sea towards the next spot. Flocks of birds wheel and dive in and out of small pockets in the rock walls. The captain directs his passengers' attention to the sea caves drilled into the cliff faces by the elements. They can appear alarmingly small, as the captain tacks a course directly towards one. Passengers experience some unease as the captain then steers the boat towards what appears to be a sheer rock face, and next heads towards a small patch of shadow that could double as a rabbit hole, and picks up speed. The boat, literally, scrapes through, whilst dramatic music plays over the PA system. With that, the boat pops back out to sea, before heading through a canal to the other side of the island. "

Chugoku

Shimane — NISHINOSHIMA 西ノ島町

👍 Must see! Kuniga Coast Hiking Track

Admire the small *torii* gate on a rocky promontory as the waves lap over the base of the rocks, and then turn to face the walk ahead of you - to the top of the 257-metre-high sea cliff, Matengai. The path leads up a grass-covered hill following the line of the cliffs. Cows and horses graze freely over the area and seem unconcerned by passersby. The path runs close to a small bay with the impressive Tsutenkyo rock arch jutting out into the sea. The route is a little steep at points, but after an hour or so you will reach the summit. From there, you can gaze down at the dramatic coastline, the green of the fields, bordered by jagged grey rocks, leading to the clear blue of the ocean. As you look out to sea, the next stop would be Vladivostok, which from here is closer than Sapporo. The coastal path showcases the best of the scenery that Nishinoshima has to offer, and should be the one thing not to miss for any visit here.

Akao Lookout and Onimai Lookout [3]

Both these lookouts are on a spit of land located a 30-minute drive from the Kuniga Coast Hiking Track. Navigate the small road up the hill and then walk out onto the lush green pastures, as the ubiquitous cattle occasionally glance in your direction. Akao Lookout offers views back over the sea and the Matengai cliff and coastline. From Onimai Lookout you can see the surrounding islands.

🏨 Accommodation - Kuniga-so Hotel [4]

Built on a small bluff overlooking Urago Town, Kuniga-so Hotel's prominent geographical position mirrors the outstanding stay you will enjoy here. The corner rooms offer superb panoramic views of the sea and the islands. As the sun sets, watch the shipping fleet head out to sea for the night's fishing. Dinner consists of a mixture of local foods - particularly seafood - and is usually a spectacular and voluminous affair.

Key dates

August 16 - Sharabune Spirit Boats Festival (constructed of straw and bamboo, and decorated with coloured paper, boats are sent off and set afloat to console the spirits of the dead)

We say

" Nishinoshima provides a beautiful glimpse of the geological forces that still shape Japan, an abundance of nature, and the role that people have carved out between the two. This island will delight any traveller. "

Recommended for

Families
Nature enthusiasts
Outdoor types

🏠 Culture Spot
Furusato-kan Museum 5

Located near the port, the Furusato-kan Museum has a number of archaeological artefacts from the island -some dating back as far as 30,000 years ago.

Despite having only rudimentary English information available, there are enough engaging objects and pictures to maintain interest until the boat arrives.

⇌ Getting there and around

✈ Oki Airport (Dogo Island). From here, take a 30 to 60-minute boat ride. Alternatively, fly to either Yonago Airport (Tottori) or Izumo Airport (Shimane) on the mainland. From here, transfer to either Sakaiminato Port (train or bus) or Shichirui Port (bus) and take a boat.

🚆 Matsue Station or Yonago Station. Travel by local train or bus services to Sakaiminato Port, or by bus to Shichirui Port, and take a boat.

Boat - From the mainland, Nishinoshima takes two hours by fast ferry, or two and a half to three hours by regular ferry (depending on the route). From Dogo Island, it takes 30 minutes by fast ferry or one hour by regular ferry. Check timetables carefully when arranging your trip. Prior booking is needed for the fast ferry.

🚌 There is a limited bus service on the island, so check in advance for routes and times. The island is small enough to make most places accessible by rental cycle, although it is very hilly. You can hire battery-powered bicycles from the tourist information office at Beppu Port. The island also has taxi and car rental services.

📖 Further information
www.100hiddentowns.jp/shimane/nishinoshima.html

Chugoku

MISASA
Tottori
三朝町

Misasa is a relaxing hot spring resort that boasts curative radium-rich waters. The characters for Misasa literally mean 'three mornings', a name that is said to have originated from a belief that a visitor who stays for three mornings in the hot springs of the town will be fully cured of any ailment they are suffering. Aside from a relaxing soak, the main draw of the town is the Nageiredo Hall of Sanbutsuji Temple, located on the cliff face of Mount Mitoku nearby.

👍 Must see! Mount Mitoku [1]

This mountain has long been worshipped as a sacred retreat for Buddhist monks. Its holy heritage dates back at least 1,300 years. Sanbutsuji Temple's Nageiredo Hall [2] is located high on the mountain. This awe-inspiring, Heian-period structure is built into the face of a cliff, and its construction remains a mystery. It is astounding to think of the dedication this involved, as even a modern-day climb requires organisation and gusto.

It is said that viewing this temple will change your outlook on life. That depends of course on how jaundiced your view is of the world, and how much adrenalin is coursing through your system after such a climb, but there is no doubting that the steep ascent is well rewarded with views of this structure and reflections on the mysteries surrounding the devotees who built it.

Though it takes less than two hours to ascend and come back down, there are sections of the climb where you will need to negotiate tree roots, and a chain section. Climbers must ascend in pairs at least, so travel with a friend or wait for the next group to come along. Rest assured, there are no especial dangers if

you are fit and equipped with firm shoes and the necessary energy.

There are several other small temples along the climb. Not as old as Nageiredo, these smaller constructs date back to the Kamakura and Edo eras. The initial approach encompasses the main temple plus a pretty bridge at the foot of the climb. The ascent is also rewarded with excellent views of the lush surrounding greenery and the Mitoku River flowing below.

Take the opportunity to imagine yourself as an ancient monk ascending to holy bliss, or simply enjoy the views and get some good exercise.

The path to the temple is closed from winter until spring, so check accessibility before your visit.

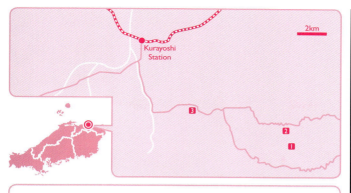

🌳 Nature Spot - Misasa Onsen 3

Misasa Onsen is a great spot to stay overnight and soothe away the aches of the Mount Mitoku climb. The town lines both banks of the fast-flowing Mitoku River, and is populated by several hot spring resort facilities. There are even some outdoor public baths beside the river, and pretty bridges with foot *onsen*.

🏠 Culture Spot - Kurayoshi

Kurayoshi, located near to Misasa, is the transport hub for trains to Tottori, Himeji and Kyoto. It has a couple of sights of note, including the gorgeous cherry blossoms around the pond of Utsubuki Park. There are also rows of warehouses nearby (the *kura* from which it is said Kurayoshi gets its name) which provide a snapshot of Edo-era tranquility.

🚆 Getting there and around

- ✈ Tottori Airport. Take the Airport shuttle bus to Misasa Hot Spring.
- 🚄 Himeji Station. Take JR rapid trains to Kurayoshi Station.
- 🚌 Buses and taxis can be taken from Kurayoshi Station to Misasa Onsen and to nearby Mount Mitoku.

📔 Further information
www.100hiddentowns.jp/tottori/misasa.html

💡 Did you know?

Monk magic

Nageiredo Hall acquired its name, literally 'throw into', because legend says the temple was thrown into the mountain by a pilgrim monk's magic. It is not the only magic found here – the shrine at the foot of the mountain emits the sound of croaking and gurgling, uncannily like the call of frogs. The noise actually emanates from buried earthenware pots, into which water drops from the shrine's well and echoes through the rocks - a feature that spawns much curiosity from visitors.

Key dates

end of July - Curie Festival (fireworks and performances)

We say

" Although I was initially nervous, the Mount Mitoku climb was easier and more rewarding than I had envisaged. Coupled with a wonderful soak and outstanding service at a local spa, it is clear why this rustic part of Tottori is so popular. "

Recommended for

Climbers

Onsen lovers

Chugoku

境港市

Tottori

SAKAIMINATO

Sakaiminato is a very pleasant port town that sits in the northwestern tip of Tottori Prefecture, with low rolling hills reaching down to the water's edge. Large fishing trawlers dock at the bay, and the sea dominates the aura of the town.

👍 Must see!
Mizuki Shigeru Road ①

Sakaiminato's most famous son, Shigeru Mizuki, created a series of internationally acclaimed cartoons, often dealing with ghosts and the supernatural. He credited his passion for the spooky to listening to the ghost stories told by a local fisherwoman of the town he grew up in. Sakaiminato has now taken Mizuki and his creations as their emblem. More than 170 statues line the Mizuki Shigeru Road, all of them strange and ghoulish, creating a kind of Japanese Gothic motif. The area is particularly well worth visiting in the evening, when the street lights cast strange hues and shadows over the kooky castings.

🌳 Nature Spot
Sakaiminato Museum of Sea Life ②

Boasting that it hosts the largest display of stuffed fish in Japan, the sea life museum does not disappoint on its promise. There is a categorised wall of sea life, and the second floor offers seasonal exhibitions, often with a local theme. Potentially worth visiting just for building up an appetite for the seafood restaurant next door.

306

Culture Spot
Yumeminato Tower

Yumeminato Tower marks the central focus of the seafront development of Sakaiminato, and offers unrestricted views in all directions. From the top of the tower, visitors can enjoy a 360° view of Lake Naka Umi to the west, the peninsula stretching away towards the mainland, and Mount Daisen glaring back from across the bay. The third floor has a permanent exhibition of cultural information relating to the various countries located on the rim of the Sea of Japan. There is a selection of exhibits from Russia, Korea, and China, as well as an adjoining room where kids can dress up in the various national costumes of these neighbouring countries.

Culture Spot
Mizuki Shigeru Museum

Dedicated to the man himself, this is a modern, interactive museum. There are plenty of displays and objects about Mizuki's life and works. It is all in Japanese though, so it's difficult to follow unless you have a good knowledge of the source material.

Getting there and around

- Yonago Airport. Take local bus or train services to Sakaiminato Station.
- Yonago Station. Take local train services to Sakaiminato Station.
- Sakaiminato is a very small, compact town, so getting around should be no problem. There is also a regular bus service to all parts of the area, centred at the train station.

Did you know?

Promoter of peace
Shigeru Mizuki was greatly affected by his experiences in the war. He almost didn't return to Japan as he was offered a wife and land by the local tribe on the Pacific island he was stationed on. He was a lifelong campaigner for peace, and stated that the characters he created could only appear in times of peace.

Key dates

July - Port Festival. (Festival for the continued prosperity and safety of the boats. It finishes with fireworks and a dancing parade. There is a sea parade with over 60 boats running through the Sakai channel.)

October - Marine Products Festival (held at the fish market, with stalls and performances, and lots of fresh seafood)

We say

" Sakaiminato's compactness means that it is easy to navigate and get around. It serves as a great gateway to the nearby Oki Islands and has enough to make it worth a day trip in itself. "

Recommended for

Lovers of seafood

Shigeru Mizuki fans

Further information
www.100hiddentowns.jp/tottori/sakaiminato.html

307

Chugoku

Yamaguchi 萩市 HAGI

Nestled against the Sea of Japan on the coast of Yamaguchi Prefecture, Hagi is a town with impeccably preserved history and more than its fair share of local heroes. Although its castle was torn down under the orders of the modernising government at the beginning of the Meiji era, the surrounding town boasts so much historical architecture that the cliché of 'being taken back in time' seems perfectly apt.

Outside the town, visitors can see the legacy of later eras, with some of Japan's earliest industrialisation efforts represented by the remains of a weaponry furnace and shipbuilding docks dating back to the end of the Edo era. Hagi is also the hometown of *Hagi yaki* pottery, renowned for its simplicity and quality.

Culture Spot
Tokoji Temple ①

This was the temple of the Mori clan, constructed in 1691. It is a large wooden complex and worth visiting for a couple of stand-out landmarks - the eerie stone graves of the Mori clan, and a large, wooden fish hanging from the ceiling of one of the cloistered corridors, which was struck to announce meals and religious services to the resident monks.

🏠 Culture Spot - Shokasonjuku Academy ②

Located in the eastern part of Hagi Town, Shokasonjuku Academy was a school set up at the end of the Tokugawa period, which is now registered as a World Heritage Site.

Shokasonjuku Academy was headed by Shoin Yoshida, a scholar of military science in the Hagi Domain. In the small one-storey wooden house with a tiled roof and *tatami* mats, he would urge pupils to be successful in life, regardless of their social status. He was later placed under house arrest (in a building adjacent to the school rooms) for ruffling the feathers of the stoic Tokugawa government of the time. Shinsaku Takasugi and Hirobumi Ito, two other local luminaries, were also students of this academy, and they later went on to play huge roles in the modernisation of Japan, as it finally accepted western influences.

👀 Did you know?

The spoils of defeat
Terumoto Mori constructed the castle and its surrounding town after his defeat at the epoch-defining Battle of Sekigahara in 1600. His domain was greatly reduced in size, but seeing where he lived in terms of natural surrounds and castle town layout, it seems he didn't do too badly!

🏠 Culture Spot - Hagi Uragami Museum ③

This modern museum showcases art and pottery of the Hagi area. Aside from the splendid displays of *ukiyoe* woodblock art prints, the main draws are the exhibits of *Hagi yaki* pottery, with pieces dating back many centuries. The wares gained fame for their recommended use in tea ceremonies, which would give rise to the key feature of the pottery – it changes colour over time thanks to the tea slowly staining the *Hagi yaki*.

Food and Drink

Fugu for you?
Ugly-looking and potentially fatal... why not try *fugu*! A speciality of the Yamaguchi area, *fugu* (blowfish) as *tempura* is a recommended treat. *Fugu* rice crackers and *furikake* (topping for rice) are also good souvenirs. Don't worry, it's safe!

Chugoku

Yamaguchi
HAGI

萩市

🏠 Culture Spot - Reverberatory Furnace ❹ and Ebisugahana Shipyard ❺

The Hagi Domain made efforts to develop a 'reverberatory furnace', a smelting device used for casting iron cannons, as part of their attempts to strengthen their coastal defences. The ruins remaining today include a portion of the chimney overlooking the sea - a testimony to the determination of the town to develop their technology, despite having very little expertise, as the country was still closed to foreigners at that time.

Close to the furnace ruins is the breakwater of the Ebisugahana Shipyard - still looking as it did in the Edo era. In 1853, spooked by the power of Commodore Perry and his black ships, the Tokugawa shogunate lifted a ban on the building of large ships, in order to reinforce the defences of each domain. Using information and techniques gleaned from Russian and Dutch shipbuilding, ships were built at Ebisugahana. The Hagi Meiringakusha visitor centre has further detailed explanations, with eager guides on hand to proudly inform you of the town's industrial legacy.

Key dates

May - Hagi-Natsumikan Festival

November - Hagi Jidai Festival (parade of participants in samurai costumes)

We say

" Hagi is a great location to spend a couple of days. English signage around the town gives clear insight into the architecture, history, and lives of the famous names of the area. A fascinating destination for history lovers, especially those who want to get a taste of how a castle town looked in the Edo era. "

Recommended for

History lovers

👍 Must see! Hagi Castle Town ⑥

Hagi Castle, once the home of the Mori clan, was constructed in 1604 and quickly gave rise to a flourishing town. Hagi has been spared damage by natural disasters and war, so the layouts of many buildings and streets from that time live on to the present day. During a relaxing stroll around the narrow lanes of the area, visitors can see samurai residences, and the distinctive white walls that remain from Hagi's days as a key area of the Choshu domain.

Set in a tranquil, wooded spot, the castle ruins are excellent for exploration - the foundations and moats are intact, and visitors can peek at the beach and sea beyond, through loopholes in the outer wall. Those with more energy can climb up the small mountain behind the ruins.

Nearby is a museum devoted to the history of Hagi, including exhibits on the Edo-era castle and samurai, plus displays on the town's young modernisers of the Meiji period, who were influential in implementing radical change throughout the country.

🔁 Getting there and around

- ✈ Yamaguchi Ube Airport. Travel by train or bus services to Hagi.
- 🚄 Shin-Yamaguchi Station. Travel by bus to the centre of Hagi.
- 🚶 The town of Hagi is quite compact, and the sights of the old castle town are easily reached on foot. A rental bicycle is recommended to expand the range of a trip to include Shokasonjuku Academy and the Meiji industrial legacy sites that lie to the east of the town.

📖 Further information

www.100hiddentowns.jp/yamaguchi/hagi.html

CHUGOKU

中国地方

OTHER TOWNS

Shimane
OKUIZUMO

Locked in a weaving mass of hills and rivers, Okuizumo is home to the traditional iron making process, *tatara*. The area was the centre of iron production until the industrial revolution, and has a number of sites and museums dedicated to the industry. The Oni-no-shitaburui Gorge offers great views of the river crashing over its boulder-strewn bed.

Culture Spot Tatara-to-Tokenkan Museum
Nature Spot Hinokami, Kamedake, and Sajiro Onsens
Must see Oni-no-shitaburui Gorge
We say The overwhelming mass of nature seems to engulf and overrun the sites in the area, and has left little trace of what was once the largest iron-working region in pre-industrial Japan. Okuizumo encompasses a large area and is difficult to get around, so a car is a must.

312

Shimane
YASUGI

Formerly well-known for its steel production, Yasugi currently draws visitors for its historical ruins, comedic *yasugibushi* dance and, most of all, for the consistently award-winning gardens of the Adachi Museum of Art.

Culture Spot Gassantoda Castle Ruins
Must see Adachi Museum of Art
We say The hike to Gassantoda Castle Ruins was worth the effort, and the gardens of the Adachi Museum of Art deserve the praise they have been showered with. Yasugi's proximity to the larger towns of Matsue and Yonago (Tottori Prefecture) makes it a great day trip if you're in the area.

Hiroshima
KITAHIROSHIMA

Kitahiroshima covers much of the central Hiroshima area, and thus its attractions are widely spread out. *Hiroshima Kagura* is a dramatic form of music and dance, linked to the Shinto religion and the agricultural seasons. Mibu-no-Hana Taue Rice Planting Festival is famous for its drums, colours and bulls. For winter visitors, there is also a series of low mountains and even a couple of snow resorts.

Culture Spot Hiroshima Kagura performances, Mibu-no-Hana Taue Rice Planting Festival
Nature Spot Yahata Marsh
We say Kitahiroshima's attractions, like the town, are rooted in the agricultural life of the area. An expansive region with scarce public transport, this is a chance to see a slice of rural life in Japan.

SHIKOKU

四国

The Shikoku Region
The smallest of Japan's major islands, Shikoku is best known for its 88-temple pilgrimage route, Meiji-era modernising historic figures, and its stunning scenery. Wonderful as a retreat from crowded, urban Japan, even its prefectural capitals have a gentle, friendly feel, with feudal castles and local eateries perfect for visitors to enjoy. Shikoku is connected to Honshu by three long bridges, including the series of double deck bridges collectively known as the Great Seto Bridge, which link Okayama and Kagawa prefectures. Encompassing four prefectures, the island is also known for its unique and wildly popular festivals, such as the Yosakoi Festival and the Awa-Odori dance festival in summer.

EHIME PREFECTURE
Ehime covers the northwestern area of Shikoku, and dozens of small islands in the Seto Inland Sea. The capital, Matsuyama, is a popular destination, thanks to its well-preserved historical sites. Matsuyama is a good base for exploring other areas, such as the tranquil countryside of Kumakogen, and the Shimanami Kaido island-hopping route, that provides astounding views of the surrounding islets - great for cyclists.

Prefectural Capital
Matsuyama City
✈ Airports
Matsuyama Airport
🚆 Main Train Stations
Matsuyama Station

Other Tourist Attractions
Matsuyama
The prefectural capital is chiefly visited for its magnificent castle, and one of Japan's oldest hot springs, the Dogo Onsen.

Uchiko
A quiet, rural time-warp, Uchiko was once a historically important producer of wax and paper. The old town area has preserved buildings from its heyday, and a *kabuki* theatre.

Dogo Onsen

Ozu City
This historical castle town still has areas with traditional houses and lanes. Cormorant fishing in the summer is another key attraction here.

Warei Taisai Ushi-oni Festival (Uwajima)
This is a three-day-long summer festival in mid-July, incorporating dancing troupes that perform the *Gaiya* carnival dance through the shopping arcade of the town, accompanied by various floats. The festival climaxes with portable shrines converging towards the town's river, surrounded by torchlight.

KAGAWA PREFECTURE

Set between mountains to the south, and the Seto Inland Sea to the north, Kagawa is a wonderful destination for a serene getaway, with pretty landscapes and a wide range of attractions for art buffs. The region is famous for its *udon* noodles - a must-try for visitors.

The prefecture is home to a number of islands of the Seto Inland Sea, including the relaxing retreats and art displays of Naoshima and Teshima. The coastal resort island of Shodoshima also has an art scene, with opportunities to enjoy outdoor installations from previous festivals.

Prefectural Capital
Takamatsu City
✈ Airports
Takamatsu Airport
🚆 Main Train Stations
Takamatsu Station

Other Tourist Attractions
Takamatsu
This historically significant port city is home to a fine castle, and the beautiful Edo-era landscaped Ritsurin Garden with its *koi* (carp) ponds and a teahouse.
Kotohira
A pleasant riverside town, Kotohira is the site of the famous Kompirasan Shrine at the top of a steep climb, and a preserved *kabuki* theatre.
The Setouchi Triennale (also known as the Setouchi International Art Festival)
This art festival is held every three years on a number of islands in the Seto Inland Sea. Ostensibly focusing on contemporary art, the festival has helped Kagawa Prefecture and the wider region gain international recognition as a key location for promotion of the arts.

Ritsurin Garden

315

SHIKOKU

KOCHI PREFECTURE

The calm, rural feel of Shikoku pervades throughout Kochi Prefecture, thanks to its beaches, mountains and rivers. Historically, Kochi is hugely significant as, under its former name of Tosa, it was the setting of much resistance and political intrigue - the young samurai looking to Japan to modernise and adapt, following the end of the country's era of isolation.

This history is proudly displayed, with statues and museums devoted to the young moderniser, Ryoma Sakamoto, dotting the prefecture. Away from Kochi City, Shimanto is worth a visit for its delightful river and countryside. The vast area of Konan provides visitors with museums and galleries to accompany its pretty natural sights.

Prefectural Capital
Kochi City

✈ Airports
Kochi Ryoma Airport

🚉 Main Train Stations
Kochi Station

Other Tourist Attractions
Kochi
The prefectural capital is small and relaxed, with a castle, temples, a beach to the south, and a museum dedicated to its most famous son, Ryoma Sakamoto.

Yosakoi Festival
This is a hugely popular summer festival in which colourfully dressed dance teams parade to a type of music that merges traditional Japanese sounds with a modern, rock style.

Extreme Seasonal Conditions
Prone to typhoons July - October.

Yosakoi Festival

TOKUSHIMA PREFECTURE

Located on the eastern end of Shikoku Island, Tokushima Prefecture is linked to Honshu Island by bridge, and is popular as a starting point for the island-wide pilgrimage route that takes in the many temples that dot Shikoku. Tokushima City is most famous for its Awa-Odori, a unique costumed dance held during the mid-August *obon* holiday. Away from the prefectural capital, Miyoshi is a must-visit for its mountains and outdoor activities.

Prefectural Capital
Tokushima City

✈ Airports
Tokushima Airport

🚆 Main Train Stations
Tokushima Station

Other Tourist Attractions
Naruto
Characterised by the swirling whirlpools found in the Strait of Naruto, the town is also known as the embarkation point for the 88-temple Shikoku pilgrimage, with its Ryozenji Temple regarded as the first on the trail.

Iya Valley
This secluded valley provides visitors with stunning views of rocky gorges and mountain slopes, as well as hot spring spots. The deceptively frail-looking vine bridges that form crossing points over the gorges are popular attractions.

Awa-Odori Dance Festival (Tokushima City)
Dating back some 400 years, this dance is one of the most fun and attractive in Japan. The females dress in elegant *yukata* (summer *kimono*) and distinctive straw hats, while the men wear festival *happi*, and both dance to compelling traditional flute and drum music. The atmosphere is fantastic, and the event is highly recommended for any visitor to the area.

Naruto whirlpools

Ashizuri-Uwakai National Park

NATIONAL PARKS

Setonaikai National Park
(see Chugoku)

Ashizuri-Uwakai National Park
Area: 11,345 ha
Features: cliffs, coral reefs, subtropical marine life, forests
Did you know? Hot weather and heavy rainfall have created distinctive plants that inhabit this park. These include the giant Picea torano trees.

317

SHIKOKU

HIDDEN TOWNS

EHIME
320   Imabari

KAGAWA
324   Naoshima
326   Shodoshima

KOCHI
330   Konan
332   Shimanto

TOKUSHIMA
334   Miyoshi

CLIMATE (monthly average temperatures)

SHODOSHIMA (north Kagawa)

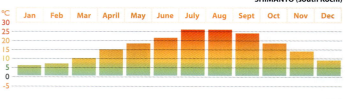

SHIMANTO (south Kochi)

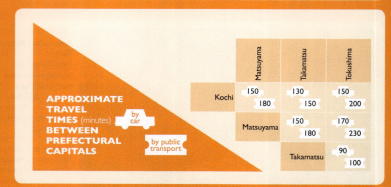

APPROXIMATE TRAVEL TIMES (minutes) **BETWEEN PREFECTURAL CAPITALS** — by car / by public transport

	Matsuyama	Takamatsu	Tokushima
Kochi	150 / 180	130 / 150	150 / 200
Matsuyama		150 / 180	170 / 230
Takamatsu			90 / 100

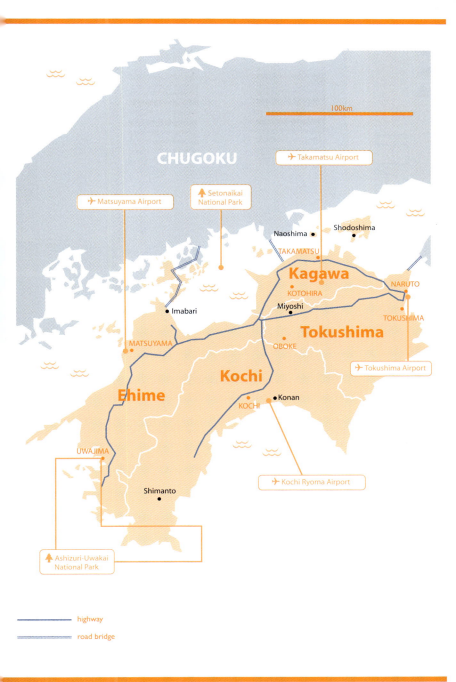

Shikoku

Ehime

今治市 IMABARI

Best known as the start (or end) point of the 70km-long Shimanami Kaido cycling route that connects the islands of the Seto Inland Sea between Shikoku and Honshu, Imabari itself has plenty of attractions to enjoy over a few hours spent in the town. The municipality of Imabari includes a number of islands in the Ehime Prefecture section of the Shimanami Kaido, that were once home to the famous Murakami Pirates, who ruled this part of the Seto Inland Sea during the Middle Ages.

🌳 Nature Spot - Kurushima-Kaikyo Bridge

The Kurushima-Kaikyo Bridge, which connects the island of Oshima to the mainland of Shikoku, is the world's longest suspension bridge structure. It was completed in 1999, after more than ten years of construction. A couple of parks in Imabari provide spectacular views of the bridge.

Kirosan Observatory Park on Oshima is known as a splendid spot for sunset views of the islands, with the bridge lit up to display the grandeur of its engineering.

Itoyama Park, on the mainland, is another recommended spot to climb to before you set off on your bicycle. It provides an up-close view of the bridge, while its observation facility houses a panel explaining the technology that was implemented during the bridge's construction.

 Did you know?

Piloting pirates

There is an ongoing debate as to the correct way to describe the Murakami Pirates. Considering their main role was as a kind of sea-guiding service, to be described as pirates perhaps does them a disservice. The Japanese words *suigun* (navy) and *kaizoku* (pirates) are used interchangeably to describe them, but the Murakami Suigun Museum argues, convincingly, that the correct translation should be 'people of the sea', which nicely defines their cultured, largely peaceful, existence.

Towel down

Alongside its maritime and shipbuilding industries, Imabari, perhaps surprisingly, is the country's largest towel production centre. Make use of their quality towels to dab the sweat off during the long Shimanami Kaido bike ride.

 Culture Spot - Oyamazumi Shrine 2

Omishima Island, the third island on the Shimanami Kaido travelling northwards, boasts the Oyamazumi Shrine – a place of worship devoted to the protection of sailors and soldiers.

The shrine is located in the centre of the island, away from the Shimanami route, but a pleasant spot to visit if time allows.

Nearby is the Omishima Museum of Art, which displays contemporary Japanese works.

 Food and Drink

Aside from the local seafood industry, Imabari also has one of the highest concentrations of *yakitori* (skewered chicken) shops in the country. The twist is that here it is cooked on a hot plate, rather than barbecued over a grill.

Must do! Oshima Island 3

The first island off the Shikoku mainland is Oshima, still technically part of Imabari City. Depending on the route, the hills may be steep for cyclists and require a certain amount of stamina. However, the peaks offer excellent views of the islands that sometimes appear to hover over these famous straits.

Shikoku

Ehime

今治市

IMABARI

🏠 Culture Spot - Imabari Castle

Occupying a wonderful location overlooking the inland sea, Imabari Castle is a must-see for visitors with time on their hands at the end, or prior to, their bicycle journey. As with many castles in Japan, Imabari's is a reconstruction of the Edo-era towers that dominated the town before the modernising zeal of the Meiji era did away with the previous structure.

What distinguishes this castle from many others is its seaside location — one of three such so-called *Mizujiro*, along with those of Nakatsu in Oita and Takamatsu in Kagawa. The moat is filled with seawater, and fish can be seen swimming in its murky shallows.

The castle was constructed by Takatora Todo in 1608, as part of his reward (like so many *daimyo* lords of the time) for backing the winning side at the Battle of Sekigahara. Todo was particularly keen on castle construction, and the beauty of Imabari perhaps indicates his passion for architectural elegance over tactical advantage.

🏠 Culture Spot - Shimanami Kaido

As the gateway to the Shimanami Kaido, most visitors either start at or end up at Imabari. If deciding to do the journey northwards, towards the Honshu mainland, there are wondrous views ahead. The islands of Ikuchijima and Innoshima (parts of Hiroshima Prefecture) are equally as rewarding as the Imabari islands. The Honshu port of call for cyclists is the well-known town of Onomichi, whose hills boast pretty temples and a laid-back, fishing-port atmosphere, reminiscent of similar towns in Europe.

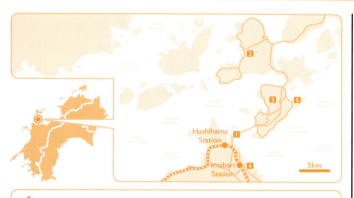

Key dates

early August - Onmaku Festival, Imabari City on the Shikoku mainland (this annual two-day festival includes dances, songs and medieval naval costumes, with a fireworks display finale)

third Sunday of October - Otomouma Festival (set at Imabari's Kamo Shrine, this festival features boys riding horses as part of a traditional prayer for familial safety and a bumper harvest)

🏠 Culture Spot
Murakami Pirates 5

Three of the islands along the Shimanami Kaido (Nojima, Innoshima and Kurushima) were long used as bases for the Murakami Pirates, who exercised huge control over the seafaring traders of the Middle Ages. Their major earnings were not from plunder, but from acting as guides through the difficult currents of the inland sea. They ruled the waves right up until the start of the Edo era.

These fast, rough currents can be witnessed today from several spots on bridges along the route. Their chaotic undertows are a bizarre sight, as the sea appears to be flowing speedily in several different directions at once. Visitors can see these currents up close by taking a boat trip around the tiny, uninhabited Nojima island.

The Murakami Suigun Museum showcases a remarkable array of objects from the period - including weaponry, boats and banners, supplemented by

scale models and maps. These displays wonderfully illustrate the Murakami Pirates' historical domination of the area.

We say

"The Shimanami Kaido cycling experience is up there with some of the best activities Japan has to offer. The Seto Inland Sea is beautiful, and if you are fortunate enough to have good weather, the ride is a dream. Allow at least two days for the trip, to properly soak up the sights along the way."

Recommended for
Cyclists
Nature lovers

⇌ Getting there and around

 Matsuyama Airport. Take local train services to Imabari Station.

Okayama Station. Travel by rapid train services to Imabari Station.

A rental car offers a speedier way to explore the area, but the main draw of the Shimanami Kaido is the biking route, which can be done in one day if you are used to two-wheeled fun. A much more leisurely pace, over two or three days, affords the time to rest at the pleasant *minshuku* and hotels that dot the area, and to soak up the wonderful views that the many viewpoints and bridges provide of this beautiful part of the world.

 Further information
www.100hiddentowns.jp/ehime/imabari.html

323

Shikoku

直島町

Kagawa

NAOSHIMA

"Red Pumpkin" ©Yayoi Kusama, 2006 Naoshima Miyanoura Port Square

Located between Honshu and Shikoku are a number of small islands that form the key features of the Seto Inland Sea. In order to invigorate the local culture and economy, a few have in recent years fostered an arts initiative. One of them - the delightful, small island of Naoshima - now complements its sandy beaches and pretty countryside with a range of galleries and outdoor exhibits that dot the island, and provide a fun search-and-discover adventure in extremely pleasant surroundings.

Culture Spot - Naoshima Fishing Park [1]

This fishing facility is a great place for both adults and children to borrow a rod and enjoy a safe, sea fishing experience. The area includes a fixed pier, a floating pier, a fishing raft and a fishing pond.

Culture Spot - Umi no Eki Naoshima (Sea Station) [2]

The marine station 'Naoshima' is a ferry terminal located at Miyaura Port, the gateway to Naoshima.

This welcoming arrival point for the island has a tourist information centre, a cafe, outlets selling local speciality products, ticket booths for the boats, and a bus terminal.

Food and Drink

Kagawa is famous for its chewy *udon*, and is the largest producer of this thick noodle in Japan, utilising locally sourced ingredients for its soup. The prefecture even has *udon* schools where you can make, then consume, your own dishes.

Must see! Galleries and Art Exhibits

There are many galleries and museums for visitors to Naoshima to enjoy, including Chichu Art Museum, Benesse House Museum, ANDO MUSEUM, and Lee Ufan Museum.

Getting there and around

🛬 Takamatsu Airport. Take local transport to Takamatsu Port and board one of the regular ferries to Naoshima Island.

🚢 Okayama Station. Take local train services to Uno Station and board one of the regular ferries to Naoshima Island.

If coming from the Shikoku mainland, boats run directly to Naoshima from Takamatsu.

🚲 It is possible to walk around from gallery to gallery on the island, but a car or bicycle will allow much more time to appreciate the art at a leisurely pace. There is a reasonably frequent and cheap bus service around the island, and plenty of signage and help in English.

Further information
www.100hiddentowns.jp/kagawa/naoshima.html

🔍 Did you know?

Art smart
The Setouchi Triennale (the region's international art festival) is held every three years. The festival in 2016 included 12 islands as well as the ports of Takamatsu and Uno.

Key dates

2019, 2022, 2025
- Seto Triennale (international arts festival with exhibits scheduled throughout the year)

We say

❝What a wonderful way to boost a local economy! Not all the art exhibits on Naoshima will be for everyone, but visitors are sure to find something that will lead to a gasp of pleasure. If you are based on Shikoku Island, or in Okayama Prefecture, Naoshima is certainly doable as a day trip. If travelling from further afield, make use of one of the many cheap lodgings on the island, run by the welcoming locals.❞

Recommended for

Modern art lovers

325

Shikoku

Kagawa
SHODOSHIMA
小豆島町

Shodoshima is a beautiful, green island located to the north-east of Shikoku, its larger neighbour, in the Seto Inland Sea in the south-west of Japan.

The island is synonymous with the olives that have been cultivated here since the early 1900s. A journey across its terrain allows visitors to marvel at staggering gorges, breathtaking rice paddies, and views of the tranquil sea and neighbouring islands.

Shodoshima is also home to a vibrant art culture - there is a recommended tour of art spots, the coastal road around Fukuda Port is lined with statues, and the 'maze town' of Tonosho houses many fascinating installations.

Local industry is dominated by the production of sesame oil and soy sauce, with the aromas from the factories around the ports of Kusakabe and Tonosho hanging heavy in the hot summer air.

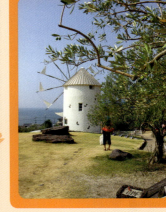

Culture Spot - Shodoshima Olive Park Roadside Station

This popular tourist spot is ideal for selecting your olive-related gifts and goods. The main buildings house an olive museum, cafeteria, accommodation and an *onsen*. There is also a picturesque windmill that stands on a lawn surrounded by olive groves.

Located a short distance away is Olive Garden, another similarly purposed area for the olive tourist trade. At this slightly newer site, you will find a shop, restaurant, an olive oil workshop facility, and some works by the designer Isamu Noguchi.

326

🏠 Culture Spot - Hitoyama Noson Kabuki ❷ Nakayama Noson Kabuki ❸

The valleys of Shodoshima have long been the home to rural *kabuki* performances. Indeed, the island once had more than 30 stages. Today, you can still see two charming outdoor *kabuki* theatres, which each date back several centuries.

Hitoyama Noson Kabuki is a grassy, amphitheatre-like setting, enclosed by a *torii* walkway and a shrine, which face towards the charming thatched wooden theatre that was originally built in 1686. The current structure is its fifth reconstruction. The troupe maintains a collection of over 1,100 costumes, but only performs at the theatre once every year, on May 3.

Nakayama Noson Kabuki is located just a few minutes away, and is equally as magical as its neighbour, but slightly busier, as visitors come to also wander around Nakayama Senmaida and to see the nearby art installations.

🌳 Nature Spot - Kankakei Gorge ❹

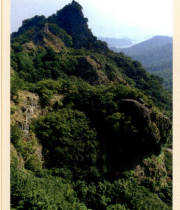

The Kankakei Gorge is considered one of Japan's three most beautiful ravines. It is famously colourful when autumn arrives in November. The area at the top is near Shodoshima's highest peak, and has observation decks with panoramic views over the gorge, the island and the Seto Inland Sea. It is a bustling spot, with a restaurant and a shop selling souvenirs along with local produce. From here, there is a choice of two hiking trails which both lead down to the bottom of the gorge. The easiest option is to descend the western trail - a slaloming concrete path that connects 12 impressive viewpoints - taking less than an hour. For a less strenuous return option, there is a cable car that joins stations at the top and bottom.

❓ Did you know?

Spirits sailing

Each year during the *obon* holiday, many locals go to Shodoshima's Angel Road to enact the charming *Shoro Nagashi* tradition of honouring their ancestors. Similar to a tradition made famous in Nagasaki, it is a private, ad hoc affair carried out by families who, after sunset, descend on the narrow spit of beach to launch candle lanterns perched upon miniature wooden boats. The boats are laden with gifts so that the spirits of deceased relatives who returned to their previous existence during *obon* are well stocked for a peaceful return to their other lives.

On the strait and narrow

The main island of Shodoshima and the smaller island of Maejima are divided by the Dofuchi Strait which, according to the Guinness Book of Records, is the narrowest strait in the world. It is 2.5 kilometres long and, at its narrowest, only 9.93 metres wide

Shikoku

Kagawa

SHODOSHIMA 小豆島町

👍 **Must see! Nakayama Senmaida Rice Paddy** 5

The central area of Shodoshima is largely used for the production of rice. As visitors journey inland, they are treated to increasingly beautiful views of contoured paddies wrapped around the feet of towering hillsides. Perhaps the most impressive of these landscapes is found at Nakayama Senmaida rice paddy.

The rough terrain here means that local farmers toil mostly by hand through the harvesting months of August and September. However, they seem happy for guests in the area to wander among the hillside paths that run between the steeply terraced, elegantly curving slopes, accompanied by buzzing dragonflies and the constant chattering of birds.

 Food and Drink

Tsukudani
Shodoshima is famed for its 400-year tradition of soy sauce production. The delicious condiment is also used for making *tsukudani* - small pieces of seafood, meat, or other foods, preserved by cooking in the sweet soy sauce. There are two *tsukudani* shops near the Marukin soy sauce museum, between the ports of Kusakabe and Sakate.

Olives
Many of Shodoshima's most famous olive-related products are not olive-based meals, but instead are a variety of delicious, rich olive oils. There are ample outlets selling these all over the island, as well as less obvious delicacies such as olive ice cream.

328

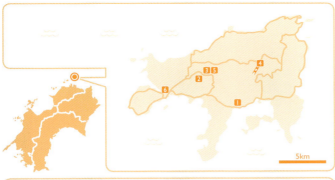

Key dates

May 3 - festival and *kabuki* performance (Hitoyama Noson Kabuki)

early July - Mushi Okuri - ceremonial fires to ward away insects, and prayers for a good rice harvest (Nakayama Senmaida and Tamonji Temple, Hitoyama)

mid-August - Shodoshima Fireworks Festival

August 15 - Shoro Nagashi lanterns on the water festival (Angel Road)

Culture Spot
Tonosho Maze Town

The district of Tonosho contains one of Shodoshima Island's main ports, located in an inlet near its western coast. A few minutes' walk from the town centre, there is a cluster of labyrinthine paths, in some places no wider than a couple of bicycles, that twist and turn between unique old farmhouses and townhouses. These narrow streets evolved as a useful foil to confuse troublemakers back in times when local pirates would wreak havoc in the town. This maze-like neighbourhood is centred around the elevated Saikoji Temple, and also houses many of the buildings that serve as galleries containing installations of the MeiPAM art collection.

We say

"While not a straightforward destination to travel to, Shodoshima promises rich rewards. Find yourself some cheap digs, rent a bicycle and venture away from the main coastal roads. Allow yourself plenty of time to soak up the Hellenic atmosphere of this beautiful location. The size of the island and the variety of attractions on Shodoshima warrant a stay of several days."

Recommended for

Art fans

Hikers

Ocean lovers

Getting there and around

- Takamatsu Airport. Travel to Takamatsu Port by bus, then by ferry or jetfoil to Shodoshima.
- Takamatsu Station. Travel to Shodoshima by ferry or jetfoil.
- Shodoshima has six passenger ferry ports that are connected by coastal bus services. Buses will also take you to many of the inland attractions. The island is large, so you might prefer to use a rental car. For the sporty traveller, cycling is also an option, although a lightweight model will serve you better in some of the more hilly areas.

Further information
www.100hiddentowns.jp/kagawa/shodoshima.html

Shikoku

Kochi

KONAN

香南市

The town of Konan encompasses several small villages (including Akaoka, Noichi and Yasu) containing a splendid mix of history, culture and nature.

The cluttered streets of Akaoka make for a pleasant stroll, and fans of Japanese art will be delighted with the opportunity to see up close the distinctive works of Ekin. The vast Actland complex in Noichi offers a family day out, with rides, games and museums that particularly focus on Kochi's ubiquitous historical hero, Ryoma Sakamoto. Visitors to Yasu can relax, surrounded by the countryside and the ocean.

👍 Must see! Ekin Museum ①

Kinzo Hirose (1812-1876) was an Akaoka-based artist who lived at the end of the Edo era and through the turbulent early Meiji period. He was given the moniker 'Ekin'. At the Actland complex in Noichi, visitors can get a taster of his vivid, amusing and colourful work from the excellent exhibits there. An even fuller appreciation can be gained at the Ekin Museum in Akaoka, where the pieces on display are supplemented by an English-language pamphlet explaining his rise, fall and rise again.

Every year, on the third weekend of July, Akaoka hosts the Ekin Festival, when his works are illuminated by candlelight and displayed throughout the town. Much of his work was painted on large folding screens, showing busy, often saucy or violent scenes. The works were previously only displayed on the festival day, but now the Ekin Museum houses them all year round. After an introductory video, step into the first exhibit, where the vast room is lit to reproduce the atmosphere of the night of the Ekin Festival.

Culture Spot - Actland

Close to Noichi Station is the Actland complex, which is a mix of amusement rides and museums. The 'Act' of Actland stands for Art, Culture and Technology, and the displays at the various museums showcase all three aspects. Technology can be seen at the classic car museum, which exhibits many designs of the last century, including the iconic Model T Ford.

Art is represented with displays of the works of notorious local artist Ekin and, in stark contrast, the sculptures of Ghanaian artist Francis Kwatei Nee-Owoo.

The main draw for Japanese tourists is the museum devoted to the life of Ryoma Sakamoto, the hero of Kochi. Sakamoto has been immortalised in numerous manga, drama and films. He was a major figure of the Meiji Restoration, and rose from youthful hot-headedness to become a vocal advocate for the modernisation of Japan, and for the removal of the shogun government.

The museum has waxwork displays showing key points in Ryoma's life from early childhood, through schooling, political discussions and diplomacy, and finally to his violent death at the hands of shogun loyalists.

Getting there and around

 Kochi Ryoma Airport. It takes approximately 15-25 minutes by car or taxi to any of the places mentioned.

Okayama Station. Travel to the area using local train services.

The Tosa Kuroshio train line offers an efficient service to reach all the places of interest. Noichi, Akaoka and Yasu all have stations on this line. From Noichi, you can rent a bicycle from the station or walk to Actland. In Akaoka, the Ekin Museum is within walking distance of Akaoka Station.

Further information
www.100hiddentowns.jp/kochi/konan.html

 Did you know?

The artist known as...
The artist Ekin had a turbulent life. Accused of forgery, he was expelled from art school and then spent several years wandering, before settling in Akaoka, using an old rice wine cellar as a studio. He was a very large, tall man and, by all accounts, a heavy drinker.

Key dates
third weekend of July - Ekin Festival (Akaoka)

We say
" There is much to do in Konan - the excellent local train service means every attraction can be reached cheaply and easily. "

Recommended for
Families

Art lovers

Shikoku

四万十町

Kochi

SHIMANTO

Shimanto is mainly famous for its gorgeous river and lush countryside, but its central Nakamura location offers plenty more to do and see, with tasty eateries, hotels, and a pretty castle within easy reach.

👍 Must do! Shimanto River

Flowing from the mountains of Shikoku into the Pacific Ocean, Shimanto River is famed throughout the country for its pure, gently flowing water which provides excellent opportunities for boat trips, canoeing, or just paddling in its shallow areas.

A leisurely cycle ride along the river bank on a battery-powered bicycle hired at Nakamura Station is highly recommended. Fishing of *ayu* (sweetfish) can be observed, including net fishing, whereby the fishers cast a large net over a school of *ayu* fish. There is also night fishing in autumn, when fishermen use flaming torches to attract the fish into the nets.

The best cycling route is upriver, where there are fewer cars and a more tranquil atmosphere, with several lookout points, and plenty of available spaces for camping. Tourists can also enjoy walking along the submersible bridges that dot the river. Although these bridges are low and have no railings, they are a wonderful and perfectly safe vantage point for watching the river flow gently by. Indulge in this sublime natural setting by timing your visit to catch the sunset dipping behind the mountains.

🌳 Nature Spot - Dragonfly Nature Park

This nature sanctuary and museum, located across the river from central Nakamura, has plenty to do for visitors of all ages.

The wide grounds and pretty ponds are wonderful for a stroll to see dragonflies and butterflies flitting around. The main building houses a dragonfly display area, as well as an aquarium containing a vast range of sea creatures of all shapes and sizes.

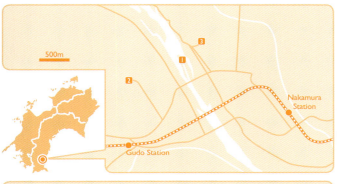

Did you know?

What a scorcher!
On August 12, 2013, Shimanto recorded a temperature of 41°C, the highest ever recorded in Japan. Although the river breezes can make the heat a little more bearable, take care if travelling here in the summer.

Shimanto shocks
Shimanto was almost entirely destroyed in the 1946 Nankai earthquake. Photographs of the area after the earthquake can be seen in the museum at Nakamura's castle, and they clearly show the extreme devastation that the town suffered just after the war. The city has of course since been rebuilt, so very few historical buildings remain.

Key dates

last Saturday in July - Shimanto Citizen Festival (dancing, lantern parade and fireworks)

early to mid November - autumn foliage in Kuroson Gorge

Culture Spot - Nakamura Castle

Nakamura Castle was initially built in 1468. Like many castles of the Sengoku (Warring States) era, it was demolished in the Edo era, when the Tokugawa shogunate specified that there should be only one castle per domain. Reconstructed in the 1960s, the current castle can be reached by a short hike from the banks of the Shimanto River.

Once at the top of the castle tower, you can enjoy excellent views which more than justify the small entrance fee. The castle doubles as the Shimanto City Museum, with pictures of the town's devastating 1946 earthquake, and details of life on the Shimanto River through the ages.

We say

" Shimanto is justifiably proud of its wonderful, long, winding river. A leisurely bike ride along its banks is a great way to admire the natural attributes of the area. "

Recommended for

Nature lovers

Water sports lovers

Nature Spot - Water Sports

Lovers of surfing can enjoy the Pacific waters on the coast of Shimanto. Both domestic and international competitions are held in Shikoku, and the different types of waves that can be found provide a choice of locations, depending on your level.

For canoeing, upriver you can find the canoe and camp facility of Kawarakko, where even beginners can enjoy the experience. Visitors are welcome to make use of the camping facilities and can experience riding a floating raft on the river.

Getting there and around

✈ Kochi Ryoma Airport. Take the limousine bus to Kochi Station and then local trains to Nakamura Station.

🚢 Okayama Station. Travel to Nakamura Station using local train services.

🚲 Once in Shimanto, if you are lacking a car, there are plenty of places where you can hire a bicycle to get around.

Further information
www.100hiddentowns.jp/kochi/shimanto.html

333

Shikoku

Tokushima

MIYOSHI
三好市

The rugged terrain of Miyoshi, in the heart of Shikoku Island, makes for an invigorating experience - mist-covered mountains, capricious rainstorms, sunlit rapids, strata-lined valley rocks and a revitalising dose of the colour green. The beautiful, emerald rivers that run between Oboke and Koboke are where most visitors begin their excursions - trips which might include trekking, rafting, pleasure boat cruises, hot spring baths and a taste of local folklore.

Culture Spot
Ochiai Village

The steep slopes facing Ochiai Village offer a wonderful vantage point to appreciate its thatched Edo-period farmhouses and winding roads. Local conservation groups maintain the area's beautiful historical feel. Don't expect a tourist Mecca, though - Ochiai is still a functioning village farm community.

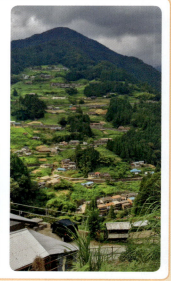

334

👍 Must see!
Iya-no-Kazurabashi (Vine Bridge)

According to local sources, this 14-metre-high vine bridge over the Iya River was originally built by the Heike clan in the 12th century, and was constructed so that it could be severed at a moment's notice, should an enemy be in pursuit.

Even the most surefooted visitor will struggle to cross without either a wobble or recourse to the twined handrail. Please note that, while not life-threatening, the gaps between the horizontal struts are wide enough for valuables to fall through. For the nervous traveller, rest assured that, despite its rustic appearance, the bridge is reconstructed every three years and reinforced with hidden steel cables.

After crossing the bridge, you can also see the Biwa Waterfall - a pretty cascade located beside steps that lead down to the river valley. In the summer months, you can walk upriver a little further from the bus tourists, and enjoy a private frolic in the cooling crystal waters.

🌳 Nature Spot
Happy Raft

If you are seeking some thrills and spills - particularly spills - the Oboke and Koboke gorges offer plenty of opportunities to try rafting, canyoning and riding on zip wires.

Happy Raft, one of about 20 companies in the area offering expeditions of this kind, are particularly well set up for visitors from overseas. Their friendly Japanese and Western staff offer a range of courses for visitors of all ages and abilities. After a brief safety chat from an instructor, rafters are soon out on the river in their life jackets and helmets, bouncing on the white waters, paddling with the rapids, swimming in the eddies and diving off rocks. Happy Raft's base also offers accommodation and a cafe with a relaxed atmosphere akin to a Thai resort.

❓ Did you know?

There be monsters
One of the *yokai* (mythological monsters) synonymous with the Miyoshi area is Konaki-jiji, whose story was made famous in an omnibus of Japanese folklore written by Kunio Yanagita in the early 1900s. The Konaki-jiji is said to be able to take the appearance of an old man or a baby, who lures unwary passers-by and allows them to hold him. After being picked up, the spirit suddenly becomes a heavy stone that crushes the victim to death. Konaki-jiji has since reappeared in 'GeGeGe-no-Kitaro', a hugely popular manga and animation series.

Shikoku

Tokushima
MIYOSHI
三好市

👬 Kids - Yokai Museum at Lapis Oboke ③

Lapis Oboke is a two-storey museum and tourist information centre, located a short walk from Oboke-kyo Mannaka.

Miyoshi's culture is rich with folklore legends and cautionary tales of local spirits, goblins and monsters - collectively known as *yokai* - who wreak misery on children trespassing into the wrong parts of the forests, mountains and rivers. The Yokai Museum houses a collection of lovingly created, garish woodland figures, with brief explanations of their evolution and magical powers. The exhibits are great for anyone who enjoys a touch of dark Japanese mythology.

Upstairs, somewhat incongruously, there is also a display of beautiful crystals and stones unearthed from the area, for those who enjoy the wonders of geology.

🏠 Culture Spot
Peeing Boy Statue And Rock ④

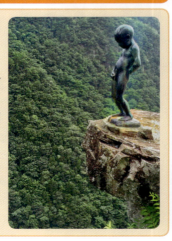

Over the centuries, this hair-raisingly precipitous spot has been a magnet for fearless and foolhardy males to test their bravado, by relieving their bladders over the giddying drop below. The rock is now separated from plucky wannabes by a sturdy safety barrier, but a little statue that stands there still allows the past to leak through to the present.

The statue is a five-minute walk from Nanoyado Hotel Iyaonsen, a beautifully located hotel, restaurant and *onsen,* with amazing views up and down the Iya valley. It also has a cable car to transport visitors to the valley floor below.

Key dates

first Saturday of April - open burning of field stubble (Shiozuka Highland, Yamashiro)

August 14-16 - Ikeda Awa Odori, Tokushima's popular dance (Awa Ikeda Station, Ikeda)

October - folk performance events (Higashi-Iya, Nishi-Iya)

late November - Yokai Festival (Yamashiro)

We say

" Stunning views, fresh mountain air, crystal clear waters, foaming rapids, and friendly people. A concerted effort has clearly been made to make the area's many charms as accessible as possible to all visitors, including those from overseas. "

Recommended for

Outdoor pursuits enthusiasts

Hot spring bathers

Folklore fans

Those seeking the soothing effects of nature

 ### Food and Drink

Iya Soba are thick, short noodles, originally made from hand-ground *soba* flour from the local area.

Try Sudachi-shu – a mild alcohol made from the green lime-like citrus fruit that is a speciality of Tokushima Prefecture.

 ### Nature Spot - Hi-Shaped Valley

On the mountain road up to Nanoyado Hotel Iyaonsen, there is a bend that affords travellers an elevated perspective of an elegantly curved gorge that resembles the shape of the Japanese character ひ (*hi*).

 ### Getting there and around

Kochi Ryoma Airport. Travel to Oboke Station using local train services. Or Takamatsu Airport / Tokushima Awa-odori Airport. Travel to Oboke Station via Awa-Ikeda Station on Shikoku Island, using local train services.

Okayama Station or Takamatsu Station. Travel to Oboke Station on Shikoku using local train services.

Carefully planned use of local buses gives visitors access to most of the main attractions in the area, although you would be hard-pressed to see all of them in one day. A rental car allows easier access to places such as Ochiai. Be warned that only the most athletic cyclists would be able to tackle the slopes in the area - a brief glimpse at a local map fails to communicate quite how dramatic the terrain actually is. Also be aware that the changeable mountainous climate can transform a sunny saunter into a sodden sally within minutes - pack a small raincoat if you have one.

 ### Accommodation
Oboke-kyo Mannaka

Oboke-kyo Mannaka is an extremely friendly hotel, located about 1.5 kilometres from Oboke Station. It has its own restaurant, both indoor and outdoor hot spring baths, and is affiliated with the nearby Oboke-kyo Mannaka Restaurant, which contains a gift shop and is the departure point for 30-minute pleasure boat tours of the Oboke ravine. As with the whole area, the hotel actively welcomes visitors from overseas with helpful signs, information pamphlets in various languages, and even multilingual staff from other Asian countries. The hotel restaurant serves traditional Japanese meals, using mostly organic, freshly farmed local ingredients.

 ### Further information
www.100hiddentowns.jp/tokushima/miyoshi.html

SHIKOKU
OTHER TOWNS

Tokushima
MIMA

Offering a mix of history and nature, Mima is a charming part of Tokushima Prefecture. The gently flowing rivers and hilly backdrop are complemented by the Edo time-warp of the unique Wakimachi area *udatsu* architecture.

Culture Spot Koyadaira District
Nature Spot Anabuki River
Must do Wakimachi Area
We say The Wakimachi area is a wonderful strolling spot and a real trip back in time. Coupled with the countryside in the region, it makes Mima an enjoyable destination.

Kagawa
KOTOHIRA

Just across from the main Japanese island of Honshu, nestled on the north coast of Shikoku, is the town of Kotohira. Though small, the town attracts a huge number of visitors all year round for its soothing *onsen* and famous Kompira Shrine, which has been a focus of tourism since the middle of the Edo era.
Culture Spot Kanamaruza Theatre
Nature Spot Kotohira Park
Must do Kompira Shrine
We say Kotohira has enough attractions to warrant an overnight stay. There is plenty of accommodation to choose from, and the town is easily accessible from larger towns in Honshu or Shikoku. The climb to the shrine requires a lot of effort, but is rewarding, especially in autumn.

Ehime
KUMAKOGEN

Kumakogen is a broad upland area in the centre of Ehime. Characterised by deep forests and valleys, this relatively unpopulated location offers chances to see unspoilt countryside, fascinating geological features, and two of the 88 temples on the historic Shikoku pilgrimage way.
Culture Spot Kuma Kogen Astronomical Observatory
Must see Iwaya-Ji Temple
We say Kumakogen's remoteness may be its biggest draw. It is a relatively undeveloped, pretty area, recommended for those who enjoy a drive in the countryside.

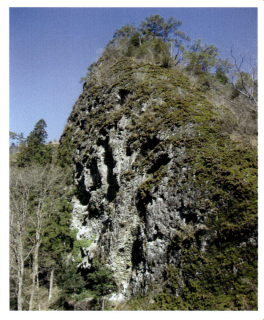

339

KYUSHU AND OKINAWA

九州・沖縄県

The Kyushu Region

The Kyushu region incorporates seven prefectures, and exhibits many of the extremes that Japanese culture and nature have to offer. The large number of national parks provide a broad range of biodiversity, active volcanoes, unique marine spots and outstanding views. The prefectures still show traces of their days as key points in the history of Japan's contact with foreign nations, and the trade and religion that entered the country through the region.

Miyakojima, Okinawa Prefecture

Aya, Miyazaki Prefecture

Okinawa

Further south, Okinawa has its own unique culture and a warm climate that distinguishes it from the other islands of the archipelago.

Japan's southernmost prefecture stretches between Kyushu and Taiwan, and is characterised by its subtropical islands, gorgeous weather and biodiversity.

KYUSHU

FUKUOKA PREFECTURE

Dazaifu

Facing the sea on three of its sides, marine trade and diplomacy have long been key to the prosperity of Fukuoka. As a first port of call in Kyushu, the prefecture is home to a number of cultural and scenic spots for visitors. Outside its lively capital, check out the fascinating mountain villages near Ukiha, and the serene waterways of the former castle town of Yanagawa.

Prefectural Capital
Fukuoka City

✈ Airports
Fukuoka Airport,
Kitakyushu Airport

Main Train Stations
Hakata Station

Other Tourist Attractions
Fukuoka City
Fukuoka is a vibrant city with plenty of entertainment for visitors. It is actually closer to Seoul than to Tokyo, and attracts plenty of visitors from the Asian mainland.

Kitakyushu City
The prefecture's northernmost city has long been an important port. Although ostensibly a centre of industry, many Meiji-era buildings remain to help give Kitakyushu a historical feel.

Dazaifu
This quiet town on the outskirts of Fukuoka has an illustrious history as the key point from which Japan established diplomatic relations and coastal defences. The town is home to several shrines and temples, including the Dazaifu Tenmangu Shrine (see photo).

Hakata Gion Yamakasa Festival (Hakata, Fukuoka City)
Portable floats race around the streets in this ancient festival held in July, while other, larger, stationary floats dot the city - some of which are up to 12 metres high.

KYUSHU

九州

KAGOSHIMA PREFECTURE

Steeped in history, and exhibiting dramatic, volcanic behaviour, Kagoshima boasts hot springs, national parks and a chain of delightful islands that runs southwards into the East China Sea, including Yakushima and Amami Oshima, which seem a world away from the stereotypical image of hyper-modern Japan. Stop by the pretty town of Tatsugo for a heady mix of nature and culture.

Prefectural Capital
Kagoshima City

✈ Airports
Kagoshima Airport
Yakushima Airport

🚅 Main Train Stations
Kagoshima-Chuo Station

Other Tourist Attractions
Kagoshima City
The lively prefectural capital is dominated by its smoky neighbour, the volcanic Sakurajima. The town has many sites related to its most famous son, Takamori Saigo, the so-called 'Last Samurai', who helped lead Japan into the modern world before then clashing with the restoration government.

Satsuma Peninsula
This district to the north of Kagoshima City retains the prefecture's former moniker - Satsuma. Hot springs and traditional culture are in abundance here.

Ibusuki
Ibusuki is a popular hot spring area, with attractions including curative hot sand baths.

Terukuni Shrine Rokugatsudo Festival (Kagoshima City)
Throughout July, the shrines and temples of Kagoshima hold a series of festivals, each with its own unique twist. (The name of the festivals, *rokugatsu*, actually means 'June', which refers to the old Japanese calendar.) The Terukuni Shrine festival event, that takes place on July 15-16, has a bubbly atmosphere, and features stalls and lanterns.

Extreme Seasonal Conditions
Prone to typhoons July - October.

Sakurajima

KUMAMOTO PREFECTURE

Located in central Kyushu, Kumamoto is a prefecture of active volcanoes, hot springs and gushing rivers. Though damaged in a 2016 earthquake, the 17th-century Kumamoto Castle is one of several pretty, traditional sites that dot the prefectural capital. Away from the city, the wonderful mix of history and nature at Hitoyoshi is highly recommended, and the countryside of Aso is a must-see.

Prefectural Capital
Kumamoto City

✈ Airports
Kumamoto Airport

🚅 Main Train Stations
Kumamoto Station

Other Tourist Attractions
Kumamoto City
Although its earthquake-damaged castle is under reconstruction, the charming prefectural capital also boasts a landscape garden and a preserved samurai residence.

Kurokawa Onsen

Kurokawa Onsen
This attractive hot spring town is known for its traditional buildings and tranquil atmosphere.

Amakusa
This scenic toll road runs from Fukushima City, and commands panoramic views of the Fukushima landscape.

Yamaga Toro Festival (Yamaga City)
Known as the land of fire - due to its spluttering, coughing volcanoes - where better to have a fire festival than in Kumamoto Prefecture? *Yukata*-clad females dance and sing with lanterns, and the festival climaxes with fireworks displays.

Extreme Seasonal Conditions
Humid in summer.

MIYAZAKI PREFECTURE

Famed for its coastal areas, pleasant climate, and mountain vistas, Miyazaki is a lovely region. Surfing, and exploring the coast by car, bicycle or on foot, are all popular pastimes. Check out the incredible rural scenery and fascinating local traditions of Shiiba, and the craft workshops and stunning bridge of Aya.

Prefectural Capital
Miyazaki City

✈ Airports
Miyazaki Airport

🚆 Main Train Stations
Miyazaki Station

Other Tourist Attractions

Aoshima
Popular for beach holidays, the main draw in Aoshima is a small island which is connected to the mainland by a pedestrian bridge. The remarkable, ribbed rock formations of the island's perimeter are known as the 'Devil's Washboard'.

Takachiho Gorge
Known as a sacred power spot, Takachiho Gorge is brimming with mythology and natural attractions.

Udo Shrine
Located on the coast, south of Miyazaki City, this pretty shrine is set in the side of a cliff, where legend says the mythical first emperor of Japan, Emperor Jimmu, was nourished by the breast-shaped rocks of the cave walls.

Yabusame (horseback archery) (Miyazaki Shrine, Miyazaki City)
Held annually on April 3rd, riders wearing Kamakura-era attire aim their arrows at targets while riding horses at high speeds.

Udo Shrine

NAGASAKI PREFECTURE

Historically a key gateway into Japan for foreign tradespeople and missionaries, Nagasaki Prefecture still displays many traces of its past. The prefectural capital of Nagasaki City has buildings in its southern hills preserved from the early Meiji era, as well as the fascinating, fan-shaped island of Dejima, which for centuries was the only Japanese location that Europeans could trade from. Nature-wise, the prefecture features volcanoes, hot springs and forested islands. Definitely worth visiting are Shimabara - a friendly town with a spectacular castle, pretty streets and local delicacies, and Iki - an island with a fine museum and fascinating marine life.

Prefectural Capital
Nagasaki City

✈ Airports
Nagasaki Airport

🚆 Main Train Stations
Nagasaki Station

Other Tourist Attractions

Nagasaki City
Set amongst devastating reminders of the 1945 atomic bomb, much of Nagasaki's earlier history is still preserved in this hilly city, and is a major draw for visitors. Dejima is a must-see, featuring reconstructions of the buildings that Dutch traders were confined to while living on this tiny island (now surrounded by reclaimed land). There are also models, and furniture from the era, as well as comprehensive explanations. In the coastal hills to the south, Glover Garden has western mansions from the 19th century. Offshore is Gunkanjima, an abandoned island which was once a vibrant coal mining town.

Hirado
The Dutch trading post before operations were swept over to Dejima in Nagasaki City, Hirado has Christian sites, historical reconstructions, and a museum.

Nagasaki Kunchi Festival
This vibrant, cosmopolitan festival in October features Chinese boat-shaped floats, dances, and many opportunities for spectators to participate in the festivities.

Dejima

343

KYUSHU

九州

OITA PREFECTURE

Best known for the hot spring resorts of Beppu, Oita Prefecture - located on the eastern coast of Kyushu - is a wonderful destination for visitors. Its coast is dotted with pretty locations such as the small town of Kitsuki, where samurai mansions and a tiny castle overlook distinctive paved slopes and the Pacific Ocean.

Prefectural Capital
Oita City

✈ Airports
Oita Airport

🚆 Main Train Stations
Oita Station

Other Tourist Attractions

Beppu
Beppu produces the most hot spring water of anywhere in Japan, and has a range of baths from typical hot springs to sand and mud baths. The so-called 'Hells of Beppu' are bubbling, belching geysers located on the outskirts of the town.

Yufuin
The hot springs of Yufuin are located inland from Beppu. The town has a leisurely atmosphere, and is home to art galleries and cafes.

Kebesu Festival (Kunisaki City)
This unique fire festival features strange mythical creatures - the Kebesu (wearing a mask) and the Touba (dressed in a white shroud). Accompanied by traditional music, the Touba try to stop the Kebesu from spreading flames in the temple grounds. It is apparently good luck for spectators to be hit by sparks from the fire!

Beppu

SAGA PREFECTURE

Widely known for its traditional ceramics and pretty coast, Saga is a small prefecture located between the more crowded areas of Nagasaki and Fukuoka. The pretty pottery town of Arita is a good port of call to experience the craft heritage of the area, through visits to its large prefectural museum, abandoned quarries, and traditional shops, which offer a great chance to purchase local wares. The scenic, small town of Ureshino is home to traditional pottery, hot springs and locally produced tea.

Prefectural Capital
Saga City

✈ Airports
Saga Airport

🚆 Main Train Stations
Saga Station

Other Tourist Attractions

Yoshinogari Historical Park
Archaeologists unearthed dozens of dwellings and tombs from the Yayoi era of Japanese history at this site, which is now an open-air museum.

Karatsu
Karatsu is a quiet coastal town known for its castle and local pottery. The nearby views of the ocean are also a draw.

Takeo Onsen
This ancient hot spring town has long been a popular retreat for the upper echelons of Japanese society, thanks to its curative waters. For a small fee, visitors can use the public baths.

Kashima Gatalympic (Kashima City)
This hilarious sports festival is held on the muddy, tidal flats of the city in early summer. Anyone can apply to enter the events, which include sliding along on wooden boards, balancing a bicycle on narrow planks in the mud, obstacle courses, and a tug-of-war.

Extreme Seasonal Conditions Humid in summer.

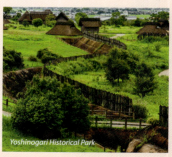
Yoshinogari Historical Park

NATIONAL PARKS

Setonaikai National Park
(see Chugoku)

Saikai National Park
Area: 24,646 ha
Features: over 400 islands, steep cliffs, volcanic landscapes, spectacular rock erosions
Did you know? The park also features places of historical interest, including Christian churches and the military ruins related to the Sasebo Naval District.

Unzen-Amakusa National Park
Area: 28,279 ha
Features: steaming volcanoes, coastal panoramas, cliffs, coral seascapes
Did you know? The seas offer astounding underwater views of colourful fish, and the park also provides excellent spots for observing birds on their migratory paths.

Aso-Kuju National Park
Area: 72,678 ha
Features: Mount Aso volcano, lakes, wetlands, hot spring resorts
Did you know? Mount Aso is active, and visitors must check local information to see how close they can get to the crater, due to the danger of lethal gases.

Kirishima-Kinkowan National Park
Area: 36,586 ha
Features: volcanoes, crater lakes and plateaus
Did you know? The iconic volcano, Mount Sakurajima, occasionally erupts and sprinkles the city of Kagoshima with ash.

Yakushima National Park
Area: 24,566 ha
Features: mountains, giant trees, rich vegetation
Did you know? Half the total of Japanese loggerhead turtles are spawned on Yakushima. Nagata Beach, the spawning site, even has its own festival, with dances imitating the movements of the turtles.

Amami Gunto National Park
Area: 42,181 ha
Features: 14 islands, subtropical forests, seascapes, hiking, water sports
Did you know? The park is characterised by its diverse wildlife, including rare species of grass-eating butterflies.

Amami Gunto National Park

KYUSHU

九州

HIDDEN TOWNS

FUKUOKA
350 Ukiha
354 Yanagawa

KAGOSHIMA
358 Amami
362 Tatsugo
364 Yakushima

KUMAMOTO
368 Aso
370 Hitoyoshi

MIYAZAKI
372 Aya
376 Shiiba

NAGASAKI
378 Iki
382 Shimabara

OITA
384 Kitsuki
388 Usuki

SAGA
392 Arita
396 Ureshino

CLIMATE (monthly average temperatures)

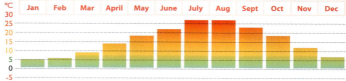

UKIHA (Fukuoka)

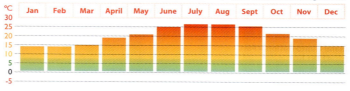

AMAMI (Amami Oshima Island, Kagoshima)

APPROXIMATE TRAVEL TIMES (minutes) **BETWEEN PREFECTURAL CAPITALS**

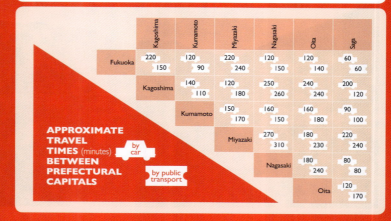

	Kagoshima	Kumamoto	Miyazaki	Nagasaki	Oita	Saga
Fukuoka	220 / 150	120 / 90	220 / 240	120 / 150	120 / 140	60 / 60
Kagoshima		140 / 110	120 / 180	250 / 260	240 / 240	200 / 120
Kumamoto			150 / 170	160 / 150	160 / 180	90 / 100
Miyazaki				270 / 310	180 / 230	220 / 240
Nagasaki					180 / 240	80 / 80
Oita						120 / 170

346

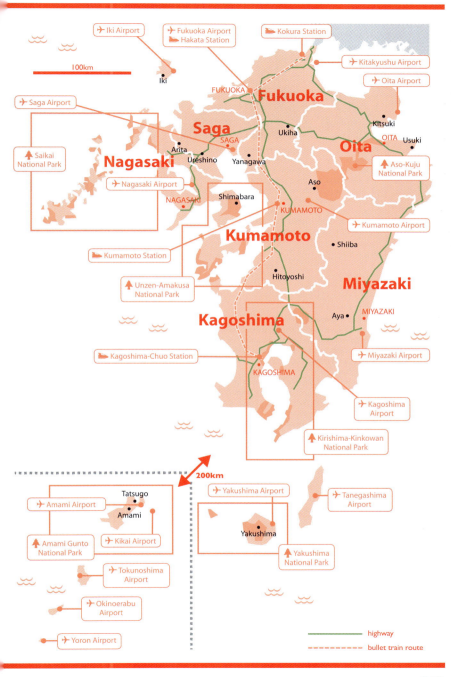

OKINAWA

沖縄県

OKINAWA PREFECTURE

Comprising over 360 islands between Taiwan and mainland Japan, Okinawa boasts a distinct climate and unique traditions. The local Ryukyu culture permeates the islands, and has been lovingly passed down through the generations. The main island has plenty to attract visitors who enjoy water sports, while the smaller islands are surrounded by white sands and cobalt blue waters above the coral reefs. Take a break from it all at the subtropical paradise of Miyakojima.

Prefectural Capital
Naha City

✈ Airports
Naha Airport

🚆 Main Train Stations
Naha Airport Station

Other Tourist Attractions

Yaeyama Islands
These southernmost islands of Japan have a relaxing, bucolic feel, with plenty of opportunities for diving and snorkelling. The islands feature jungles and preserved Ryukyu villages.

Kumejima
This small island has everything that beach lovers and diving enthusiasts could ever want. The lengthy white sand bar of Hatenohama Beach is the island's most popular attraction.

The Naha Great Tug of War Festival (Naha City)
Tug of war contests have long been held throughout Okinawa to give thanks for a bountiful harvest. Held every October, this festival features banner performances, and climaxes with the tug of war competition.

Extreme Seasonal Conditions Prone to typhoons July - October.

NATIONAL PARKS

Yambaru National Park
Area: 13,622 ha

Features: unique flora and fauna, mangrove forests, hiking, canoeing

Did you know? The park is home to unique biodiversity, including the Okinawa Woodpecker, Okinawa Rail and the Ryukyu Long-Haired Rat.

Keramashoto National Park

Keramashoto National Park
Area: 3,520 ha

Features: white beaches, transparent waters, diving, snorkelling, whale-watching

Did you know? The park has plenty of tradition and history, including unique festivals and World War II battle sites.

Iriomote-Ishigaki National Park
Area: 21,958 ha

Features: forests, coral reefs, trekking, animal watching, water sports

Did you know? Iriomote-Ishigaki is Japan's southernmost national park, and has Japan's largest coral reef. After the archipelago separated from the continent, unique species such as the Iriomote wild cat evolved here.

HIDDEN TOWNS

OKINAWA

402   **Miyakojima**

CLIMATE (monthly average temperatures)

MIYAKOJIMA (Okinawa)

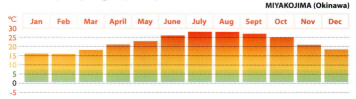

348

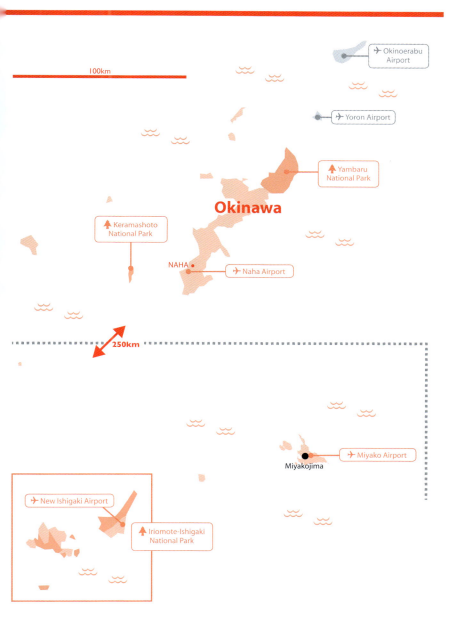

Kyushu

UKIHA
Fukuoka
うきは市

The rural town of Ukiha evolved as a well-to-do area of farmers and industrialists whose advantageous location allowed their businesses and wealth to expand so much that they were also able to patronise a local, creative culture.

Visitors to Ukiha have access to three very distinct attractions. Amid the canals and narrow streets of the old centre of commerce, there is still an area where the iconic, white-walled merchant houses of the town's forefathers have been tastefully maintained, and which are now home to a variety of thriving local businesses, such as independent coffee shops, bakeries, and bookshops.

A little further to the south, at the foot of the Minou mountain range, is a quiet cluster of chic boutiques known as Budo-no-Tane.

After all your retail therapy desires have been satisfied, head even further into the mountains to experience thatched farmhouses, breathtaking views of paddies, and the warm hospitality of the villages of Tagomori and Niikawa.

 **Food and Drink**

Riverwild Ham Factory ❶

An international award-winning shop and cafeteria, bedecked in Gothic chic and run by a rock and roll fanatic, selling mouth-watering, ham-based products. The flavours tasted here are a world away from the usual supermarket fare.

🏠 Culture Spot
Budo-no-Tane [2]

Budo-no-Tane is a collection of boutiques in the wooded Nagarekawa area at the foot of the Minou mountains.

In this enclave of stylish emporiums, selling the best handicrafts of local designers, potters and carpenters, there is not a high street brand to be seen. Very much for the discerning hipsters and artisans, these restored, wood-floored farmhouses, cool, adobe-walled coffee shops, art galleries and shops selling hand-made delicacies, are run by a family to support young craftsmen and producers. While you are here, take the opportunity to stretch your legs and walk a little further up the hill to see the ungroomed splendour of the Suwa Shrine.

❓ Did you know?

Cooking Papa

The proprietor of Minshuku Baba (one of Ukiha's mountain inns) - a Mr. Dairiki - was an inspiration for one of Japan's enduring manga characters, *Cooking Papa*.

The story is about a salaryman who is an excellent cook, but is anxious to keep this secret from his co-workers. He lets them believe that his wife, who in the story is actually a disaster in the kitchen, cooks all his meals. Full recipes for the dishes featured are provided at the end of each chapter.

The comic has run in the manga magazine 'Weekly Morning' since 1985, and has also been adapted into an anime television series and live-action TV drama.

The irony is that Mrs. Dairiki is, in real life, a great cook!

Kyushu

Fukuoka
UKIHA 市
うきは

👍 Must see! Tsuzura Tanada [3] and Tagomori [4]

Tsuzura Tanada is a 300-allotment paddy, located in a beautiful, winding valley, deep in the heart of the Minou mountains. Because of the extreme terrain, these terraced rice fields are very time intensive to farm. The misty valley and the multi-hued farmland make for a splendid spectacle.

Within a short drive from the paddies, there are several small villages. Here you can see traditional thatched farmhouses lining the banks of the gurgling mountain river. As well as the residences of the local farming community, there are small coffee shops, bakeries and even galleries to be found.

One local family in the village of Tagomori, the Hirakawas, have opened their beautiful ancestral home to the public. Visitors (by appointment) can gain valuable insight into rural ways, by walking around this historical building.

For those who wish to stay overnight in the mountains, there are a few families operating *minshuku*-style accommodation for groups of two or more. Here, guests can enjoy delicious local dishes made from mountain vegetables indigenous to the area.

🏠 Culture Spot - Seisuiji Temple [5]

The caretakers charged with the upkeep of this zen temple have thankfully resisted the temptation to renew or modernise, and have instead allowed the complex to age organically, permitting mother nature to enrich the character of the statues, paths and footbridges around the temple. The temple was established on this site because of the clear water that springs from the earth here, which was taken as a sign of the location's spiritual purity.

352

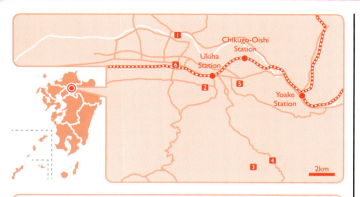

Culture Spot - Chikugo Yoshii Shirakabe Streets 6

Throughout Ukiha's history, the Chikugo River enabled local commerce to thrive. A neighbourhood of striking, white-walled merchant houses grew up amid the narrow streets, canals and dams of the town centre. Some local family names still reflect the long history of trade with Korea and China in this westernmost region of Japan.

These days, the town centre is experiencing a renaissance, as the younger generation take inspiration from the area's creative heritage. Innovative business ventures are housed in the traditional buildings, which have been restored to their original state, and exude Edo-era elegance and charm. Visit here to saunter amongst charming bakeries, cafes, bookshops and galleries, wander around the narrow waterways and visit the beautifully maintained Igura-no-yakata and Kagamida Yashiki local museums.

Getting there and around

✈ Fukuoka Airport. Travel via Hakata Station to Ukiha Station using local train services.

🚆 Hakata Station. Travel to Ukiha Station using local train services. Trains are infrequent, so plan carefully.

🚶 The streets of Chikugo Yoshii Shirakabe are within a short walk of Chikugo Yoshii Station, but a car or taxi is needed to visit the other attractions mentioned.

Further information
www.100hiddentowns.jp/fukuoka/ukiha.html

Key dates

February-March - Hina doll displays (Yoshii Historical District)

April - traditional Shinto festival (Ukiha Okunchi)

May - opening event of Chikugo River fishing

June - firefly viewing

July - summer festival and Ukiha Chikugogawa Onsen Fireworks Festival

October - traditional Shinto festival (Yoshii Wakamiya Okunchi) parade

October/November - Ukiha Matsuri Festival

December - mountain light-up festival in Kojio valley settlements

We say

" Ukiha seems to welcome visitors with a genuine desire for them to enjoy the local sights and creative, rural culture. Many links with international organisations and art groups have been formed, and performers from overseas are regularly invited to give concerts and workshops. A sense of creativity and community is palpable in this pretty town. "

Recommended for

Folk art and handicraft lovers

Fans of rugged terrain and simple cuisine

353

Kyushu

Fukuoka

YANAGAWA
柳川市

The town of Yanagawa, located about two kilometres inland from the Ariake Sea on the west coast of Kyushu, is threaded by a network of serene canals that date back to the Edo period, when these waterways surrounded Yanagawa Castle.

Criss-crossed by lanes lined with Meiji and Taisho-era commercial buildings, and festooned during February and March every year with traditional *sagemon* decorations that hang throughout the town, Yanagawa continues to exude an old-world charm.

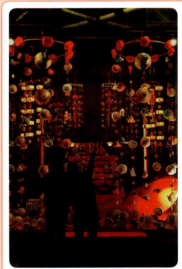

🏠 Culture Spot - Sagemon

During the annual *hinamatsuri* doll festival season from February until the end of March (see *Did you know?*), Yanagawa shows off traditional *sagemon* hanging ornaments. Local houses, shopfronts, museums, and even the waterways of the town, are richly decorated with these brilliantly coloured, hand-sewn, hanging balls and figures. Suspended from above, the *sagemon* perfectly complement the more common displays of aristocratic *hinaningyo* dolls below. The tradition is said to have originated in Yanagawa, but similar displays can be found beyond Kyushu. Almost all of the town's attractions are decorated during this period.

🏠 Culture Spot - Yanagawa Ohana

This site - the former home of the Tachibana family who ruled the area during the Edo era - is the centre of Yanagawa culture. Just a stone's throw from the tourist information centre and the last pier of the *donkobune* sightseeing boats, here visitors can enjoy exhibits displaying the local history and culture.

The **Tachibana Museum** contains artefacts from the family history of these feudal lords, including gorgeous fabrics, suits of armour, helmets, muskets, folding screens depicting fantastical images, and tiny hand-crafted *hinaningyo* dolls.

The **Seiyokan** is a large, western-style building constructed in 1910, with sumptuous furniture, fittings and joinery that provide a fascinating window into the grandiosity and elegance of the Meiji-era aristocracy. Adjacent to this, and no less grand, is the traditional Japanese architecture of the **Oh-hiroma**, which was constructed at the same time.

Measuring 100 *tatami* mats in size, this space can be converted into a *noh* stage when the mats are removed. Both buildings look out onto the peaceful **Shoto-en Garden**, which contains a large, ornamental pond surrounded by garden rocks, stone lanterns, and about 280 Japanese black pine trees.

Also within the grounds is the **Ohana** hotel and restaurant, which serves local specialities such as *unagi-no-seiro-mushi* (eel steamed in bamboo) and seasonal delicacies from the Ariake Sea.

💡 Did you know?

Ghibli connection
In 1987, a video documentary about Yanagawa's canals and their restoration, titled 'The Story of Yanagawa's Canals' (*Yanagawa Horiwari Monogatari*), was created by Studio Ghibli, the makers of the world-famous *anime* films 'My Neighbour Totoro' and 'Spirited Away'.

Get dolled up
Each year, a set of ornamental dolls (*hinaningyo*) depicting the Emperor and Empress, with various court attendants and musicians from the Heian period, are displayed in girls' homes throughout Japan during the weeks preceding *hinamatsuri* (Doll Festival or Girls' Day).

Popular poet
Hakushu Kitahara was raised in Yanagawa in the late 19th century. He is regarded as one of the most important poets in modern Japanese literature. Kitahara published many books, and also wrote children's songs and anthems for high schools. Many of his poems remain popular today. An annual festival celebrating his life and work is held in Yanagawa during the month of November, where enthusiasts read his poems to passersby at night from stages along the town's canals.

Kyushu

Fukuoka — YANAGAWA / 柳川市

👍 Must see! Yanagawa Canal Boat

All visitors to Yanagawa should ensure that at least 60 minutes of their stay is set aside for a lazy boat excursion along the pretty canals that run around the site where the town's castle was formerly located.

A popular tourist attraction, passengers can luxuriate in the dappled sunlight in a *donkobune* boat as it glides past the town's traditional homes, gardens and old traders' warehouses, under drooping willow trees and low, foliage-covered, stone bridges that punctuate the twists and turns of these nostalgia-soaked waterways.

Boatmen in traditional punter garb regale their customers with the history of the town (in Japanese) and occasionally serenade them, making use of the natural reverberations beneath the bridges to enhance the beauty of their lullabies. These natural raconteurs also exchange friendly jibes as their boats pass each other.

Visitors can pre-book a boat for the evening and bring their own picnic for an illuminated tour. Rainproof ponchos and *kotatsu*-style under-table heating are also available for inclement conditions.

There are several companies operating these boat rides which conclude at the *Ohana* guest facility, a pretty and convenient port to step ashore. A ticket also includes the bus ride returning passengers to their point of embarkation.

Key dates

mid-February - early April - Yanagawa Doll Festival (*Sagemon Meguri*)

late April - early May - Nakayama Ofuji Festival (wisteria)

4th Saturday in July - Nakashima Gion Festival

early October - Onigie (Mihashira Shrine Autumn Festival)

November 1-3 - Hakushu Festival and Water Parade

Culture Spot - Hakushu Birthplace and Memorial Hall / Folk Museum

Yanagawa was the birthplace of Hakushu Kitahara (1885-1942), one of Japan's best-known poets. The home of his wealthy, *sake*-brewing family was destroyed by fire, but has since been restored, and now this elegant wooden building, located on one of the town's old thoroughfares, serves as a memorial to Hakushu's life and works, displaying samples of his writings and sheet music. Unlike many poets, Hakushu enjoyed great celebrity during his lifetime, as evidenced in the large number of striking, black-and-white photos of his life. There is no English signage, but an English-language pamphlet is available at the entrance.

Behind the house, there is a large, modern, three-storey building that houses the Yanagawa Folk Museum. Artefacts focus on local history and fishing traditions, and include an old fishing boat kept in dry dock. The low ratio of fascinating exhibits per cubic metre suggests that this should be kept as a 'rainy day' option.

We say

"Yanagawa is a delightful town, with its attractions all within convenient proximity of each other and Nishitetsu Yanagawa Station. Try to plan your trip to coincide with the *hinamatsuri* (Doll Festival) period of February/March, and allow yourself at least a whole day to imbibe the local atmosphere amongst the quiet lanes and canals."

Recommended for

Families

Early spring breaks

Food and Drink

Unagi-no-Seiro-Mushi (eel steamed in bamboo)

This delicacy is a speciality of Yanagawa. It is the signature dish of more than ten competing restaurants, each using their own methods of grilling, steaming, and seasoning the eel, which is served on a soy-flavoured bed of rice.

Getting there and around

🛬 Fukuoka Airport. Travel by local train services via Nishitetsu Fukuoka Station to Nishitetsu Yanagawa Station.

🚅 Hakata Station. Travel by local train services via Nishitetsu Fukuoka Station to Nishitetsu Yanagawa Station.

🚶 Yanagawa can be covered on foot quite easily, but don't miss the chance to explore the waterways in a canal boat.

Further information

www.100hiddentowns.jp/fukuoka/yanagawa.html

Kyushu

Kagoshima
Amami Oshima Island — AMAMI
奄美市

While hordes of summer holidaymakers join an annual exodus from Japan to the tropical climes of Hawaii, Guam and the like, more prudent travellers might be better advised to stay a little closer to the mainland, and visit the island of Amami Oshima, 380 kilometres from the southern coast of Kagoshima.

Complementing the turquoise waters that lap the huge stretches of sandy beaches, the island is covered in swathes of mountain forest, and boasts a wide range of speciality cuisine and tropical fruit. Add to these attractions Amami's hot springs, and rich tradition of handicrafts, and you have a perfect island getaway.

Culture Spot - Thalasso AMAMI-no-Ryugu (Spa Therapy Resort)

This picturesque resort on a sandy white beach near to Ohama Seaside Park, is one of the island's most popular spots to watch the sun go down.

The spa centre is designed for one purpose only - relaxation. As well as a suite of therapies including seaweed packs, dry or wet saunas, and massages, there is a large walking pool and an assortment of mineral baths and jacuzzis, each designed to provide relief to a specific part of the body. There are also outdoor lounging beds, submerged in gurgling baths from which you can gaze upon the ocean. The resort is popular with the more senior locals, who use the facilities regularly, but also welcomes day visitors. If you want to enjoy a massage, ask your hotel to make an advanced booking.

Nature Spot - Kinsakubaru Virgin Forest

Deep in the heart of Amami's mountains, visitors to this forest can enjoy tours of the native flora and fauna.

The foliage that covers the mountain slopes is mostly made up from Amami's iconic gigantic fern trees, craning skywards in competition for the sun. This forest area is home to a wide variety of birds, insects and frogs, many of which can only be found on Amami.

Be warned that much of the wildlife often remains hidden, because of the disturbance caused by the sound of groups of tourists with their tour guides, so your trip might be mostly an appreciation of the foliage. However, depending on your luck, you may be able to observe any of the following - green pigeons, red sparrows, hawks, red kingfishers, short-eared Amami black rabbits (*Amami-no-kurousagi*), turquoise-winged large tree nymph butterflies, mice, lizards and poisonous habu snakes.

It is recommended that you take a pre-arranged minibus and guided tour, hosted by an expert guide (most hotels can arrange this for you) due to the risk of encountering poisonous snakes, becoming lost, and the likelihood of damage to your car by tree branches. Although the tours offer only Japanese-language explanations, some guides use photos and audio on a tablet device to help visitors identify the native animal and plant species hiding in the forest.

The tours aim to explain how different species coexist in the forest as part of a sensitive natural balance.

Visitors should do a little homework about the forest prior to their visit, to ensure that their enjoyment does not solely depend on comprehension of Japanese botanical terms.

Did you know?

Rare rabbit

Amami Oshima is home to the Amami black rabbit. These short-eared mammals can only be found on the remote islands of Amami Oshima and Tokunoshima. They have been legally protected for nearly a century, initially in response to overhunting. These native rabbits became further endangered when 30 mongooses were introduced to Amami in 1979 to control the habu snake population. By 1999 almost 10,000 mongooses inhabited the island, preying on various local animals, and putting the Amami rabbit on the endangered species list. Thankfully, recent efforts to control the number of mongooses have allowed the Amami rabbit population to recover.

Kyushu

Kagoshima — Amami Oshima Island — AMAMI — 奄美市

👍 Must see! Ohama Seaside Park ❸

Ohama is renowned as one of the most beautiful spots to watch the sun set on Amami. This beach is located in the middle of the north coast of the island. The area also features a campsite, a seaside museum, and an aquarium in which visitors can touch the sea turtles that are raised here and released into the sea.

Other recommended locations to enjoy watching the end of the day are Nishikomi, Taenhama Beach, Kuninao Beach and En Kaganbana Tunnel.

🌳 Nature Spot - Mangrove Park ❹

A leisurely paddle through Amami's Virgin Mangrove Forest is an excellent way to enjoy the Yakugachi River.

Groups of visitors in kayaks that seat one or two people are chaperoned by guides who explain (in Japanese only) the botany of the tropical swamp.

Note that high tide allows greater access to some of the nooks and crannies of the park. Amongst the wildlife found here are small black crabs that you can see scuttling up the trunks of the submerged trees. The park also has a restaurant, gift shop, and a mini-golf course.

Key dates

late July/early August - Amami Festival (firework display, boat competition, parade)

November - Amamioshima Challenge Cycling 240k

We say

"While exploring the warm mangrove forests and rugged mountains heighten the enjoyment of a visit, Amami is primarily a beautiful place to enjoy the relaxing benefits of a tropical island beach holiday."

Recommended for

Families

Marine sports enthusiasts

Sunbathers

Food and Drink

Amami's best-known speciality is *keihan*, a delicious rice dish usually cooked with chicken and a choice of egg, pickles, dried *shiitake* mushrooms, *tankan* (a type of orange) peel, *nori* (seaweed), soup stock and *sake*. Another local favourite is pork belly and bones, simmered with *miso*, rice wine and vegetables. Tropical fruits grown on the island include banana, passion fruit, papaya, and the small citrus fruits of *ponkan* and *tankan*.

The native brown sugar is used in many sweet dishes, and also in the local alcohol, *kokuto shochu*.

Kids

If museums and botanical tours do not appeal to your children, playing and swimming on Amami's beautiful beaches is a wonderful way to spend your time on the island.

Culture Spot
Amami Park 5

This park houses the Tanaka Isson Memorial Museum of Art, and the Amami-no-sato museum, which provides tourist information about the Amami islands, and an exhibition of the traditional folk culture.

Getting there and around

Amami Airport.

From Kagoshima-Chuo Station, travel by bus to Kagoshima Airport and then fly to Amami Airport. Alternatively, travel to Naze Sea Port by boat from Kagoshima. There are no passenger trains on the island.

Although many of the hotels can arrange transportation to the main tourism hubs of the island, hiring a car (available from directly outside the airport) will afford a far greater degree of freedom. Bicycles are an option, but visitors may find cycling around Amami's hilly terrain challenging.

 Further information
www.100hiddentowns.jp/kagoshima/amami.html

TATSUGO

Kyushu — Kagoshima — 龍郷町 — Amami Oshima Island

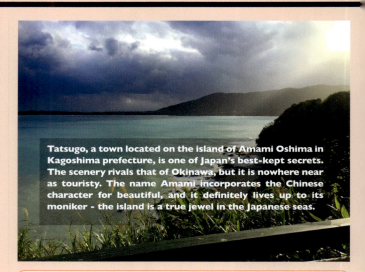

Tatsugo, a town located on the island of Amami Oshima in Kagoshima prefecture, is one of Japan's best-kept secrets. The scenery rivals that of Okinawa, but it is nowhere near as touristy. The name Amami incorporates the Chinese character for beautiful, and it definitely lives up to its moniker - the island is a true jewel in the Japanese seas.

👍 Must do! Tsumugi (Pongee – mud-dyeing of kimonos) ❶

At the Amami Oshima Tsumugi Sightseeing Garden, you can see extraordinary kimonos being dyed and woven by the locals. It can take over two years to complete some of these beautiful garments. The process of dyeing and weaving is all done by hand for maximum precision. The kimonos are extremely expensive to buy, but visitors can try them on for a more reasonable fee.

🌳 Nature Spot - Heart Rock ❷

On the east coast of Akaogi, there is a heart-shaped pool that appears only at low tide. This charming natural phenomenon is popular with visitors. Within a short walk, the rocks lead on to a lovely stretch of beach that is ideal for swimming.

362

 Food and Drink

Local dishes include peanut-flavoured *miso* paste with seaweed, the chicken and rice *Keihan* dish, the local brown sugar of *kokuto* which is used in gelato, and *kokuto shochu* liquor.

 Nature Spot - Kurasaki Beach 3

With white sands, and a sea seemingly tinted with every shade of blue, this beach in the Tatsugo area is a hidden gem. It is often deserted and is great as a private retreat.

 Nature Spot Amami Nature Observation Forest 4

Visitors who make the one-hour hike to the summit of this natural getaway are rewarded with a breathtaking view. The path is well-maintained, but there are warnings about poisonous snakes that sometimes appear from the deep recesses of the slopes.

It is about 30 minutes by bicycle from the town centre to the start of the hiking path, so a car may be a better option if you want to conserve your energy for the hike.

 Getting there and around

🛬 Amami Airport.

🚌 From Kagoshima-Chuo Station, travel by bus to Kagoshima Airport and then fly to Amami Airport. Alternatively, travel to Naze Sea Port by boat from Kagoshima. There are no passenger trains on the island.

🚍 Bus services on the island are infrequent. Rental cars are recommended, although a rented bicycle is another option for the energetic traveller.

 Did you know?

Dirty tricks
It is said that the mud-dyeing on Amami Oshima originated when islanders buried their kimonos in the muddy ground, to hide them from the invading samurai, only to discover upon recovering them that the cloth had turned a beautiful dark brown.

We say
"Without a shadow of a doubt, Amami is in this researcher's top three favourite places in Japan. Although not very well known, it is certainly a hidden jewel among Japan's many islands. With a very Okinawan feel, but with less tourism and more untouched seaside beauty, Amami Island is the perfect place for a getaway from chaotic daily life."

Recommended for

Those looking for a quiet retreat

Japanese culture buffs

 Further information
www.100hiddentowns.jp/kagoshima/tatsugo.html

Kyushu

屋久島町

Kagoshima
YAKUSHIMA

Beaches, diving, hiking, mountain climbing, *onsen*, seafood and waterfalls - Yakushima has something for everyone.

The regular rainfall on Yakushima renders the whole island green. Allow as many days as possible to ensure you can get at least one clear day to appreciate all of its beauty.

Nature Spot
Yakusugi Land

A variety of hikes are on offer here, to see the gorgeous cedars and forest canopy. There are many huge stumps of Yakushima cedar trees that were chopped down during the Edo period for use as timber for wooden tiles. The sheer strength of nature is overwhelming, as the vegetation wraps around and snakes over the stumps. A fabulous chance to see the natural environment in all its power and glory.

👍 Must see! Oko-no-Taki ❷

Simply, one of the most beautiful waterfalls in Japan. Get up close and feel the refreshing spray. Easily accessible by road, and just a short walk from the car park, Oko-no-Taki is recommended as part of a day-long island tour.

🌳 Nature Spot - Kigen Sugi ❸

While not as old as the legendary Jomon Sugi, the *Kigen* (B.C.) *Sugi* (cedar) tree is thought to be 3,000 years old. Its accessibility and beauty make it a must-see.

Visitors can get there by local bus, or join a tour. The top of the tree was lopped off either by lightning or in a typhoon many, many years ago, but its sheer girth and beauty make it an awe-inspiring spot to visit.

❓ Did you know?

Princess Mononoke
World-famous animator Hayao Miyazaki was seen sketching around the island in the late 1970s, and the locals wondered what he was up to. The answer came with the animation classic 'Princess Mononoke'. The film, which was clearly inspired by the Yakushima countryside, became an instant hit on its release in 1997.

Top heavy
The Yakushima residents would protect their houses from typhoons by putting large stones on the roofs. Examples of such houses can still be found dotted around the island.

🌳 Nature Spot - Nagata Inakahama Beach ❹

This beautiful beach is best known for the sea turtles that lay their eggs there in the summer. It is well worth a visit at any time for its gorgeous mountain backdrop and yellow sands. For the romantically inclined, the sunsets can be exquisite.

Kyushu

屋久島町

Kagoshima — YAKUSHIMA

🌳 Nature Spot
Jomon Sugi Hike 5

Most of those who embark on this ten-hour hike have the ancient Jomon cedar as their goal. The wild vegetation on the way makes all the effort worthwhile.

An early morning start is essential.

🍶 Food and Drink

The local seafood of Yakushima is fantastic. Especially recommended is a succulent set of local sushi or *sashimi*. Salted or deep-fried flying fish is another smart choice.

Since Yakushima is part of Kagoshima, *shochu* alcohol is found everywhere too.

The laid-back atmosphere at the restaurants ensures you will end up chatting with the convivial staff and other customers.

Yakushima is famous for its tea, and a short walk inland will reward visitors with picturesque views of tea plantations, framed by spectacular mountain backdrops.

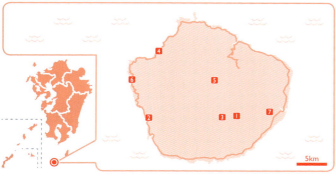

Key dates

August - baby sea turtle viewing season

We say

" Everything they say about Yakushima is true, from the changeable weather to the lush green forests and jungles. I really felt the power and endurance of nature here in this untouched part of Japan. A unique island with the usual high level of Japanese hospitality and cuisine. Really worth a visit, but allow four days minimum. "

Recommended for

Hikers
Nature lovers
Beach lovers

👍 Must do! Island Bus Tour

A bus tour is a relaxing way to do a circuit of the island and cover most key sites. The journey is breathtaking, with magical views of the mountains and forests. Local tour company Matsubanda Kotsu offer a full-day tour. The guides are knowledgeable and clearly proud of their home island. Lunch is also included. The pick up and drop off is at your accommodation, and English-speaking guides are also available.

🌳 Nature Spot
Seibu-Rindo forest path 6

Up in the highlands, monkeys and deer roam freely. Visitors can get up really close and enjoy staring contests with the wildlife on the Seibu-Rindo forest path. Feeding the animals is banned, so they won't trouble you because they know they are out of luck! Seeing these two very different mammals peacefully co-exist is fascinating.

🏠 Culture Spot
Yakusugi Museum 7

This museum is worth a visit to learn about the beautiful trees of this island. You can hold some of the tools from various eras that were used to chop the trees down, as well as enjoy many local exhibits, including a branch from the celebrated Jomon Sugi.

 Kids

Kids will love the gorgeous beaches to the north of the island, and the sight of turtles laying eggs in the summer is both magical and educational.

⇌ Getting there and around

✈ Yakushima Airport. There are flights from Osaka, Fukuoka and Kagoshima airports. Then take a taxi or rental car to your destination.

🚢 Kagoshima-Chuo Station. Take a local bus to Kagoshima Port to then travel by jetfoil to the island, alighting at Anbo or Miyanoura.

🚗 The best way to get around the island is by car. However, there are sporadic bus services and rental cycles are also available.

 Further information
www.100hiddentowns.jp/kagoshima/yakushima.html

Kyushu

阿蘇市 ASO
Kumamoto

Aso, located approximately an hour's bus ride from Kumamoto Airport through rows of hills, mountains and volcanoes, is a wonderful spot in Kyushu. It is dominated by Mount Aso, the living and breathing volcano of the region.

👍 Must see! Kusasenrigahama

Across the road from the Aso Volcano Museum there is open grassland in a crater at the foot of Mount Eboshidake, with the billowing smoke of Mount Naka not far away. Horses can be seen grazing around the ponds in the centre of these craters. There are several hiking routes along which walkers can experience breathtaking panoramic views. Guided horseback rides are another way to take in the spectacular scenery. A ropeway (closed when the volcano is particularly active) leads to the crater. For the truly adventurous, there are helicopter tours that offer unparalleled bird's eye views of the area.

🏠 Culture Spot - Fire Festival

Throughout the month of March, fire festivals take place at a number of places in and around Mount Aso. The most famous sight of these festivities is the Dai Himonjiyaki, a beautifully lit, 350-metre Chinese character which decorates the slope of Mount Aso.

Another event is the Hifuri Shinji Festival, held around the middle of March, when crowds flock to Ichinomiya Aso Shrine. Bundles of straw, bound together with rope, are lit from the fires that line the streets around the shrine. These are swung around to celebrate the marriage of the gods, and to pray for a good harvest. Booming drums and the drone of traditional Japanese instruments create an incredible atmosphere that draws spectators ever closer to the proceedings. The rings of fire make for spectacular viewing, and part-way through the three-hour-long festivities, onlookers can even join in and swing their own flaming straw bundles.

Following the 2016 earthquake, the westward-bound train line between Aso Station and Higo-Ozu Station was closed.

🏠 Culture Spot
Aso Volcano Museum 2

This museum offers insight into the volcanic activity of the surrounding area, as well as more general information on volcanoes around the world. The museum has free headsets which translate the exhibit commentaries into other languages. The second floor has permanent exhibitions, while the third floor broadcasts a film about Aso, with subtitles available in multiple languages.

🌳 Nature Spot
Uchinomaki Onsen 3

Uchinomaki Onsen is the name of the hot springs in Aso. It is an area where many hotels or Japanese-style inns (*ryokan*) can be found. Many of them offer both public and private bathing experiences.

⇌ Getting there and around

✈ Kumamoto Airport. Travel by bus to Aso Station Bus Stop.

🚅 Kumamoto Station or Oita Station. Travel by bus to Aso Station Bus Stop.

🚌 There is a limited bus service to get around the area. Taxis can be expensive, so renting a car from Kumamoto Airport is recommended.

📖 Further information
www.100hiddentowns.jp/kumamoto/aso.html

❓ Did you know?

Heavy smoker
Mount Aso is the largest active volcano in Japan, and in fact consists of five peaks, one of which, Mount Naka, continuously emits smoke.

Key dates

March - Fire festivals
mid-March - Hifuri Shinji Fire Festival (Aso Shrine)

We say

" An area of spectacular nature, made all the more enjoyable by the wonderful *ryokan* accommodation in Uchinomaki Onsen, and its steaming hot baths, gorgeous food, and welcoming atmosphere. "

Recommended for

Hikers
Geology enthusiasts

Kyushu

人吉市

Kumamoto

HITOYOSHI

Bordering the rapid-flowing Kuma River and surrounded by the mountains of southern Kumamoto, the historical castle town of Hitoyoshi has an abundance of attractions for visitors.

Known as 'Little Kyoto', thanks to the temples and shrines dotted around the town and its periphery, the town also boasts the ruins of Hitoyoshi Castle, once the residence of the long-ruling Sagara family.

Boat rides on the Kuma River, or biking and strolling along its banks, are recommended to fully appreciate the town. Follow all that up with a soak in one of Hitoyoshi's many *onsen*, and the town is perfect for a two- or three-day stay.

👍 Must see! Hitoyoshi Castle Ruins ❶

Dating back over 700 years, Hitoyoshi Castle was the proud home of the Sagara clan, who ruled the town until the Meiji era - an unusually lengthy period of time in Japanese history. The vast grounds of Hitoyoshi Castle, across the Kuma River from the town centre, provide a large area to explore. Renovated stone walls mark the approach to the castle. Once in the grounds, the remaining walls and steep steps evoke the rich history of Hitoyoshi in its days as a thriving castle town.

Explore the castle grounds at leisure and enjoy views of the Kuma River, the town to the north, and the surrounding mountains of Kyushu - a splendid spot in any season.

Drop by the Castle History Museum at the foot of the castle hill to see large-scale models of the town in its heyday, as well as a variety of local paraphernalia such as festival masks, palanquins, and temple drums that were used to mark time in the Edo era.

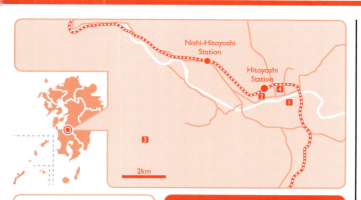

😯 Did you know?

He got there first!
In his famous work *Kaido wo Yuku* ('on the road'), the author Ryotaro Shiba dubbed Hitoyoshi 'Japan's most vibrant hidden village.' Sounds like a good working title for a book...

Key dates

October 3-11 - Okunchi Festival (Aoi-Aso Shrine)

August 15 - Hitoyoshi Fireworks Festival

We say

" A fantastic small town. Whether travelling alone, as a couple, or with kids, Hitoyoshi has much to offer in a manageable area. Top marks to this town! "

Recommended for

Everyone

🏠 Culture Spot
Aoi-Aso Shrine 2

Aoi-Aso Shrine (see main image), built in the early Heian period, is a gorgeous spot approached via an elegant red bridge over a lotus-leaved pond. Entering through the red *torii* gate reveals the distinctive thatched roof of the shrine, a style that predates later wooden structures.

🏠 Culture Spot
Kajiyamachi Street 4

Kajiya means blacksmith, and this narrow stone-paved street has featured workshops and factories since Edo times. These days, visitors can observe *miso* and soy sauce being made, and sample some of the local produce.

🌳 Nature Spot - Kaname Waterfall 3

Venturing further from the town centre, a visit to the Kaname Waterfall is a treat. Nestled deep in the hills, several kilometres to the south of Kuma River, it is a spectacular sight, as the water tumbles off the right-angled rock face.

🔁 Getting there and around

✈ Kagoshima Airport. Travel by expressway bus to Hitoyoshi Interchange, or by local train services to Hitoyoshi Station.

🚄 Shin-Yatsushiro Station. Take local train services to Hitoyoshi Station.

🚶 The attractions in the town are all close to each other, so sightseeing on foot is possible. Renting a battery-assisted bicycle from the tourist information centre at Hitoyoshi Station is highly recommended to facilitate access to sights a little further afield.

📓 Further information
www.100hiddentowns.jp/kumamoto/hitoyoshi.html

Kyushu

綾町

Miyazaki AYA

Aya is a town located a short distance from Miyazaki Airport and Miyazaki Station, and is endowed with a rewarding combination of local handicraft culture, a beautifully reconstructed castle, and an awe-inspiring suspension bridge that spans the plunging, evergreen valley of the Ayaminami River.

Nature Spot
Aya Biosphere Reserve

Aya proudly vaunts the official 'Biosphere Reserve' status bestowed by UNESCO upon its subtropical forests. The health and biodiversity of the mountain wildlife here is strictly monitored and maintained, and this pervading eco-friendly philosophy has engendered a thriving local organic farming industry, as well as attracting many craftspeople to the area. During the springtime, wild cherry blossoms punctuate the evergreen forests with splashes of pink.

Nature Spot
Kawanaka Natural Park Course

Kawanaka Natural Park is a 20-minute drive from Aya town centre.

There are two hiking courses (1.5km / 3.5km) for a therapeutic, leisurely stroll through the forest. Caution is recommended, so consider walking with a paid guide (reservations required one week in advance through the town hall). Hikers should wear walking shoes, and carry water supplies. It is also wise to cover exposed skin during humid periods, in case of leeches and snakes.

🏠 Culture Spot - International Handicrafts Pavilion ❷

Situated a stone's throw from Aya Castle, the pavilion is a lovely wooden structure given over to the display and sale of the handicrafts of local artists.

Goods on sale include pottery, carved wooden household implements, hand-dyed and woven fabrics, and ceramic tableware. In recent times, Aya has become a magnet for nature-inspired artists and craftspeople. Each year in late November, a handicrafts festival featuring approximately 40 workshops attracts about 20,000 visitors to the town.

Next door to the pavilion, there is a workshop area for visitors to try their hand at pottery, weaving and traditional fabric dyeing.

The pavilion also contains a fascinating museum of Japanese pop culture, with magazines, electronic household goods, and posters dating back to the 1960s - a treat for fans of retro kitsch.

One of the outbuildings of the pavilion is an old elementary school that has been moved to the site wholesale, and now contains exhibits showing the history of domestic life and agricultural equipment used in the area.

🏠 Culture Spot - Aya Castle and Museum ❸

This five-storey reproduction of Aya's beautiful, historical castle (originally constructed in the 14th century) has a deep brown, wood-panelled exterior, in contrast to the white of many other Japanese castles.

Inside, visitors to the museum can soak up some of the town's history, and learn about its feudal warriors. Artefacts include muskets, samurai armour, swords, and archery equipment. The top floor has a balcony all around the tower, offering grand panoramas of the surrounding plains and the mountains beyond. Note that there is no English signage inside, although a rudimentary English-language pamphlet is available.

❓ Did you know?

Shy Buddha

The Kawanaka Shrine houses a wooden statue of a seated Buddha that was carved over 500 years ago. In the 19th century, there was a move to abolish Buddhism, and the statue was rescued and hidden in a cave by local people. These days it can only be viewed by the public once a year!

Kyushu

綾町

Miyazaki AYA

👍 **Must see! Aya Teruha Suspension Bridge** ④

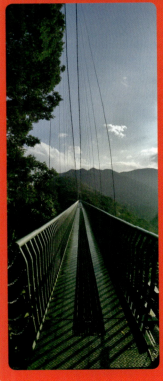

The bridge, which was originally opened in 1984 and strengthened in 2011, was constructed to allow visitors access to the flora and fauna around Aya's waterfalls and evergreen hardwood forest.

Its state-of-the-art design feels reassuringly robust, but all but the bravest of visitors will experience at least a hint of vertigo as they stand in the middle of the 1.2-metre-wide bridge, looking down at the valley floor 142 metres below, where the mountain river wends its way towards the town. Make sure you have a firm grip on your camera if you're taking photos as you cross the bridge.

For visitors with an hour to spare, there is a two-kilometre walking path through the valley woodland that loops back to the starting point, but be aware that the route features some fairly slippery wood and stone steps, and wet conditions might also add the risk of encountering leeches to your arboreal expedition.

The approach road to the suspension bridge has time restrictions due to its precarious nature after dark, so ensure that you set off with plenty of time to complete your hike.

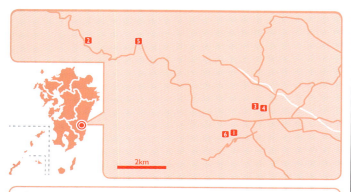

Key dates

late February-early March - Aya Hinayama Festival (doll festival displays around the town)

mid-September - Fireworks display

first Sunday in November - Aya Horse Race

We say

" The high point of my visit was the Aya Teruha Suspension Bridge – an impressive spectacle in its own right, but also a great gateway to the mountain forests on the other side of the Ayaminami River valley. Spending a night in the luxury of the Ryoyoutei Hotel was an indulgence that made the trip even more memorable. "

Recommended for

Nature lovers

 ### Accommodation - Ryoyoutei Hotel

Guests of the Ryoyoutei Hotel can look forward to a luxurious experience. The large suites are composed of traditionally styled rooms containing a sofa area, an escritoire, an en-suite cypress bath, a view out to your own stone and moss garden, and a main room where multi-course Japanese meals are served by kimono-clad hotel staff. The hotel also has a large, communal, hot spring bath, and within the hotel complex there is a glass art gallery, a winery, and outlets selling glassware, wine, various *sake* and craft goods.

 ### Food and Drink - Unkai Brewery

Shochu and wine are brewed in the area, and the Unkai Brewery, located beside the Ryoyoutei Hotel, welcomes visitors to taste as many varieties as they wish, and also to view wine production processes such as bottling and storage.

 ### Getting there and around

- Miyazaki Airport. Travel to Minami Miyazaki Station by train, then to Aya town centre by bus.
- Miyazaki Station. Travel to Minami Miyazaki Station by local train service, then to Aya town centre by bus.
- Aya is a compact town, and many places of interest are within walking distance of its centre. A trip to the suspension bridge or to the Kawanaka Natural Park requires some planning and effort, though.

 ### Further information

www.100hiddentowns.jp/miyazaki/aya.html

Kyushu

椎葉村

Miyazaki SHIIBA

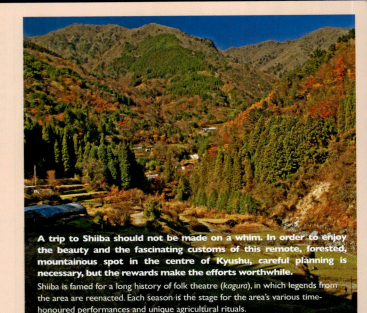

A trip to Shiiba should not be made on a whim. In order to enjoy the beauty and the fascinating customs of this remote, forested, mountainous spot in the centre of Kyushu, careful planning is necessary, but the rewards make the efforts worthwhile.

Shiiba is famed for a long history of folk theatre (*kagura*), in which legends from the area are reenacted. Each season is the stage for the area's various time-honoured performances and unique agricultural rituals.

The many festivals and customs here are intertwined with the traditional agricultural practices associated with rotation farming of buckwheat and millet, as well as production of other delicacies such as *shiitake* mushrooms, soy beans, plums, mountain potatoes, *yuzu* and freshwater fish.

🌳 Nature Spot - Yakihata

Travel even further into the mountains to visit Yakihata, an outlying village, where the air is often silent except for the call and response of birdsong.

Visitors here can stay at a large family guesthouse, and enjoy hands-on experience of traditional Japanese mountain farming techniques.

The owner runs workshops for groups, where attendees can make authentic mountain dishes such as konjac and *mochi* rice cakes, from vegetables farmed in the surrounding area.

🔖 Must see! Shiiba Museum of Folk Performing Arts ②

This museum should be the main focus of every visitor's trip to Shiiba.

Allow yourself ample time to absorb the information collected here. There are four floors of exhibits, photographs and videos - almost all with translations in English - that introduce and explain the large number of historical customs particular to this profoundly rural location.

The museum contains a display of the numerous masks used in Shiiba's *kagura* performances, that range from the beguiling to the terrifying.

The building's multi-functional design also enables it to be used as the home for some of the *kagura* performances during the several event seasons of the year.

Much of the building is devoted to the traditions that relate to the local farmers' entreaties to the gods for bountiful harvests and good health. These traditions include dances, hunting, archery, and burning of the fields.

⇄ Getting there and around

✈ Miyazaki Airport. Travel to Hyugashi Station by local train, then on to Shiiba by bus.
🚆 Miyazaki Station. Travel to Hyugashi Station by local train, then on to Shiiba by bus.
🚌 Access to Shiiba is extremely challenging as it is a 150-minute bus ride from the nearest travel hub (Hyugashi Station) and buses are very infrequent, so be prepared to commit at least two days of your time to justify the journey. That said, the route is through stunning mountain scenery. A rental car picked up from Hyugashi will allow you the most freedom. Ensure that your accommodation is booked in advance if you plan to stay overnight.

📍 Further information
www.100hiddentowns.jp/miyazaki/shiiba.html

💡 Did you know?

Tragedy and history
According to legend, after defeating the Taira clan in the battle of Dan-no-ura in 1185, a Minamoto warrior, Munehisa Nasu, pursued them into Shiiba's forests. However, when he saw the impoverished conditions they had been reduced to, he felt great compassion for the clan. He soon fell in love with Tsurutomi, a Taira nobleman's daughter. The lovers lived happily together for three years, but were forcibly separated by order of the Shogun. The heartbroken princess gave birth to a daughter, and generations of their descendants continued to live on in Shiiba, taking the Nasu family name.

Key dates

second weekend in November - Heike Matsuri (commemorating the tragic romance between General Munehisa Nasu and Princess Tsurutomi)

We say

" Commit yourself to a few days enjoying the delicious food and the fascinating customs that are unique to this mountain village. Shiiba displays a tightly packed slice of old Japanese mountain life perched on a beautiful valley slope. Ensure that you plan your trip carefully to coincide with festivals in or around the town. "

Recommended for

Fans of traditional Japanese theatre

Lovers of rustic food

Kyushu

壱岐市

Nagasaki — IKI

Iki island is located in the Korea Strait between Kyushu and Korea. This hilly island is a pivotal location in the history of Japan's trade with the rest of Asia, and has long been a stop-off point for merchants, with a vibrant community existing here for at least 2,000 years.

The influence of Chinese and Korean culture can still be seen today. The perimeter of this beautiful, green island is dotted with small towns and beautiful beaches, which are popular in the summer months with marine sports enthusiasts.

🌳 Nature Spot - Devil's Footprint Rock Formation [1]

This iconic rock formation, created by the collapse of the edge of a sea cave, is an attractive spot on a grassy headland on the west coast of the island - perfect for picnics and gazing out to sea. It is said that its evocative name comes from the local legend of a huge demon who planted one of his feet here while trying to catch a whale.

🌳 Nature Spot - Monkey Rock [2]

From the tranquil parking area at the end of a series of narrow, winding country roads, visitors are immediately faced by this craggy coastal rock formation that closely resembles the profile of a huge monkey deep in thought. While here, take a little time to wander around the neighbouring headland which provides great sea views.

Kids

Iruka (Dolphin) Park [3]
The dolphin park is in the north of the island, just a few minutes' drive from Katsumoto Town. The venue has a mini-museum, and performances during which, for an extra fee, visitors can feed and touch the dolphins.

Ikikoku Museum Kids' Institute Of Archaeology [4]
In this hands-on section of the museum, there is a range of workshops and activities designed to engage inquisitive children in the world of history and archaeology.

Food and Drink

Iki is famous for many locally produced delicacies, including beef and sea urchin (*uni*). Miuraya restaurant, just five minutes from Gonoura port, is renowned for its fresh *uni* dishes - both raw and cooked.

The island is also home to seven breweries, producing variations of Iki's distinctive *shochu* alcohol.

Did you know?

Art imitates life
The faces of all of the characters in the dioramas at the Ikikoku Museum were modelled on the faces of contemporary Iki residents. Mini telescopes at the museum allow visitors to see the incredible faithfulness to detail achieved by the creators.

Nature Spot - Takenotsuji Three Viewpoints [5]

Takenotsuji, Iki's highest point, provides three great viewpoints within close proximity of each other, each offering impressive but distinct views over the island. From here, visitors can fully appreciate the verdant beauty of the island and its ocean setting. There are parking areas which can be accessed either from the steep road that runs from the north, or from the gentler southern slope.

379

Kyushu

Nagasaki — 壱岐市 IKI

🌳 Must see! Ikikoku Museum and Haranotsuji Ikikoku Park [6]

This beautifully designed, modern museum is a great place for visitors to contextualise the importance of Iki in the history of Japan.

There are pamphlets and interactive audio guides available in a range of languages including English, which enable a relaxed learning experience. The suggested route begins with a short movie projected onto a 180°, curved screen, that narrates a brief history of the island. When the movie concludes, the screen descends to reveal a panoramic window looking out over Haranotsuji Ikikoku Park, a recreation of the village located here, as it was in the Yayoi period - a lovely touch.

Inside the museum there are a large number of exhibits, including a recreation of a wooden *junkozo* seafaring vessel, ancient farm tools, earthenware pots, and glass beads, which reflect the impact that international commerce with China and Korea had on the island.

There is also a fantastic, meticulously made diorama which recreates the lives of locals in the Yayoi period. The figures have been made with jaw-dropping attention to detail. The diorama allows visitors to experience life in the period through the sights and sounds of the residents going about their daily activities of fishing, trading, playing, hunting, and fortune-telling.

Elsewhere in the museum, kids can learn some rudimentary skills of archaeology through hands-on workshops. There is also a huge, beautifully appointed repository for the large number of artefacts found on the island.

The museum's centrepiece is a four-storey tower from which you can take in the 360° spectacle of the island's forests, fields and the ocean.

The whole building - its organic curved shape, grass-topped roof, panoramic tower and imaginatively displayed exhibits, is a superb architectural achievement. This is just how modern museums should be done.

No less impressive is the nearby reconstruction of Harunotsuji - the capital of the Ikoku kingdom. This area was a rich site of archaeological discoveries, and today visitors can walk around accurate copies of some of the buildings used during the Yayoi period.

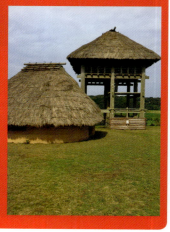

Key dates

second Sunday of January - Iki Island New Year Marathon

first Sunday of June - Iki Cycle Festival (road race)

end of July - Gion Festival

first Saturday of August - Iki Dai-Dai-Kagura Performance (folk theatre)

We say

" Iki is a wonderful place to visit. I was left with many memorable impressions – from the wildlife (I saw a swooping buzzard fly away with a snake hanging from its talons), the people (I experienced a strong sense of friendliness from everyone I encountered - schoolkids, municipal workmen, kiosk vendors), the interesting culture (small shrines pepper the country roadsides), the smells (the fragrant aromas of rural farms), and the terrain (coastal country roads that dip and climb - something like Cornwall meets Hawaii). Although it is possible to explore Iki in one busy day, to do proper justice to the island you will need to stay for at least one night. "

Recommended for

History buffs

Marine sports enthusiasts

Nature Spot - Beaches

As you might expect, the beaches on Iki are one of the main attractions for visitors, who can enjoy diving around the coral reefs, fishing, and also more rigorous pursuits such as jet-skiing. Some of the most popular beaches are:

Tsutsukihama (family beach), Ohama (popular with surfers and windsurfers) and Nishikihama (banana boats, jet skiing and scuba diving) in the Ishida area, the Twins Beach in Gonoura, Kuyoshihama (popular with surfers) in Ashibe, and Tatsunoshima (accessible only by a small ferry from Katsumoto harbour during the tourist season).

Culture Spot
Yunomoto Onsen 7

Yunomoto is the island's hot spring village resort. There are 17 hot springs in the village. The Kokuminshukusha (municipal hotel) is good value. Although the bath in the hotel is modestly sized, its silky brown waters relax the tiredest of muscles. Perfect for unwinding after a hike or cycle trip.

Getting there and around

Fukuoka Airport. Travel to Iki Island by ferry or jetfoil from Hakata sea port. Alternatively, fly to Iki Airport (two flights per day from Nagasaki Airport – though the plane takes only eight passengers). Travel onwards by local bus services.

Hakata Station. Travel to Iki Island by ferry or jetfoil from Hakata sea port. Travel onwards by local bus services.

It is a 70-minute journey to Iki by jetfoil from Hakata sea port, or just over two hours by ferry.

The island measures around 15km top to bottom, and east to west. It is well signposted, has few cars, and no prohibitively steep slopes, so cycling is a great way to get around.

Bicycles can be rented from the tourist information centre beside Gonoura ferry terminal. A car is the next best option, as buses are infrequent.

Further information
www.100hiddentowns.jp/nagasaki/iki.html

381

Kyushu

島原市

Nagasaki

SHIMABARA

Located on the east coast of Nagasaki Prefecture on the Ariake Sea, and backed by the fearsome Mount Mayuyama, the castle town of Shimabara offers plenty of historical and cultural delights.

Ideal as a day trip from Nagasaki City, or for a one-night stay in one of the nearby *onsen* hotels, Shimabara provides a slice of Kyushu's relaxed hospitality.

Culture Spot - Shimabara Castle

Originally built in 1624, Shimabara Castle dominates the town's skyline. Just a short walk from the station, the castle caters for both adults and children, with plenty of interesting displays, opportunities to dress up, and hands-on exhibits. Each floor covers a different period of the town's history, with displays including the Shimabara Rebellion, local samurai, Christian symbols, swords, and other paraphernalia. All of the exhibits have a brief English explanation, and the fifth floor offers amazing 360° views of the town and its surroundings.

Be warned that there are no lifts in the castle.

Nature Spot
The City of Swimming Carp

'The City of Swimming Carp' is actually just a few streets that are lined with carp-filled streams, providing a nice spot in the south of the town for a stroll. Clap and the carp will swarm towards you. The Yusui Teien is a water villa in the area. Free to enter, you can walk around the house and enjoy watching the carp darting around the ornamental pond.

382

👍 Must see!
Bukeyashiki (Old Samurai Houses) 🏯

It is not uncommon for Japanese towns to claim that they offer an experience where visitors can 'travel back in time', but Shimabara's *bukeyashiki* are the real deal. Located a short walk north-west of the castle, a narrow stream runs along the street of the *bukeyashiki*. This man-made stream provided drinking water for the low-ranking samurai who resided in the area during the Edo era. Several houses are maintained in their original state, with displays depicting samurai family life, and can be entered for free. A wonderful window into the past.

Food and Drink

Guzoni is a healthy dish of dumplings, seafood and mountain vegetables in a slightly salty soup - recommended as a stamina-boosting daytime pick-me-up. The dish dates back to the Shimabara Rebellion, where the under-siege local Christians, reportedly at the insistence of their 16-year-old leader Shiro Amakusa, concocted the dish from any ingredients they could forage.

⇌ Getting there and around

✈ Nagasaki Airport. Travel to Shimabara Station by bus or train.

🚄 Hakata Station. Travel via Isahaya Station to Shimabara Station by local services.

🚶 Shimabara can be covered on foot in a day. All the major spots are within walking distance of each other in the town centre.

If wishing to venture further afield, it is worth renting a car to visit Shibazakura Park, or the various observatories related to the devastating disaster of the 1991 Mount Unzen eruption.

❓ Did you know?

Last stand

The Shimabara Rebellion of 1637 was the last stand of Catholic Christian leaders in the Edo era. Christianity had flourished in Nagasaki Prefecture until the Shogun's fears about the religion's growing popularity led to it being increasingly suppressed. The rebellion was a reaction to both this persecution and the high tax demands of Edo. The quashing of the rebellion ushered in much stricter policies against Christians, driving them underground.

Legend

Shiro Amakusa was the teenage leader of the Shimabara rebels. His execution at such a young age earned him enduring fame, through modern manga and video games.

Key dates

April - Shibazakura Flowers (Shibazakura Park)

August - Shimabara Water Festival (*bukeyashiki* stream is lit with bamboo lanterns)

August - Shimabara Port Fireworks Display

September - Ariake Crab Festival

October - Shimabara Castle Autumn Festival

December-January - Shimabara Winter Night (illuminations)

We say

❝ As well as all the cultural and culinary experiences, Shimabara had some of the chattiest, friendliest locals that I have met in Japan. ❞

Recommended for

History buffs

 Further information
www.100hiddentowns.jp/nagasaki/shimabara.html

Kyushu

杵築市

Oita

KITSUKI

Kitsuki is well known for its beautifully preserved historical buildings and streets. Many small towns in Japan describe themselves as 'Little Kyoto', but in Kitsuki's case this is totally justified. A stroll around the town will reveal several fascinating spots for lovers of Japanese history, including what is claimed to be Japan's smallest castle, several outstandingly maintained samurai houses, and cobbled slopes that have connected the various areas of the town since the Edo era.

👍 Must see!
Ohara Residence

The mansion of the Ohara family, who served the local lords of the Matsudaira clan, is perhaps the most famous samurai residence in Kitsuki.

Visitors can walk inside the building and around the grounds to get a feel of the home life of a typical samurai family. The separate entrances, one for the master of the house and any dignitaries, and the other for less important family members, show the clear divisions of authority in the Edo era.

Fascinating rooms in the house include a chamber with a higher ceiling than others so that the residents could practice archery, and the wooden-floored rooms of the servants.

🏠 Culture Spot - The Isoya Residence 2

This spot, just up the Kanjoba slope from the castle, is one of the major attractions for visitors to Kitsuki. The Isoya Residence was once used as a place of relaxation for lords of the town - and it's easy to see why. The rooms open out onto a spectacular garden with tranquil mountain views, which are especially pretty when the plum trees blossom during the spring.

🏠 Culture Spot - Kitsuki Castle 3

The architecture and location of this castle - which claims to be the smallest in Japan - is wonderful. The view from the castle tower over the town and the inland sea is fabulous. There are several elevated spots in the town from which visitors can view the castle against its coastal backdrop. Inside, there are displays of samurai paraphernalia which belonged to the Matsudaira clan that once ruled the domain. Artefacts include armour, coins, maps, palanquins, and weaponry.

 Did you know?

Sandwich-shaped castle town

The town promotes several dishes made with local ingredients. One of these is known as the Kitsuki Sandwich, which was developed because the town is, apparently, shaped like a sandwich. In fact, the local pamphlets mention that Kitsuki is 'the only sandwich-shaped castle town in Japan' - an interesting claim to fame.

385

Kyushu

Oita — KITSUKI (杵築市)

🏠 Culture Spot
Commercial District 4

The commercial district of the town runs between its two characteristic slopes. There is plenty of interesting architecture to enjoy in this area, with some of the stores having remained in business for many years. This area is also a good choice for dining.

🏠 Culture Spot
The Clan School Gate 5

Located along the road of former samurai residences, another wonderfully preserved construction is the gate of the school where the local samurai would educate their offspring in academic studies and martial arts.

🏠 Culture Spot - Suya-no-saka 6 and Shioya-no-saka 7

Suya-no-saka and Shioya-no-saka are well-known slopes in the town, that connect the north and south samurai districts with the commercial district. All the areas still retain plenty of Edo-era buildings to help create the feel of stepping back in time. The slopes provide excellent photo opportunities, although the area is often crowded with tourists. These inclines are often used for scenes in TV commercials and dramas - a testament to their authentic historical feel.

There is another slope called Tenjin-zaka, which provides excellent views of the tiled roofs of shrines and temples in the Teramachi area.

Food and Drink - Kitsuki Don-to-Don

As well as the Kitsuki Sandwich, the town has developed other unique dishes to showcase local produce. One of these, the Kitsuki Don-to-Don, comes in a large bowl containing local meat or seafood produce on a generous bed of rice. Great as a stamina boost before tackling the town's famous slopes.

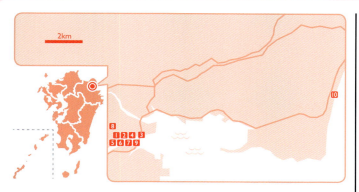

Key dates

May 4, 5 - Castle Festival

July 24, 25 - Tenjin Festival (the 'fight' where the floats collide with each other is a highlight)

We say

" I found Kitsuki to be delightful. It is clear the town is proud of preserving its heritage and, though many towns claim to protect their history, Kitsuki really feels like a taste of Edo. Fantastic for a leisurely half-day trip. "

Recommended for

History lovers

Culture Spot
Rental Kimono Warakuan 8

If you wish to augment your visit to this wonderful historical town by dressing the part, the knowledgeable staff at Warakuan can help you choose a kimono to wear. Wearing the kimono will earn free admission to the sightseeing spots of the town.

The town also offers various other Japanese cultural experiences, including making a postcard with pressed flowers, and tea ceremonies.

Culture Spot - Kitsuki Castle Town Museum 9

This small museum is a pleasant diversion to take in cultural artefacts and historical items. There is a diorama showing how the town looked in its heyday, and it is interesting to compare it with the present day view of the famous slopes, which still maintain their original appearance by being kept free of power lines and gaudy signs - an all too common distraction in historical areas of Japan.

On the ground floor of the museum stands one of the large floats used at the Tenjin Festival in July.

Nature Spot - Nada Beach 10

On the opposite side of the bay from the castle is Nada Beach. Designated as one of the 100 best beaches in Japan, not only does it have white sands, but if you are lucky, you might get the chance to see the decidedly primordial-looking Horseshoe Crab, sometimes used as a symbol of the town.

Getting there and around

 Oita Airport. Travel by taxi, rental car (approximately 30 minutes), or by local bus services to Kitsuki.

Kokura Station. Travel by local train services to Kitsuki Station.

This small town is perfect for leisurely strolls, and its famous slopes aren't too tough for most visitors to tackle.

Further information
www.100hiddentowns.jp/oita/kitsuki.html

387

Kyushu
Oita
USUKI
臼杵市

Usuki lies in one of the birthplaces of Japanese culture and history. Kyushu has often been at the forefront of political and religious changes, and these are reflected in the area. There is a wide choice of historical and religious sites, some dating back thousands of years. Many of the sites offer more questions than answers, and their origins are often obscure.

Culture Spot
Usuki Shrine

What appears to be a low hill on the outskirts of town is actually one of the classic lock-shaped, Kofun-period tombs that dot the ancient areas of Japan.

These earthworks were commonly built around 1,500 years ago to inter contemporary bluebloods. At Usuki, when they delved into the low mound, they found two stone coffins, which contained bones from the skeletons of a male and a female, who are thought to have been a married couple. There is now a shrine built on the site, but the stone coffins are on open display.

Also on the site is an ancient rice mortar from which the town derives its name, Usuki.

👍 Must see! Usuki Stone Buddhas [2]

In an innocuous field outside of the town and off the main road, lies the site of Usuki's main attraction. Follow the path from the entrance up a slight rise, and tucked into slight enclaves in the side of the hill are groups of large stone Buddhas, each with a unique face. Radiating a variety of emotions, they sit in clusters of three or four at different points on the path. The motivation behind their creation has been lost to time. They appear to have been built in two different eras - the Kamakura period (1185-1333), and the Heian period (794-1185). Carved from malleable volcanic rock, they were vulnerable to the elements and erosion. Following a long period of neglect, they have now all been restored, and are designated as national treasures.

The mysterious origins of the statues stimulates a sense of wonder regarding the artisans who quietly toiled away in this unremarkable part of Japan, over a thousand years ago.

❓ Did you know?

First landing

The island of Kuroshima in Usuki is the site of the first landing in Japan of an Englishman - William Adams. He ended up making his home in Japan, and became an advisor to the legendary shogun Ieyasu Tokugawa. His life was later immortalised in the James Clavell book 'Shogun'.

🏠 Culture Spot - Inaba Residence [3]

Actually two for the price of one here. The main house was the second home of Usuki's ruling family, presumably for times when they tired of life in their castle. It has traditionally laid out Japanese rooms, a gated entrance and decorative gardens. There is also a second, earlier, samurai residence on the same site. Visited together, they offer a well-preserved glimpse of the past. The buildings are located a short distance from the tourist information centre [4].

Kyushu

臼杵市
Oita
USUKI

🌳 Nature Spot - Furen Limestone Caves

The town of Usuki spreads out from the coast and into the hills and forests of the interior. As you head through quiet countryside and smallholdings sitting in anonymity, you can understand why one of the most impressive limestone caves in Japan remained undiscovered here until 1926. The fact that the caves were completely sealed off until that time has turned out to be a piece of good fortune, as the caves have not been subject to any weathering processes, and are in a near-pristine state.

The entrance, concealed behind rocks, leads you into a series of passageways going deeper into the mountain. These eventually open out into the main grotto, a large cave filled with stalagmites and stalactites of all manner of shapes. Emerging into the bright lights again after, you are left to wonder what other treasures may lay hidden in these mountains.

🏯 Culture Spot
Usuki Castle

When Usuki Castle was first constructed in 1556, it stood on an island in the bay. Chosen originally for its location, which was easy to defend from attack, this island has been transformed through land reclamation projects over the years, and is now connected to the mainland. Today the castle itself has also been moved, and there is a park in its place. The original walls and gate still enclose the park, which provides a pleasant view over the town.

Culture Spot
Ryugen-ji Temple and Pagoda 7

Just on from Nioza Historical Road, is a very pretty temple with an accompanying three-storey pagoda. Worth stopping by if you are in the area.

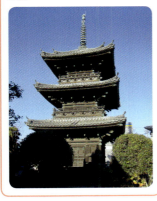

Culture Spot
Nioza Historical Road 8

This road winds up the hill, past temples and residences. Starting near the modern town centre, effort has been made to maintain the historical integrity of the area, and all the buildings have a period aesthetic. The road is narrow in places, and any sight of modern life is blocked out. There are also a couple of historical residences along the route which visitors can peer inside.

Key dates

end of March / beginning of April - Usuki Castle Ruins Cherry Blossom Festival (over 1,000 cherry trees are lit up into the evening on the grounds of Usuki Castle)

mid-July - Usuki Gion Festival (floats and parades fill the streets)

end of August - Fire Festival (1,000 burning torches light up the Usuki stone Buddhas)

first Saturday and Sunday in November - Takeyoi Festival (the town is lit up using traditional bamboo lamps)

We say

❝ Usuki seems at first glance to be a sleepy, seaside town, but it is a place that rewards a little exploration. As well as the samurai period houses in the town centre, the surrounding areas also offer glimpses of an even older Japan. ❞

Recommended for

History enthusiasts

Urban walkers

Getting there and around

- Oita Airport. Travel by bus to Oita Station, then by local train services to Usuki Station.
- Kokura Station. Travel by local train services to Usuki Station.

There are regular ferry services to Usuki Port from Yawatahama (Shikoku).

The castle and samurai district are in the middle of town, the stone Buddhas are a little way out of town, but reachable by rental bicycle. Getting to the caves will require a car.

Further information
www.100hiddentowns.jp/oita/usuki.html

391

Kyushu

有田町
Saga
ARITA

Arita, the home of Japanese porcelain, celebrated its 400th anniversary of porcelain production in 2016. The town itself still retains the architecture and layout of its Edo-era prime, and boasts many lovely nature spots.

🏠 Culture Spot - Tozan Shrine ①

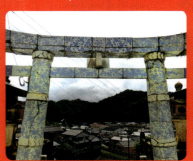

To the south of the railway tracks (in fact the shrine entrance doubles up as a railway crossing!), you can ascend to Tozan Shrine, the home of several monuments to local luminaries, including Ri Sampei. The real draw of the shrine, though, is the porcelain sculptures that line the path to the altar and, best of all, the gorgeous porcelain *torii* gate - a one of a kind. The crest of the hill affords a fantastic view of the town and its surroundings.

Food and Drink

Godofu is the local *tofu* (bean curd). Accompanied by various tasty sauces, its full flavour and chewy texture make for a delicious snack or side dish.

Arita's local delicacy, served in only four eateries, is the Aritayaki Gozen - a reasonably priced selection of locally produced delicacies, served with the staples of rice, soup, and a side dish of the excellent *godofu*. Perfect for lunch or dinner.

Nature Spot - Izumiyama Quarry

At the Izumiyama Quarry, visitors can observe the place where Korean immigrant Ri Sampei (Korean name: Lee Cham-Pyung) discovered kaolin (porcelain's raw material) for the first time in Japan, in the early 17th century. Though unused now, it's not difficult to imagine the quarry's bustling past, when thousands of tons of kaolin clay were dug out with simple pickaxes.

Adjacent to the quarry is the History and Folklore Museum, which displays pictures of the town's famous buildings, as well as exhibits illustrating the porcelain production process, including tools used to quarry the clay, design and paint the products, and make baskets for shipping.

Aside from typical tableware, there are several more spectacular exhibits, such as bathtubs and bowls made from the kaolin clay. An annexe displays fragments of porcelain which show the evolution of porcelain ware design over time. The museum provides a fascinating insight into the craftsmanship involved in porcelain production.

Also backing on to the quarry are the Ishiba Shrine, with a statue of Ri Sampei, and the site of a large sumo ring where quarry workers would relax on their days off by cheering on their favourite wrestlers.

Did you know?

Korean master

Ri Sampei was said to have been forcibly brought to Japan by then ruler Hideyoshi Toyotomi, after Japanese invasions of the Korean peninsula in the 1590s.

Ri's search for suitable clay to produce porcelain wasn't successful until the Izumiyama Quarry was discovered at the beginning of the 17th century. In honour of his achievements, he was allowed to take the Japanese name Kanagae Sanbee.

Kyushu

有田町 ARITA — Saga

🌳 Nature Spot - Arita Dam ③

Just north of Kami-Arita Station, and within easy hiking distance of Uchiyama, is the Arita Dam. This impressive feat of 1950s engineering created a reservoir which now hosts an abundance of wildlife.

Further out of town, the Ryumon valley is worth a visit if time allows. Visitors can walk the circumference of Ryumon Dam and enjoy the peaceful setting.

🏠 Culture Spot - Kyushu Ceramic Museum ④

Just south of Arita Station is the Kyushu Ceramic Museum, which contains a number of works by contemporary ceramic artists. The museum also has a room of exhibits donated by the Shibata family, who collected ceramics over many years. The clear explanations in the Shibata collection provide an engaging introduction for newcomers to the charms of porcelain production.

The museum's exhibits cover all eras of the history of Arita porcelain, including the early Edo period, and trade with the Dutch East Indies Company, as well as the history of porcelain production in China and Korea prior to its development in Japan.

Octagonal Lidded Jar with Underglaze Cobalt-blue and Overglaze Polychrome Enamel Design of Peony and Phoenix / Kyushu Ceramic Museum, No. 63-0761

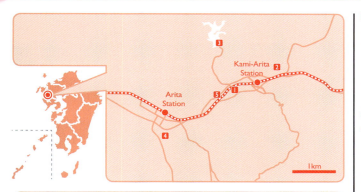

Key dates

April 29 - May 5 - Arita Ceramics Fair (the main thoroughfare is closed to vehicles, and the street is lined with stalls selling porcelain wares)

We say

" Even if you have little interest in porcelain, the architecture and natural setting of Arita are attractions in themselves. Arita's pride and enthusiasm for its history as the birthplace of Japanese porcelain is infectious. Book accommodation early, as the town has a limited number of rooms for visitors. "

Recommended for

Lovers of pottery, architecture and nature

👍 Must see!
Uchiyama District

The main road between the stations of Arita and Kami-Arita is decorated with gorgeous buildings from various eras dating back to Edo times. Such a well-maintained collection of architecture is rare in Japan, and is a real must-see of the town. Many of the buildings are still used as stores for selling porcelain wares.

There are signs in English throughout the area, indicating points of interest, and explaining their historical relevance.

Other places of note in the Uchiyama area include the Tombai walls, which have lined the alleys of the town for centuries. These walls were constructed from the used fire bricks of kilns. Nearby, a giant, thousand-year-old ginkgo tree adds to the ambience.

⇌ Getting there and around

✈ Saga Airport. Take a limousine bus to Saga Station and then the train to Arita Station, or a Limousine Taxi from Saga Airport directly to Arita (reservation necessary).

🚆 Hakata Station. Travel by local train services to Arita Station.

🚲 Getting around is easy, as most sights are within walking distance of Arita Station or Kami-Arita Station. Hiring a bicycle from Arita Station is recommended to make the trip even smoother, especially if planning a little time to visit the outskirts of the town.

📱 Further information
www.100hiddentowns.jp/saga/arita.html

Kyushu
Saga
URESHINO
嬉野市

Tucked away in the quiet northwest of Kyushu, Ureshino is more than just a hot spring resort town, providing fine dining options and a pretty town centre. Famed for its tea and pottery, it has a slight ambience of a European resort, possibly due to its historical links to Nagasaki and the West.

🏠 Culture Spot - Hizen Yoshida-yaki

Hizen Yoshida pottery boasts over 400 years of history. It originated here in 1577, when the distinctive white stone, crucial to the process, was discovered in the bed of a local river. Hizen Yoshida-yaki Pottery Hall is on a low hill, a short drive outside the town. The hall displays various types of pottery and porcelain and, with prior booking, visitors can try their hand at using a potter's wheel.

Explore the narrow streets surrounding the area, where there are a number of kilns and workshops - some operational, some disused - which give you a feel for how bustling the industry would have been at its height.

Must see! Ureshino Onsen

Ureshino Onsen (see main photo) was first mentioned in chronicles from 713AD, when it flourished as a stop on the Nagasaki Kaido. The 3,000 tons of piping hot, mineral-rich water pumped out every day, is famous for giving skin a lustrous shine. There are many *onsen* hotels in the area offering lovely views over picturesque gardens, giving guests a perfect way to relax after exploring the town, and a chance to try the famed Ureshino Onsen waters.

Kids - Hizen Yume Kaido – Ninja Village

As you step through the wooden gate and the pounding ninja pop theme blasts out, you know this is going to be a high-octane experience. The theme park itself could do with some renovation in places, but offers a lot of interactive elements. Visitors can try out a wide variety of different ninja skills, such as using a ninja blow pipe, throwing a ninja star, avoiding hidden traps in a ninja house, making ninja pottery, and even feeding ninja chickens and horses.

The fully costumed staff provide plenty of family fun, and there are shows every two hours. For an extra fee, children can dress up as ninjas for the whole day. While not necessarily a treat for all adults, it is well suited for little ninjas - or the little ninja in you.

Nature Spot - Kasuga Valley

Kasuga is a pretty valley surrounded by fields and wooded hills, leading down to a dam. Best enjoyed in its autumn colours, there is a variety of flora in the area, including Japanese knotweed on the river banks. Japanese knotweed is unfortunately an invasive plant in the west, and was introduced to Europe by former Ureshino resident, Philipp Franz von Siebold. Stop off at the dam on the way back, to enjoy the views from the top of the tea plantations which stretch back to Ureshino.

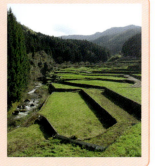

Did you know?

Wonderful, wonderful waters
The legendary third-century ruler of Japan, Empress Jingu, is said to have noticed how rejuvenated her soldiers became after taking the local baths. At this, she is said to have exclaimed '*Ureshii!*' ('how wonderful'), and that is how the town got its name.

Kyushu

Saga — URESHINO
嬉野市

🍶 Food and Drink

Onsen Yudofu

A local speciality is *tofu* cooked in water from the *onsen*. The *tofu* is served boiling in a pot, and enjoyed with a number of different sauces. The cooking process gives the *tofu* a creamy taste and texture.

Ureshino Tea

Award-winning Ureshino tea is considered by many connoisseurs to be the best in Japan. The tea plants are a ubiquitous feature of the low, rolling countryside around the area. Dozens of tea shops - selling tea, kettles, teapots, and cups - are spread throughout Ureshino.

🏠 Culture Spot
Todoroki-no-Taki Park 4

Just on the edge of town, the main feature at this park is the river that gushes through a small rock canyon, and then over a number of waterfalls, before flattening out and ambling towards the town. There are a number of interesting rock formations and pools to be found here. Near the park, Kinsarankan is billed as an interactive facility for green tea. Here, via an advance booking, visitors can try selecting the best leaves and the proper way to brew them.

🏠 Culture Spot
Siebold's Onsen 3

Philipp Franz von Siebold was a German botanist and physician. He was one of the few westerners to visit Japan before the opening of the country to the outside world in the 1860s, and he helped introduce Japanese studies to the West. He stayed in Ureshino whilst travelling to the court in Edo (Tokyo), a trip which concluded with him being accused of spying for the Russians and expelled from the country. Siebold's Onsen is a European-style building in the centre of town, bearing his name. With the feel of a European spa hotel, this bright, airy *onsen* has wood panelling and white walls. Check out the second floor, which has exhibits explaining the history of the town, and a pretty balcony area with views across the town.

🏠 Culture Spot - Onsen Park 5

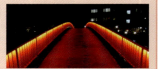

Onsen Park is beautifully situated beside a river, and offers sights of the older buildings of the town. It is especially pleasant to walk through the park in the evening, when the bridges are lit up.

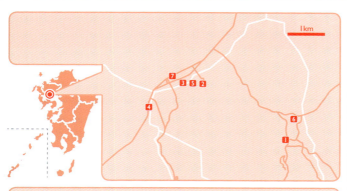

🌳 Nature Spot - Hyakunenzakura 6

Ancient cherry trees are fairly uncommon, so it is worth taking the short walk from Yoshida-yaki Pottery Hall to visit the Hyakunenzakura ('100-year-old cherry tree'). Perched on the side of a hill with views across the valley, the tree is in full bloom from late March to early April. Despite its name, when the tree was actually planted, and by whom, is not known.

🏠 Culture Spot - Toyotamahime Shrine 7

Mythical princess, Toyotamahime, was a daughter of the sea god, and was renowned for her beautiful, white skin. This pretty shrine is best approached from the south. Its main attraction is the white catfish statue just to the side of the main building. Pour water over the statue, and it is said that visitors will be granted skin as beautiful as that of the princess.

🚋 Getting there and around

✈ Fukuoka Airport. Travel by local train services to Takeo Onsen. From Takeo Onsen, take a bus to Ureshino Onsen.

🚆 Hakata Station. Travel by local train services to Takeo Onsen. From Takeo Onsen, take a bus to Ureshino Onsen.

🚲 Most of the main attractions are fairly central. There is bicycle rental available at the bus terminal, to help you get around. You will need a car to get to the pottery area, or Kasuga Valley.

 Further information
www.100hiddentowns.jp/saga/ureshino.html

Key dates

last Saturday in March - Ureshino Brewery Sake Festival

early April - Ureshino Tea Summit (new tea festival)

early August - Ureshino Onsen Summer Festival (fireworks and events)

early November - Ureshino Onsen Autumn Festival (a chance to try onsen yudofu, the town's signature dish)

We say

" A wonderful *onsen* town offering many of the charms of a city break whilst being deep in the countryside. Ureshino provides a variety of sights and activities for all visitors. "

Recommended for

People interested in traditional Japanese crafts, tea and pottery

KYUSHU
九州

OTHER TOWNS

Fukuoka
ITOSHIMA

Itoshima is located on the northern coast of Fukuoka prefecture. Itoshima's townsfolk are historically an international mix, owing to the area's long history of trade with China and Korea. Within just a few miles, visitors can experience a drastic difference in climate between the seafront and mountains. Itoshima has stunning countryside, and a town centre dotted with small restaurants.

Culture Spots Itokoku Historical Museum, Sakurai Shrine
Nature Spots Shiraito Falls (mountain waterfall)
Must see Sakurai Futamigaura (beach)
We say Itoshima is an excellent day trip for visitors staying in Fukuoka City. Head north from Chikuzen-Maebaru Station for gorgeous coastal scenery, or head south for breathtaking mountain terrain.

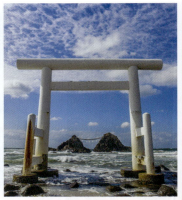

Kagoshima
HIOKI

Hioki is a town most famed for its ancient tradition of Satsuma-yaki pottery and ceramics. The town stretches south, down to the difficult-to-access area of Fukiage on the coast. Hioki retains the identity of a traditional old Japanese town, with a number of hot springs scattered around Yunomoto Station, and its community of potters in Miyama Village.

Culture Spot Tanoyu Onsen
Must do Miyama Toyukan Pottery Centre
We say A relaxing place to visit for pottery enthusiasts.

Kagoshima
TARUMIZU

Tarumizu faces the prefecture's eponymous capital city across Kagoshima Bay, and is watched over by the neighbouring volcanic island, Sakurajima.

Tarumizu's busy coastline is a rich breeding ground for Japanese amberjack (*buri*), and its waters are busy with fishing boats. Just a short distance away, the land rises steeply up to mountainous terrain, where some of its better-kept secrets can be found.

Culture Spots Yachiyoden Shochu Brewery, Tarumizu Roadside Station and foot *onsen*
Nature Spots Senbon-Ichou - 1,000 Ginkgo Trees (autumn only)
We say The sight of Sakurajima, the fresh air of the rugged highlands, and the camping resort of Morino-eki Tarumizu, all combine to make Tarumizu an enjoyable diversion for visitors to Kagoshima who have some time on their hands.

Miyazaki
TAKANABE

Just along the coast from the ancient rock formations of Aoshima, is the town of Takanabe. Surrounded by serene countryside, and sites of historical interest, visitors can hire a bicycle or go for a leisurely drive around this town to enjoy its far-flung sights.

Culture Spot Maizuru Castle ruins
Must see Mochida Tomb Group
We say On the outskirts of town, the eerie Mochida tombs, jutting from the surrounding paddy fields, are an interesting spot, and the old castle hill makes for a pleasant hike. A good base from which to explore the wider Miyazaki area.

Kumamoto
MINAMATA

The town of Minamata is synonymous with Minamata Disease, a neurological disorder caused by industrial waste that contaminated the nearby waters over many years, and which poisoned the sea life that was consumed by the locals. While the event is remembered as an important part of Japan's history, this strikingly beautiful area has since successfully met a set of environmental objectives, and is now an official Japanese eco-town, with a museum and eco-park showcasing its revitalisation.

Culture Spots Eco-Park Minamata
Must see Yunoko Island
We say Minamata is an inspiring town, which educates visitors about the legacy of unregulated industry, and which has re-invented itself as an eco-town, providing a compelling model for the future. The tranquility of Yunoko Island at night is a particular highlight.

Okinawa

MIYAKOJIMA
宮古島市

Okinawa

Miyakojima is one of the most iconic of the Okinawa islands. While it has many other distractions and places of interest, one of the main draws for visitors to Miyako is its coastline, which features some of the most beautiful tropical beaches in all of Japan. Miyako is perfect for water sports enthusiasts, as well as families seeking some rest and recuperation.

If all the soaking up of the sunshine on white, sandy beaches, and swimming in crystal-clear cobalt blue waters isn't enough for you, Miyako also has many golf courses, fabulous restaurants and a lively musical tradition.

The majority of the island is used for the cultivation of sugar cane, tobacco, and mangoes, and it is easy to get lost in the labyrinthine roads that run inland between the fields of these tall, local crops.

Wildlife thrives, and the sights and sounds of scuttling crabs, insomniac frogs and giant bats are fairly commonplace.

👍 Must do! Marine activities

Miyako offers a wide range of marine-based activities. Divers can choose between snorkelling or scuba diving around coral reefs that lie just a few metres from the coast, or make a reservation to travel further out to sea on a boat expedition.

Sea kayaks are a peaceful way to paddle around the island's ocean trenches and caves (you might even encounter sea turtles), while those who are interested in more adrenaline-fuelled activities are catered for by jet skiing, wakeboarding, water skiing, and tube or banana boats.

Fishing, either from the beach or offshore angling from boat cruises, is another way to unwind.

🏠 Culture Spot - Muikaga Ido ❶

There are several historical wells that dot the area around the centre of Miyako City. One of these is Muikaga Ido, a well found in a deep cave, that was used from 1720 until the end of the last century. The low walls that enclose the area are made from chunks of long-dead coral.

🌳 Nature Spot - Irabu Bridge ❷, Irabu Island ❸ and Shimoji Island ❹

Irabu Bridge, the longest toll-free bridge in Japan when it was completed in 2015, added a huge amount of convenience to the lives of locals and visitors, who used to have to take the ferry that connected the main island to Irabu Island and its smaller neighbour, Shimoji Island. The bridge itself is an elegant and hugely impressive feat of engineering, 3,540 metres long, and curving along both axes.

The coastline that surrounds Irabu Island is not long, but still manages to squeeze in many beautiful sights. One of the most notable of these is Sawada Beach, a quiet shallow dotted with huge, isolated rocks which look fabulous when backlit by the sunset.

Irabu Island is connected to Shimoji Island by several bridges, each only a few metres long. The island is the site of the area's original airport.

❓ Did you know?

Stone me!
On Miyako Island it is a common sight to see graves lining the roadside. Unlike their counterparts in Honshu, the graves here are relatively large, hut-like stone mausoleums where families will come to share a meal with their deceased ancestors on occasions like *obon*.

Sleeping policemen

The corners of many of the road junctions on the main island are policed by a slightly creepy-looking statue of a black-lipped policeman known as Mamoru-kun, who silently warns motorists against the temptations of reckless driving.

Daiko!
Don't drink and drive on Miyako! The island has an authorised service called *daiko*, where local, sober people will drive you and your car home for a reasonable fee.

403

Okinawa

Okinawa — MIYAKOJIMA 宮古島市

🍶 Food and Drink

The residents of Miyako Island are a hardy bunch, and many congregate in the evenings for the drinking custom of *otori*, where members of a group take turns to make a pronouncement on life and the world, which all the others will then discuss, and then down a drink of *awamori*, the local liquor.

Popular local soft drinks are banana and brown sugar milkshakes, and bitter melon juice.

Another Miyako staple is *Goya Chanpuru* - a dish made from chopped up *goya* (bitter gourd), *tofu*, egg, and spam (the processed meat which became popular locally in the post-war rationing years).

🌳 Nature Spot - Beaches

Yonaha Maehama Beach

This is Miyako Island's most famous beach. The golden sands and deep blue sea stretch out along the south coast of the island. Some sections of this coastline are owned by hotels, but most of this family-friendly expanse is open to all. From here you also get a great view of Kurima Island (which is accessed by the Kurima Bridge). Yonaha Maehama Beach is particularly recommended for its beautiful sunsets.

Aragusuku Coast 6

The east coast of the main island has wonderfully tranquil waters, and its relatively difficult access and absence of local hotels ensure that the beaches are usually fairly quiet. This side of the island is popular for snorkelling and paddle boarding.

Sunayama Beach 7

This secluded but popular family beach is known for its iconic rock arch and its coral reef, which is not far out to sea. It is an ideal location for snorkelling.

🏠 Culture Spot - Kurima Island 8 And Kurima Bridge 9

A 1,690-metre-long bridge connects the main island to Kurimajima.

Visit the Ryugujo Observatory, from which you can gaze down at the bands of aquamarine and sapphire waters below, and across to the fine golden sands of Yonaha Maehama beach. The recent development of Kurimajima has led to a surge in cafeterias and stylish boutiques.

Key dates

April - All-Japan Triathlon Miyakojima

May - Koinobori (carp kite) Festival (Ueno German Culture Village)

June/July - Tour de Miyakojima (cycling road race)

July - Miyakojima Summer Festival

October/November - Pantu Festival (locals dress as evil *pantu* spirits, covered from head to toe with mud and foliage, to drive out demons and cleanse the island of bad luck... and to terrify small children)

We say

❝ Miyako is a beautiful island with a range of activities to suit all visitors. The local culture is notably less restrained than in many other parts of Japan, which makes for a fun-filled experience. Here you can enjoy nature, the sea, history, sports, traditional music and dance, and fresh, tropical food and drink. ❞

Recommended for

Diving and water sports enthusiasts

Holidaying families

Sunbathers

Golfers

 Food and Drink

Shima-uta Rakuen Bunmya - Izakaya and Live House ⑩

The initially intimidating proprietor is the star of the show here, as he and his backing singers entertain diners with a mixture of relaxing and rowdy local standards accompanied by the *sanshin*, a traditional Okinawan instrument with a snakeskin-covered body and three strings. By the end of the night, the performance can sometimes transform the evening meal into a singing, dancing village hoedown, with all the diners getting in on the *kuichaa* (Miyako's distinctive song and dance tradition) action.

⇄ Getting there and around

✈ Miyako Airport. Flights to Miyako Island leave from Tokyo Haneda, Kansai, Chubu Centrair and Naha airports.

🚲 The island is too large and usually too hot for most people to circumnavigate by bicycle. Bus routes are generally only between the airport and the hotels. Rental cars and taxis are therefore the most convenient way to get around. Many leisure and water sports companies will pick up their customers from hotels free of charge.

 Further information
www.100hiddentowns.jp/okinawa/miyakojima.html

TRAVEL ADVICE

other information

The recommendations in this book are only made possible by the remarkably swift and efficient Japanese public transport network. The bullet train and domestic plane services will get you to a major train station or airport within the vicinity of any chosen destination, in just a few hours.

Once into the lesser-populated parts of Japan, visitors without access to a rental car are reliant on sporadic local trains or buses, unmanned stations, or lengthy taxi rides.

PLANES

As a major economic power, it is no surprise that Japan has airports dotted around almost every prefecture. Predictably, the main hubs are based around the major cities, with millions of travellers every year landing in Fukuoka, Chubu Centrair, Kansai, Narita and Haneda International Airports.

Depending on your starting and leaving point, some of the more remote prefectures may be more easily reached by train. Flights to rural airports are frequent and can be much cheaper and less time-consuming than using the *shinkansen* bullet train system. This book lists the main access points for each town and each prefecture, but check online for up-to-date, precise information.

BUSES

Using buses in Japan is safe and inexpensive, but can be a little challenging at first, since there is often a lack of English information, and the payment systems differ depending on the route you use. Here, as with trains, the purchase of a travel card such as IC or Pasmo might make life easier, as on some buses you can just swish the card over the device by the door when boarding and alighting. Often, though, you will need to have coins to hand. Although the fare requires the right change, you can convert your notes into the appropriate coins via a device next to the driver. Be warned that these devices don't take the larger notes (¥5,000 and ¥10,000), so if you are planning to travel by bus, stock up on coins or ¥1,000 yen notes.

For the rural areas such as those showcased in this book, even the remotest will likely have a bus service of some sort, though make sure you are aware of the times, as they may come as rarely as just once or twice a day.

Overnight buses

For longer trips, overnight buses are a much cheaper option than the bullet train. Several bus companies run such services between major cities and prefectural capitals.

BOATS AND FERRIES

Including the four major islands of Japan, the archipelago totals over 6,850 islands, of which 430 are inhabited, and several are featured within these pages. Naturally, many of the islands of Japan can only be reached by sea, and access can be heavily affected by the weather.

Check out English-language websites of your island of choice, for details on getting there and back. Depending on the destination, there may be a choice of services, from plodding ferries to zipping jetfoil boats.

TRAINS

Japan's bullet trains provide an awesome travelling experience due to their speed, convenience and comfort. When aboard, it is easy to forget just how fast you are travelling, but if you have the chance to be at a station that bullet trains often pass through, it is a jaw-dropping sight to see one flash past. While the bullet trains are all run by JR (Japan Railways), local train services are operated by a mixture of JR and private companies, which can sometimes make purchasing tickets a confusing proposition. That said, the oft-mentioned Japanese hospitality shines throughout the system, and helpful station staff, websites and English-language ticket machines all combine to make buying tickets a painless process.

Holidaymakers from overseas qualify for some excellent, money-saving travel deals such as the Japan Rail Pass (continue reading for more details). Bone up before you come, to ensure getting the best deals on offer.

The further into the countryside you get, the more infrequent the train services become, with some stations operating just a few trains a day. To make sure you can catch the return train you want, consider photographing the station timetable when you arrive.

How to book tickets:

- The much-lauded Japan Rail Pass must be purchased outside Japan. It will save you from having to fiddle about with coins and notes, as well as saving a lot of money if you are planning to use many trains during your stay. The seven-day pass is so cheap that its price is almost the same as just one round trip from Tokyo to Kyoto. For longer-stayers, the 14-day pass is also available, as well as child passes. Kids under six travel for free.
- You can reserve *shinkansen* (bullet train) tickets up to a month in advance of your trip. Slightly cheaper, non-reserved seats are available, but there is always the risk that you may have to stand for the journey if travelling at peak season or on busy weekends.
- Reservations can be made at the *midorinomadoguchi* (green window) of major JR stations. The staff will usually have enough English to be able to process your booking with ease.
- *Shinkansen* tickets can also be purchased on the day of travel, but may involve a wait at the *midorinomadoguchi*.
- Tickets for during the peak travel seasons of Golden Week and *obon* should be booked as soon as possible.
- For non-bullet-train rapid services that require a reservation, the *midorinomadoguchi* is also the place to go.
- For local trains, most stations have automated ticket machines. Many lines make use of travel cards which can be purchased at ticket machines through English-language guidance. There is a variety of prepaid cards available (e.g. Pasmo, IC, Suika, Icoca, etc.), but they are all used in the same way. A purchase of one of these is highly recommended to save you time and anguish before boarding your train. Take note that the more rural a station is, the less likely it is to accept such cards, and you might need to creak open the wallet.

TAXIS

Taxis in Tokyo and other major cities can be prohibitively expensive, but the cheaper fares charged in more rural areas make them a reasonable option. Some Japanese language skills will get you a long way (figuratively speaking), as most drivers will have only the most rudimentary level of English. Try out our *Useful Phrases* (see page 412) to avoid a trip to the wrong end of town.

other information

TRAVEL ADVICE

RENTAL CARS

Stop! In Japan, they drive on the left! Got it? OK - then we can continue. We mention in our *Getting there and around* sections of each town whether a rental car is necessary - inevitably, many trips will definitely benefit from having four-wheeled transport.

The process for renting a car is straightforward in Japan, with companies such as Nippon Rentacar and Toyota providing services at every major transport hub. You will need an international licence, but all the booking can be done online in English, and the documentation, including insurance, is usually available in English (and other languages) at the rental location.

Once behind the wheel, some highways require tolls. It is recommended to purchase an ETC Card from the rental company, which will enable you to automatically go through the toll booths.

All rental cars will come with a satellite navigation device (*nabi*), but double check to see whether it has an English-language option (these can sometimes be pre-arranged when you book online).

Parking at many rural spots and hotels is free, but not always, so have some change available for when you return to your car.

RENTAL CYCLES

From our experiences, some of the best visits involved the use of rental bicycles. You can check beforehand whether a town has such a service. A passport is necessary for identification, and advance booking may be required, but once saddled up, it's difficult to imagine a better way to see a town than to leisurely cycle around it. The recent proliferation of battery-powered bicycles has made such visits even easier, though be sure to check how quick the battery is going down (such bicycles have a display to show the remaining battery life) because riding a dead battery-powered bike is quite a heavy burden! Rental cycles are often available directly from a town's tourist information office, but it is unusual to be allowed to rent one overnight.

WALKING

Our *Getting there and around* sections give visitors some advice on navigating their way around the towns. Many of the towns have our recommended attractions within walking distance from each other, but equally, many towns have them at disparate locations, requiring use of wheeled transport, as mentioned above. Japan is, of course, mountainous. For climbers and hikers, the country is utopian. Thanks to the public transport service, one is never too far from a mountain to climb or from a pretty hike. However, be aware that the changeable Japanese climate can cause particularly hazardous conditions in mountainous areas.

GENERAL ADVICE

Day-to-day life in Japan remains mostly problem-free, due to Japanese society's adherence to its many rules. There is a certain amount of leeway and sympathy for the travelling foreign visitors, as the locals realise we can't know all the regulations and etiquette. Try to keep a look out for the many illustrated warning icons and signs that are provided to help visitors avoid hazards (e.g. wild beasts or dangerous slopes) and cultural faux pas (e.g. flash photography or inappropriate clothing).

NATIONAL HOLIDAYS

Japan has a generous amount of national holidays throughout the year, which may affect the convenience of your travel. Certain times to be especially wary of are the New Year period, the mid-August *obon* holiday period, and the series of national holidays at the end of April and early May, known as Golden Week, when the entire country hits the roads and rails for a getaway, the accommodation prices (if indeed you can find any accommodation during Golden Week) skyrocket, and the convenience of travel is severely affected.

TRAVELLING WITH KIDS

In each of the town chapters, where relevant, we include a Kids section. Some towns are more kid-friendly than others, with attractions unambiguously aimed at the young crowd, while certain destinations are strictly for the more mature. Below is some general advice for those travelling with kids.

Transport

In general, travelling with kids is extremely easy in Japan. Logistically, the amazing train service ensures that getting from A to B is smooth. Try to avoid the rush-hour trains of the bigger cities, as kids can get lost and squashed amongst the sullen salarymen. For the bullet trains, it's a great, fun ride for the kids as much as for adults. Children aged 5 or under travel free on buses and trains, and those aged 6-12 travel at half-price.

Food

Food-wise, there is usually plenty to satisfy fussy youngsters, with a variety of restaurants, even in smaller towns. Be warned that staying at a *ryokan* may mean the food is *very* Japanese and, often, seafood-based, so perhaps not ideal for the toddler palate. Some *ryokan*, though, have a kids menu or a buffet meal option, so it really is a case of checking out websites in advance. Also, convenience stores help to ensure that kid-friendly dishes and snacks are never far away.

Activities

Japan places great emphasis on education, and museums are designed to engage curious young minds. There are plenty of hands-on displays even in the more rural museums. Cultural activities can often attract the kids even more than the adults, with opportunities to try their hand at pottery, sweet-making and various arts and crafts.

TRAVELLING WITH PETS

Japan is tolerant of pets, especially dogs, though their living conditions and general treatment can differ markedly from other countries - don't be surprised to see a proud owner pushing their much-loved mutt around in a pram, wearing a bow in its fur. If you want to bring your own extended family member to Japan, there are several hoops to jump through. Contacting your outbound airline will glean such information, including quarantine procedure and travelling conditions. Once in Japan, it is generally not possible to bring pets onto public transportation, except small pets that can fit in a box lighter than ten kilograms.

There are plenty of pet hotels for visitors to leave their pet if necessary, and even some hotels that allow guests to stay with their furry friend.

JAPAN FOR THE DISABLED

Japan has improved hugely over the last few decades in providing access and services for the disabled. For wheelchair users and others with motion difficulties, most stations in the bigger cities have lifts and helpful staff on hand to get you on and off your desired train. Some buses in major cities, known as *non-step* buses, have facilities for wheelchair users to board and alight safely. However, the more rural that one goes, the less likely that barrier-free facilities exist on public transportation, so plan accordingly. Urban Japan has excellent toilet facilities, with their anyone-can-use *daredemo* toilets that are spacious and have up-to-date equipment. Again, though, there can be discrepancies between every *daredemo* toilet you use, so don't always expect the same high standards each time.

For visually impaired visitors, train platforms and most pavements in big cities have the raised dots and lines known as tactile paving, and traffic lights provide melodies to help with crossing the road safely.

Once outside the major cities, such provision becomes less adequate, and any visit will need a great deal of planning.

LGBT JAPAN

For Asia, Japan is a tolerant environment for lesbian and gay travellers. The more rural areas, while unlikely to have a gay scene, are simple to stay at for gay and lesbian couples, thanks to the accommodation options of hotels with twin rooms and shared Japanese rooms in *ryokan*, which make staying as a couple uncomplicated.

other information
GENERAL ADVICE

RELIGION
There is an increasing awareness in Japan regarding the requests of travellers with religious requirements, such as Halal or Kosher food, and accommodation catering for prayer. The level of awareness and adequate provision differs from area to area, so plan accordingly and, if visiting one of our recommended hidden towns, it may be wise to bring what you need with you.

SAFETY
Japan is often described as the safest country in the world, with low crime rate statistics to support such claims. That said, like anywhere across the world, it never hurts to exercise customary caution during your visit. Non-human hazards can include earthquakes, tidal waves and wild beasts. Any visitor staying in Japan for a length of time is likely to experience at least a mild seismic tremble. The key is to not be alarmed, take cover under a table or something solid and, when the shaking ceases, calmly exit the building. For serious quakes, television, radio and electronic devices should provide any necessary information in English.

Be aware that, in the occurrence of an earthquake, the majority of injuries are caused by fires or *tsunami* that might subsequently occur, rather than people being hurt by falling objects.

If necessary, follow any locals towards the designated evacuation area.

There are also weather-related hazards to be wary of. Typhoon season (typically at its height from May to October) can cause flash floods and mudslides, and disrupt travel plans. Again, up-to-date weather information can accurately inform you of the path of any typhoons, so you can plan accordingly.

There are many wild animals in Japan, so if you're venturing into the mountains, be wary of snakes and bears. Follow the guidance of locals, keep to the major paths, and take necessary precautions, such as carrying a small bell to deter any inquisitive bears in the vicinity.

CLIMATE
Japan experiences extreme weather conditions, with the northernmost areas cloaked in snow throughout winter, and the southernmost islands of Okinawa warm all year long. In between, aside from Hokkaido, the rest of Japan has very hot and humid summers. August is the most uncomfortable month to visit unless you are planning to chill on a sheltered beach. Take precautions to avoid the dangers of heatstroke, sunburn, dehydration and insect bites (particularly mosquitoes).

Outside the middle of summer, spring and autumn are pleasant, with warm, comfortable weather. June and early July, before the stickiness hits, is the rainy season, which sweeps across Japan from west to east. The extremes of winter differ depending on which part of the country you are in, and can be mild towards the south, and very cold if in the north or facing the chilly Sea of Japan.

Weather forecasts are usually extremely accurate, and visitors can plan schedules well in advance. One final tip is that, if the forecast says rain, then expect rain. Unlike many countries, the rain may not relent, so a good, strong umbrella is recommended.

ACCOMMODATION
Japan has a wide range of accommodation options, including high-end traditional *ryokan* inns, homely *minshuku*, hotels, and hostels. Be warned that accommodation can get full very quickly, especially during peak season, weekends and holidays. Book as early as possible to avoid disappointment. Here we list the main different types of accommodation, and briefly explain what to expect:

Ryokan: traditional inns. Fantastic for a traveller wishing to experience the real Japan, and rest up like a weary aristocrat. Expect *tatami* mats, hot springs, *futons* and astonishing meals - and a bill to match. Be warned that *ryokan* charge per person rather than per room, so even if you are sharing with a number of friends, the bill will be massive, and many *ryokan* don't offer rooms to lone travellers, so if you are travelling solo, it may be necessary to find alternative accommodation.

410

Minshuku: *Minshuku* is the name given to (usually) family-operated bed-and-breakfast establishments. Many of these do not have their own websites, but don't let that put you off - *minshuku* provide some of the most welcoming accommodation in Japan. There is also the option of 'experience stays', such as at religious retreats or farmhouses - highly recommended as a chance to chat and dine with locals.

High-end Hotels: Here is where Japan is homogeneous with the rest of the world. A five-star hotel is much the same the world over, after all. Naturally, the 100 towns in this book are short on five-star accommodation, but if you really need to splurge on luxury, any nearby major city will undoubtedly provide such an option.

Standard Hotels: Many of the towns will have a reasonable, standard-priced hotel. Such accommodation provides excellent service and comfortable amenities, the price usually reflecting the popularity of the location.

Business Hotels: Even the smaller towns may have one or two of these, as the besuited, travelling Japanese salaryman can be found even in the remotest spots. A good budget option, with simple but sufficient amenities. Dining is rarely included in the price, so visitors are at liberty to explore the town for meal options. For non-claustrophobic travellers, capsule hotels are an even cheaper option in some larger towns.

Love Hotels: Do we need to explain these? While purpose-built for couples requiring romantic privacy, as an option for simple, reasonably priced accommodation, they can be quite sufficient. You may get a strange look if you enter alone, though.

FOOD

Menus

For those who cannot read Japanese, navigating the menus in some high-end restaurants can be a frustrating task, with many only written in *kanji* characters, potentially making choosing a meal an expensive, slightly risky, experience. That said, staff can often provide rudimentary English explanations of the dishes on offer.

Many restaurants and Japanese-style bars (*izakaya*) have English menus, or menus with photos to reassure visitors, though the literal translations can occasionally be bizarre and off-putting.

Vegetarianism

Being a vegetarian in Japan is tricky. Many bakeries, delis, and cafes take a vague approach to listing ingredients. As such, you may often be surprised with stealth bacon or other meat in a seemingly 'vegetarian' meal. That said, food service staff will be very helpful when they know what you want, even if they're taken aback or puzzled by your requests. Learning a few expressions to explain your needs will come in useful (see page 413).

There are many delicious Japanese foods that vegetarians can enjoy, and whole restaurants dedicated to such delights as *tofu*, and vegan *ramen*. Be adventurous, and don't be afraid of asking for help or more information about menus and meals. With a bit of online research, vegetarians can eat out very well in Japan. Family restaurants, *tempura*, *soba* and (if able to eat fish) sushi bars are great places to start while you find your way.

Tipping

Japan doesn't tip. In fact, tips would be flatly refused or just cause confusion, so enjoy the chance to not worry about offending the server or getting your maths wrong!

MOBILE PHONES AND INTERNET

As with anywhere, the progress and development of wi-fi services and electronic gadgetry moves apace (so much so that anything we could write here would probably already be out of date when you read it). Suffice to say, wi-fi services abound in Japan, but the quality of the connection can be sporadic or non-existent, especially if you're headed for the deeper, mountainous areas.

OTHER TIPS

Left Luggage

Most train stations and tourist offices will have coin lockers or some kind of left-luggage service. Even if there isn't an official service on hand, most accommodation or tourist office staff will be happy to look after your luggage when asked.

Convenience Stores

Convenience stores are ubiquitous in Japan. Even some of the smaller towns may have a 24-hour convenience store with snacks, ATMs and toilet facilities.

Shopping

Japan has a consumption tax, so the price tag you see may not match the actual amount you pay - but you are extremely unlikely to be ripped off in a Japanese shop. There are tax-free shopping opportunities for foreign visitors - check government websites for details.

Rubbish

One thing that many first-time visitors to Japan mention is its cleanliness, despite the vast urban sprawls. However, there is a lack of bins, except outside some convenience stores and on some train station platforms, so people are expected to take their rubbish home with them.

Etiquette

It never hurts to bone up on the do's and don'ts prior to any visit. The basics in Japan include not wearing shoes indoors, using the hot springs properly, eating according to the local etiquette, and avoiding speaking loudly on trains.

USEFUL PHRASES

other information

BASICS

Good afternoon.	こんにちは。	Konnichiwa.
How are you?	お元気ですか?	O-genki desu ka?
Fine, thank you.	はい、元気です。	Hai, genki desu.
What's your name? (lit. "Your name is...?")	お名前は?	O-namae wa?
My name is John.	ジョン です。	Jon desu.
Please.	…ください。	…kudasai.
Thank you.	ありがとう。	Arigatō.
Excuse me.	すみません。	Sumimasen.
I'm sorry.	ごめんなさい。	Gomen nasai.
Goodbye.	さようなら。	Sayōnara.
I can't speak Japanese.	日本語が話せません。	Nihongo ga hanasemasen.
Do you speak English?	英語は話せますか?	Eigo ga hanasemasu ka?
I don't understand.	分かりません。	Wakarimasen.

EMERGENCIES

Is there someone here who speaks English?	誰か英語が話せますか?	Dareka eigo ga hanasemasu ka?
Please help!	助けて!	Tasukete!
Where is the toilet?	トイレはどこですか?	Toire wa doko desu ka?
I'm lost.	道に迷いました。	Michi ni mayoimashita.
I lost my wallet.	財布をなくしました。	Saifu o nakushimashita.
I'm sick.	具合が悪いです。	Guai ga warui desu.

TRANSPORTATION
bus and train

How much is a ticket to ____?	____ までいくらですか?	____ made ikura desu ka?
A ticket to ____, please.	____ までお願いします。	____ made onegai shimasu.
Where does this train/bus go?	この電車(バス)はどこに行きますか?	Kono densha/basu wa doko ni ikimasu ka?
Where is the train/bus to ____?	____ の電車(バス)はどこですか?	____ no densha/basu wa doko desu ka?
Does this train/bus stop in ____?	この電車(バス)は ____ に止まりますか?	Kono densha/basu wa ____ ni tomarimasu ka?
When does the train/bus for ____ leave?	____ 行きの電車(バス)は何時に出発しますか?	____ iki no densha/basu wa nanji ni shuppatsu shimasu ka?
When will this train/bus arrive in ____?	電車(バス)は何時に ____ に着きますか?	Kono densha/basu wa nanji ni ____ ni tsukimasu ka?

taxi

Take me to ____, please.	____ までお願いします。	____ made onegai shimasu.
How much does it cost to get to ____?	____ まではいくらですか?	____ made wa ikura desu ka?
I'd like to hire a tourist taxi for a few hours.	観光用タクシーお願いします。	Kankō yō takushii onegai shimasu.
Can you wait here until I come back?	ここで待ってもらっていいですか?	Koko de matte moratte ii desu ka?

DIRECTIONS

How do I get to ____?	____ はどこですか?	____ wa doko desu ka?

ACCOMMODATION

How much is a room?	一泊いくらですか？	Ippaku ikura desu ka?
Is breakfast/dinner included?	朝食(夕食)は付きますか？	Chōshoku/yūshoku wa tsukimasu ka?
What time is breakfast/dinner?	朝食(夕食)は何時ですか？	Chōshoku/yūshoku wa nanji desu ka?
I want to check out.	チェックアウトします。	Chekku auto (check out) shimasu.

MONEY

Do you accept credit cards?	クレジットカードは使えますか？	Kurejitto kādo wa tsukaemasu ka?
Where can I get money changed?	お金はどこで両替できますか？	Okane wa doko de ryōgae dekimasu ka?
Where is an ATM?	ATMはどこですか？	ATM wa doko desu ka?

EATING OUT

A table for one person/two people, please.	一人(二人)です。	Hitori/futari desu.
Do you have an English menu?	英語のメニューありますか？	Eigo no menyū arimasu ka?
Do you have _____?	_____ はありますか？	_____ wa arimasu ka?
Excuse me (to waiter)!	すみません!	Sumimasen!
The check, please.	お会計おねがいします。	O-kaikei onegai shimasu.
Do you have a vegetarian menu?	ベジタリアンメニューありますか？	Bejitarian menyū arimasu ka?
Is there any meat in this?	これに肉は入ってますか？	Kore ni niku wa haitte masu ka?
Have you used meat stock?	肉の出汁は使っていますか？	Niku no dashi wa tsukatte imasu ka?
Is this a local dish?	地元の食べ物ですか？	Jimoto no tabemono desu ka?
A beer, please.	ビールを下さい。	Biiru wo kudasai.
A glass of red/white wine, please.	赤(白)ワインを 一杯下さい。	Aka/Shiro wain wo ippai kudasai.
Can I have another plate (for sharing)?	取り皿をください。	Torizara wo kudasai.
Can I have a knife and fork?	ナイフとフォークをお願いします。	Naifu to fōku wo onegai shimasu.
What is this in English?	これは英語で何と言いますか？	Kore wa eigo de nan to iimasu ka?

SHOPPING

How much is it?	いくらですか？	Ikura desu ka?
Do you have this in my size?	私のサイズありますか？	Watashi no saizu arimasu ka?
Do you ship overseas?	海外に送れますか？	Kaigai ni okuremasu ka?

DRIVING

| I want to rent a car. | レンタカーお願いします。 | Rentakā onegai shimasu. |
| Can I get insurance? | 保険入れますか？ | Hoken hairemasu ka? |

IN THE TOWN / AT THE TOURIST OFFICE

Where is the tourist office?	観光案内所はどこですか？	Kankōannaijo wa doko desu ka?
Do you have coin lockers?	コインロッカーはありますか？	Koinrokkā wa arimasu ka?
I'd like to rent a bicycle.	自転車を借りたいんですが。	Jitensha wo karitai desu ga.
Do you have this _____ in English?	英語の_____はありますか？	Eigo no _____ wa arimasu ka?
What time do you open/close?	何時に開きますか(閉めますか)？	Nanji ni akimasu ka/shimemasu ka?
A receipt, please.	領収書お願いします。	Ryoshusho onegai shimasu.
Where can I _____?	_____ はどこで出来ますか？	_____ wa doko de dekimasu ka?
Can you look after my luggage?	荷物を預かって下さい。	Nimotsu wo azukatte kudasai.
What _____ do you recommend?	お薦めの _____ は何ですか？	Osusume no _____ wa nan desu ka?
Can it be reached on foot?	歩けますか？	Arukemasu ka?

Index

Aichi Prefecture *180*
Akashi *240*
Akita Prefecture *36*
Amami *358*
Aomori Prefecture *37*
Arita *392*
Ashikaga *156*
Aso *368*
Asuka *246*
Atami *222*
Awara *196*
Aya *372*
Bibai *22*
Central Hokkaido *15*
Chiba Prefecture *90*
Chihayaakasaka *254*
Chubu-Hokuriku Region *180*
Chugoku Region *272*
East Hokkaido *16*
Ehime Prefecture *314*
Esashi *32*
Fukui Prefecture *181*
Fukuoka Prefecture *341*
Fukushima Prefecture *37*
Gero *208*
Gifu Prefecture *181*
Gunma Prefecture *91*
Hachinohe *54*
Hagi *308*
Hakuba *124*
Hakusan *210*
Hatsukaichi *278*
Hikone *264*
Himi *226*
Hiroshima Prefecture *272*
Hitoyoshi *370*
Hokkaido Region *14*
Hokuto *172*
Hyogo Prefecture *234*
Ibaraki Prefecture *91*
Iki *378*
Ikoma *250*
Imabari *320*
Inuyama *188*
Ise *214*
Ishikawa Prefecture *182*

Itako *114*
Iwaki *62*
Iwate Prefecture *38*
Izumisano *258*
Izumo *292*
Kagawa Prefecture *315*
Kagoshima Prefecture *342*
Kamiichi *228*
Kamishihoro *30*
Kamoenai *24*
Kamogawa *98*
Kanagawa Prefecture *91*
Kansai Region *234*
Kanto-Koshinetsu Region *90*
Kasama *118*
Katsushika *162*
Katsuyama *198*
Kawagoe *150*
Kitsuki *384*
Kochi Prefecture *316*
Komoro *128*
Konan *330*
Kosaka *42*
Koshu *176*
Kumamoto Prefecture *342*
Kumano *218*
Kurashiki *284*
Kusatsu *106*
Kyoto Prefecture *235*
Kyushu Region and Okinawa *340*
Masuda *296*
Matsushima *74*
Mie Prefecture *183*
Mikasa *26*
Mimasaka *288*
Minabe *266*
Misasa *304*
Miura *122*
Miyagi Prefecture *38*
Miyakojima *402*
Miyazaki Prefecture *343*
Miyazu *244*
Miyoshi *334*
Mutsu *58*
Nagano Prefecture *92*
Nagasaki Prefecture *343*

Nagatoro *154*
Nakafurano *20*
Naoshima *324*
Nara Prefecture *235*
Nihonmatsu *66*
Niigata Prefecture *92*
Nishinoshima *300*
North Hokkaido *15*
Nozawaonsen *132*
Numata *28*
Oga *46*
Ogasawara *164*
Ogawa *136*
Oita Prefecture *344*
Okayama Prefecture *273*
Okinawa Prefecture *348*
Ono *202*
Osaka Prefecture *236*
Oshima *168*
Rikuzentakata *68*
Sado *142*
Saga Prefecture *344*
Sagae *82*
Saitama Prefecture *93*
Sakaiminato *306*
Sakata *84*
Semboku *50*
Sera *282*
Shibukawa *110*
Shiga Prefecture *236*
Shiiba *376*
Shikoku Region *314*
Shimabara *382*
Shimane Prefecture *274*
Shimanto *332*
Shimoda *224*
Shimosuwa *138*
Shiroishi *78*
Shizuoka Prefecture *183*
Shodoshima *326*
Soni *252*
South Hokkaido *16*
Suita *262*
Tateyama *102*
Tatsugo *362*
Tochigi *160*
Tochigi Prefecture *93*

Tohoku Region *36*
Tokamachi *146*
Tokoname *192*
Tokushima Prefecture *317*
Tokyo Prefecture *94*
Tono *70*
Tottori Prefecture *274*
Toyama Prefecture *184*
Ukiha *350*
Ureshino *396*
Usuki *388*
Wajima *212*
Wakasa *204*
Wakayama Prefecture *237*
Yakushima *364*
Yamagata Prefecture *39*
Yamaguchi Prefecture *275*
Yamanashi Prefecture *94*
Yanagawa *354*

Published by Nellie's Ltd.
Kenkyusha Fujimi Bldg. 3F
2-11-3 Fujimi Chiyoda-ku
Tokyo 102-0071 Japan

© Nellie's Ltd. 2018
All rights reserved; no part of this publication may be reproduced, stored in a retrieval system, or transmitted in any form or by any means, electronic, mechanical, photocopying, recording or otherwise, without the prior written permission of the publishers.

ISBN: 9784905527497
Printed in Japan

Editor: Anthony Gardner
Designer and Second Editor: Brian Smith

The publishers would like to thank the following for their invaluable contributions:
Chairman: Atsushi Takahashi
Vice Chairman: Hiroyuki Yamamoto
John Antone
Yoshino Antone-Ishibashi
Kunio Hirata
Masataka Koreeda
Sumiho Ohta
Unokichi Tachibana
Atsushi Takahashi

Kazuo Hamano
Taiji Kansai
Fumihiro Okazeri
Haruhiko Okinobu
Hiroshi Takehana
Aya Yamazawa

Fuyuko Addison, Gavin Addison, Jonathan Boyle, Jonathan Cant, Matthew Chadwell, Alex Cox, Angela Gardner, Rachel Gardner, Josh Grisdale, Ian Holden, Nao Nishitsuji, Richard O'Neill, Natasha Paterson, Michael Rayner, Stephen Rowley, Maria Sethi, Darrel Stein, Andrew Wilkinson

JTB - http://www.japanican.com/en/
JAL http://www.jal.co.jp/en/
ANA http://www.ana.co.jp

JR Hokkaido : http://www2.jrhokkaido.co.jp/global/index.html
JR East : http://www.jreast.co.jp/e/
JR Central : http://english.jr-central.co.jp/
JR West : https://www.westjr.co.jp/global/en/
JR Shikoku : http://www.jr-shikoku.co.jp/
JR Kyushu : http://www.jrkyushu.co.jp/english/

All Japan Rent-a-car Association : http://www.rentacar.or.jp/en/

Image copyright:
Japan map: AQ_taro_neo

15: siro46, feathercollector **16:** San Hoyano, nengniwaa **17:** San Hoyano, Tatsuo Nakamura
36: krit_manavid / shutterstock.com **37:** takahashi_4 / shutterstock.com, tk312001
38: yspbqh14, mTaira / shutterstock.com **39:** Sean Pavone, yspbqh14 **52:** PixHound / Shutterstock.com **75:** Em7 / shutterstock.com
91: Olga Kashubin, shihina, bondjb / shutterstock.com **92:** GUDKOV ANDREY, siraphat / shutterstock.com
93: Tupungato / shutterstock.com, Natapat2521 **94:** f11photo, Shuttertong **95:** f11photo, Shuttertong **147:** Tokamachi Tourist Association
180: finallast **181:** Wizard8492, Matsumoto **183:** mokokomo, Chomphuphucar
184: Navapon Plodprong / shutterstock.com **185:** kyogan **236:** twoKim images / shutterstock.com, yoko_ken_chan
237: cowardlion **274:** tipwam / shutterstock.com, mokokomo **275:** 10max **314:** Sean Pavone
315: MrNovel / shutterstock.com **316:** YOHEI TAKASHINA / shutterstock.com
317: Net Ohhayo, KPG_Payless **342:** wdeon, T Chareon **343:** kan_khampanya, KPG_Payless
344: Sean Pavone, kan_khampanya **348:** photoNN **348:** takerunosuke, nikosto **400:** Takayuki Ohama
©2017 Used under license from Shutterstock.com.

Front cover image: Shiiba, Miyazaki Prefecture by Brian Smith. Back cover image: Oga, Akita Prefecture by Stephen Rowley.

Although we have taken all reasonable care in preparing this book, we make no warranty about the accuracy or completeness of its content and, to the maximum extent permitted, disclaim all liability arising from its use.

Unokichi Tachibana

Tachibana School (Yose Characters and Edo Characters) Chirographer
UNOS Corp. Director

Unokichi Tachibana was born in Tokyo in 1950. From 1965, he studied
under Ukon Tachibana, master of the Tachibana School. Since then, his
work has included pieces for kabuki and theatre, logos for a variety of
shrines, temples and organisations, and illustrations for CDs and books.

http://www.unos.co.jp